Film and Television in Education

This book is to be returned on
or before the date stamped below

Film and Television in Education

The handbook of the British Universities Film & Video Council

Second edition

Edited by Chris Dry

BLUEPRINT
An Imprint of Chapman & Hall
London · Glasgow · Weinheim · New York · Tokyo · Melbourne · Madras

Published by Blueprint, an imprint of Chapman & Hall, 2–6 Boundary Row, London SE1 8HN, UK

Chapman & Hall, 2–6 Boundary Row, London SE1 8HN, UK

Blackie Academic & Professional, Wester Cleddens Road, Bishopbriggs, Glasgow G64 2NZ, UK

Chapman & Hall GmbH, Pappelallee 3, 69469 Weinheim, Germany

Chapman & Hall USA, 115 Fifth Avenue, New York, NY 10003, USA

Chapman & Hall Japan, ITP-Japan, Kyowa Building, 3F, 2-2-1 Hirakawacho, Chiyoda-ku, Tokyo 102, Japan

Chapman & Hall Australia, 102 Dodds Street, South Melbourne, Victoria 3205, Australia

Chapman & Hall India, R. Seshadri, 32 Second Main Road, CIT East, Madras 600 035, India

First edition 1991
Second edition 1995

© 1991, 1995 British Universities Film & Video Council

Index compiled by Marilyn Sarmiento

Typeset by Chris Dry

Printed in Great Britain by Alden Press, Oxford

ISBN 1 857130 16 2

A catalogue record for this book is available from the British Library

∞ Printed on permanent acid-free text paper, manufactured in accordance with ANSI/NISO Z39.48-1992 (Permanence of Paper).

Contents

vi

Foreword

The British Universities Film & Video Council was founded in 1948. During the last 47 years we have seen enormous changes both in the technologies of the media delivering moving pictures and sound and in the ways in which education has harnessed their use. Many of the most significant changes have come about during the last two decades. Indeed, during the last five years there have been so many radical technological developments that there has been a danger of these diverting attention and jeopardising proven methods for the sake of innovation.

In a time of such change it is important for educationalists to keep their feet firmly on the ground. History shows that few if any new developments in audio-visual media have been implemented effectively in education before their widespread adoption in the public domain.

This is not to say that educators and researchers should not investigate the potential in all innovations – both technological and methodological. However, it is possible to be carried away by R&D before the real benefits of innovation can be delivered through successful implementation.

The content of this handbook in part reflects the diverse nature of the developments in audio-visual media which are currently being investigated from the educational standpoint. In addition the handbook provides lists and sources of basic information of a more conventional nature which should be of benefit to teachers, lecturers and academic support personnel.

As linear and analogue methods of one-way communication give way to the non-linear, the interactive and the digital, the BUFVC will continue to provide information and services which support the use of proven methods in education while at the same time keeping track of the latest innovations.

The council has an established role in supporting the use of audio-visual archives for scholarship and research. The continuous process of technological innovation should not be allowed to overshadow the real value of our audio-visual archives for learning at all levels. In 100 years' time the words 'film and video' may well be historical novelties, but there can be little doubt that the libraries of material we create and retain now will be essential for use by educationalists in the future. While we need to accommodate innovation we have a responsibility to future generations to value, preserve and provide access to the audio-visual materials created during the last 100 years.

This second *BUFVC Handbook* therefore is a slice in time – a summary of information and a brief account of some of the diverse interests in our evolving field of work.

Murray Weston
Director, British Universities Film & Video Council

Introduction

It is clear that the role of film and video, together with the rapid introduction of information and communications technologies into the classroom, is becoming an essential element in innovative education provision as we move towards the 21st century. The collection of articles drawn together for this handbook highlights the practical value that creative use of these resources can provide. It appears that the use of non-book media, and the central role played by the British Universities Film & Video Council, have come of age.

Theory and Practice   The possibilities for using non-book media in education have mushroomed in recent years. But, if the equipment cupboard is locked and you do not have the key, there may as well be nothing. Access is everything – but what should you do when you *do* have the key? In this section, Chris O'Hagan, from the University of Derby, starts with a practical overview to using educational media as it stands today.

Dr Robin Moss, Head of Education at the Independent Television Commission, continues with an appraisal of the schools television service, arguing that in spite of the sell-off of ITV franchises and the Birtist approach to economics at the BBC, we enjoy not only the best but the two best schools education services in the world.

Medical sciences have exploited the use and potential of recorded images more successfully than any other academic discipline. Michael Clark, Audio-Visual Resources Manager at the Wellcome Trust, offers an insight into the history of medical illustration as a training tool.

Andrew Hart, from the University of Southampton, closes the **Theory and Practice** section, airing his concerns and explaining how the PGCE course at Southampton copes with the teaching of media studies, a popular and over-subscribed discipline which meets with ambivalence from curriculum administrators.

New Technologies   But what of the future? Information and communications technology has frustrated, delighted, irritated, and enthused individuals and institutions since the first desktop PCs entered the classroom in the early 1980s. **New Technologies** aims to clarify some of the issues about the implementation of IT in higher education. From Tana Wollen's linear narrative about the potential of interactivity, through the myriad possibilities explored by the Open University Production Centre for distance learning, to specific projects and activities such as SuperJANET and the Advisory Group on Computer Graphics, there is enough here to augment the frustration. But, as Keith Yeomans points out in his article comparing the use of the Internet in education in the USA and the UK, the complexity '...is not a case for ignoring or rejecting it. Rather it is an argument for those who believe in extending access to brief themselves on the strategic issues and work towards resolving them appropriately'.

Archives and Centenary Celebrations The centenary of cinema neatly bisects the projected life of this publication. The year 1995 is likely to see a wealth of discussion as the UK moves towards its own film centenary in early 1996. For our part we focus on the history of cinematography in education and the importance of film archives. Murray Weston, Director of the BUFVC, asserts that the first cinema was one of scientific research and discovery and it set the trend for other innovations to find a niche in higher education before other more commercial uses are applied. The release of Virgilio Tosi's ORIGINS OF SCIENTIFIC CINEMATOGRAPHY strengthens this argument and makes one wonder at what audiences must have thought in those pioneering days.

Film archives need not concentrate on the professional image; amateur film can give precious clues to past traditions and has something to say about virtually all of the academic disciplines. The only problem is locating relevant material. In her article Gwenan Owen, from the Wales Film Archive, makes a case for amateur film and, by extension, the archiving of film in general. Gwenan's article is preceded by a short introduction by Phill Walkley from the UK's centenary coordinating body Cinema 100.

Daniela Kirchner has worked in the BUFVC offices for nearly two years collecting and collating the data for the ambitious MAP-TV project. In her article 'Europe Against the Odds', Daniela describes the highs and lows of producing what, in future years, I am sure will be referred to as the bible of European film archives.

Directory The **Directory** section aims to provide a practical guide for those producing, acquiring and using non-book media in higher education – a response to the many requests for information we receive at the BUFVC. It is hoped that the directory will save time for researchers, academics and producers of audio-visual programmes in higher education. If we fall short in any respect, or you can think of other listings which may be of practical use, please let us know and we shall endeavour to include your suggestions in future editions.

Acknowledgements The first edition of this handbook was described by BUFVC Director Murray Weston as 'a truly joint effort involving all of the BUFVC'. This edition is no different with the exception of some changes in personnel.

Two staff members who have 'moved on' must be mentioned: Jim Ballantyne, former Head of Information, for his contribution of the legislation section and my predecessor, Nick Wray, former Head of Communications, who kick-started this edition.

Chris Dry, Editor

 The Open University

Open University Educational Enterprises Limited

UNLIMITED ACCESS TO ONE OF THE WORLD'S GREAT EDUCATIONAL RESOURCES

Subscribe to the Open University's annual UK Off Air Recording Scheme OR purchase individual videos as you need them.

Open University broadcasts are:

COMPREHENSIVE - over 1,000 programmes are available across a wide range of undergraduate and business subjects

CLEAR - learning points are clearly communicated

ACCESSIBLE - complex concepts are conveyed in a way that is often difficult with print alone

ACCURATE - programmes are reviewed by external assessors prior to transmission

TIME-SAVING - using Open University teaching resources can help cut down on course preparation time.

Well-presented audio and written support materials are also available.

NEW FOR 1995
Video cassettes are now available of broadcasts from the following courses:

Art, Society and Religion in Fourteenth-Century Siena, Florence and Padua, 1280-1400
Astronomy and Planetary Science
Materials: Engineering and Science
Studying Family and Community History: Nineteenth and Twentieth Centuries
The United States in the Twentieth Century
The Growth of Religious Diversity: Britain from 1945
Understanding Music: Elements, Techniques and Styles

To find out more - complete the coupon below.
--------✂--✂--✂-----------
❏ Please send me further details of the UK Open University Licensed Off Air Recording Scheme
   Please send me a copy of your catalogue giving details of videos and support material covering:

❏ Arts   ❏ Social Science and Education   ❏ Maths, Science and Technology

Name _____

Organisation _____

Address _____

_____

Postcode _____ Telephone Number _____

Please indicate your type of organisation:
❏ Secondary School   ❏ Sixth Form College /FE/HE   ❏ Other

Please return to OUEE Limited, 12 Cofferidge Close, Stony Stratford, Milton Keynes MK11 1BY, UK.
Telephone 01908 261662; Off Air Enquiries 01908 262612 or Fax 01908 261001.

Marketing code BUFVC95

Educational Media in Practice: the Myth and the Reality

CHRIS O'HAGAN

The Console for the Video auto-Editing System for Open Learning which allows lecturers to video their presentations in real time without any technical assistance.

There it was, glistening and gleaming, a work of technological art, itself capable of creating great works of art – a Bolex 16mm camera. I reached out to touch it, and bang, my hand hit the glass. I tried the door. Locked. Who had the key? The Principal?.. Why did I want it? For one of my classes, for the students to make a film. The students? I wasn't serious, was I?

No one ever got to use that camera. It's probably still there in its cabinet, gathering dust, like the two Bolexes and the completely unused Beaulieu Super 8 system I found at one of the teacher training colleges my current institution merged with some years ago. Fortunately, we run degrees in photography, film and TV so those cameras did find a use rather later in life than had been intended by the enthusiastic purchaser.

At another institution, it was quite the opposite. Students and staff could be set free on the TV studio, and after a few minutes of dos and don'ts, were making programmes. The technical staff didn't intrude unless asked. I learned a big lesson for the day I was to become responsible for audio-visual facilities myself: access is all.

Well, not quite all. Technology has to be usable and controllable with a minimum of effort. Not 'user-friendly'! That expression should be consigned to the dustbin with the equally horrible phrase 'human-resource management'. Both suggest that human beings are objects to be manipulated. No, 'user-friendly' is a term for technocrats. It is part of the answer to the question 'How can I get you to use my system?' while the real questions 'Will it do anything useful?' and 'Who is really in control?' remain too awkward to ask. Autonomy rather than user-friendliness is the key to usability. Educational technology can only realise its full potential if students and teachers can take possession of a system, personalise it, own it. It will fail if its users feel manipulated, however 'friendly' that manipulation.

Unfortunately, technocratic attitudes have created a gulf between the nature of teaching and audio-visual systems. I don't mean that lecturers rarely use slide-projectors, video or computers, but that these are seen as trimmings, as icing on the cake, rather than as integral to processes of teaching and learning. This, then, is the myth and the reality: the myth of technology liberating educators

1

and the reality of a glossy veneer over the mass of routine education in universities.

I exaggerate for effect, of course. There are many remarkable specialist uses of technology, particularly where the focus is on training rather than general education. However, the real goal for many educational technologists is the ubiquitous system which impacts right across disciplines and specialisms. Only a few technologies have had that kind of impact – the overhead projector and the videocassette for example.[1] Some experts would claim that the computer is one such system, but the jury is still out here, I feel, and will probably remain out for some time yet. The potential is there. But how many times have we heard that phrase since the burgeoning technological enthusiasms of the 1960s, and how much of that potential now lies covered in dust?

Which brings me full circle. I believe the key to ubiquity, to the centrality of audio-visual systems in higher education, lies in easy access with autonomy. If teachers, learners, and service staff all understand this, particularly service staff, then the myth may become the reality and technology in higher education may become truly liberating.

In the next few pages I hope to suggest how you can take control, with some help, and how you can make technology work for you. I am going to examine the possibilities offered by the overhead projector, the rostrum projector, the slide projector, the videocassette, the computer, and finally, multimedia systems. At the end of each section you will find a few extra hints for effective use.

The Overhead Projector This is one of the great success stories in education. It is cheap enough to be found in every teaching room, so access is straightforward, and it is very easy to learn how to use. It is so commonplace that it is possible to overlook its importance. In a recent review of the excellent *Handbook of Educational Technology*[2] one finds the following observation: 'When it is stated that the "OHP is probably the most versatile visual aid that can be used to support mass instruction methods" it suggests that the authors are unaware of the power of computer-aided learning'.[3] This non-sequitur suggests rather that the reviewer is unaware of the power and influence of the overhead projector as well as badly infected himself with a dose of computer-hype, believing in the myth while blind to the reality.

In fact, curiously, the computer has extended the influence of the OHP. Overhead transparencies (OHTs) of high quality are quickly and cheaply produced using both specialist software (e.g. Pagemaker) or common word processors (Word, WordPerfect). This is generally better than using hand-written OHTs if a good size lettering is used. (As a rough guide 25 characters maximum to a line in portrait format – though of course it does depend on the size of the room and the power of the projector.)

Some lecturers believe that specially prepared transparencies do away with spontaneity. This need not be the case because you can still add to them during the actual presentation, using an erasable pen so they can easily be restored for re-use afterwards. (If you want to add to hand-written OHTs prepare them first with a permanent pen.) As an alternative you can write on a transparent plastic sleeve containing the transparency.

OHTs can substitute for your notes by providing cues for what you intend to say, and more importantly can provide key structural information to the students. It is this facility for pre-planning your lecture in a visual way that makes the OHP so powerful and flexible as a tool for communication. In fact, the overhead projector is one of the most effective inanimate staff developers because in learning to use it lecturers develop and improve on a wide range of skills – preparing, structuring, economical use of language, visual literacy, and seeing the presentation more from the audience's point of view. Research has shown that information presented both visually and verbally is more readily recalled than if only one of these media is used. So the overhead projector has probably had more impact on effective formal learning than any other technology since the invention of the printing press. And what is more it still does have, despite the overblown assertions of the computer lobby.

Learning to use the OHP for communication is one of the most effective ways of preparing staff to use more sophisticated learning technology including computers. The overhead projector is an embodiment of my axiom: ease of access with autonomy is the key to ubiquity. Lecturers can experiment and learn on the job, and develop a style or styles of their own. The OHP is so versatile that one is always learning new tricks. Commonplace it may be, but its power as an educational technology is very uncommon.

Tips for use
- don't overfill, keep the lettering large
- walk to the back of the room and see if you can read it
- avoid photocopied transparencies
- stick post-its over sections you want to 'reveal'...
- or stick an old ruler to the top edge of a piece of paper to stop it slipping off towards the bottom
- use introductory (plan) and concluding (summary)

transparencies amongst others
- don't provide hard copies of your transparencies before the lecture – it reduces attention...
- unless you have them incomplete with sections to be filled in during the lecture
- cut up transparencies into eight or 10 pieces and give one piece to each individual or group of students, with a pen, for responses that can be quickly collected and spread across the top of the projector for everyone to read (anonymously)
- 'animate' your transparencies by moving pieces of shaped card (silhouette) or coloured acetate across a clear background, or by simply overlaying one sheet on another to build up an image or pattern.

The Rostrum Projector We should not forget that one of the great advantages of the overhead projector is that it is specially designed for use in relatively high ambient light conditions – so students can see to take notes at the same time. Other systems such as the rostrum projector and slide projector require that the lights are lowered and/or dark blinds cover the windows. This applies equally with computer-based presentation systems using an LCD tablet or projector. The lights must be continually raised and lowered and it is harder for students to read and write. Nevertheless, these other systems have their particular advantages.

One of the most flexible is the rostrum projector. A remote-control video camera is hung from the ceiling above a flat lectern and what it sees is sent to the main lecture theatre screen through a video projector. At the University of Derby we have designed one so that when the projector is switched on the lights automatically dim, and vice versa when it is switched out. Two forms of illumination are also provided for – from below and above.

The camera can be focused and zoomed by the lecturer using pairs of up/down buttons on the lectern. This means a much bigger and closer image can be generated than with the average overhead. A small monitor allows the lecturer to set up the image before switching the projector in. Normal printed opaque materials can often be used without special preparation, as well as transparencies. A particular advantage is the wide depth of field generated if the camera is three or four metres above the lectern, such that solid objects can be scrutinised with great clarity. Even small live creatures can be observed.

A rostrum camera is no more expensive than an episcope (£1,500) if there is already a video projector in the theatre, but a lot more versatile, and there is no risk of damaging valuable books.

Antiquarian and art materials can be used as the lighting generates very little heat. It is a bit harder to use than an OHP but soon mastered, and as with the OHP the presenter has complete autonomy in the creation and choice of materials for projection. The imagination is the limiting factor.

Tips for use
- prepare your materials in landscape format to better fit the television screen proportions...
- or materials prepared in portrait format can be 'rolled' up the screen like TV credits
- move solid objects around very slowly and deliberately, it looks 'twitchy' otherwise.

The Slide Projector Like the rostrum projector this has the disadvantage of requiring a darkened room. Also, unless compact back projection is used the presenter is often a long way from the slides, if, for example, one is in upside-down!

A big advantage is quality of image. You get better clarity and colour density with slides than with any other system. There is usually good access to equipment and the 35mm format provides for considerable user autonomy in the provision of material – you can often take the shots yourself, and most institutions have slide-making services as well.

A supply of opaque slides is useful to separate the carousel or cassette into sections, though modern projectors close down the lens when a gap appears in the sequence, making blank slides unnecessary.

Projectors can be linked together with a dissolve unit to produce a seamless transition from one slide to the next – very effective if the essence of your presentation is the slide show itself.

Tips for use
- make sure before that your screen will take both landscape and portrait shots (if you are mixing them) without 'guillotining' one or the other.
- run through your slides to check order, right way up and right way round (a mirror image can give not just a reversed but a completely false impression as well).

The Videocassette We have so far been in the land of reality of very powerful and highly usable systems, but now we are about to enter the land of myth, where the technocrats, the technofreaks and technohypists reign supreme... if we're not careful.

The videocassette is, like the overhead projector, one of the great success stories. It liberated educational television from a cumbersome connection to broadcast schedules and opened up a

Pandora's box of possibilities, particularly with the recent changes in copyright law in the UK and the advent of satellite television. Unfortunately, as with Pandora's box, a lot of educational 'ills' were also let loose.

Many, many years ago, in the early days of the videocassette (actually open reel at that time), I took my first steps as an educational media facilitator. I created a catalogue with brief summaries of videotapes for the general studies department, by both title and subject, some 300+ programmes in all. It was so effective it was a disaster! I discovered that some lecturers were using a video just about every week, as a substitute for proper class preparation, and in fact lecturers across the institution were using it to provide some light relief from their turgid lessons. Whenever those of us with a more integrated approach to using video wanted a machine or a tape, it was already booked!

The problem was not the catalogue, but the way lecturers approached and still approach the use of video: as light relief, as relaxation, as unstructured illustrations, as half an hour or 50 minutes to do some marking. At the end of the tape comes the question, 'Now what did you think of that?' followed by a sudden silence then a brief and awkward, general and platitudinous debate.

That is a caricature, but nevertheless, there is more than a germ of truth in it, because both lecturers and students bring something of the television's domestic flavour into the classroom – its passivity, its generality, its 'opiate for the people'. So that if a video is presented in a way similar to a domestic showing – without preparation, without preliminary discussion, without breaks for questions – the students will quickly become passive and forget the beginning before the end is even reached. Worse still, their viewing will be completely uncritical and unanalytical.

Of course, how a video is presented will depend on the nature of the programme. But a major problem with off-air programmes is that they often have a diffuse and wide-ranging nature in an effort to maximise the audience. Usually lecturers and students need more clearly focused or edited material, and this demands one of a range of approaches.

Selective Use of the Programme Here the lecturer has logged the extracts he wishes to show to the students and uses the revolution counter and fast-forward button to edit the material 'live', so to speak. Continuity is provided by structured discussion of prepared questions between the extracts. It is still not easy to use this approach smoothly, but that may not be important in the end, if the learning is effective.

6

Use of Educational Videos Both off-air and commercial straight educational programmes are very variable in quality, and except in highly specialist cases are rarely exactly what is needed for a particular point in an instructional schedule. Much play has been made by producers of educational programmes of the need for 'broadcast quality' of image and of their skills to produce quality in educational terms as well. There are some excellent examples around, but nevertheless educational videos often suffer from having to maximise potential users for commercial reasons, and are therefore often little better than so-called serious entertainment programmes in terms of focus. Selective use within the video is often necessary.

ExtrActive Video I don't believe that a video needs to be of 'broadcast quality' any more than a handout needs to be printed at 2,000 dots per inch rather than 300. Students will tolerate all sorts of awful presentation if they feel they are learning effectively – even the hand-written back of a cigarette packet can be a vital item in one of their files! This is not an argument to design down to some basic level, but rather to see quality as 'fit for purpose'.

It is possible to physically edit off-air programmes and so produce an edited version of acceptable image quality and much better educational quality and usefulness. (Note: this must be within the terms of any copyright licence applicable to the off-air material.) Captions and instructions can be added to the tape, which can also mean that it can be used for independent learning by students. I have called this ExtrActive video, because it extracts the relevant material from the general confusion, but also as a pun on Interactive Video.

The interactive video lobby is another part of the myth generation in educational media and it has hijacked the concept of interactive learning using video as being exclusive to non-linear systems. This is a version of naïve realism. It assumes a direct relationship between 'reality' and the observer and believes that the two can interact by simply pressing buttons and switching pathways. Another caricature, but all good teachers know that interaction is something that ultimately occurs in the mind if there is to be deep rather than surface learning. Much of what passes for interactive video implies a 'bucket theory' of the mind rather than a 'searchlight theory', to borrow Karl Popper's graphic descriptions from a different context.

Both linear and non-linear video can be interactive in the deep learning sense, just as one can be interactive with a book when reading it linearly or non-linearly – effective learners use both approaches. So linear ExtrActive video can be used interactively.

In principle, one could say that it is an ideal to always use video in an interactive way – the simplest being to stimulate structured discussion between students, and with their teachers if present. For more on ExtrActive video see O'Hagan 1994a.[4]

Produce Your Own Video This is hardest of all, or rather was hardest of all. Technocracy rears its head most perniciously in the television studio. The lecturer is usually powerless, under the control of floor manager and producer, swamped by lights and surrounded by unfamiliar technology. Likewise in the edit suite the budding programme-maker is often at the mercy of the technical staff. It is also all so very time-consuming and expensive. A long way distant from easy access with autonomy, so it is no wonder that few lecturers commission material.

Outside the studio, the hand-held camcorder has revolutionised filming and is remarkably effective without special lighting. But editing in camera is a hit-and-miss affair, and good sound is always a problem without sophisticated add-ons. And it still is time-consuming.

The trick is to adapt lecturers' teaching skills to the visual medium and adapt video production technology so that it is easily operated by non-technical staff. In pursuit of this I invented the concept of VESOL, Video auto-Editing System for Open Learning, which has since been realised at the University of Derby with the help of a grant from the Higher Education Funding Council under the Teaching and Learning Technology Programme (TLTP) Phase II.

VESOL is a system which allows lecturers to video their presentations in real time without any technical assistance, producing a fully edited tape by switching between cameras while giving the presentation. Four cameras make a typical system: 1) close/medium shot of lecturer 2) long shot 3) overhead projector 4) main screen and whiteboard. Video and computer outputs can also be switched in if required. It sounds impossible, but in fact is relatively easy to use. Almost every lecturer who has received initial training (just 30 minutes) has managed to cope with it and has become hooked on the idea. Super VESOL, which uses a rostrum projector to great effect rather than the overhead projector, and VELAB, Video Enhanced Laboratory, are further developments of the system.

Copies of the presentation can be made in both S-VHS and domestic VHS formats, the former providing a master tape for duplication or editing together with other material (say, shot with a camcorder) if required. However, the system is designed to produce a final and edited tape in the same time it takes the

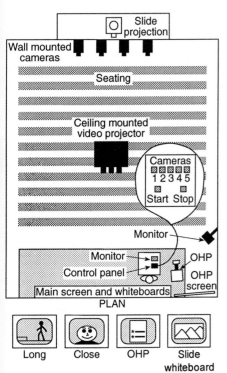

A graphic displaying the Video auto-Editing System for open Learning (VESOL).

lecturer to give the presentation. This can be of any length from a few minutes to a standard 55-minute lecture. What is more, the lecturer is in a familiar environment, using familiar presentation systems, and within limits can behave quite naturally. He can practice on his own without anyone else seeing the initial mistakes, until happy with the product. Programmes can be made with a live audience or in the empty amphitheatre. This really is access with autonomy. For more details of the system see O'Hagan.[5]

Tips for use
- find autonomous ways of using or creating video, so that there is real ownership of both teaching and learning
- break up your programme into short sections
- integrate the video with other media – handouts, slides, OHTs – for reinforcement of learning
- try dividing the students into groups to discuss different aspects of the programme
- always critically examine who made the programme, who it was made for and why
- don't try to develop too much at a time; try showing the programme twice with different preambles creating different contexts
- while video is good at simple illustration, remember in higher education this should be coupled with critical analysis.

The Computer The ubiquity of the computer in general might lead one to believe it was a powerful tool in teaching and learning. This is a long way from the case as yet, at least in the way that the technologies covered so far play major roles in delivering teaching or facilitating learning.

However, there is no doubt the computer is playing an increasingly important role in communications – word processing, desk-top publishing, databases, data transfer, e-mail etc. – for both teachers and students, and is clearly now indispensable in the office, library, and media and resource centre. But as a teaching or learning machine, the computer has a long way to go to turn the mythology and hype into reality. A lot of money and even more time has been wasted on systems that simply don't deliver anything useful in what might be termed 'programmed learning' over the past few years. But there does seem to be some light at the end of the tunnel with some of the latest developments, and I will deal with a few of these in the next section on hyper and multimedia.

When talking about computer-assisted learning it is necessary to distinguish between information systems and learning systems. CD-ROM can store massive amounts of information – textual, graphical, video and sound – which are easily called up for reference or study on the screen. The Internet and World Wide

Web provide access to an enormous variety of material and services. But, in general, these are exploratory rather than focused. Attempts to harness them to specific learning objectives have been rather mixed, except where very precise training requirements can be identified, and a very deep pocket for funding is available. Flight simulators, stock exchange simulators, engineering process training, and cytology training have been very successful, but the massive cost has been justified by the lives saved, the expensive plant preserved, the poor financial speculation avoided. In higher education the search has rather been for a versatile, low-cost way of generating computer-assisted learning across the board.

The main thrust has been to find a very flexible and usable authoring programme. The difficulty has always been the long learning curves to become proficient in using software like Authorware Professional or Authority, which has meant that most teachers have balked at the prospect. Instead the dreaded expert has appeared offering to 'do it for you'. The results have been less than ideal in most cases because the educational component and authoring abilities have been embodied in very different people who find it hard to communicate effectively. The proliferation of TLTP projects has improved matters, but let us not kid ourselves that much progress has been made beyond the specialist enthusiasts who were always there – though a few of the projects have enormous potential (that word again!). I regret that this is not an area that yet measures up to my axiom. There is little access, less autonomy. But I believe it is coming, and it is up to us to beat the technocrats and create autonomy for lecturers. For me that means generally controlling both the educational content and the authoring. For a taste of what this could be like you can create a simple computer-based tutorial in a few hours (in a staff development seminar we've done it in half an hour) by getting hold of a copy of ELFSoft which was developed by the Electronic Learning Factory at Bradford University. It is in the public domain, so completely free to educational institutions.

Nevertheless I suspect that computer innovations in communications like e-mail and the Internet will continue to overshadow developments in computer-assisted learning. In universities these meet the access and autonomy criteria right now – the possibilities are fantastic. For a taste, just get the list of lists from Mailbase. Send one or more of the following messages to mailbase@mailbase.ac.uk: 'lists' or 'lists full' or 'send mailbase user-guide' – type accurately, this is an automatic system. When you join a list you will be in touch with a world-wide community of scholars in any field that interests you. And Mailbase is only one of the many list servers on the Internet. There's freeware here as well. Eudora, which works in Windows or on a Mac, is a nifty programme for handling your mail and attachments. Someone somewhere will get you a copy.

Tips for use
- be sceptical but not negative
- eat a healthy diet of reality sandwiches
- or simply ask, 'Who's got the time and where's the money?'
- better still, think through, 'Will it work and what will they really learn?'

Multimedia This is the name given to computer systems that can deliver a variety of audio-visual media out of a single box, without lots of add-ons like video players. The key to this is of course the reduction of all sources to the purely digital data that computers can deal with. Unfortunately, converting images, particularly moving images, to digital format takes up very large quantities of memory. The problem has been partially solved using innovative software which compresses the data, rather than by expanding memory capacities. It is still only a partial solution, however, and for multimedia to really take hold in higher education much larger memory in more compact form will be necessary. This is not too far distant. Some would claim that CD-ROM is the embodiment of large memory in a small space, but personally I feel that CD-ROM is just a stopgap on the way to a more sophisticated electronic read-write system.

Nevertheless, if full-motion video is largely ignored, multimedia is highly usable right now – without recourse to the complexities of preparing, editing and pressing a CD-ROM. Such complexities limit access and remove autonomy.

One approach is through hypermedia systems, a development of hypertext systems that provide much more than just text. Some of the most interesting work currently being done in this area is to provide open, networked hypermedia across a campus. Students can follow particular tutorials from a workstation, or more serendipitously explore planned and unplanned connections between tutorials and information packages. This open-ended, divergent approach to learning through computer technology is closer to the goals of higher education than the highly convergent use of technology in industrial training. For more information I direct you to the Hypertext Campus Project at the University of Kent or the Interactive Learning Centre at the University of Southampton for details of Microcosm.

Before we get too enthusiastic, a word of caution. Research has shown that the lack of a clear structure for learning in open hypermedia systems causes difficulties for students who are not already familiar with the field.[6,7] It is easy for the inexperienced student to become confused and disillusioned. It can be helpful to give such students structural models to guide them. Books implicitly offer a range of structural models, including many variations on the linear model. There is a real danger that in moving to electronic media this 'initiation' into different models for structuring learning will be forgotten, disadvantaging in particular all the so-called non-traditional students we are seeking to attract into the universities.

Most lecturers can quickly understand the principles of hypertext. (Incidentally, I once saw Wilma Strang from Kent use OHTs to show how hypertext worked to the complete understanding of a novice audience, where a 'real' demonstration might have mystified them – the power of the overhead projector again!) It is much harder for lecturers to grasp how to work authoring software like Authorware Professional, which would let them create much more structured tutorials than in hypermedia. A solution to this is to create 'shells' which restrict the options available, making a template into which the lecturer can easily insert the learning materials, particularly if they can have them readily converted into a digital format.

At the University of Derby the TLTP Project TOTAL, Tutor Only Transfer of Authored Lessons, is creating a set of graded shells which will allow lecturers to create tutorials of increasing complexity. In this way, lecturers will control both the educational material and the software, and will acquire authoring skills while producing usable material. The shells enable staff to use readily available teaching materials from lectures and seminars and tutorials, including VESOL tapes, to create multimedia packages for independent learning. Technical staff and facilities have been put in place to provide on-demand digitising services for graphics, photos, video, as well as a design service, if needed. The daunting prospect of having to go through 100 hours plus of training before being able to create real learning resources is overcome. The lecturer is empowered and developed simultaneously through access with autonomy.

Tips for use
- begin simply, have a modest aim like a five minute reinforcement tutorial
- work out ways of using readily available materials, don't create everything from scratch
- start developing your conventional teaching materials as you go along with an eye to the new media.

Conclusion There has been much talk of how teaching and learning will be transformed through technology. This is the hype and it will also remain a myth unless the technocrats become facilitators who help teachers and researchers to take control themselves.

I have calculated that even a very powerful and expensive Learning Technology Unit or whatever your university wants to call it, could not hope to affect much more than 5% of all the teaching and learning going on in an institution over a 5 – 10 year period before it was bogged down in replacement, renewal and debugging – that is, unless it is prepared to seriously address access with autonomy in the ways I have suggested. This means being prepared to surrender power and influence of the common bureaucratic kind.

It is easier said than done. No one likes to be labelled a technocrat. If everyone who is one knew he or she was one, there wouldn't be any left. Technocrats and bureaucrats don't see themselves that way. That is the problem.

I hope this article will help both teachers and technical staff find more and better ways to create access with autonomy. Only then will the myth of technology liberating teachers and learners come closer to reality.

Chris O'Hagan is Head of Educational Methods and Media at the University of Derby. He has taught in secondary education as well as FE and HE. His subjects have included maths, physics, chemistry, communication studies, English literature, philosophy and sociology of science and the economics of technology. Today he works in staff and educational development as well as managing a department providing services in educational media across the university – TV, photography, graphics, cartography, reprographics and printing. He would be pleased to discuss this article or provide further information. C.M.OHagan@derby.ac.uk

References

1. Gayeski DM (1989) Why Information Technologies Fail. In *Educational Technology* **29** (2), pp. 9-17.
2. Ellington, Percival and Race (1993), *Handbook of Educational Technology*, 3rd ed, Kogan Page, London.
3. Rawlinson G (1994) review of the *Handbook of Educational Technology* (1993) op. cit. In *The New Academic* (**3**) 2.
4. O'Hagan CM (1994) The Use and Abuse of Video in Education. In *Designing for Learning: Effectiveness With Efficiency*, R Hoey (ed), Kogan Page, London.
5. O'Hagan CM (1995) Video Auto-Editing System for Open Learning (VESOL). In *Computer Assisted and Open Access Education*, F Percival (ed), Kogan Page, London. See also *Audio Visuality* **1** (2) Dec 1994.
6. McKendree J and Reader W (1994) The Homeopathic Fallacy in Hypertext: Misconceptions of Psychology in Design of Computer Courseware. In *ALT News* (April 1994).
7. Charney D (1994) The Impact of Hypertext on Processes of Reading and Writing. In *Literacy and Computers*, Hilligoss and Selfe (eds), MLA, New York.

ROUTLEDGE

Essential Reading

The Newspapers Handbook
Richard Keeble

The first comprehensive guide to becoming a newspaper journalist. It gives practical advice on the processes and skills needed when working for a newspaper, and examines the theoretical, ethical and political issue of the job.

Media Practice Series

September 1994: 368pp illus. 40 b&w photos
Hb: 0-415-08990-5: £45.00 Pb: 0-415-08991-3: £12.99

The Radio Handbook
Pete Wilby and Andy Conroy

Discusses the theoretical and ethical aspects of radio journalism, as well as its practical side, enabling students to develop an informed understanding of how and why radio works. It is essential reading for anyone studying or hoping to work in today's radio industry.

Media Practice Series

September 1994: 320pp illus. 30 b&w photos
Hb: 0-415-09466-6: £40.00 Pb: 0-415-09467-4: £12.99

English for Journalists `2nd Edition`
Wynford Hicks

'*English for Journalists* is a jolly useful book. It's short. It's accessible. It's cheap. And it tells you what you want to know.'
– *The Journalist.*

An invaluable guide not only to the basics of English, but to those aspects of writing – reporting speech, house style, jargon, cliches – specific to the language of journalism.

September 1993: 80pp Pb: 0-415-09493-3: £6.99

Still Reaching Out: The Future of Educational Television

ROBIN MOSS

We have seen a fair amount of radical change in educational television in the past five years. The pace of change will quicken and deepen in the next five years and beyond. It is as if we have been sailing down a broad and placid river and as we realise suddenly that the current is flowing faster and the banks of the stream are closer and less friendly than before, we catch the sound of rapids round a distant bend.

It has to be said at once that the two British schools television services are in excellent health. Research into teacher use of television programmes shows that it is high and perhaps even rising. Funding of programme production is more than adequate and seems well-protected for the foreseeable future. Certainly both the BBC and Channel 4 schools service have very detailed plans, fully costed, for the commissioning of programmes right to the end of the 1995/6 school year. Legislation protecting both services runs to the end of the century, and in the case of the BBC, beyond.

There are some alarming features about this situation and the roar of distant rapids must not be ignored. First, there is the extraordinary resonance in the phrase 'the two British schools television services', which is amplified by the general retreat, and in some places extinction, of public service broadcasting elsewhere in the western world. As Paul Ashton, Commissioning Editor for the Channel 4 schools service pointed out in the October 1994 edition of *Spectrum*, '...it is really little short of folly that Britain not only has easily the most comprehensive and best-funded television service for schools in the world, but easily the best two such'. When one adds that collaboration between the two is honoured more in the breach than the observance, there is clearly room for improvement. There is now a spice of urgency to the UN-style negotiations that traditionally bedevil attempts to bring sanity to this matter. It is possible to imagine that schools might in a few years time find cheap videodiscs or CD-ROMs so attractive in supporting learning that they ended up praising the television resources to the skies (as research shows most of them do) but using them hardly at all.

There is great excitement in some quarters about the information superhighway and what it means for education and training. To listen to some people, you would think that the information revolution has already occurred and that television is completely finished as a medium for communication, let alone as a useful educational resource. It is worth remembering that in real life highways may not reach every part of a country, that they can get badly jammed, and that people drive at differing speeds and with differing skills on the roads that they use. In Britain, for instance, access to the Internet is presently restricted not only by the varying range of equipment and the different levels of interest shown by teachers in schools, but also by factors as crucial as telephone connections being busy at key moments, and other structural problems. This is all very obvious and it is no doubt true that in a decade for many of us such problems will seem laughable pre-history.

Nevertheless, these are wise words:

'Just because something is possible certainly does not mean that it will be done. Nor does it mean that social or economic benefits that can be imagined will actually occur.'

In case you think these are merely the words of an elderly television producer stubbornly keeping his head in the sand, let me assure you that they are not my own words. In fact, they were spoken by Barbara Beckett, General Manager of British Telecom Cable Television Services, in a speech delivered at a recent conference in London. The conference entitled *Windows on the Future* was organised by the Labour Party and attended by several members of the shadow Cabinet as well as senior figures in British higher and further education. Many of the speakers at the meeting spoke more enthusiastically than Barbara about the inevitability of change and the urgency of Britain moving to the forefront in the development of the information superhighway. Several warned that if the investment was not made in the next two years, all would be lost.

Barbara Beckett, by contrast, was less strident and reminded delegates that all forecasters are, by definition, fools. This is probably more true now than it has ever been, precisely because the range and pace of change is so speedy and so powerful that uncertainty about the future is certain.

We hear that the speed of development in the microelectronics industry is now so fast that a given unit doubles its power and halves its cost every two years. This gives great strength to the research and development wing of any organisation working in this or an allied industry. It also means that anybody who can afford to wait and see before investing in a particular product might as well wait if he or she can. This sort of attitude can be a bit of a drag on economic progress and there certainly does appear to be consumer resistance to information technology which even the marketing pull of the software giants has difficulty in overcoming. It does not mean that a revolution is not occurring. It simply means that it will not be such a tidy business as some prophets suggested it might be. Indeed, what revolution ever was a tidy, clean, simple affair?

So where are we? If we look back over the past five years in British television, a great deal of forecasting has proved to be quite wrong. Commercial television in Britain has continued to supply not only an excellent television service for schools, but also an enormous range of quality programmes, particularly in drama. More of that in a moment. Many have been surprised how well the audiences for the four terrestrial television channels have held up. They should not be. The four channels have made good programmes in the past and so they continue to do so. Naturally, there are changes: subscriptions for satellite and cable television continue to increase but still constitute only a fraction of the whole population and even within these homes, the established channels remain the most heavily viewed. One of the more successful cable channels in Britain is UK Gold, which by drawing on old BBC and ITV programmes are only repeating what has been seen several times over on terrestrial television. One of the most famous commercial companies in Europe, Thames Television, lost its licence to provide a transmitted programme service in the 1990 application process. Many predicted that the company would wither away. Five years on it is so successful as a programme-maker that it has become the biggest independent producer in Britain, earning more annually from this and from its programme library than it did as a contractor.

Five years ago, television sponsorship in Britain was worth £2 million annually, a trivial sum compared with advertising revenue. Now it is worth £30 million, and rising. Five years ago, most commercial television and almost all BBC television was produced in-house. In early 1995, one third of ITV's new productions, all of Channel 4's, and nearly one quarter of the BBC's, are commissioned from independent companies, most of them relatively small.

There have been significant changes in ownership, too. When applications were being considered for licences for regional television on Channel 3 only three years ago there were 16 licences to be won, all to be separately owned. Now there are effectively 10 licensees and several of them have interests in each other's companies and engage in a certain amount of co-production. The richest of these companies is part of a conglomerate that is now one of the largest media organisations in the world – Carlton Communications. Three years ago, Murdoch's News Corporation owned a satellite television service that was losing hundreds of millions of pounds of revenue each year. Now it is so successful that it is about to seek a stock-market flotation at around £450 million: News Corporation revenue is already equivalent to about one third of the combined revenues of Channels 3 and 4 and it is rising sharply.

Not all of these changes have been wholly to the good for educational broadcasting, but the interesting thing about them is that they form a bag of contrasting developments of which, few, if any, were forecast to be in place by the end of 1994. Apart from the difficulty of forecasting technical change over the last five years, corporate and industrial change in the world of television has proved swift and unpredictable, or at least unpredicted. More is bound to follow, faster.

Meanwhile, educational television in Britain is in excellent health. Pardon? What else can be said, when apart from the doubly unique and doubly excellent schools services, both the BBC and Channel 4 fulfil a responsibility to inform, educate and entertain. In the case of Channel 4, over seven hours of material is commissioned to be broadcast each week. This is supplemented by an average of over three hours of other material, all of which is supported by print or other forms of opportunity for the viewer to follow up interest aroused by programmes.

Reaching out to the viewer remains the most important and remarkable feature of independent television's contribution to education and training over the past decade. Despite widespread expectations to the contrary, the ITV companies, released by the Broadcasting Act (1990) from the legal requirement to include educational material in their output, have maintained a quantum of programming in their schedules and retain the appropriate staff to make its effects felt far beyond the moment of transmission. These 'community education officers' are unique to British independent television. Their role is to familiarise themselves with the educational (and social) needs of the region and community they serve and to link up with the production and commissioning staff to encourage suitable responses from the television company. It seems laughable now to recall a purple-faced ITV executive protesting in 1981 that these new-fangled officers would be coming between the production staff and the public! Those were the days when executives could come a line in pomposity to match the best you will see in the Palace of Westminster.

These members of staff have survived – as all educational initiatives in a commercial venture must survive – on competitive merit. During a period when ITV has had to shed scores of staff across the country, there are no fewer community education officers now that there were in 1990. It makes sound commercial sense to use these excellent links with the region, and to maintain some regional education and training initiatives as examples of services cable manifestly cannot match at present.

Channel Four has also gone from strength to strength in reaching out to the viewer. Experiments have been introduced to develop 'clubs' to give viewers advance notice of forthcoming output that will interest them and to supply them with particular support information or activities. The Gardening Club is now well-established. Others include the Science Club. Following its establishment Channel 4 has taken a leading role in setting up the National Science Line, a telephone hotline to resolve scientific queries. This is supported not only by the Royal Society and the Royal Institution, but by a host of benefactors including the Wellcome Centre for Medical Science.

There can be no doubt of the continuing strong relationship between the independent television sector's programme-makers and commissioners and the viewers. Indeed it is no accident that the British company invited to demonstrate the practical interface between the public and the information superhighway at the *Windows on the Future* Conference was the broadcaster currently leading the way in the development of CD-ROM, Anglia Television. Like Thames Television and all British broadcasting, Anglia's power lies in its programmes, particularly in the case of educational CD-ROMs, the SURVIVAL natural history series. Those broadcasters who continue to make educational material of the highest quality are laying down treasures for their future.

'The electronic infrastructure of the advanced economies will have six distinct features:

- interactivity
- mobility
- convertibility
- connectivity
- ubiquity
- globalisation.

That is not my prophecy. It comes from Alvin Toffler's latest book, *Powershift*. Those six features apply to the devices that will emerge as market leaders in the next few years, not just in the

North, but in such markets as India, where Hyundai has just invested in a plant to assemble and market cheap video CD players to play discs costing as little as 99 rupees each, only half the cost of videocassettes. The six features apply to high-quality education and training and to high-quality educational programmes too.

The current is indeed flowing fast, and there are not only rapids but sharp rocks on the banks of our river. What should we do as our boat gathers speed? Sitting still and praying is not really an option. Nor is pretending that nothing is really happening out there. To turn against the current or across it at once is to lose our ability to handle our ship. If we go with the current and plan our course we stand a good chance of spotting a safe anchorage and reaching it, by seizing the opportunity when it arises. Those qualities that have always made educational television magical can carry it forward into the 21st century, through the rapids that we are approaching and into a period when audio-visual resources can perhaps at last effectively support learning as well as teaching.

Dr Robin Moss is Head of Educational Broadcasting at the Independent Television Commission.

Audio-Visual Training Materials in Medicine

MICHAEL J CLARK

Introduction

Douglas Fisher filming Dr L G Goodwin at work on the chemotherapy of experimental ameobiasis in. (Wellcome Film Unit 1947).

The place of medical audio-visual programmes and of medical film-making* in the culture of modern British medicine is at once complex and precarious. On the one hand, society's perennial concern with matters of health and ill-health, the importance of medical institutions in society generally, and the accumulated wealth, prestige and sheer size – not to mention *amour propre* – of the medical profession have throughout much of this century provided a strong underlying basis for medical film-making as a specialised activity. Medical films, videocassettes, audiocassettes and tape-slide programmes have become familiar, if not essential, elements in professional medical and surgical education, while medical documentary films and television programmes are among the principal sources of public information (some would argue, misinformation) about health and medicine. On the other hand, it can scarcely be denied that, for all but a few cine-enthusiasts and specialists in medical illustration or medical imaging, medical audio-visual programmes and film-making *per se* play only a very small part in the overall activity and outlook of the medical profession and biomedical research community. Though generally acknowledged to have some, usually rather ill-defined, role in professional medical training and in health education for the general public, the production and use of audio-visual programmes are hardly among the profession's most pressing concerns, while even in the more purely educational sphere, medical film and video face increasing competition from more glamorous computer-assisted interactive learning packages.

Film (and, to an even greater extent, television) has usually been regarded primarily as an entertainment medium, and for this reason has tended to be looked down upon by the medical profession, in common with most other skilled professionals and scientists. However, as the recent series THE ORIGINS OF SCIENTIFIC CINEMATOGRAPHY (1991-93) has made abundantly clear, the origins of the 'seventh art', and the development of many standard

* Throughout this article, the expressions 'medical film' and 'medical film-making' are used as a kind of shorthand to refer to audio-visual programmes and production generally, though as will be apparent from the context, in some places they do refer specifically to film.

cinematic techniques such as slow-motion and time-lapse photography, are to be found as much in the world of late 19th-century scientific and medical research as in that of popular entertainment.[1] Many of the most famous medical scientists and practitioners of the past 100 years – men such as Emile Roux, Ivan Pavlov, Sir Henry Dale and, more recently, Max Perutz, John Kendrew and Charles Fletcher – have made notable contributions to medical and scientific film-making, and broadcasting, whether as authors, advisors or presenters.[2] Nor has the scope of medical film-making been limited to clinical-medical teaching and biomedical research. Although many early medical films were clearly intended to serve as aids to teaching or as records of clinical or biomedical research, many pre-1945 medical and health films were made primarily to record some noteworthy medical event, famous personality or interesting case, or to publicise and raise funds for the work of some voluntary hospital, municipal or private clinic or other philanthropic institution, rather than specifically as teaching materials. As well as constituting an important resource for medical education, medical audio-visual programmes thus form an integral part of the historical record of 20th-century medicine and medical science, while their importance in helping to shape public perceptions of health and medicine and attitudes towards the medical profession and medical practice can hardly be exaggerated.

Medical Audio-Visual Materials in Higher Education

Although studies of the use of film in medicine have tended to ignore earlier still-image presentations, the origins of medical film are closely bound up with much earlier developments in medical illustration, still photography and image projection systems. As early as the 1840s, lecturers such as Richard Owen sometimes used magic lantern slides and other visual aids to supplement the use of models, specimens and demonstrations in anatomical and medical lectures.[3] By the 1880s and 1990s, notable improvements in the resolution of high-magnification microscopic images, the introduction of more sensitive photographic plates and improved histological staining techniques were enabling bacteriologists such as Robert Koch and Paul Ehrlich to make extensive use of slides to record and display the results of microbiological research.[4]

Following the invention of true cinematography, some of the earliest uses of film to record interesting and unusual medical and surgical cases highlighted its potential value for medical education,[5] and as early as 1912 the *Journal of the American Medical Association* published an interesting discussion of the role of medical films in education.[6] By the 1920s, a large number of clinical-medical and surgical films were being made and shown regularly in teaching hospitals and (more rarely) at meetings of medical societies, and in 1930 an article by Oswell Blakeston in *Close Up* singled out medical film-making as '[one] branch of cinematography in which England [sic] is not totally outclassed'.[7] However, as the preface to the Scientific Film Association's 1952 *Catalogue of Medical Films* observed, 'The early history of... medical films in Great Britain reveals a number of enthusiasts each making films largely for the interest and joy in making them',[8] and right up to the Second World War and beyond medical film making in Britain remained very largely a localised, *ad hoc* and essentially amateur affair, the work of a large number of isolated enthusiasts rather than the product of any concerted professional initiative.[9]

Despite this fragmentation, however, the 1930s saw the first serious attempts to evaluate and organise the amorphous mass of existing medical and surgical film for educational purposes, under the auspices of the International Institute of Educational Cinematography and the Medical Panel of the newly-established British Film Institute. In 1934, the Medical Panel sent out a questionnaire on medical films to every university medical school and teaching hospital in Britain and in 1936 the Institute published its first *Catalogue of British Medical Films*, which listed over 300 medical, surgical and dental films of educational value, together with many research films on biomedical science.[10] While very few of the films listed in the BFI's catalogue had been made with any definite curricular requirement or application in mind, their orderly classification and presentation according to the 'pre-clinical science' or clinical-medical/surgical speciality to which they referred undoubtedly expressed a desire to see a much greater and more systematic use of film for teaching purposes across the whole medical curriculum.

This aspiration was maintained and even strengthened in the immediate post-war period. In 1944, the Medical Committee of the Scientific Film Association joined forces with the Royal Society of Medicine and subsequently with the British Medical Association to create an embryonic permanent organisation under Dr Brian Stanford for the cataloguing and evaluation of both existing and new medical films, and in 1948 a new *Catalogue of Medical Films* containing some 800 titles was published jointly by ASLIB and the SFA.[11] To the publishers' surprise, the first edition of 1200 copies sold out in just 18 months, and in 1952 a new and much enlarged edition was published with financial support from the BFI.[12] The immediate post-war years also saw the formation of several new professional medical and scientific film units by major pharmaceutical and medical equipment companies such as ICI and

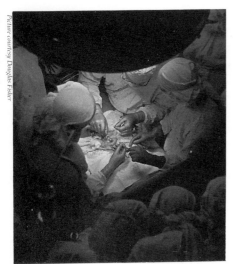

Picture courtesy Douglas Fisher

This photograph shows closed-heart surgery using d-Tubocurarine, an early muscle relaxant. This Wellcome Film Unit production was used to demonstrate the clinical applications of the new drug.

the Wellcome Foundation, and just as in the case of the documentary film-makers of the 1930s, these units soon began to collaborate successfully with distinguished medical research scientists and clinicians to produce high-quality teaching and research films of a non-promotional character.[13]

Much of this activity was maintained and even increased during the 1950s and early 1960s, but as early as 1952, the editors of the second edition of the *SFA Catalogue* were forced to admit that the sheer volume of new medical film production had made it impracticable to maintain the system of detailed appraisal set up in 1945-46.[14] The rapid growth of medical specialisation and expansion of student numbers during the 1950s and 1960s made it still more difficult for the BFI to maintain a time-consuming panel system of educational appraisal which depended largely on voluntary work. Except in a few specialised fields such as studies of the microcirculation[15], no new educational guides to medical and health films (as distinct from library catalogues) have appeared in Britain since the early 1970s, and Bernard Chibnall's invaluable *British Film Guide: Medicine* (1967) remains the last attempt to produce a truly comprehensive survey of British medical film.[16]

Though much of the increased activity in medical film-making during the immediate post-war years seemed to have spent itself by the mid-1950s, the end of the decade saw a radical new departure in the form of the Medical Recording Service Foundation (better known as the Graves Medical Audiovisual Library), founded in 1957 by Drs John and Valerie Graves in collaboration with the nascent College of General Practitioners.[17] Hitherto, nearly all medical audio-visual programmes had been made primarily to serve the training needs of hospital doctors and surgeons, and film and slides had been the media of choice because of their suitability for use with large student audiences in medical school lecture theatres. By contrast, Graves Medical's programmes were intended primarily to serve the needs of continuing and postgraduate education for GPs meeting in small groups in clinics and surgeries, and they formed part of an increasingly widespread concern to improve educational standards in general practice as a step towards enhancing its professional status. Working at first with gramophone records and later with audiocassettes and tape-slide programmes rather than film, and only very much later turning to videocassettes and videodiscs, Graves Medical rapidly established itself as one of the principal sources of materials for continuing education in general practice, the tape-slide format in particular proving extremely well-suited both to small-group teaching and discussion and to individual self-directed learning. Nor were the range of subjects dealt with limited to problems of general medical practice. Already by the end of the 1960s, the library included many audiocassette and tape-slide programmes made primarily for use by nurses, midwives, health visitors and other paramedical occupations, and by the 1980s it constituted a comprehensive source of materials on almost every conceivable social and psychological, as well as medical and paramedical, aspect not only of primary care, but of many hospital-based specialities.[18]

The Brynmor Jones Report of 1965 envisaged a much enlarged role for audio-visual media and materials of all kinds in higher education, including medical education[19], and was strongly supported by influential medical figures such as Professor Sir John MacMichael. However, it soon became apparent that some of its recommendations, such as the suggestion that academics should be encouraged to go on short courses in audio-visual production and presentation methods, were never likely to be implemented, while the Brynmor Jones model of central audio-visual service provision may well unwittingly have contributed to the isolation of media services from academic teaching and research by taking production activity away from individual departments and widening the gulf in status between mere technicians and potential medical and scientific authors. Moreover, even where (as, for example, in the University of London) a serious attempt was made to put the spirit of Brynmor Jones into practice, the results were not always terribly inspiring. In medicine as in other subject areas, a good many of the new programmes produced in the 1970s and early 1980s took the form of televised lectures to camera rather than genuine educational programmes, and failed to reconcile the conflicting demands of up-to-date scientific and medical contents, low production budgets and the need for attractive presentation. Within 20 years, the actual activity of audio-visual production has been almost completely transformed by the enormous improvements in analogue and, more recently, digital media technology during this period. But many of the most fundamental problems of medical audio-visual programme-making, especially those of educational design, identifying relevant audiences and understanding their specific needs, remain much the same and, in many cases, apparently as far from solution as they were in the 1960s and 1970s.

The Structure of Medical Film-Making in Britain

Professionally speaking, medical film-making has long suffered from the relatively weak institutional and professional infrastructure of medical and scientific film-making generally in the UK. Unlike (for example) Germany or the Netherlands, there is no national institute for scientific film in Britain, no professional association for scientific film-makers since the demise of the old Scientific Film Association, and only one major festival and set of awards specially devoted to medical films – the BMA's annual film competition. By the same token, there is no overall co-ordination of educational programme-making either with respect to curricular needs or to quality standards, and no truly comprehensive information sources on new or existing programmes. Much medical film-making remains semi-amateur in character, while professional medical film-making is very largely confined to a few university-based audio-visual and television centres with strong links to local medical schools (Sheffield, Southampton, Newcastle), a few well-established teaching hospital departments of medical illustration (St Mary's, St George's and St Bartholomew's Hospitals, London; University of Wales College of Medicine, Cardiff) and a small number of independent producers with extensive experience of medical documentary programme-making and/or corporate video production, such as Medi-Cine, Meditel and InCA. Though there have been some outstanding new productions in recent years from university medical school-based units such as the Leicestershire Health Authority Health Education Video Unit, these have largely been concerned with health education or the training of paramedical personnel rather than with medical education in the narrower vocational sense. Such public funding as is available in the university sector is almost entirely directed towards new technology-based, computer-assisted learning initiatives, while the continued downward pressure on funding both in higher education and the National Health Service has greatly increased the pressure on audio-visual centres either to become purely 'service' departments or to concentrate more on outside commercial work than on educational programme-making – if, indeed, they manage to survive at all.

Nor is the position very much better from the professional – medical standpoint. Whatever their medico-scientific or clinical interest, medical audio-visual programmes are not normally numbered among those forms of scientific communication which confer academic or professional distinction upon their authors, nor are they usually included in the research 'outputs' held to justify continued public funding for academic departments in university medical schools. Moreover, the competing demands of staff, patients, and students and continual pressure on resources in both the NHS and higher education inevitably make audio-visual programme-making appear a luxury that hardly any teaching hospital or university medical school departments can afford. Consequently, very few clinicians and medical educators either have the incentive or can afford the largely unpaid time to write, produce or even appear in new medical audio-visual programmes. Nor is it surprising if they often fail to make the best use of already existing audio-visual media and materials in their own teaching and research. In these circumstances, it is scarcely to be wondered at if in the audio-visual field most senior clinicians, medical educators and biomedical research scientists confine their attention largely to hi-tech diagnostic imagery on the one hand, and to traditional 35mm slides and still photographs on the other, leaving both conventional medical film and video and multimedia productions in limbo.

Conclusion Despite the sheer cumulative volume of productions in this area, the history of medical and surgical films as teaching and learning materials is to a large extent one of missed opportunities and unfulfilled potential, and the outlook for conventional medical audio-visual programme-making appears increasingly bleak. Yet at the same time, the demand for good, relevant audio-visual teaching and learning materials, not just in professional medical education but in health education and paramedical training, has never been greater or more urgent. It remains to be seen how far this demand can satisfactorily be met by new technology-based interactive learning packages. The problem is not so much one of a lack of opportunity or even of resources *per se* as of finding the right combination of technology and educational content to meet particular educational needs.

Viewed in this perspective, however, both the recent history and future prospects of medical audio-visual programme-making appear in a very different light. It would be all too easy to write the history of audio-visual media and materials in medicine simply in terms of a linear technological progress from one new medium to the next, culminating (perhaps) in the development of digital multimedia. However, as well as ignoring such inconvenient facts as the persistence of apparently 'outdated' media and formats, this would be to perpetuate the naïve faith in the unaided capacity of technology to 'solve' educational problems which has itself been responsible for so many inappropriate and unsuccessful applications of audio-visual media in medicine. Rather, a more effective *use* of audio-visual media and materials in medical education needs to be informed by a more critical *theoretical* awareness of their specific educational roles and particular advantages and disadvantages.

Medicine itself is entering a period of great uncertainty and far-reaching change, while medical education is also facing growing pressure for radical reform. The growing emphasis on 'self-directed' learning in medicine points to the increasing use of video and interactive learning packages, but far from rendering more traditional media obsolete, the development of digital multimedia may well give some older medical audio-visual materials a new lease of life. However, technological progress needs to be matched by a parallel process of reflection involving medical educators, programme-makers and educational technologists on the precise role – or rather, roles – and indications for use of audio-visual media and materials in medical education and practice, if the opportunities which the new technology offers are not to be wasted.

Michael J Clark is Audio-Visual Resources Manager at the Wellcome Centre for Medical Science, London.

References

1. Virgilio Tosi (author and director), Hans-Karl Galle and Ulrike Schwab (producers), THE ORIGINS OF SCIENTIFIC CINEMATOGRAPHY (3 parts) (Insitut für den Wissenschaftlichen Film, Göttingen, CNRS Audiovisuel, Paris, and Istituto Luce, Rome, 1991-93). See also Virgilio Tosi, *Il Cinema Prima di Lumière* (Rome, ERI, 1984).
2. See, for example, WILLIAM HARVEY AND THE CIRCULATION OF THE BLOOD (Royal College of Physicians, London, 1927, 1957) and THE PROPERTIES OF ACETYLCHOLINE (ICI Pharmaceuticals, 1947) [Sir Henry Dale and Sir Thomas Lewis]; CONDITIONED REFLEXES (Russia, 1925) [Ivan Pavlov]; THE STRUCTURE AND FUNCTIONS OF HAEMOGLOBIN (University of London, 1979) [Max Perutz]; and THE THREAD OF LIFE (BBC-TV, 1961) [John Kendrew]. I owe this last reference to Drs Tilli Tansey and David Gordon (The Wellcome Trust). Professor Charles Fletcher's work for YOUR LIFE IN THEIR HANDS is too well-known to require detailed referencing, but see also his three part series THE CHANGING FACE OF MEDICINE (BBC-TV, 1976).
3. I am grateful to Professor Phillip Sloan (Dept. of History, Notre Dame University, Indiana) for this information.
4. For some of the more controversial implications of this practice, see especially Alberto Cambrosio, Daniel Jacobi and Peter Keating (1993), Ehrlich's 'Beautiful Pictures' and the Controversial Beginnings of Immunological Imagery, *Isis*, **84** (4), 662-699, especially pp. 662-666, 670-683.
5. See THE ORIGINS OF SCIENTIFIC CINEMATOGRAPHY, Part 3: EARLY APPLICATIONS: MEDICINE (1993), especially the early surgical films of the French surgeon Clement-Maurice Doyen.
6. Weisenburg T.H. (1912), Moving Picture Illustration in Medicine with Special Reference to Nervous Diseases. In *Journal of the American Medical Association*, **59** (26) pp 2310-2312
7. Oswell Blakeston (1930), England's Strongest Suit. In *Close Up*, **VII** (2) pp. 125-130, on p. 125. I owe this reference to James Patterson (National Film and Television Archive).
8. Scientific Film Association (1952), *Catalogue of Medical Films* London, Harvey and

Blythe, p. ix.

9. Ibid. See also Brian Stanford (1948), A Review of British Films in Medicine During the Last Decade. In *Science in Films I: A World Review and Reference Book* Blodwen Lloyd (ed) London, Sampson, Low, Marston, pp. 35-41, especially pp. 36-37, and Florence Anthony and Douglas Fisher (1952) The Film in Medical Science. In *Tabloid Memoranda*, I (4) pp. 101-108, especially pp. 105-106.

10. *Catalogue of British Medical Films of Technical Interest to Medical Practitioners and Students* (1936) The story of the BFI's involvement in the International Institute of Educational Cinematography's initiative is briefly described in the introduction, London, BFI, pp. 3-7.

11. Royal Society of Medicine and Medical Committee of the Scientific Film Association (1948) *Catalogue of Medical Films*, London, ASLIB, p. v.

12. Medical Committee of the Scientific Film Association (1952) *Catalogue of Medical Films* London, Harvey and Blythe, p. x.

13. See, for example, BLOOD STREAMS IN THE BASILAR ARTERY (1949) (Wellcome Film Unit with Professor K J Franklin, Department of Physiology, St Bartholomew's Hospital Medical College); THE PROPERTIES OF ACETYL CHOLINE (1947) (ICI Film Unit with Sir Henry Dale); CARDIAC OUTPUT IN MAN (1951) (ICI Film Unit with Professor John MacMichael, University of London); THE JUGULAR VENOUS PULSE (1957) (Wellcome Film Unit with Dr Paul Wood, Institute of Cardiology, University of London).

14. Medical Committee of the Scientific Film Association (1952) *Catalogue of Medical Films* London, Harvey and Blythe, pp. x-xi.

15. Stephen D Carlill (comp) (1972) *The Microcirculation Film Catalogue*, London, BLITHE (British Life Assurance Trust for Health Education) with the British Medical Association. See also, however, the BUFVC's two subject-catalogues *Audio-Visual Materials in Physiology* (1985), London; BUFVC, and *Discovery and Invention: A Review of Films and Videos in the History of Science and Technology* (1985), London, BUFVC, both of which contain many titles of interest for biomedical science and medical history teaching respectively.

16. Bernard Chibnall (ed) (1966) *The British Film Guide, Vol. I: Medicine and Allied Subjects*, London, Film Centre International. See also, however, *Medical Films 1973 Selected for their Educational Value*, (1973) London, British Life Assurance Trust For Health Education with the British Medical Association and *HELPIS-MEDICAL; A Catalogue of Audio-Visual and other Educational Materials in Medicine and Allied Fields*, (1974) London, Council for Educational Technology.

17. See *Graves Medical Audiovisual Library* [brochure] (1986), Chelmsford, Graves Medical Audiovisual Library, for a brief history of the organisation to the mid-1980s.

18. See *Graves Medical Audiovisual Library, Catalogue* (1989) Chelmsford, Graves Medical Audiovisual Library. A revised, updated and enlarged version of this Catalogue was issued by the Concord Video & Film Council in 1993. The Graves Medical Audiovisual Library continues to operate but since April 1993, Graves programmes have been distributed by the Concord Video & Film Council, Ipswich.

19. For a general overview of the Brynmor Jones Report and its impact on higher scientific education, see Martin Hayden and Michael Clarke (1991), Brynmor Jones and After. In *The BUFVC Handbook for Film and Television in Education 1991/92*, London, BUFVC, pp. 15-21.

Wellcome Trust Film and Video Collections

Do you

need a medical film urgently for
teaching or research?

Are you

looking for biomedical or medical—historical footage
for a new documentary film or television programme?

Have you

ever despaired of finding any
scientifically literate film documentation or user support?

The Wellcome Trust Film and Video Collections
183 Euston Road London NW1 2BE

A working library of more than 600 contemporary and archival medical and medical–
historical films and videos, with free viewing facilities, customized information and advice
geared to the needs of medical educators, research scientists, medical historians, and
documentary film and television producers. Film researchers welcome by appointment.

**For further information, contact Michael Clark or Marie Williams on
0171 611 8596/7; Fax: 0171 611 8765**

Media Studies: Innovation and Intervention in Education

ANDREW HART

Media studies is a popular option with students but meets with ambivalence from curriculum administrators.

Undergraduate media studies courses are still among the fastest growing and most over-subscribed courses in the UK higher education system. Some courses (especially those with a vocational dimension) report a selection ratio as high as 200:1. Yet this dynamic growth has occurred predominantly in the new universities. The University of Southampton is typical of the older universities in having no undergraduate courses at all in media, communication or cultural studies. It is unusual, however, in offering postgraduate taught and research degrees in these areas, mainly for practising teachers. An MA(Ed) in Language, Literature and Media Studies has been running for nearly two decades and new specialised certificate courses have recently been developed in both part-time and distance-learning modes. At the same time, there has been a rapid increase in the number of researchers undertaking MPhil and PhD research in media studies. We have also incorporated media studies into the core curriculum offered to one-year graduate trainees on our English, Drama and Media Postgraduate Certificate in Education (PGCE).

This article explores the apparent paradox that professionals in education are developing their academic expertise in media studies at a time when the requirements of the National Curriculum and Department for Education (DfE) interventions in initial teacher education appear to be repressing its growth. It suggests that official curriculum interventions are in conflict with current curriculum innovation in the area of media studies and that this conflict needs to be addressed by university departments of education.

In spite of the continuing expansion in A-level and GCSE provision, with four different examining bodies now offering syllabuses and the number of candidates for some examinations increasing exponentially, the post-Dearing revisions to the original Cox-based National Curriculum for English do not say much about media studies or media education.[1,2] Even the references to the study of media texts alongside literary ones are less evident than previously. At the same time, one of the key effects of the requirement for higher education institutions to form partnerships with schools for initial teacher education has been to repress curriculum innovation. Although there are obvious gains in the fact that trainees are able to spend more time in schools, they are disadvantaged by being more detached from the latest research findings and curriculum innovations which flow from them. Because teachers are extremely busy in their classrooms and increasingly involved in the burden of National Curriculum paperwork, trainees are likely to encounter much more conservative and centrally driven models of teaching and learning.

Media Education in Secondary Schools The Autumn 1993 issue of the British Film Institute's (BFI) *Media Education News Update* suggested that:

'There is still much confusion over whether media education just means that the media are a convenient way of bolstering traditional English teaching, or that it entails specifically studying the media themselves. We think it must mean the latter because the former takes no account of existing knowledge and how it ought to be developed during schooling. To develop this effectively, teachers must receive adequate guidance; the production of such guidance must, in the long term, be based on the knowledge, skills and understanding that media education should be building.'

One of the main reasons for this confusion is not specific to media education but shared by most other disciplines. It is what has been called the 'enormous lack of descriptive work in classrooms'.[3] The research discussed later in this article sets out to provide some of the necessary detail for descriptions of classroom activities and to analyse the strategies, styles and achievements of different teachers' approaches.

Study of the mass media has been growing in popularity in English schools at least since the 1960s. The main impetus for this growth came from teachers of English, many of whom saw themselves as protectors of children from the 'false consciousness' that the media were believed to inculcate. It was this invasion of consciousness which Marshall McLuhan perceived in the 1960s. He saw education as a form of 'civil defense' [sic] against 'media fall-out'[4] (p. 208). The invasion was a subliminal one, operating beneath the threshold of consciousness. In a famous phrase, he warned that the content of the media was 'like the juicy piece of meat carried by the burglar to distract the watchdog of the mind'[4] (p. 26). This fear of the seduction of the innocent was to dominate the early years of studying the media.

In the 1970s and 1980s, media education in the UK grew rapidly, with the creation of new secondary-level courses in film studies and later with new courses in media studies and national examinations at ages 16 and 18. The availability of the videocassette recorder gave an enormous boost to media work and made the study of television the dominant focus. However, there was a tension over what kinds of texts were legitimate objects of study: those valued by teachers or those valued by students? This tension led many teachers to examine their own attitudes in more personal, less theoretical ways, and some recognised the hypocrisy in routine condemnations of what were major sources of information and pleasure for themselves as much as for their students, especially when they formed an important part of students' cultural identities.

The growing importance of media education has been underlined by the Department of Education and Science (DES)-sponsored report *Popular Television and Schoolchildren*,[5] by two BFI/National Foundation for Educational Research (NFER) surveys[6,7], by the BFI's detailed curriculum documents[8,9], by the attention paid to the subject by broadcasters and by the publication of *Media Education: An Introduction*.[10]

However, there has not been a corresponding expansion of training and development opportunities for trainee or practising teachers. In addition to the restrictions of the National Curriculum and initial training structures, changes in the funding and administration of INSET have meant that the major costs have been passed from the DES to local education authorities (LEAs) and, most recently, from LEAs to schools. Limited school funds mean that many teachers who wish to enhance their expertise have to do so at their own expense and in their own time. Others are obliged to work in isolation with little more than examination syllabuses to guide them. Some have inherited responsibility for media courses from enthusiastic teachers who have moved on. Although some of these substitutes often become enthusiasts themselves, they can too easily find themselves overwhelmed by the scope of the subject and by the unlimited material from which to choose.

What we offer in the Southampton PGCE course goes some way towards providing a basis for developing media education and media studies in schools, in spite of the current trends. All PGCE students are given a basic introduction to media education in the context of a language, communication and media module in their first term of study at the university. Those who are training as English teachers (currently 34) also follow a more in-depth course on media education in their first term, with two further option courses later in the year. They are all required to teach the whole range of the English curriculum, including media and drama, during their professional experience in schools.

The range of the English curriculum was helpfully defined in the influential Cox report *English for Ages 5-16*[11], which outlined five different but related perspectives:

a personal growth view • focuses on the child: it emphasises the relationship between language and learning in the individual child, and the role of literature in developing children's imaginative and aesthetic lives.

a cross-curricular view • focuses on the school: it emphasises that all teachers (of English and of other subjects) have a responsibility to help children with the language demands of different subjects on the school curriculum; otherwise areas of the curriculum may be closed to them. In England, English is different from other school subjects in that it is both a subject and a medium of instruction for other subjects.

an adult needs view • focuses on communication outside the school: it emphasises the responsibility of English teachers to prepare children for the language demands of adult life, including the workplace, in a fast-changing world. Children need to learn to deal with the day-to-day demands of spoken language and of print; they also need to be able to write clearly, appropriately and effectively.

a cultural heritage view • emphasises the responsibility of schools to lead children to an appreciation of those works of literature that have been widely regarded as amongst the finest in the language.

a cultural analysis view • emphasises the role of English in helping children towards a critical understanding of the world and cultural environment in which they live. Children should know about the processes by which meanings are conveyed, and about the ways in which print and other media carry values.

The Cox report suggested that 'media education has often developed in a very explicit way concepts which are of general importance within English'[11] (section 9.9). It defined media education as asking the crucial questions:

'Who is communicating with whom and why; how has the text been produced and transmitted; how does it convey its meaning?'[11] (section 7.23).

Media within English is most easily identified with the 'cultural analysis' perspective. It offers ways of understanding a wide range of texts and the contexts in which they are produced and consumed. Students learn practical ways of exploring some of the social and cultural issues which the media raise in a way that relates to their own cultural and social experience. They study the media as institutions which reproduce and reinforce dominant values. The statutory provisions and voluntary codes that are designed to protect the public from misrepresentations are a necessary background to understanding the nature of media texts. But this does not imply that the media are simply manipulators of audiences. On the contrary, media audiences are active makers of meaning and the media need to be seen as potential agents of education and change.

Knowing about the context of production and consumption of texts is a necessary basis for understanding how to read them. The fact that texts are constructed rather than discovered is central to the process of reading. The essential task of English teachers is not so much to make qualitative distinctions between literary and media texts nor to place them on some form of hierarchical scale; rather, it is to help students learn how to evaluate for themselves any kind of text according to content and context.

The specialist PGCE Media within English course involves consideration of such central topics as:

- Media studies and the National Curriculum; planning and assessing lessons; problems, processes and practical work
- Media languages: signs, codes, conventions and forms
- Children's and adults' uses of media; responses to media texts
- Categorising, researching and reaching audiences
- Documentary media: newspapers, television and radio news
- Media organisations: technologies, production and distribution
- Forms of fiction: comics, film and television serials
- Promotion, persuasion, public relations and advertising
- Representations and ideology: race, gender and class in the media
- The development of media studies in the curriculum.

The post-Dearing revisions to National Curriculum English[2] have simplified the specifications which arose out of the Cox-based order.[1] The 10-level scale has been reduced to eight over Key Stages 1 to 3. The attainment targets have been reduced to three (Speaking and Listening; Reading; Writing). Each attainment target and programme of study is organised into three strands: Key Skills, Standard English and Language Study, Range.

As has recently been pointed out, the post-Dearing curriculum can be read literally or 'between the lines':

The confident and enthusiastic English teacher who scours the text for ways of incorporating media into English will find many opportunities...But the less confident or inexperienced teacher looking for direct references to justify and support media education will find them excessively cautious.[12]

Whilst the range of references to media work is welcome, it is regrettable that these references come mainly in the form of examples. If they are not tied in with assessment and not mandatory, they may, unfortunately, be ignored. Unless there is a systematic expectation of assessment right across the English curriculum (to include media) it is unlikely that media will feature effectively in teaching and learning. This would be a great pity, because media texts actually provide accessible, real and exciting opportunities for the development of the basic reading, writing, speaking and listening skills which most of us agree are necessary within English.

An opportunity for creating a much more comprehensive and effective basis for literacy amongst all secondary pupils may be lost unless teachers themselves grasp the potential for developing media work within English. It is not enough to hope that media issues will be tackled adequately in other parts of the curriculum: English teachers are experienced in textual analysis; no other subject has 'literacy' as a central focus; media education has a complex conceptual structure that English teachers have worked hard to get to grips with in recent years. It is only within English lessons that the media are likely to be subjected to the sort of rigorous analytical scrutiny that living in a 20th-century democracy requires.

However, if we examine the revised curriculum more positively, three critical developments are clear:

- References to media now occur in all the attainment targets, rather than being confined somewhat defensively to Reading
- Throughout each attainment target and each key stage, the sections on Range (which are unfortunately placed near the end of each attainment target and key stage) indicate explicitly that 'text' means much more than 'written text'. It specifically includes 'television and radio programmes (news and documentaries, narrative and drama), newspapers, brochures, leaflets, reports, guidebooks, pamphlets, reviews, advertisements, playscripts and screenplays'. (Oddly, however, there is no mention of film, magazines or music at any point.)
- Because of the generalised use of 'text', it follows inescapably that 'read', 'listen' and 'write' must also be understood liberally, not literally.

Nevertheless, few teachers have been formally trained in media education or media studies.

There is inevitably a wide variation in theoretical understanding and classroom practice. Notions of media education may vary from showing a video recording of a Shakespeare play to the critical study of media institutions and audiences. Some teachers have rejected analytical approaches in favour of creative or technical ones. Others justify the subject for its implicit methods alone, arguing, for example, that its emphasis on group work and projects develops social skills. However, little is known empirically about teachers' actual classroom practices. The self-selected examples described in the BFI's curriculum documents are not the products of systematic research, although such accounts might well be useful in the context of action-research projects designed to enhance teachers' roles as reflective practitioners.

The Models of Media Education Project

The aim of the Southampton *Models of Media Education* project[13] was to illuminate some of the similarities and differences in media teaching styles of a small group of secondary English teachers. We wanted to explore their conceptions of media education in an English context. We also tried to document some of the perceived problems and rewards of teaching and learning about the media. We explored teachers' attitudes to media education both as a theoretical discipline and as a classroom subject, their aims for their students, the experience they brought to the work, the key concepts with which they felt most confident and the sources from which their understanding of these concepts derived, their favoured resources and the ways in which these are used, and their expectations for the future of media education. In the process, we were identifying models which might make some sense of the wide range of practice amongst English teachers, rather than trying to devise or recommend models of our own.

There are certainly some problems, as David Buckingham has pointed out, in incorporating work on the media within English.[14,15] Redefining 'texts' to include non-literary ones was difficult enough for Cox and the National Curriculum Council and might also be difficult for some English teachers. The BFI secondary curriculum document suggests that English teachers are ill-equipped to deal with the issues that surround the production and circulation of media texts and that they harbour prejudices about media in relation to literacy. The BFI predicts that:

'Media education in its most developed sense will be more likely to happen only in conjunction with other subjects because of the limited frame of reference in the English statutory order which gives preference to literary values and literary works over other media such as film, television and photography'[9](p. 65).

This approach creates a dilemma. It acknowledges the breadth and quality of media work within English but rejects it as a specialist base for media education:

'In our view, it is important that secondary schools do not leave full responsibility for media education to the English department. All subject areas share the potential for a wider-ranging use and study of media technologies, products and institutions. This means that schools will have to plan for whole school development'[9](p. 3).

The first BFI/NFER questionnaire survey (Twitchin and Bazalgette 1988) revealed a very wide range of understandings of and attitudes towards media education within schools in all phases, but offered little insight into the detail of classroom practices. We suspected that when asked to describe their own practice by questionnaire, teachers were likely to trawl through their memories to highlight significant moments in their own growing awareness of the implications of media education which they have shared with current or past pupils but have often been unable to integrate into a coherent programme of studies. At the same time, we were encouraged by the insights which had been generated in the *Understanding the Media* project interviews with teachers[13, 16-19] and we therefore chose structured interviews to investigate teachers' motivations, aims and anxieties in greater depth than seemed possible from a questionnaire.

So we were able finally to define the main research question in our project as:

What are English teachers doing when they say they are doing media education at Key Stage 4 (ages 14-16) in secondary schools?

The process of observation, discussion and analysis illuminated some of the convergences between English teaching and media education and enabled us to examine a range of classroom strategies in some detail. Unlike Buckingham[20] in his work on media education in classrooms, we were only incidentally concerned with pupils' learning. Buckingham offers a critical look at the claims made for group work in developing social skills, learning to work under pressure, understanding team structures, providing opportunities for self-reflection and exploring the idea that reading texts is a process of negotiation. He endorses the view that if pupils share their pleasure in texts with their peers, their understanding is developed. Similarly, his most recent research[21] is concerned with the growth of children's evolving understanding of television modes and processes, particularly in terms of how this operates in informal social settings. Although the questions of what and how children learn are also central to understanding how teachers teach, the focus of this project was explicitly on the latter.

Our basic research question was made operational by focusing on two major sub-questions:

- What media education aims are apparent?
- What forms of media education are apparent?

The research methods were structured pre-lesson interviews with selected teachers at Key Stage 4 and systematic lesson observation. In the classroom setting, the focus was on the teachers' instructions, questions, responses and other actions. Coding of teachers' strategies was carried out according to a systematic observation schedule, but not according to a given time-frame. Because the judgement of an event's significance was entirely in the hands of the lesson observer, observations were necessarily high-inference. But, as with all systematic observation processes, they had the distinct advantage of being made explicit.

The main variables were:

- Declared teacher aims
- Key concepts (implicit or explicit reference)
- Lesson introduction
- Content items
- Method (structure/organisation/development)
- Teacher-defined tasks/pupil activities
- Resources
- Lesson conclusion.

More detailed indicators of these variables included, for example, lesson follow-up, room, furniture, equipment, noise, interruptions, response, timing. The 'key concepts' identified were based on the BFI's 'signpost questions' shown below. These provided a robust but flexible framework for coding different conceptual focuses in both the lessons and the interviews.

Signpost Questions
- *Who* is communicating and why?   Media agencies
- *What type* of text is it?   Media categories
- *How* is it produced?   Media technologies
- *How* do we know what it means?   Media languages
- *Who* receives it and what sense do they make of it?   Media audiences
- *How* does it *present* its subject?   Media representations

Teachers' Aims   One of the benefits of the recently created GCSE and A-level examinations in the UK has been that syllabuses have had to provide clearly expressed aims and objectives. English teachers, as pragmatic as most, have often become so used to basing their teaching on past examination papers and taking many of their aims for granted that this approach had considerable novelty. The introduction of explicit aims and, in particular, learning objectives enabled teachers to re-examine their work and to remind themselves of a discourse which had perhaps become under-used. With the new emphasis on coursework, teachers found that each assignment needed to be justified in terms of objectives, but that in the case of media work the concepts were sometimes unfamiliar.

Although our teachers listed between them 29 aims for the 11 lessons we observed, it was clear that some were uncomfortable with identifying specific media concepts and saw the lessons in terms of textual approaches familiar from literature work. Our analysis suggested that of the 11 lessons, three declared no media aims at all, five aimed at a balance between media and English (mostly literature) aims and only three conceived of the lessons purely in media terms.

Lesson Content	Key concepts central to lessons	Frequency
	Audiences	5
	Language	3
	Image analysis	3
	Institutions	2
	Mediation	2
	Representation	1
	Narrative	1
	Genre	1
	Categories	1

The last four aims were mentioned specifically by only one teacher, a probationer who had recently completed a media course and whose lesson did address her aims; it was also, at one hour 40 minutes, the longest lesson we observed. There is scope for some difference in how these aims are classified, e.g. is 'design pictorial representations' image analysis or representation? Clearly, it is both, but here we have to trust our coding category during the observation of the lesson.

Conclusions Teachers' aims which referred directly to audiences and language made up nearly half of the specifically media ones. Awareness of 'audience' as a concept is probably the borrowing from media education that English teachers in general have most enthusiastically embraced. Its relevance to literary study, to imaginative writing and to oral work has been a valuable extension to English studies and it has linked closely with recent emphases on language registers.

Overwhelmingly, the teachers believed that media education should be a part of students' education throughout their secondary education and possibly before. There was very little anxiety about the subject proliferating into other disciplines and most felt secure about their own contributions to any cross-curricular initiatives. On the other hand, none of the schools concerned had yet developed a school policy for media education and in some cases the teachers interviewed proved to be unaware of media work being done in other departments. Some expressed anxiety about attitudes of colleagues in their own departments and feared some disapproval of what was sometimes seen as the study of ephemera.

It can be argued that teachers were interested in the concept of 'audiences' at least as a direct response to these uncertainties and anxieties. The study of audiences may have featured as much for its value in studying the written and spoken word as for its centrality in studying the media. What was happening, perhaps, was that English teachers were seizing on this area as a more accessible way into aspects of media studies where they felt less secure.

Some of the teachers had trouble bridging the gap between their own experience of the media and the varied experiences of their pupils. Some had found that there was scarcely any, or even no, overlap. With the best will in the world, attempts to draw from pupils observations on their tastes in programmes, music, newspapers, etc. with which the teachers were largely unfamiliar proved intimidating. By focusing on audiences, the teachers seemed to find a way of gaining acceptance for their own tastes while helping pupils to value their own experiences.

Work on images seemed to mark a movement away from a language-directed approach to specifically media concerns. What was striking about these lessons, though, was that the work was almost entirely 'uncritical' in that the emphasis was on seeing the images studied as models of good practice on which to base pupils' own work. Indeed, comparisons with poetic imagery were often made without irony. This approach extended into the next category, 'institutions', where pupils were presented with accounts of media institutions as having their own imperatives which were apparently perceived as inevitable or even to be copied. The idea that institutional ethics might be in any way problematic did not emerge. In one case the approach seemed to be linked to the school's own attempt to promote itself in the local community, each being used to justify the other.

This model of institutional acquiescence seemed to be general except in the two schools which dealt with the next concept on our list: 'mediation'. In both cases, mediation was interpreted as bias and pupils were warned of its effects. The similarity to work on literary texts is obvious, though both teachers were imaginative in their approaches: one showing that a Bible story would inevitably be distorted by media presentation and the other encouraging pupils to compare their real-life experiences with the fantasy representations of their age-group in colour magazines.

Even those teachers most dedicated to the need for media education tended to value it initially for its insights into, and new approaches to, language study and literary texts. They brought with them to the study of media texts habits learned from teaching literature, recognising (with Dr Johnson) that the first duty of the critic is to praise. What they did not praise, they were inclined to accept as inevitable, viewing existing institutions as representing a hegemony which seems irresistible. There was some recognition that bias and distortion might occasionally appear in media texts as they do in literary ones, but there was little sign of any awareness that these distortions might be ideologically determined.

Most of the teachers showed limited experience of media processes and agencies. This meant a restriction of range to relatively familiar areas. Like media texts they studied with pupils, they were strongly constrained by their own institutional and 'production' contexts. Agency, industry, institutions and production, which are arguably most central to teaching about the media, were rarely addressed by teachers. At the same time, although there is as yet no research to substantiate it, these are probably the areas in which pupils have least expertise.

For the future, it seems that it will not be enough for English teachers to be, as Raymond Williams put it, 'determined not to be determined'.[22] The critical question for curriculum research and development in media education is how can systematic training and staff development enable English teachers to gain the confidence and expertise to move beyond the limits of the known and familiar territory of English teaching into the more problematic areas of media education?

Southampton's new distance-learning Certificate in Media Education, run this year on a pilot basis, is an attempt to provide some of the help which teachers need. Although over 100 written enquiries were received from teachers in many different parts of Britain, including Northern Ireland, and overseas, a small cohort of students has been registered initially in order to enable close monitoring of their performance in relation to the new learning mode and materials. Before admission, all students were required to write a 750-word statement about their qualifications, experience and motives for doing the course. In many cases, initial telephone contact was made and individual discussions with students took place. The quality of this original batch of applications has been high, judging from their written statements and from the kind of questions they asked by telephone. They seem to be highly motivated but unable to gain convenient access to equivalent courses and qualifications elsewhere. The fact that the certificate can count towards a modular MA(Ed) is also no doubt an attraction for prospective students.

So far, it seems that students are managing the course well and finding it useful in their professional development. The specially designed distance-learning materials and the course guide are working effectively. Those students who have made contact since registration seem to be making good progress in their reading and self-assessment activities. The success of the course will ultimately be measured by the formal assignment which has to be submitted at the end of the course. The assignment, a curriculum audit of media education work in teachers' own institutions, is a substantial project which some students have now satisfactorily completed. It has clearly been vital to provide extensive and detailed feedback for students who lack the conventional contact with their tutors. Formal evaluation of the first year of operation, with a view to expanded recruitment, is currently planned.

It is clear from our experience in Southampton with both practising and trainee teachers that we need to be as flexible as possible in the range and modes of courses on offer. In spite of the constraints imposed by interventionist DfE policies for the National Curriculum and for initial teacher education, there remains a great demand from teachers and a great challenge to provide innovative ways of ensuring their development. The quality of such development depends crucially on the linking of teaching and research which university departments of education uniquely provide.

Andrew Hart is Senior Lecturer in the University of Southampton's School of Education, where he teaches media studies on MA(Ed) and PGCE courses and supervises research students. He has published widely on media education, works closely with teachers through the Southampton Media Education Group and directed the Models of Media Education *project. He wrote, with Gordon Cooper, the BBC Radio 4 series* Understanding the Media *and a book of the same title based on the series. He is currently working on a book for secondary*

English teachers on media education. He recently became Director of the Southern Media Education Research Network.

The published reports of the Models of Media Education project are available from Dr Andrew Hart, School of Education, University of Southampton. The book *Understanding the Media* and cassette package of the six BBC Radio 4 programmes is available from Southampton Media Education. Details of the courses referred to here are obtainable from the Assistant Registrar, Faculty of Educational Studies, The University, Southampton SO17 1BJ.

References
1. DES (1990) *English in the National Curriculum*. HMSO, London.
2. DfE (1994) *English in the National Curriculum*. HMSO, London.
3. Brumfit CJ and Mitchell RF (1990) The Language Classroom as a Focus for Research. In *Research in the Language Classroom*, CJ Brumfit and RF Mitchell (eds). Modern Language Publications/Macmillan, Basingstoke, p. 6.
4. McLuhan M (1973) *Understanding Media*. Abacus, Falmouth, p. 208.
5. DES (1983) *Popular Television and Schoolchildren*. HMSO, London.
6. Twitchin R and Bazalgette C (eds) (1988) *Media Education Survey Report*. BFI/NFER, London.
7. Dickson P (1994) *A Survey of Media Education*. BFI/NFER, London.
8. Bazalgette C (ed) (1989) *Primary Media Education: A Curriculum Statement*. BFI, London
9. Bowker J (ed) (1991) *Secondary Media Education: A Curriculum Statement*. BFI, London.
10. Alvarado M and Barrett O (eds) (1992) *Media Education: An Introduction*, BFI/Open University, London.
11. DES (1989) *English for Ages 5-16* (The Cox Report). HMSO, London.
12. Bazalgette C (1994) Initial Response to the Draft Proposal for English. In *English and Media Magazine* 30 (Summer), p. 8.
13. Hart A and Benson T (1993) Media in the Classroom. Southampton Media Education Group, Southampton.
14. Buckingham D (1990) English and Media Studies: Making the Difference. In *English Magazine* 24, pp. 8-12.
15. Buckingham D (1990) English and Media Studies: Getting Together. In *English Magazine* 24, pp. 20-23.
16. Cooper G and Hart A (1990) *Understanding the Media: Interview Transcripts*. Southampton Media Education Group, Southampton.
17. Cooper G and Hart A (1990) *Understanding the Media*. BBC Radio 4, London.
18. Cooper G and Hart A (1991) *Understanding the Media: the Radio Series* (cassette package). Routledge, London.
19. Hart A (1991) *Understanding the Media: A Practical Guide*. Routledge, London.
20. Buckingham D (ed) (1990) *Watching Media Learning*. Falmer, London.
21. Buckingham D (1993) *Children Talking Television*. Falmer, London.
22. Williams R (1976) *Keywords*. Fontana, London, pp. 90-91.

Interactivity and the New Media

TANA WOLLEN

It may seem strange in a publication as specialised as this to be calling for a meeting of minds occupied in very disparate areas of work, but this needs to happen more regularly lest the speed of media developments leaves our comprehension behind.

For those of us comfortable with a singular focus, the prospect is daunting: not only are the proliferating developments in film, television and video to be harnessed somehow, but the arcane worlds of computing also need to be entered into without fear. Those whose work is devoted to the study of film and television and their respective histories can no longer afford to ignore the consequences of computer-generated images or texts; nor can software designers ignore for much longer the emotional and cultural pull film and television narratives have had on their audiences for so long.

In a world where images, sound and text can be produced, edited, stored and transmitted digitally, computing, media and telephony are converging into formidable forces. Whilst the rumblings of massive media combines such as Time-Warner or Microsoft carry on in the background, there can be very few people in the industrialised world who have not had their work, if not yet their leisure, radically altered by digital technology. The blinking screen and waiting keyboard have replaced most of our typewriters and banks of index cards. Cataloguers, researchers and archivists amongst the readers of this publication will appreciate only too well the storage capacities and 'smart' searching capabilities of their computer tools. We don't actually need to understand the mathematical principles or electronic dynamics which make a computer obey our commands any more than we need stop to think about how a telephone works before we pick it up and dial, but it is worth considering how, or indeed whether, new forms of media are going to change our cultural habits as radically as they have affected our working lives.

Before long, the effects of new media forms such as CD-i or computer games on older media will be readily accepted simply because they will exist in profusion. However, amidst all the hype surrounding new media technologies two promises are being made. The first is the omnivorous nature of the new media: there will be no sound, image or graphic which cannot be digitised. The second is that there will be much greater scope for interactivity. Thus there will be any number of virtual worlds – from rain forests to molecular structures – into which we shall be able to enter and act. Moreover, this interactivity will not be limited to responding to a 'given' set of characters or landscapes: we shall be able to form shapes, plot narratives; to construct, influence and change the worlds in which we move and which will, undoubtedly, be moving around us.

A closer consideration of 'interactivity' will show this to be a rather hollow promise at the moment. Anyone who has donned the helmet and/or goggles of a 'virtual reality' machine will know that as yet the actual experience does not amount to the excitement generated by its potential. Image definition is still lumpily pixellated and the choice of action limited to stretching out a robotic hand which, with some time lag, you can use to pick up a computer-generated teapot or open a car door. Interaction with a digital text can take other forms: guiding a joystick or pushing buttons to move Sonic or Mario along to the right place at the right time and the right speed; punching your PIN number into the banking cybernets to pull out real cash (at the end of the day, there will never be anything 'virtual' about the experience of having no money!).

For many years a good book or film has offered the most impressive of virtual worlds. You can get into them, they hook you, you can't put them down, you're transported. The conjured world has to be convincing but the narrative has to be its driving force. These older media forms of virtual worlds (increasingly dubbed 'linear narratives') are, according to the critical hype surrounding new media technologies 'regressive modes', because you just sit there and lap them up. All those elements of colour and music, of description and character, of editing and plot, are designed to enthral and trap you. Nothing wrong with that, in my view. New modes of interactivity, especially when they are market-driven, cannot simply be hailed as inherently 'progressive' in order to make us more readily dismiss the old.

Interaction, like any dialogue or conversation, can range from the banal to the provocative, from the intellectually challenging to the simply exciting. What is proving to be a decisive, even troubling, factor in the media convergences which are getting such an airing, is not the fact that the new products engage their audiences but the nature of that engagement. Narrative may be universal but some narratives are better than others. Even computer games are rated by their aficionados according to the 'gameplay' they offer and the search is on for game designers who can script a game worthy of those who have honed their decoding skills by watching countless movies.

This point where technology intersects with markets is a crucial one at the moment. Gone are the days when getting a small, computer-generated ball to bounce back and forth across the screen occasioned great acclaim. Annual sales of computer games may be worth more than box office takings (a difference of $1.2 billion in the US, according to *Variety* 18-25 July 1994), but the mass markets still know movies and television programmes and still want them. If you are 'under the spell' of a writer, a director, a cinematographer or film score composer, so what! You might like it like that! It has to be a moot point whether the desire to be enthralled by a book, a film or a game is any different, even though the actual experiences might differ enormously. The point is that across the whole gamut of media products – film, video, television, computer games, multimedia – the spectrum between maker control and user autonomy is now a very wide one. How we relate to media texts and what we are able to do with them (the modalities of our interactivity, so to speak) will simply vary much more than they used to and producers will be able to exploit that variety, branding here, carving out niche markets there. Some might want to better their personal bests at blitzing demons or ducking bombers in bedrooms or arcades, but others – perhaps more executively stressed – may not always want to be taking a barrage of options or decisions at speed.

Different kinds of audiences/player engagement will emerge as game designers adopt more cinematic techniques and as movies develop plots and characters which lean more favourably to games licensing. In this respect, variety may give way to conformity as these industrial synergies recycle the same product in different guises – JURASSIC PARK saturation is a case in point.

On the other hand, interactivity may well be technologically driven to become ever more personalised, and to such an extent that, ironically, the industrialisation of interactivity could make the personal as a singular point of identity disappear altogether. In cyberpunk fantasies such as Pat Cadigan's novel *Fools*, a plethora of identities, memories and dreams can be accessed, borrowed or exchanged. It is as though everyone's neural networks are a hum of mobile videophones. There are no fixed boundaries, no geographical, historical or biological certainties. There are certainly no linear narratives. This future is portrayed as a vast amniotic state in which we cyborgs float, receiving and transmitting any number of messages in full-motion video and

47

digital stereo immediately to and from the cranial matter of any number of identity patterns. In these almost unimaginable levels of media noise, what will 'interactivity' mean then? Who will block out, flounder and drown? Who will find themselves evolved into new, polydextrous and antennaed forms?

Tana Wollen is Senior Projects Officer at the British Film Institute. With Philip Hayward she co-edited Future Visions, New Technologies of the Screen, *published by the BFI in 1993.*

Interactive Product Development at the OUPC

CATE ACASTER

The BBC Open University Production Centre has quietly but rapidly achieved some ground-breaking results in the field of interactive media technology. While other parts of the BBC are quickly gathering pace and developing larger-scale (and more commercial) projects of this nature, the centre's Interactive Media Group has been involved in specialist broadcasting-based product development for the last year. This article examines interactive media research at the Open University Production Centre, beginning with an introduction to the centre and its relationship with the Open University.

The OUPC The Open University Production Centre (OUPC) is the BBC department which has produced the audio and video programmes for the Open University (OU) for 25 years. The OUPC is a dedicated BBC Education Directorate department operating from a purpose-designed building on the OU campus in Milton Keynes. Some 160 half-hour television and 350 radio programmes are conceptualised, developed and produced each year. They are transmitted on BBC2, Radios 3 and 4, and on SSVC satellite to the armed forces in Europe. The BBC and the OU have a partnership which incorporates issues of policy, copyright and transmission, and as the OUPC is funded entirely by the Open University, no BBC licence fee money is involved.

The centre's strategic aim is to be the most effective and innovative higher education media production house in the world – *The Only Place* that the Open University will want to use for any of its audio, video, interactive multimedia or broadcasting requirements. It is staffed by academically qualified programme-makers who have specialised experience in translating complex concepts into effective higher education learning materials that are accessible to both their target and 'drop-in' audiences. As well as current interactive media research, the OUPC is also credited with earlier technological achievements including the invention of the video rostrum and CUEDOS - now an industry standard for auto-conforming. In addition, the Centre produced the first HDTV studio programme, and boasted the first Lightworks non-linear editing system in the BBC.

In early 1994 the OUPC's Interactive Media Group (IMG) was formed out of an existing, interactive laserdisc unit. The group was set up primarily to exploit the opportunities offered by digital technologies and to develop ideas for products relevant to open learning in the higher education sector. Projects are designed in a multi-platform environment and a range of CD-ROM, VideoCD and CD-i projects have been initiated which are working to realise the potential of multimedia in the educational environment.

The IMG is a versatile multi-discipline team exploring a range of issues in areas like intelligent management of access to multi-media resources, how video can be further exploited within the medium, broadcast quality animation using desktop computers, and interactive satellite transmissions. Huw Williams was appointed Project Co-ordinator of the group, bringing a background in commercial multimedia and enthusiasm for innovative educational ideas.

In 1995, interactive television experiments are planned to take place from the centre. The aim of the exercise is to enable programme presenters to gain direct access to an extensive database of video material that can be called up on demand to illustrate an argument or concept by replaying the audio/video clip over satellite. Future developments will allow the recipients of these transmissions to interact with the database using phone lines, and control the data flow via satellite. Obviously, getting the user interface right is essential in a project of this type. The controlling component will be a tone dialling pad that is both cheap and simple to send out to the potential student audience. Because it is recognisable, this will have the added advantage of being user friendly, as well as being easy to use.

As well as compact discs and interactive television, the IMG has also been researching how multimedia technology can contribute to the production of broadcast output. Experiments have already taken place which create complex multi-layered animation using the Macintosh computer and After Effects software (used in several Hollywood productions). While this method of production is slower than a specialised professional graphics edit facility i.e. Harry or Henry, it allows a greater degree flexibility as all the animation occurs within the digital domain. If changes are required, they are entered and the final animation is then re-rendered, usually overnight. Although slower than the equivalent on-line process, the end result should cost the producer less and allow more space for experimentation.

Terrestrial broadcasting provides a convenient and widespread method for disseminating audio-visual course materials, and accessibility is one of the key policy imperatives for both the OU and the OUPC. University research shows that 40 % of students first became aware of the OU through broadcasting, and a 1994 Gallup Poll found that 45 % of its sample had actually watched a programme[1]. How the issue of accessibility will alter with the advent of interactive technology is thus a delicate issue. Working on the theory that interactive products and services may eventually replace some of the Open University's broadcast output, issues of access, cost to the student and user-friendliness are paramount. Naturally, projections for technological growth in the domestic environment provide a vital planning aid for the group to help them assess whether interactive products will address these accessibility concerns. In the longer term, the group anticipates that CD-based products will eventually be overshadowed by interactive cable delivery and is actively involved in researching such developments.

Products and Projects For its first consumer-driven project, the group was commissioned to translate the BBC Schools' Programme Catalogue for 1994/5 to a CD-ROM for reference use in secondary schools, where PC CD-ROM drives are becoming a standard resource. Produced in-house in less than three months from inception to completion, the disk enables teachers to search for information on every television and radio programme produced by BBC Education for schools in 1994/5. The product is designed to be easy and fast to use, allowing the user to access content and transmission details for any programme. The user can also view a video clip from their chosen television programme, or hear an audio excerpt from their chosen radio programme, and print off a form to order support resources such as recorded and printed material. The product features over 3,000 photographs, 40 minutes of video, 10 minutes of audio and the entire text of the existing print catalogue. The disc was pressed in October 1994 and distributed to every secondary-level educational institution in the country free of charge.

A second project, specifically designed for the OUPC, was the development of a Macintosh CD-ROM video show disc. Over 40 minutes of high quality video was incorporated to create a demonstration product for information or promotional purposes. The user is introduced to three different access paths which allows them to look at a sample of Open University programmes on offer, be it by faculty, subject heading or geographical location. Ultimately, a more comprehensive product of this nature could be used by students to review programmes, by academics to search for clips on key words and by broadcasters to search for clips by location.

The OUPC Showdisc main-menu: users can search by subject, faculty or location

The product has already been used in an external exhibition and to demonstrate to visitors to the OUPC the range of academic programmes produced.

Another demonstration product that has been developed is a 'shotbase' or a multimedia database. This was designed to explore issues such as the optimum sampling strategy and compression algorithms of video data when used for archive and reference purposes. It examines how text-based programme details existing on electronic production files can be dynamically integrated with the pictures. It also looks at the concept of a central networkable product that allows multi/simultaneous users, and how to minimise network traffic and increase application speed within such a system. This research is currently the subject of a bid to central BBC funds for further development.

For the Open University, the needs of the student are paramount. The OUPC's Interactive Media Group has examined the needs of students, and looked at how multimedia can aid their learning experience. To this end, the group is working on a 'Moviewriter' which would allow the student to write an essay and illustrate relevant points by attaching multimedia resources (graphics, sound and video) to parts of their assignments which have been culled from a course CD-ROM. This will create a multimedia course assignment that can then be sent to the tutor on floppy disk for assessment. A further research project will examine how help functions can guide a new user through the dense information web of a multimedia product . This will be designed to instil confidence in the users and ultimately enable them to get maximum use out of a product.

Various other projects remain pending on the mouse-mat, for example a CD-i application that enables the quality of encoding available under the MPEG 1 standard to create interactive digital video. (MPEG 1 allows full screen full motion video playback from CD-ROM with a suitable decoder card.) The unit is a registered developer of ScriptX, a new multimedia language initially developed by Kaleida Labs, and will start to port existing and new products over to this format soon. The group is supplying all the graphics for a consortium of 40 universities producing a CD-ROM series on biodiversity in natural life. As an in-house service, IMG has also worked with BBC staff to provide technological support materials when presenting their work at conferences and trade events.

The Future The OUPC Interactive Media Group is not alone in research and development in multimedia and interactive learning. The

University's own Academic Computing Unit has been researching and developing comprehensive CD-ROM course products which combine audio-visual and textual materials for home teaching purposes. In addition, the University's Human Cognition Research Laboratory piloted a virtual summer school in 1994, and has been running a master's course using the FirstClass Computer Conferencing Service. This year it is piloting a course on the Internet – a project that was immediately over-subscribed by interested students. The Institute of Educational Technology also has a strong research programme in multimedia aiding in the development of a virtual microscope, and continuing its pioneering work on electronic aids for disabled students.

At the time of writing there are exciting new developments within the university associated with plans for a Knowledge Media Institute that has been designed to enhance and accelerate the many separate initiatives across OU and OUPC in areas such as multimedia, video conferencing, computer conferencing and other interactive on-line initiatives. The university has developed and produced a coherent and focused technology strategy for the future – an Open University for the electronic age.

Cate Acaster is a researcher who worked as Special Assistant to Colin Robinson, Head of the BBC Open University Production Centre.

Reference 1. Ballard A (1994) *Public Awareness and Image of the Open University - Report on Findings for 1994.* Open University Business Development and Marketing Office. Open University, Milton Keynes.

AV Voyages on SuperJANET

JOHN DYER

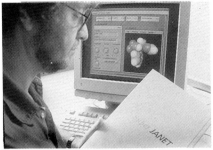

Networked terminals provide a means to share teaching resources, and can also allow for increased collaboration between higher education institutions

The United Kingdom Education and Research Networking Association (UKERNA) in Oxfordshire is currently developing SuperJANET, a telecommunications initiative for higher education and research, which could provide an 'information superhighway' for teaching and learning. Based on the already widely-used Joint Academic Computer Network (JANET), SuperJANET's high speed and broad bandwidth aims to establish a channel for sophisticated conferencing and communications among universities and other institutions, and to provide an on-line means to view and study digitised libraries, ranging from archive manuscripts to important film and television collections.

The Technology

Advances in telecommunications technology now mean that complex information incorporating text, sound, pictures and moving images can be delivered over computer networks. The measure of the volume of such data that can be moved over a network in a specific period of time is called bandwidth, and it is measured in bits of data per second (each character, such as the letter 'a' or 'g', typically requires 8-bits to describe it). Other useful measures of network performance are transit delay, which represents the time taken for a single data bit to traverse the network, and jitter, which is the variance of transit delay over time. These are all vitally important characteristics when real-time video data, for example, is being transmitted.

Academic networking in the UK has progressed over the last ten years from an initial bandwidth of 9,600 bits per second (often written as 9.6 kbps), through 64 kbps, up to the recent 2 Mbps. SuperJANET is bringing a massive increase in bandwidth up to 144 Mbps – with the prospect of further increases up to the gigabits per second range. In terms of specification, SuperJANET has high bandwidth, low transit delay, low jitter, and uses fibre optic digital technology. The consequence of this is that users of SuperJANET are able to access very large amounts of data over the network in real time.

Although, in essence, SuperJANET is simply a communications wire, the pace of development in the electronics industry is leading to the gradual convergence in the capabilities of telecommunications, computer and entertainment equipment. This is already extending the scope of the potential uses and applications of the network.

The Pilot Projects   During the last 12 months the Joint Network Team has run a programme of pilot applications spanning many disciplines to demonstrate the capabilities of the network. SuperJANET currently links the Rutherford Appleton laboratory with seven other sites: Hammersmith Hospital, Imperial College London, University College London, the University of London Computer Centre and the universities of Cambridge, Edinburgh and Manchester. These centres have been the testbed for applications which fall into four broad areas:

- Distributed or distance teaching
- Group communications
- Remote access
- Information and electronic publishing services

Distributed or Distance Teaching   With the increase in the number of students attending UK universities, some lecturers are now looking for more effective ways of delivering teaching materials than through purely traditional means, such as lectures. One way of enhancing teaching could be through the use of professionally developed multimedia teaching packages which can provide an environment that engages the student in a stimulating interactive process. First-generation multimedia teaching packages supporting text, sound, and still and moving images are already available for a range of stand-alone computers. These multimedia publications often contain 'hypertext links' that allow a reader to navigate between related parts of a text. A description of a film may, for example, provide on-screen 'buttons' which may open a 'window' showing, say, a cast list, or which may play a short extract from a film in the form of a QuickTime movie. Such links are typically used for providing more detailed information about an item, for cross-referencing or for bibliographies. Traditionally both the software and data are supplied on read-only optical CD-ROM discs, which are played from a drive attached to the computer.

SuperJANET, however, makes a more distributed approach possible. Teaching courseware may be created and held on-line by institutions with particular expertise in a given subject area or topic. If the machine hosting the material is connected to the network then the course may be made available to students at other institutions. The advantage of this model is that students can access the most suitable teaching material for their purposes, regardless of its physical location, and therefore without the need to travel. SuperJANET has sufficient bandwidth to allow the transmission of all the necessary data types for education including full-motion video in real time. However, further development of applications will be needed to monitor control and record access, and to provide coherent indexes so that materials which are available on the network can easily be identified and located.

Group Communications

Group communications covers applications that provide support for individuals collaborating on projects who may not necessarily all be located on the same site. SuperJANET is capable of carrying desk-top video conferencing sessions between computers, allowing staff and students to collaborate face-to-face despite being many miles apart. Group communications currently requires a workstation equipped with a video camera and video grabber board. Because of the volume of data which moving images represent, various compression algorithms are used to reduce the amount of information which needs to be transmitted. At present, this does mean that any video-conferencing computer must possess sufficient power to compress and decompress video signals in real time. However, these kinds of facilities on computers are already becoming more widespread and we believe they will soon be available as standard add-ons, even on low-end computers.

Personal contact through video may seem something of a luxury, but there are many ways in which this technology can be exploited. Specialist pathologists, for example, are often called on by smaller general hospitals to make a diagnosis. In such cases tissue sections are usually sent by post or courier between hospital sites, but the process is prone to delay and high costs. Through video conferencing, however, an image from a microscope could be transmitted across SuperJANET from one hospital to another within seconds. There are clearly many other disciplines ranging from engineering and chemistry to the study of fine art where this kind of facility could prove to be very useful.

Remote Access

SuperJANET can also provide a means to access scarce and expensive resources including supercomputers, medical scanners and satellite and imaging data. Researchers already use the network to browse graphical surface temperature information data from the Along Track Scanning Radiometer (ATSR) satellite.

Before the installation of SuperJANET users had to request specific segments of data to be sent to them on tape. In contrast, SuperJANET provides access to all of the many gigabytes of data that are held on-line.

Another example is the transfer of patient data from medical scanners to specialist centres for expert analysis and opinion. Software has been developed to correlate data from positron emission tomography (PET) scanners showing representations of brain activity with images from magnetic resonance imagers (MRI), which show the fine details of brain structure. Specialists can thereby make deductions about the correlation of dysfunction and physical damage that may be present in the two types of scan, without the patient needing to travel from one hospital to another.

Information and Electronic Publishing Services

The development of information and publishing services via SuperJANET will probably have the most significant impact on the way in which lecturers keep up to date in their subject areas. It is clear that ever increasing volumes of information are now originated – or are at least stored – in the digital domain. This means that, technologically, it could be a relatively simple task to make the information available for browsing and consultation across the network. Again the high bandwidth of SuperJANET permits the transmission of text, sound, high-quality still images and full-motion video.

There has already been a massive rise in the amount of data that individuals and institutions are making available globally on-line. This has been stimulated by the widespread availability of public domain information systems such as Gopher, WAIS and the World Wide Web (WWW). Of these, WWW is the most advanced, because of its hyperlinking capability. The Joint Network Team provides a SuperJANET information service using a WWW server which is accessible 24 hours a day. This information is updated regularly and provides details of the pilot applications on the network. Access to this service can be made from any IBM-compatible Windows computer, UNIX workstations running X-Windows, or Apple Macintosh computers running the public domain software called Mosaic.

There is also great interest in the more formal publishing of refereed works (such as learned journals) in electronic format. A SuperJANET project that has been running since 1993 permits users to browse on-line copies of real published journals. The articles involved are from some of the major publishing houses. The intention is ultimately to develop this pilot into a fully fledged alternative to printed journal publishing. Of course, other types of data sets can also be published in this manner, ranging from picture catalogues to scientific film libraries. However, before such uses become commonplace, important issues such as copyright and access accounting will have to be addressed.

The Future The Joint Network Team is always interested in hearing about applications that could make good use of this developing network. Applications relating to the transfer of multimedia information are particularly interesting, as are projects which provide a means of disseminating information to the higher education community at large. We believe that SuperJANET has the potential to become a powerful telecommunications infrastructure which will help to serve many of the needs of lecturers, researchers and students in the UK and beyond.

John Dyer is Technology Manager, United Kingdom Education and Research Networking Association.

A SuperJANET information pack is available from the UKERNA which also produces the newsletter *Network News*, which provides regular updates about work on SuperJANET. Further details are available from the Liaison Desk, Rutherford Appleton Laboratory, Didcot, Oxfordshire, OX11 0QX ☎ 0235 445517 or e-mail: JANET-LIAISON-DESK@jnt.ac.uk

This is a slightly modified version of an article which first appeared in the BUFVC magazine *Viewfinder* (No. 20, February 1994). For subscription details ☎ 0171-734 3687.

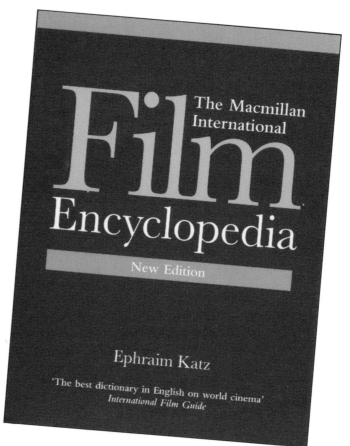

Using Computer Graphics

ANNE MUMFORD

Introduction The Advisory Group on Computer Graphics (AGOCG) provides a single national focus for computer graphics, visualisation and multimedia within the UK higher education community. AGOCG is concerned with the handling of visual information and its processing.

Its terms of reference are:

- to advise the relevant bodies on all aspects of computer graphics, visualisation and multimedia
- to be aware of advances in relevant software and hardware technology and in related standards
- to liaise with the community to identify requirements in computer graphics, visualisation and multimedia
- to make recommendations to the funding bodies on options for improving the environment available to the community for computer graphics, visualisation and multimedia
- to ensure the availability of facilities for education and training on the benefits and use of computer graphics, visualisation and multimedia including standards.

Visual information processing is a rapidly evolving area which underpins many current activities and initiatives within the higher education (HE) community. AGOCG's experience of the core technologies of visual information processing places it in a strong position to inform and advise local sites, other services and relevant committees in this strategically important area.

How AGOCG Works AGOCG works on the principle of active co-ordination as the most effective and efficient method of achieving its objectives. This has extended from the initial appointment of Dr Anne Mumford as the AGOCG Graphics Co-ordinator to subsequent appointments of Support Officers for Visualisation and Multimedia (Steve Larkin and Sue Cunningham at the University of Manchester). A co-ordinated approach helps to avoid unnecessary duplication within the community and leads to better use of the available resources.

Another consistent theme in AGOCG's operation has been that of involving expertise within the community wherever possible through open workshops and meetings to help guide the programme, and open invitations to bid for funded projects. Almost every UK Higher Education Institution (HEI) has been involved in one way or another in an activity organised by AGOCG.

AGOCG Activities These are very widespread, but concentrate on helping support staff in central support services and in departments to carry out their jobs effectively. Recent activities include:

Software Evaluations This involves getting a group of people together to evaluate a series of packages in an area (for example visualisation software, image processing software) resulting in an evaluation report and an agreement with a supplier (or suppliers) for a special price for UK HEIs.

Development of Training Materials This is often a joint initiative across sites allowing expertise to be pooled. This activity is frequently related to a software deal with sites then being able to obtain the software and an associated set of training materials making support much easier.

Support Services AGOCG funds the support of electronic mail and bulletin board services to ensure that questions get answered and information input to lists.

Workshops, Meetings and Courses Getting people together is always important and AGOCG has used workshops to help direct its activities and to advise the community on areas of new technology. Workshops have included multimedia, document exchange, multimedia file formats, visualisation, IT in art and design. The recommendations have proved invaluable to AGOCG and to the community it serves.

Standards Standards are important in our networked world where information exchange is vital to many activities. AGOCG has funded some participation in the development of standards and has a commitment to the adoption and promotion of standards. The area of standards is one which the Joint Information Systems Committee (JISC) of the HEFCs is committed to.

High Quality Output Devices One problem that many sites find is being able to justify the purchase of expensive output devices for high quality (or unusual) forms of output. This has been addressed centrally for some years by the higher education funding organisations who have funded microfilm and 35mm film recorder services at the University of

London. More recently, AGOCG and JISC have made contributions towards the setting up and enhancement of video facilities at the University of Manchester and the Rutherford Appleton Laboratory. Files can be sent across the network in various formats for video output. Slide making facilities are now offered by a number of sites. Large format colour output (up to A0) is also offered by some sites. One job carried out by AGOCG has been to try and put people who have a service to offer with spare capacity in touch with those with some demand, but perhaps not enough to justify the investment in the equipment.

AGOCG Library   AGOCG is currently funding library provision for some slide and video material which is of interest in the computer graphics area. This includes the Siggraph videos (the full set), some educators' slides and videos of lectures by leading practitioners. It also includes tutorial material and other 'grey' literature. This is hosted by De Montfort University and the materials can be obtained through inter-library loan.

Supporting Multimedia   As part of its concern to underpin the provision of computer graphics, visualisation and multimedia, AGOCG held a workshop in December 1993 to address the issues of 'Multimedia in Higher Education: Networking and Portability', the results of which are published as AGOCG Technical Report 24. This workshop tied in with the proposal from AGOCG for the Support Initiative for Multimedia Applications (SIMA) which has now been funded by the JISC New Technologies Initiative. The New Technologies Initiative is expected to be a three-year initiative of JISC. This has funded projects in a range of areas which reflect new areas of technology and their application. The projects are concerned with demonstrating the use of new technology to the higher education community through example, setting up services, training, and dissemination of good practice.

The main elements of SIMA are:

- a support officer who will offer help to the community, run courses, survey activities nationally, disseminate information about national initiative and other deliverables, and be a source of information for the community – Sue Cunningham of the University of Manchester has been appointed to this post
- workshops
- a series of evaluations leading to reports and recommendations
- a series of pilot projects.

SIMA aims to build on the model of AGOCG which will act as a steering group for the initiative. The projects in the first year will implement some of the recommendations of the AGOCG workshop. These recognise that multimedia is a technology which will be vital to many areas in higher education, yet the main developments will be industry-led. In higher education we need to be looking to support people using the new technology and to assist them in setting up an infrastructure with appropriate hardware and software.

The following projects have been funded in the initial phase and reports will be available between August 1994 and April 1995:

University of Liverpool	Evaluation of Video Conferencing Products on UNIX Systems to Support Help Desk and Advisory Activities in a Computing Service Environment
Heriot-Watt University	Meeting Teachers' and Learners' Support and Training Needs – Use of Video Conferencing with PCs.
University of Derby	Desktop Video Conferencing on Apple Macs.
University of Bristol	Report and Guidelines on Image Capture.
University of Aberdeen	Report and Guidelines on Image Capture.
Robert Gordon University	Survey of Uses of Software and Hardware for Multimedia Applications in UK Higher Education.
HUSAT Research Institute, Loughborough	Dos and Don'ts of Video Conferencing.
Heriot-Watt University	Dos and Don'ts of Video Conferencing for Teaching in Higher Education.
University of London	Dos and Don'ts of Video Conferencing – Experience from LIVENET.
Liverpool John Moores University	A Review of Multimedia Networking Developments.
Heriot-Watt University	Report on the Provision of CBL Material over Network Information Servers.

A subscription service is being set up for the output of SIMA (£50 to UK higher education) for all the output from the first year of the SIMA project. It is hoped that funding for a further year will be made available. If you would like to subscribe, please contact Anne Mumford at the address below.

An open meeting to discuss the use of information technology (IT) in art and design departments was held in mid-1994. This resulted in a lively discussion with many points emerging. A brief report of the main points which came out of this meeting is given below.

The Community   It was noted that the community involved both HE and further education (FE) institutions. JISC (and thus AGOCG) is primarily concerned with HE. The community is very variable with some art and design departments being small departments in large institutions and others dominating in small institutions. In small institutions it may be hard to acquire the skills necessary to introduce and support IT aspects and use of network tools. This may be easier in large institutions, but in these it is often the science/engineering-based subjects that dominate resource provision and not the art and design departments. Thus, graphic art and design can suffer in both.

IT Strategy for Art and Design   The requirements of art and design departments are different from those for science and engineering. This needs to be recognised in IT strategies in institutions. The differences include the following. There is a major bias towards Macs. Art and design departments would rather have high specification equipment capable of running industry-standard software than lots of lower specification equipment. Art and design is not moving towards a lap-top for every student but towards shared high-end equipment. There is also a difference in terms of the measured output of work – this may be a work of art and not an academic paper. Institutions – and assessors – may not consider this to be quite as 'serious' as papers and a culture change is needed if resources are to be allocated to graphic art and design.

Software Agreements   It was agreed that the CHEST-style agreement and contacts with suppliers sounded as though they would overcome some problems experienced by sites. The inclusion of documentation copying and the development of associated training materials was felt to be beneficial.

Information Exchange   Most sites did not know what other sites were doing. People tended to meet according to their particular craft interest.

Network Connection   This was seen as a major problem for many sites. Most sites are in the 'new' sector. Connections to all HE sites are expected by the end of the year.

A number of sites reported favourable experience with this means of accessing information across the network. It was felt to be an appropriate interface. It was proposed that a WWW server for this community could be set up through AGOCG.

Apple Macintosh Bias   It was noted that there was a general bias towards the use of Macs in many departments and in the industry. This was with the exception of the design tools where CAD packages tended to be used on PCs and UNIX workstations.

Use of Mailbase   It was agreed that a discussion list would be useful. There is a need for people to be able to find others working in their subject domain. Mailbase and other network tools might help.

Training People to Use
the Network Services   There is a need to show people how they can use available network services. This could be done at a future AGOCG event for this community.

Teaching the Students   People should be encouraged to include training on network tools and services as part of their courses. Students are coming into HE with more IT skills than before. There was a feeling that creating and updating training materials was unrealistic given funding and changes in software. It was felt that what was required were study skills for both staff and students in how to use manuals supplied with software – give them the courage to open manuals!

Design Librarians   It was agreed that we should make contacts with design librarians.

Resource Sharing   This is needed for shared output. Stereo lithography was mentioned.

Case Studies   It was suggested that a series of case studies of what people are doing would be useful. This might cover tools being used and site policies.

Teleworking   There was interest in this area and in the area of video conferencing. There are clearly a number of people working in this area and it would be useful to share experience. Video conferencing has been used at Ulster and some useful experience gained. It was noted that the Support Initiative for Multimedia Applications being funded by the JISC New Technologies Initiative is going to look at this area and to produce reports through AGOCG.

Datasets of Information and Images There is a need to continue to have on-line catalogues of information. The information is visual as well as textual and image databases with supporting text are needed. There is a need for curatorial and co-ordinating effort in this area. JISC, through its Information Services Sub-Committee is considering these issues.

Multimedia Authoring There is interest in multimedia authoring and an agreed need for evaluations of the market. The University of Hull has recently carried out an evaluation of popular packages as part of its ITTI project. The Mac/PC crossover is important to the art and design community and tools are needed to go across platforms.

AGOCG is now looking to act on some of the comments made. The need for institutions to take account of the needs of art and design departments in their information systems strategies has been raised with JISC. An invitation to express interest in submitting case studies on the use of IT in art and design departments has received a good response. It is intended to ensure greater promotion of information services available to higher education art and design departments.

AGOCG – Part of a Larger Picture AGOCG is funded by the Joint Information Systems Committee (JISC) of the Higher Education Funding Councils. JISC is a joint venture between the funding councils for England, Scotland and Wales with the Department of Education for Northern Ireland participating in some of the initiatives.

JISC Information Services JISC and its Information Services Sub-Committee funds a number of services which include:

CHEST – Combined Higher Education Software Team Negotiates agreements for UK HE. These are often based on community recommendations. CHEST tries to negotiate site licences for software which includes maintenance and upgrades.

NISS – National Information Services and Systems Provides information services over the UK Joint Academic Network, and acts as a focus for computer disseminated information for the academic community. It contains a wealth of information on the bulletin board and the WAIS server and access to other services in the UK and round the world.

Mailbase An electronic discussion list service for exchange of ideas between people via e-mail. Lists are set up for specific discussion topics.

HENSA – Higher Education National Software Archive   An archive for public domain software for PCs and for UNIX systems.

BIDS – Bath Information Data Services   Offers bibliographic data services to the academic community across the network.

MIDAS – Manchester Information Datasets and Associated Services   Offers on-line access to many large and complex datasets, including the 1991 and 1981 census data. The funding for many of these sets comes jointly from JISC and the ESRC with associated work taking place at the ESRC data archive.

National Services   Offered by a number of sites including ULCC (microform and slide production), University of Manchester (video, slide output), and Rutherford Appleton Laboratory (video output).

Linking via the Network   The link for all these services is the network via JANET. The extension to SuperJANET to offer more bandwidth is important for people in graphics, art and design with work involving images and multimedia data. The SuperJANET brochure notes:

'The knowledge, skills and resources exist at different locations. What's needed is some way to bring this information together without having to bring the people together.'

SuperJANET offers part of the solution to an integrated 'information highway' for all UK HE.

IT in Training, Teaching and Learning   The need to use IT in teaching and learning has been recognised by the Higher Education Funding Councils with a number of initiatives. Many of these are looking to use new technology in training, teaching and learning. Much of this work, particularly in the Teaching and Learning Technology Programme (TLTP) uses multimedia techniques. The Computers in Teaching Initiative (CTI) is a subject-based initiative for the support of teachers.

IT and the Library in UK HE   The Libraries Review Group of the funding councils, chaired by Professor Sir Brian Follett, has reported. JISC is working on implementing the IT-related recommendations in the near future. The report notes that the 'exploitation of IT is essential to create the effective library service of the future'.

Further Information   If you would like more information about AGOCG or any of the services above, please contact the AGOCG Co-ordinator: Dr Anne Mumford, Computing Services, Loughborough University, Loughborough LE11 3TU e-mail: a.m.mumford@lut.ac.uk

Navigating The Cybercampus:

Who's on Board and Whose Hand Is on the Tiller?

KEITH YEOMANS

Access tends to be seen as a marginal issue in higher education. A whimpering survivor from the participatory politics of the 1970s, manifest in a range of special courses held in great suspicion by some academics, the idea seems to have little relevance to the market driven, globally competitive, resource starved realities of higher education at the end of the 20th century. Yet the principle of access has a much wider relevance to the future of the sector as a whole than ever before as information and communications technology (ICT) speeds our passage into the information economy. Our concern now has to be not just finding ways for disadvantaged students to enter higher education but also ensuring that the sector itself has sufficient access to the global communications environment to maintain its traditional strengths and grow new ones.

It may seem odd to question the strength of higher education's position in this environment. Inter-university ICT networks were, after all, the source of Vice-President Gore's information superhighway (ISH) vision. SuperJANET, the UK version run by and for higher education, is in the forefront of European developments in this area. Academics move in and out of administrative and commercial policy-making at the highest levels and have always played a leading role in industry research and development. More recently, the ERSC-funded PICT programme, linking six university-based research centres, has carried out substantial research into the impact of ICT, now being fed into national decision-making. The rhetoric flowing from the ISH vision sets education at the vanguard of the benefits resulting from its implementation. So how could the sector's reign be challenged and in what ways?

A study tour of policy-making and practice in education on the ISH in North America* added questions about this wider dimension of access to those already arising from my work in this area here. A brief review of these questions and the context in which they arose may help to shift slightly the emphasis in the continuing debate about the future of higher education and, more directly, help to strengthen the contribution of those groups in higher education served by the BUFVC.

The conversation about access and ICT should start on the conventional campus with the academics who currently control the content, delivery and accreditation of higher learning. Here, as elsewhere, it is often quickly reified into hardware and system issues which quickly generate hard statements about cost and relative utility. But wider themes must be tackled if access to learning and research resources via the technology is to be realised evenly across disciplines. While most academics will give some space to ICT in their work, if only as a better typewriter, its use for research and teaching still varies widely between disciplines. Developments in interactive multimedia are liberating the technology from domination by text and data but the implications of these changes for their work need to be fed quickly through to academics if differences in ICT use between disciplines are not to grow. These differences will be reflected not only in departmental budgets but also in the range of course choices available to remote students. If ICT-based teaching materials have not been developed they cannot be distributed to this increasingly important group. The Higher Education Funding Councils' (HEFC) Teaching and Learning Technology Projects are a step in this direction but Snow's two cultures still have a role in shaping cyberspace.

Differences in attitude and aptitude, cutting across both teachers and learners, also inhibit the equitable spread of ICT across the sector. Eighty per cent of the students enrolled at the University of Phoenix's on-line campus, where teaching and student support are conducted almost entirely by e-mail, are men, in spite of a broad range of courses offered. This may, to some extent, reflect the university's recruitment methods but it is tempting to argue that gender-based differences in attitude towards access to and use of ICT have their part to play. Age and culture-based differences, though perhaps less well researched, are also likely to play a part in the decision to either generate or use ICT-based learning systems. These differences may appear less critical if they did not apply to key target groups for distance, flexible and lifelong learning.

Issues like these are not new; some are the subject of current research. Policy makers and those who run higher education institutions (HEIs) should be concerned with their rapid resolution. In the US the ISH vision and the train of interventions flowing from it have made a large but unquantifiable contribution to change by establishing the role of ICT in higher education (in this case) as a priority to be addressed by professionals and managers at all levels. The pressure to adapt quickly is evident in initiatives like the Western Cooperative for Educational Telecommunications, a programme set up by the Western Interstate Commission for

Higher Education. It includes among its awareness-raising activities toll-free audio conferences for state higher education executive officers, who are encouraged to discuss questions such as, Who are (and will be) the new providers of post-high school learning? What are the new teaching and learning approaches we might adopt from these non-traditional providers? How can we fund and support these new approaches while wrestling with accountability and productivity concerns?

In a public environment in which HEI managers and professionals feel obliged to address questions like these it is hard to ignore or marginalise ICT concerns. But the deliberate absence so far of an ISH-style vision from central government in the UK and the more focused impact of the European Commission's strategic programmes in this area call for different strategies for change in our HEIs. How many have prepared development plans which include ICT strategies spanning all faculties, are related to predicted changes in student population size and structure and based on a quantified analysis of ICT needs? It is still apparently possible, at the time of writing, to conduct a public debate about the long-term future of higher education without mentioning the technology's role and the resources needed to develop it. Yet the Open University has been with us for a quarter of a century and few broadsheet articles on the ISH now fail to invoke variations on electronic or virtual universities.

One danger of isolationism in higher education is apparent in the fate of campus audio-visual production facilities, all too familiar to BUFVC members. Clarke and Hayden's article in the last Handbook entitled 'Brynmor Jones and After' shows how, in spite of their comparatively rich circumstances at the time and the bold claims made for it, the technology's impact in HEIs was limited by '...the snooty and instrumental view of audio-visual aids ...' and the Brynmor Jones Report's reflection of 'the era's insufficient understanding of what has become known as "the management of change"'. For all our knowledge now in this field and for all the research undertaken, by the PICT not least, into the implementation of ICT in organisations Clarke and Hayden's gloomy hindsight appears all too relevant to this technology's fate. Nor has ICT yet had its Brynmor Jones (perhaps its *fin de siecle* equivalent sits in a PC in an office on the Microsoft campus). Yet the scope and impact of this technology on higher education's future is infinitely greater.

Attitudes towards and aptitudes in ICT on campus may be important short-term factors in determining who may benefit from what kind of higher learning via the technology, but they occupy only a small corner in the wider picture of learning in the 21st century. In the US today's new universities are run out of small, quiet office blocks set, for example, in the scrub lands of Colorado. A dish farm in the yard beams their academic wares to thousands of students across the US and, increasingly the Asia-Pacific. At one site a handful of young people sit in booths selling courses and dealing with students' problems on toll-free lines: no sherry parties, no freshers' fair. At another they charge more for master's degree courses than conventional universities on the grounds that keeping students in the workplace while they are learning is more cost-effective. At another, based on one floor of a small office block in San Francisco, all seminars are conducted by e-mail among students and tutors across the nation. It is reasonably argued that this exploded, non real-time exchange of ideas improves dialogue by allowing time for reflection and allows full participation by students who would be intimidated around a table.

These are reputable universities whose courses are accredited in the same way as traditional ones. They buy academics on short, part-time contracts, monitor their performance and do not renew with the ones who fail to make the grade. They have ambitious but careful marketing plans which include Europe. It is not likely that they will sweep aside traditional HEIs but their presence in the market place will add to the pressure on existing provision, especially for the 'new business' group of adult home learners. The economics of this new approach to learning must affect the whole sector, through competition as well as economies of scale. One academic economist at a prominent traditional university in the US pointed out that its reputation meant it had to turn away two out of three applicants because space constraints and building costs prevented physical expansion. The university is investing in ICT as a cost-effective means of absorbing the demand.

The principles are the same as those by which ICT has transformed retailing and financial services, but how much strategic analysis has been carried out on the impact these delivery systems will have on the size and composition of the market for higher education as well as the cost and quality of its provision? It may be argued that quality will be maintained as long as academics control accreditation, but how resistant can accreditation mechanisms be to a market-driven system serviced by academics on short-term contracts? The Open University experience would seem to suggest that it is possible to extend provision via new means of distribution without loss of quality, but is this process infinitely extensible? These, too, are questions about access. The term is conventionally understood to mean entry to a more or less homogenous tier of provision. But how likely is it that the new delivery systems will dilute quality in the pursuit of scale economies or erode the traditional HEI's position by niche marketing? In this case, issues of access merge with those of control. Now that 'cyber' is routinely prefixed to words to do with ICT it is worth being aware that the Greek root of 'cybernetics' means 'steersman'. The issue of control is central to the meaning of the term we use to describe the study of the person/machine interface. ICT adds even wider dimensions to the access/control nexus in higher education than those outlined above.

Set among the wooded hills of Seattle's outer suburbs, the campus is similar to that of a modern university almost anywhere in the world. The buildings scattered around its 150 acres are more prosperous looking than those most universities could afford but, clad in jeans and trainers, some of the people working in them could be students or faculty pretty well anywhere. Yet this campus is fundamentally different from others. It is not owned by a university, even a rich, private one, but by a multimillion-pound company. The discussions taking place around its tables, however, could radically reshape education into the next century as their antecedents transformed business and commerce over the past decade. Planners on the Microsoft campus, together with those in a handful of other communications industry headquarters, are dreaming their role in the organisational environment of the next century. They argue that their company's impact on institutional education would be at least as great over the next 10 years as it has been on business in the past decade. Their entry to this market, like that of other communications industries, will be decided by the business case: will the profits from it justify the investment?

The cable, computer and telecoms industries see the learning market as a whole. They have equal access to campus, home and workplace. Distinctions between these learning sites or between institutions are historical jetsam. The products they sell in this market will be shaped by consumer demand and profitability, not academic fiat. Accreditation is a selling point. The high table will be courted for its capacity to add value. Similar issues have long obtained in the relationship between academics and print publishers but, like many others, the marriage has survived on a mixture of quarrels tempered by mutual dependence. Both partners are now staring uneasily into the gaping maw of the multimedia monster, uncertain whether to bolt the door, call the police or try to keep it as a pet. The decision will not be theirs.

As higher education in the old social democracies returns, apparently irresistibly, to the 'user pays' principle, direct government intervention in access to higher education is receding. HEIs may still control the academic criteria for entry but the dungeons and dragons of the virtual university computer game are delineated by decisions far removed from the senate and senior common room. If academics and the friends of higher education are to widen and patrol the paths into and through the electronic labyrinth they must be more aware of what these decisions are, how they are made and their relevance to higher learning. It is also vital to realise that plans now being laid by governments and communications companies world-wide about what in the US is called the National Information Infrastructure will directly affect not only access to education but also the commerce in research and its dissemination among universities, companies and the public sector.

The Internet is an important instance. Defining the ISH vision, this decentralised, open (in principle), international system has been extolled as a panacea for and a microcosm of the western, liberal academic community. It has been promoted in the US as the model for the massive broadband networks that will reach into homes and workplaces across the union. Its formulation influences more or less directly electronic communications development plans world-wide. Yet the signs of strain are already showing. The traffic in multimedia juggernauts is apparently already causing jams in some areas. Demand for access has led to temporary overload for some service providers. Effort is going into configuring the network and making it secure to cope with growing demand to use it for business transactions. Scarcity, therefore commercial opportunity, lies not yet in the network's capacity but in the control of access to it.

The ISH vision carries with it an assumption of universality. But access to the superhighway requires not only the means to pay for the hardware, software and running costs but also the competence, need and patience to enter and navigate it. These two sets of constraints alone are sufficient to exclude a high proportion of most countries' populations. But further inequities of access have already been observed here and in the US through the practice of 'redlining' - the exclusion by cable and telecoms companies of economically and socially disadvantaged areas because their investment in infrastructure is unlikely to yield an acceptable return. ISH watchers in the US note with concern the shift in telecoms regulatory language from 'universal service' to 'universal access' as a further retreat from an equity of provision more strongly asserted in the US than here. They are aware, too, of the hurdles to providing interactive broadband capacity to rural areas.

Add these concerns to the problematic and unresolved pricing and intellectual property rights factors shaping the content and availability of multimedia products and the complexity of using the ISH to improve access to higher education is clear. This, however, is not a case for ignoring or rejecting it. Rather, it is an argument for those who believe in extending access to brief themselves on the strategic issues and work towards resolving them appropriately. It is also a case for those in the academic community with the relevant expertise, skills and facilities – and this must include the entire BUFVC membership – to contribute to the cause while enhancing and safeguarding their own positions by systematically making these resources more available within their own institutions and outside to their wider communities.

In the US independent watchdogs like the Benton Foundation, the Center for Media Education and the Electronic Frontier Foundation research into and campaign on issues, such as the ones outlined above. Federal and State administrators are making efforts to identify and assert equity issues in the development of the National Information Infrastructure. The Western Cooperative for Educational Telecommunications is only one body within the higher education sector negotiating with the communications industry to obtain favourable rates for HEI needs it has helped to identify, raising awareness of critical ISH issues in the teaching unions and on campuses through conferences including, for example, sessions on federal telecommunications legislation and funding initiatives and state planning models for connecting to the national information highway.

The absence of a national initiative and the decision to focus telecoms competition at local level are both strong arguments for HEIs to stimulate thinking and action on these issues in their local areas among politicians, administrators and the private sector. The debate should start, however, on campus among the faculty whose future will increasingly depend on its outcomes and, perhaps most importantly, among the students whose lives will be shaped by it.

*Keith Yeomans is an independent consultant working in electronic communications and education. He recently visited the USA where, courtesy of a Winston Churchill Fellowship, he examined the role of the information superhighway in promoting access to education.

A Hundred Years of Moving Pictures and Education

MURRAY WESTON

Jean Comandon with his technician Pierre de Fontbrune using special techniques for filming the growth of plants at the Institute Pasteur. (CROISSANCE DES VEGÉTAUX c1940).

Writing at the end of 1994, as we enter a period celebrating the centenary of film, it might be appropriate to apply a historical perspective to the use of audio-visual media for education since the 1890s.

A re-examination of the early development of moving pictures in the late 19th century shows that many of the 'pioneers' were not entertainers, but academic researchers and educationalists. The early chronophotographers such as Janssen, Marey and Muybridge recorded movement for scientific research and then used the images to educate and inform. The projection of their pictures was made to academic audiences and students – particularly those with an interest in human and animal physiology. The military also took a special interest in 'chronophotography' for the design of infantry equipment and the study of ballistics. This was some years before the Lumière brothers presented the first commercial cinema performances for entertainment in Paris in 1895.

The users of 'film as instrument,' the educators, were there at the start. In fact, there are surviving films from around the turn of the century which were made to record subjects in medicine, surgery, anthropology, psychiatry, botany and zoology. The early academic film-makers explored in a surprisingly sophisticated manner the properties of film for recording time-lapse, high-speed and cinemicrography. All this was achieved before 1910. Examples of these early films have now been collected and re-released in a film series entitled THE ORIGINS OF SCIENTIFIC CINEMATOGRAPHY, which has been compiled by Virgilio Tosi in a co-production with the Institut für den Wissenschaftlichen Film, Göttingen; CNRS Audiovisuel, Paris; and the Instituto Luce, Rome. This excellent compilation clearly demonstrates that the early use of film by the academic community, one of the keys to the development of the genre of the 'documentary', was essentially a European phenomenon.

The British documentary movement of the 1930s was a further expression of this European interest in factual film, and saw the founding of many important new groups and institutions. It also laid the foundations for specialised 'educational film'. In 1930 the Empire Marketing Board Film Unit was formed. The British Film

Institute was established in 1933 as was the Shell Film Unit, which, under the guidance of John Grierson, was properly launched with the release of Edgar Anstey's AIRPORT in 1934. This use of film by an industrial company came about through the farsighted support of Public Relations Officer Jack Beddington at Shell. His feeling was that industry had a responsibility to its public to educate and to inform without promoting products. In the 1920s 16mm film arrived, and this, the first practical system which could bring moving pictures into the lecture theatre or the classroom, allowed Shell films to reach a specialist market without necessarily being distributed via cinemas. Shell was not the only organisation to see the advantage of using film in this way. The Coal Board, British Railways and the GPO, along with specialist educational production companies such as GB Instructional, all added quality productions to the growing catalogue of material available.

The subsequent influence of Britain's documentary movement on the style of factual film production around the world cannot be overestimated. The nascent medium of television was also influenced in the way it approached documentary programmes – especially after the British service was re-launched in 1946.

During wartime, documentary film production was controlled and came under the Ministry of Information. Paradoxically, this was an important period for the creative development of documentary film-makers. The evidence of the strides made in wartime was soon to be shown in the quality and quantity of production post-war.

By the late 1940s film was being used for educational purposes for all age groups. In 1947 the Scientific Film Association was formed and 1948 saw the foundation of the British Universities Film Council. At that time it was mainly teachers of science who recognised the value of film both as an instrument of research and for communication.

It might be surprising to learn that university scientists who tried their hands at film-making were later to have considerable influence on British television programmes. For example, people like Nicholaas Tinbergen and Gerald Thompson at the University of Oxford were among those who helped to establish the reputation of BBC TV's natural history programme output through contributions to programmes including LOOK.

In America the rise of the influence of behavioural psychology in the study of learning started to have an influence on educational theory and the use of various media for teaching. This broad academic subject area became known as educational technology and it was later to have a significant influence on the innovative use of audio-visual materials and new media in education.

Interest in the use of film and television for teaching at all levels increased throughout the 1950s and 1960s. At the Scottish Central Film Library, one of Britain's largest 16mm film libraries which served a predominantly schools market, a former manager used to tell how, at the height of activity during the early 1960s, all the film prints (and they held thousands) would be out on loan by Tuesday night every week.

Live use only could be made of television, there being no means readily available for recording off-air, so any broadcasts for education were made at times intended to fit in with school timetables. In the early 1960s, universities rapidly increased in size and number as a result of major investment by the Labour government. Part of this investment, following the publication of the Brynmor Jones Report in 1963, included the provision of film and television production facilities in a number of the larger universities. Some also installed cable distribution networks.

Although the Brynmor Jones Report focused on 'higher scientific education', those working in the arts, the humanities and the social sciences were soon to recognise the value of film and television in their teaching – either through the production of new materials or through the study of archival material. In 1966 the InterUniversity History Film Consortium was formed (and is still operating to this day) to make archive film more widely available as a prime source for study.

In 1969 the Open University was launched and this brought innovative teaching methods into higher education along with broadcast television. The Open University has since been one of the great success stories of British educational innovation and the use of broadcasting in partnership with the BBC played an essential part in establishing this success.

The next real revolution in the use of audio-visual materials in education came with the general availability of low-cost video recorders and videocassettes for use in the lecture theatre, the classroom and the home. Even though the first videocassette machines appeared in 1969 their real influence was not felt until they were widely available through high-street shops; 1981 was arguably the year when this happened. Paradoxically, this development was not immediately helpful. It offered the potential for low-cost access and flexible use of television and pre-recorded material – but at that time it was illegal to record most general output television programmes 'off-air' and it took a little time for enough good quality teaching material to be released on cassette.

In addition, as a direct result of growing competition, the 16mm film libraries started to decline rapidly and print quality went downhill. The television companies released relatively few programmes for educational use (finding it too much trouble for too little return to clear relevant rights for cassette distribution) so something needed to be done. The *Copyright, Designs and Patents Act, 1988* included a special section (No. 35) which allowed educational establishments to record general television and radio broadcasts off-air. This enabled universities and schools legitimately to accumulate large libraries of broadcast programmes from 1989. Indeed, in the future, these libraries may become important stores providing access to the broadcast record to complement the holdings of the established national and regional archives.

The early 1980s saw the introduction of microcomputers into education at all levels. This development, combined with the control of optical videodisc player devices, offered the potential for random access and interactive control of moving pictures, which could be useful for certain types of educational application. Assumptions about the value of interactivity came from the results of behavioural psychology and educational theory. The impact of this development using videodiscs largely failed – partly because the content of the material was not always well constructed and partly because there was simply not enough appropriate software available. Without good supplies of software very few player devices were purchased.

Similar problems have already been met in the development of computer-based multimedia courseware. Rapid changes in computer equipment and software have not helped to establish the general use of computer-based multimedia courseware, although development work has shown much promise during the last five years.

The gradual drift in technology from analogue to digital and from linear to non-linear is gathering pace and it is clear that these changes are likely to have a fundamental effect on the distribution and use of moving pictures and sound for learning. It is not yet clear, however, where these developments will bring their greatest impact.

If one allows oneself the opportunity to look ahead from this point there are various broad conclusions about the future which may be drawn.

Moving pictures and sound sourced from computers are likely to have a significant impact on teaching and learning in the not-too-distant future. Quite how the material will be delivered, what system it will use and how it will fit in with conventional teaching are yet to be seen. The ubiquitous videocassette is likely to stay around for many years. Even though digital will soon replace analogue, it is highly unlikely that non-linear works will replace linear media.

Interactive and 'on-demand' services appear to offer new opportunities for broadcasting and cable transmission and these may provide new forms of access to educational material.

Whatever happens, the main challenge will be to ensure that these burgeoning media will continue to deliver material of value to those who wish to improve learning. Whether the delivery is by computer, television, cinema screen or holographic virtual image it matters not – from the educationalist's point of view, it is essential that the heritage of moving pictures and sound recorded during the first 100 years of the audio-visual industries (and in the future) is catalogued and held safely with provision for easy access and use. Without libraries there can be no organised study. Indeed, some would go further – the measure of a civilisation is shown by the size and content of its libraries. The next hundred years will really prove whether we value our audio-visual records (and our civilisation).

Murray Weston *is Director of the British Universities Film & Video Council*

A Hundred Years Young

PHILL WALKLEY

It was just a fragment, no more than 30 seconds: The Euston Road, hansoms, horse drawn trams, passers-by glancing at the camera but hurrying by without the fascination or recognition that came later. It looked like a still photograph, and had the superb picture quality found in expert work of the period, but this photograph moved!

In the three weeks before Christmas 1994, the National Film Theatre showed all the National Film Archive's holdings of pre-1900 films, and of course the variety was very wide: the first Lumière films from 1895, Robert Paul's and Birt Acres' pioneering 1895 and 1898 titles, early actuality subjects through to the first attempts at narrative cinema. In these first years there were neither professionals nor amateurs in the world of film-making. Everything that survives has a place simply because of its age and rarity. While some very early material astonishes in its beauty and technical proficiency, not all of it is exemplary. It was surprising to see that the earliest Irish material (the work of Robert A Mitchell during 1898) was limited both visually and in its subject matter.

During 1994 and 1995, we have been celebrating the Countdown to Cinema – those events, people, experiments and ideas which generated such an excited atmosphere of competition in 1894 and 1895, culminating in the Lumière brothers' victory in getting film onto a screen on 28th December 1895 in the Grand Café in Paris. The UK will commemorate its celebration in 1996 because that is when our centenary falls. The Lumière show at the Regent Street Polytechnic on 20th February 1896 will be commemorated on the same date and in the same place in 1996 with a performance of the first programme on an original Lumière machine. We shall then move to Leicester Square in early March 1996 to recall the Lumières' arrival at the Empire on 7th March 1896 and Robert Paul's at the Alhambra on 25th March. The Leicester Square events mark the arrival of commercial cinema via the music hall, with 100 simultaneous premieres across the UK.

Gwenan Owen's stimulating article which follows makes an argument for the serious consideration of what is the real 'people's cinema' – amateur film. Cinema 100, the British commemoration of the centenary of cinema, shares this passion. Perhaps uniquely in Europe we want to have a genuinely popular celebration of what has been the most accessible and popular of visual art forms. In addition to the national projects (premieres, open days, media series), 13 area committees are coordinating local events all over the kingdom. The First Screenings initiatives of Cinema 100 aim to celebrate, and also renew, the enthusiasm for picture going that marked the last century.

A travelling show will feature a mixture of compilation film (including archive material) and live actors; nominations for commemorative plaques are being invited from people all over the country; there are plans for a book of first screenings, and a number of education packs and reminiscence projects are ready. Archive shows making accessible treasures of the regional film archives as well as the National Archives will be an important enrichment of centenary screenings, with a joint European project currently under consideration to examine the continent into which the cinematograph came by using last century film from a number of EU partners.

Cinema recorded, entertained and enthralled the last century. It changed the way we viewed the world. Its technology has passed into everyone's homes through the video recorder and into everyone's hands with the video camera. Most subtly, experience of film watching has influenced the way people use the film and video cameras which are in increasing ownership. As we commemorate the cinema's first hundred years we treasure, even revere, the fragments that remain from the first years of film-making. Gwenan's article makes an impassioned plea for the proper recognition and preservation of film made by ordinary people. How rich a celebration we shall have in 2096 if her ideas are followed!

Phill Walkley *manages the First Screenings initiative of Cinema 100, the coordinating body for the 1996 UK centenary of cinema celebrations.*

Moving Views:
The Study of Amateur Film

GWENAN OWEN

VERZET IN GRONINGEN (RESISTANCE IN GRONINGEN), 1947. *An amateur film which provides insight into the way our perceptions of the past change. In this picture the resistance group deliberates with the leader, uncle Rudolf, in his living-room.*

The recent publication of *Wales and Cinema – The First Hundred Years*[1] prefaces its contents with the following words from Luis Buñuel's autobiography:

'You have to begin to lose your memory, if only in bits and pieces, to realise memory is what makes our lives. Life without memory is no life at all. Our memory is our coherence, our reason, our feeling, even our action. Without it we are nothing.'

Memory is our past, our individual past and our collective pasts. It is also our history, and just as there are many memories there are also many histories. The past is a complex and changing kaleidoscope, as constantly changing as the present and constantly requiring airing and re-assessment.

Our collective memories, our knowledges of the past are derived from many different sources ranging from early tools and instruments to manuscripts and visual representations, legal documents, diaries and letters as well as secondary sources and interpretative historical texts.

Film and photography have also, more recently, played their part in shaping our interpretations of the past. And while all historians are aware that no historical source can be considered totally objective, the image, and in particular the moving image, is a potent representation of the past and a historical source which needs to be handled with extreme care. If the camera never lies, it certainly does not tell the whole truth and nothing but the truth.

The value of the moving image as an historical source was one of the many issues raised and discussed at a recent conference organised by the Wales Film and Television Archive at Chapter Arts Centre, Cardiff. Moving Views – An Amateur Film Forum was an attempt to draw attention to the valuable visual heritage created by the amateur film-makers of the 20th century – a heritage which until recently has been regarded by film archives as the black sheep or poor cousin of our film culture, and which, as a consequence, has been rejected as a serious historical resource.

Now the balance is shifting and the poor cousin seems to be coming into its own. Television producers, documentary makers, film archivists, historians, geographers, ethnographers and anthropologists are increasingly convinced of the need to preserve and assess this very varied and inconsistent hybrid which is our amateur film culture. This growing interest has been reflected on a European level by the creation of the Association Européene Inédits (AEI) whose aim is to 'stimulate, promote, co-ordinate and organise, at an international level, all activities related to the research, archiving, preservation, safeguarding, enhancement and propagation of unpublished or unofficial moving images...'.

The creation of this association was a direct result of a conference, Images Memoire de l'Europe, held in Spa, Belgium, in 1989. The subsequent commitment to the preservation of the amateur and unofficial moving image heritage of Europe was a direct response to guidelines issued by UNESCO in October 1980. The association holds a conference once a year during which the three main aspects of its work – preservation, academic research and production – are advanced in various ways. Workshops, seminars and multiple screenings provide a stimulating environment for exchange and discussion. Issues which may arise from the conflicting aims of film archives, whose main priority will always be preservation, and television producers, whose aim is always to provide original and visually stimulating programmes, may lead to confrontation, but it also leads to greater mutual understanding and to the creation of working practices which will ensure that amateur moving images are conserved for future generations and also viewed and evaluated by contemporary generations.

One of the features of the annual AEI conference is the 'atelier universitaire' (university workshop). The aim of this seminar is to stimulate the debate on the academic value of amateur film and to establish whether or not it merits our attention and the investment required for its long-term preservation.

Such questions are fundamental to the existence of the association, but are also questions which need to be addressed regularly in these times of ever-decreasing budgets. Film archives need to be able to justify their selection and preservation policies, while university departments need increasingly to demonstrate the value of their research into any given field. More importantly, if these films do have a value, then awareness of their existence, their value and their contents needs to be shared and propagated, and decisions as to how best to achieve this have to be made. The forum Moving Views was a step in this direction, an attempt to bring the debate about amateur film to the public platform, but also an opportunity to screen the very wide range of amateur films so far preserved by some of Europe's film archives.

The forum was opened by Jo Sherington of the Scottish Film

Archive whose talk 'The Entrepreneurial Spirit' was a discussion of the social and industrial value of the 1930s' film collection of an industrialist and his family. The family owned clay mining and brickwork manufacturing works in central Scotland. This film collection, which includes images of working practices as well as social and family occasions, offers 'important historical evidence in the fields of industrial archaeology, economic history and social history', and reflects the multi-disciplinary nature of amateur film.

A selection of images from the collection was screened including footage of industrial and technical processes. Attention was drawn to the use of hand labour, of women workers and to details of dress and safety precautions, features specific to this locality. The use of slow motion, it was suggested, was an indication of the film-maker's delight in the images he was shooting and of his pride in the functioning of his enterprise, and was interpreted as being as much an indication of his aspiration as of his achievement. This latter point is an extremely important one: any analysis of the amateur film as historical evidence needs to take into account fundamental questions such as the films context and provenance – who shot the films? Why did he/she shoot them? Who were the films made for? Answers to these questions are sometimes surprising and inevitably change our reading of the images presented.

Two of the films screened by Klaas-Gert Lugtenborg in his presentation 'The Key to the Past' illustrated this point very clearly.

An extract from OOGST TIJD IN HET VERLEDEN (HARVEST TIME IN THE PAST) 1926 shows the threshing of rape seed in the northern province of Groningen (The Netherlands). The images showed traditional and rather primitive harvesting methods; the atmosphere was one of conviviality – tired workers sharing a hearty meal at the end of a hard day's work. Although the viewer might be aware of the impact the camera's presence may have had on the workers, it came as somewhat of a surprise to learn that this 'amateur' film was a long way from being a true representation of harvesting methods in the northern Netherlands in 1926. The film-maker Van der Veu was far from being a naïve cinematographer documenting daily life. His film was in fact a construction. The threshing block used in the film, which came from a museum, had been made in 1730 and had last been used for harvesting in 1860 – 65 years before the making of Van der Veu's film!

In fact, Van der Veu, a folklorist from the west of Holland had wanted, for political reasons, to create an image of the north of Holland which was far removed from reality. At a time of great social and economic change Van der Veu's aim seems to have been to hide the truth from his colleagues in the centre of Holland about what was really going on in the north. His film suggested a happy society free of labour unrest or poverty. Moreover, it suggested that this was due to that society's adherence to traditional agricultural methods and social traditions. In fact, the agricultural crisis was at its height in 1926 and the province of Groningen was suffering a great deal of agricultural unrest and strikes! The image of the amateur film as being an authentic representation of the past is immediately undermined by this film.

The second film used to question the validity of amateur film as historical evidence was VERZET IN GRONINGEN (RESISTANCE IN GRONINGEN). This film was made in 1947 by two ex-Resistance fighters, Tiddeus and Van der Meij, their aim being 'to keep memory alive and show the absolute reality of how things happened'.

However, other documentation recording the Resistance suggests a reality rather different from that represented by the film, with much less heroism and much more danger. What the film does, however, is to provide an insight into the way our perceptions of the past – even the immediate past – change. Subsequent events had made this dangerous time a moment of heroic sacrifice – a perception of the past which could well have been very different had the outcome of the war been otherwise. Despite the distortions Klaas-Gert Lugtenborg does not reject this film as a serious historical document; rather he sees it as 'a beautiful and very interesting production and also a very welcome addition to the sources to be [sic] needed for study of how in post-war society people tried to cope with their war-time experiences'.

Nevertheless, the historical evidence it provides is perhaps not what we might immediately expect but something which is far more complex. We learn as much about how our perceptions of the past can be distorted by its outcome as we do about what the past was really like. We learn as much about the nature of memory as we do about the nature of history.

Although all historical evidence needs to be handled with investigative restraint these two films are graphic reminders that the moving image requires careful scientific analysis. Somehow its immediacy and its accessibility suggest an authenticity which, because it seems to mirror life and all its perspectives, is somewhat more credible. In the words of Dr Heather Norris Nicholson, 'The transformation role of the camera can... have contradictory effects: film through memorialising a past moment can transform something ephemeral into normality while also having the potential power to concretise ordinariness into something unique'.

Despite these justified reservations, Klaas-Gert Lugtenborg, who is director of the History Bureau at Groningen University, is a fervent advocate of the value of amateur film as historical evidence. The History Bureau is involved in a wide range of research commissions covering a whole spectrum of historical themes specialising in local and regional history. Its interest in the history of image and sound has led to a number of research projects which have attempted to evaluate or assess amateur film as an historical source.

Klaas-Gert Lugtenborg points out that amateur film has often been ignored by historians who considered these films to be snapshots of the past rather than serious documents worthy of historical analysis. The poor academic reputation of the amateur film is, he argues, seriously compounded by the dearth of material available for study and he insists upon the need for closer relationships between academic establishments and regional film archives – 'No research is possible without a well established and proper archive. In a reverse order [sic] a proper archive will lead to more and better research'.

The importance of preserving these documents in regional rather than national archives is closely linked to Lugtenborg's argument that these films are of particular value to the study of local or regional history. Preserving them in their locality is likely to facilitate research work. Establishing the film-makers' links with a given area may help to provide a fuller context for the material while it is also likely to facilitate the identification of the film's contents. The very specific and localised content of these films means also that exhibiting them in the locality of their origin may result in a greater consciousness of the importance of such material, the discovery of more information which will lead to a better understanding of the nature of the material and the possible discovery of other material.

Such an approach is far removed from the traditional analysis of film as historical document. The mass-medium approach often used to analyse film has, says Lugtenborg, no relevance for amateur film, for although it may be screened to audiences, amateur film was never intended or created as a mass medium.

A more satisfactory model of analysis, tried and tested by researchers at the History Bureau is that proposed by the American professor John E O'Connor in his book *Image as Artifact – The Historical Analysis of Film and Television*.[2] O'Connor proposes a model of film analysis that connects film research to more traditional historical methods. Once the provenance of a film has been established (and fundamental questions about its contents, production and reception dealt with), a wider exploration of the relevance and significance of these films can be undertaken.

O'Connor suggests that the moving image, in this case the amateur film, may be analysed for its value as evidence for social and cultural history, as evidence for historical facts and as a representation of history.

The fourth premise suggests analysing a document from the point of view of the history of amateur film as 'industry' and art form.

While Klaas-Gert Lugtenborg is convinced that O'Connor's model provides the most useful basis for research on amateur film, he is also convinced that the link between amateur film and local history is a mutually beneficial one. Although the general attitude of the academic world towards the study of local history as a discipline is rather negative, there does seem to be a shift of attitude. The role of local history in 'refining existing [historical] generalisations and prejudices' is at long last being recognised in historical research.

Why this shift in attitude has come about, and why the amateur film seems to be coming into its own, is a very complex issue and not unrelated to the nature of late 20th-century developments. Undoubtedly the revised attitude towards amateur film is closely linked to the renewed interest in local and regional history which is becoming evident in contemporary western Europe. Our modern western society is becoming increasingly complex; its moral standards and values are constantly changing, often leading to confusion and loss of direction. It has been suggested that this apparent renewed interest in local or regional history is a direct result of this and directly related to the need to be able to identify with something small, recognisable and tangible in an increasingly complex and anonymous society.

Dr Patricia Zimmerman, Associate Professor in the Department of Cinema and Photography at Ithaca College, New York, has written extensively on amateur film, and like Klaas-Gert Lugtenborg is acutely aware of the importance of preserving amateur film for future generations. In her presentation 'Localised Knowledges: Amateur Film and History', Dr Zimmerman suggested that one of the difficulties with the academic analysis of amateur film was the messy nature of these documents and the fact that they do no lend themselves easily to 'the neat lines of philosophical or artistic research'.

'Film professionals', she says in her article 'Home Movies, Home Truths',[3] 'often view amateur film-making as the debris of film production and film studies the lowest form of all representational modes, a kind of flotsam and jetsam of visual culture ...To call a film "amateur" is to banish it forever to the inconsequential and the meaningless. It is also in the world of film preservation to erase it from the historical record.'

Dr Zimmerman's argument centres around relationships of power. She argues that the rejection of amateur film is 'part of a significant cultural struggle over who has power to create media to invent images...The struggle to include amateur film within the lexicon of film studies and film preservation is quite simply a struggle between public sphere and the private sphere, one of the central debates of our century'.

The word 'amateur' derives from the Latin word 'amare' – to love. As leisure time expanded from the mid-19th century amateurism in all spheres of activity grew. Nevertheless, these activities, like the home, family, reproduction, child rearing, celebrations and mourning, belonged to the private sphere of life; they were disregarded by historians whose analysis of the past was essentially based on an economic and political perspective and for whom an amateur film was nothing more than 'the visual equivalent of a diary'. While applauding this shift Dr Zimmerman recognises the problems associated with the use of amateur films as historical documents. Screening her own parents' family films from the 1950s, she refers to her parents' consumerism and the way in which Christmas is represented on celluloid not only as a religious holiday and a family gathering but as a symbol of the family's growing material success as represented by the substantial gifts offered to the children. These messy, multi-faceted images are therefore difficult to analyse, while what the film is saying now is not necessarily what it was saying then.

This remark points significantly at another problem concerning the analysis of amateur films. They can be fragments of life, they can be fantasies and memories; but whatever they are they are likely over time to become different things. The way we read images is of necessity shaped by our knowledge of the context in which the images were created. To recognise their value we may need to be experts in any one of a number of disciplines.

During the last AEI conference held in Brest in Brittany in May 1994, the university workshop's discussion centred around the statement, 'You can't see what you don't know'. Member film archives were asked to select one or two amateur films from their collections, and to invite academics from different disciplines to comment upon their contents and assess their value to their particular discipline. The Wales Film and Television Archive selected two films – MAYFAIR AT RHEADR (late 1920s) and BRYNSIENCYN SUNDAY SCHOOL TRIP (1950s). Geographer Gwilym T Jones and folk historian Beth Thomas were then invited to comment on the contents of these two films independently of each other.

This attempt at an interdisciplinary approach to the appreciation of amateur film was repeated at the 'Moving Views' forum. Beth Thomas, who works at the Welsh Folk Museum at Saint Fagan's, pointed to the strengths and weaknesses of amateur films from the point of view of the ethnographer, for whom the 'prime requirements in the film documentation of folk life are authenticity and accuracy'.

For an ethnographer, one of the strengths of amateur films is that they are generally made by ordinary people recording events in their own lives, which are of personal significance and importance. Despite this seeming quality of authenticity, for the ethnographer there is a certain ambiguity, for in choosing to film the significant the film-maker may have omitted to film what to the ethnographer is of most importance – the mundane details of everyday existence.

Referring to the film of the Sunday school trip, both Gwilym T Jones and Beth Thomas referred to the importance of knowing that in Wales in the 1950s Nonconformist chapels were not only centres of religious life, but also the focus of the majority of social activities. Ignorance of this fact would result in an incomplete understanding of the significance of the contents of the film.

Commenting on the powerful impact of the moving image Beth Thomas noted that this silent film brings the past to life and 'captures the fun and excitement of such an occasion in a way which cannot be reproduced by still photographs'.

The absence of sound can in certain cases be compensated by the existence of oral recordings of the same or similar events. Combining these sources can, according to Beth Thomas, 'create a whole which is greater than its constituent parts'. Oral history recordings can often provide the ethnographer with the mundane details of everyday life as well as information about special events. 'Its weakness is that the past is seen through the filter of subsequent experiences' (cf RESISTANCE IN GRONINGEN). Amateur film on the other hand 'has the benefit of immediacy', but it is often lacking in 'detail and documentation'.

A significant aspect of the analysis of amateur film referred to by a number of contributors to the 'Moving Views' forum was the economics of amateur film-making. Jo Sherington referred to the things which people chose to film as a reflection of both their aspirations and the way in which they wished to project themselves. While frequent reference has been made to amateur film as being a document which helps us to analyse history from below – the history of the common people or of the working people – it is also true to remember that very often those who possessed the ciné cameras belonged to a certain milieu and that though they may have filmed the lives of the working classes, the working classes might well have preferred to represent themselves on film in a different way.

An indirect consequence of the economics of amateur film-making and of the evaluation of technology is pointed out by Dr Heather Norris Nicholson. Dr Norris Nicholson argues that familiarity with the camera (both from the point of view of the person filming and of those being filmed) is a factor which can greatly affect the end product – the film. 'Did the changing cost and greater familiarity with ciné cameras during the first half of this century gradually produce a different type of representation, or had the subject matters of home, street scene and community already acquired such iconic character that the apparently typical scenes of everyday occurrence become part of an established genre shaped by earlier visual artists?' Such a question perhaps relates directly to the fourth model of John O'Connor's analysis of amateur film as industry and art form.

The 'Moving Images' amateur film forum brought together a varied cross-section of people and interests including historians, ethnographers, archivists and film-makers. The concluding plenary session raised as many issues as it resolved, suggesting that this burgeoning subject has a fertile future.

The presence of members of the Cardiff Ciné and Video Society (originally the Cardiff Amateur Ciné Society) was a refreshing reminder that for members of such clubs, making films was a hobby which might involve social documentation, artistic expression and technical expertise, but above all it was a pleasure, as the many images projected during the weekend testified. Family films, amateur documentary, amateur fiction and amateur art film of varied length, quality and gauge showed what the amateur film heritage holds in store for future researchers.

Although many questions remained unanswered there is no doubt that we have much to learn from our amateur film heritage and that what we learn is likely to change our perceptions of both our history and our film heritage. Unless these films are preserved quickly, the opportunity to challenge perceptions of the past through them will be lost.

In an ideal world every region would have its film archive and every amateur film acquired would be preserved and copied.

However, in the economic realities of the late 20th century selection becomes necessary in terms of budgets, storage space and logging time. Once a selection policy becomes a necessity then questions of how and why material is selected and by whom are inevitably raised. Given the multi-faceted nature of amateur film, it would seem that any valid selection policy would require an active collaboration between film archivists, local historians, ethnographers, linguists, geographers and other interested disciplines. Academic research and film preservation can benefit mutually from closer collaboration – the future of amateur film depends on the successful creation of such networks and partnerships and needs serious consideration.

We need also to reflect on how best these images can be exhibited. Challenging ways of screening this material which is not traditional cinematic fodder need to be found so that audiences come to appreciate these images as something more than just a light-hearted home movie. Presenting a newsreel of a given event alongside an amateur film of the same event can be both provocative and enlightening. While such an exhibition may highlight the strengths and weaknesses of both documents it also questions basic assumptions about how we create our understanding of the past.

In her résumé of the workshop 'You Can't See What You Don't Know' held by the AEI at Brest in 1994, the amateur film historian Susan Aasman concludes that if, as one scholar has pointed out, 'amateur film is a footnote', then we should not forget that footnotes are essential for academic research but 'better than to speak of footnotes... it [sic] is to value amateur film for the different perspectives it offers, which can raise new questions and therefore provide new answers. In order to find these answers we have to know what we're looking for because "you can't see what you don't know"'. For Heather Norris Nicholson, recognising the many attributes of amateur film 'is a beginning towards relocating their position as evidence and points to their unrealised potential interest for researchers working in interdisciplinary ways'. The future of amateur film is, it would seem, assured.

Gwenan Owen is Education and Outreach Officer at the Wales Film and Television Archive.

References

1. Berry D (1994) *Wales and Cinema – The First Hundred Years.* University of Wales Press
2. O'Connor JE (1990) *Image as Artifact – The Historical Analysis of Film & Television.* Mallabar
3. Zimmerman P (1994/5) *Home Movies, Home Truths* . Sgript (0), Wales Film Council.

Further Reading   Aasman S (1994) *Reflections on 'You Can't See What You Don't Know: Ten Scholars on Amateur Film as Evidence'*. Film Research Foundation SFW, Amsterdam; AEI, Charles Roi, Belgium.

Europe against the Odds

Researching Film and Television Collections in Europe: The MAP-TV Guide

DANIELA KIRCHNER

Coordinating a project which involves 20 teams in over 40 European countries may seem a nightmarish task which one would consider bound to fail. However, as it is often the case in life, things seem to work out especially when you least expect them to. It is in precisely this way that the MAP-TV Guide project has proved to be a very successful one.

The Project The MAP-TV Guide project was set up to document the existence of archive film and television collections throughout Europe: from the Atlantic to the Urals. In comparison with other similar publications this project wanted to locate not only the big and well-known national film collections, television archives and stock shot libraries, but also smaller and hitherto less well-known collections held by local and regional authorities, industrial companies, museums, universities and private individuals.

MAP-TV (Memories Archive Programmes), an initiative of the MEDIA programme of the Council of Europe, is an association created to encourage the production of film and television programmes about the history of Europe and also to enhance the value of audio-visual archives. MAP-TV regroups producers, film-makers, broadcasters and archive holders, sets up co-productions of archive-based projects, and grants development loans. This unique initiative was launched with the commitment to contributing to a better understanding of Europe's audio-visual heritage.

A typical German filmbunker, one of many included in the MAP-TV Guide.

BUFVC The British Universities Film & Video Council (BUFVC) was commissioned by MAP-TV to coordinate the project. BUFVC has long-standing experience in the field of archive research and has been for many years a focus for researchers in the UK. It holds the Slade Film History Register which contains valuable data about the British cinema newsreel companies and published in 1981 the first ever *Researcher's Guide to British Film & Television Collections* which is now in its fourth edition.

Calling Europe Any project aiming to locate film and television archives across the entire continent of Europe cannot be carried out by just one country or organisation. Because of this, Jim Ballantyne, former Head of Information, and Murray Weston, Director, at BUFVC, developed a devolved structure for the MAP-TV Guide project. Teams were to be set up in as many countries as possible in order to carry out local research. The data collected would then be included in a guide covering all of Europe. Simultaneously, teams could also publish the data collected in their own country in the appropriate language. The project was given the final go-ahead by MAP-TV after a questionnaire had been devised in collaboration with the first established teams which were in France, Germany and Portugal.

The Job It was at this point that BUFVC advertised the position of coordinator for the project. Applicants were tested for language skills and were warned that the job would involve extensive travelling throughout Europe during the proposed year of employment.

Needless to say, the travel never materialised. Having been offered the job, my work was confined to BUFVC's offices in Soho, central London. Instead of travelling I spent a lot of time phoning different countries and trying to send faxes across Europe, experiencing all of the joys of telecommunication and language problems.

When I started work on the project the task seemed to be overwhelming. In most countries coordinating teams still had to be set up. Those interested in coordinating the research in their own countries had to prepare and submit a budget. This might sound mundane but actually involves complex bureaucratic procedures which vary from country to country. Once budgets had been approved by the MAP-TV board and an agreement with each team signed, a 'MAP-TV Kit', containing the questionnaire and sample letters in three languages together with a floppy disk of a database specifically developed for the project, were sent out.

Picture courtesy the Russian State Archive of Film and Photo Documents

A Russian cameraman filming during World War II

Eastern Europe All in all 18 teams were set up covering the research and collection of data in 21 European countries. Additional funding was provided at this stage by Eureka Audiovisuel to help support the research in Eastern European countries. Teams were established in Russia, Belarus, Ukraine, the Baltic States, the Czech Republic and Albania.

Research for the remaining 24 countries was undertaken by the BUFVC. Mailing lists were established and 2,000 questionnaires in either English, French or German were mailed direct from London. The entire project involved more than 15,000 questionnaires sent out across the whole of Europe.

Europe's Answer The mailing, however, was only the first and most straightforward part of the project. As expected, archives were not especially keen to complete a complicated four page questionnaire, and all of the teams had to make a lot follow-up telephone calls in order to get the questionnaires completed. In some cases teams actually visited staff in archives. To keep teams informed about the progress of the project, and to remind them in the most diplomatic way possible of the deadlines for the delivery of the data, a newsletter was also sent out on a regular basis.

Ideally teams were supposed to translate the data and enter it on the database we provided for them, so that the data gathered had only to be ordered when we received it. This was indeed the case with the three established teams. Others would translate the data and enter it onto their own database and some would only send us the data in the local language.

The complexity of the project together with the tight deadlines led to severe scepticism and I doubted whether information would be forthcoming from all of the teams. I had worked out a series of reasons why I would not receive some of the data collected: coordinators would fall ill; data would be lost in the post; some teams and archives might disappear altogether. I was in for a series of surprises, most of them very pleasant ones, which demonstrated to me at least how misleading stereotypes of different countries can be.

Teams participating in the project submitted the data they had received and most of them collected an enormous amount of information. The reply to the direct mailing from BUFVC's offices in London was also good, considering that we were asking representatives of archives to complete a questionnaire which in most cases was in an alien language.

Data arrived of course not quite within the time schedule we expected it but it was so exciting to receive all the data collected throughout Europe that I would not dream of complaining. However, this left us only a short time for translation, entering the data onto the MAP-Base and editing it in order to meet our deadline with the publisher.

Receiving the first data was a revelation in itself; it became apparent that certain aspects of the questionnaire were not quite clear to those who completed them and in some cases questions had been completely misunderstood. It was the moment when you wanted to redesign the questionnaire, but this was obviously too late. This is also the moment when you discover the idiosyncrasies of the English language and the different ways countries use and interpret it. At times I wished that I was a native

English speaker, but on the other hand, my non-English languages helped me to understand what the translations were supposed to mean. With the help and good will of a native English speaker, Suzanne Hoefkens, we established our own interpretation of the data and it seemed to work.

Countries were also asked to submit photographs to illustrate the information and we received an interesting and varied selection from over 40 countries.

The Book
All in all detailed information on 1,900 film and television collections throughout Europe has been collected for the first edition. *Film and Television Collections in Europe: The MAP-TV Guide* lists addresses, telephone and fax numbers of the archives as well as contact names and details relating to the history of the collection, the holdings, catalogue systems, access conditions, viewing facilities and the copyright status of the material held.

The book includes details about many smaller collections and some real curiosities such as the Gan Bull Fighting Archive in Madrid, the German Museum of Hygiene in Dresden and the Videoteca Pasinetti collection of films relating to the myth of Venice. Next to detailed descriptions of major professional archives researchers will also find useful data on amateur film collections, and an additional section lists 200 film researchers currently working in Europe.

The data was submitted for publication in September 1994 and the printed version of the *MAP-TV Guide* will be published by Blueprint/Chapman and Hall in Spring 1995. An electronic publication (CD-ROM), containing additional information on all the archives as well as new entries, is planned for the near future. There are certainly more European film and television archives to be unearthed for future editions and the updating process has already started.

What seemed to be impossible ultimately proved to be achievable. The commitment of the local teams was excellent and the cooperation of the different institutions in individual countries, especially in central and eastern Europe, where no national teams were established, was extremely positive. There were of course occasionally hurdles to overcome and communication was more difficult with some countries than with others, but clearly I was the difficult one, as I did not speak their language.

I thought that coordinating so many countries and teams throughout Europe, across so many languages and cultures would be an impossible task. My fears proved to be unfounded. The MAP-TV Guide project has showed to me that communication and

Picture courtesy the Centre Valaisan du Film et de la Photographie

Emile Gos filming the CROIX DU CERVIN, 1922

cooperation are not defined by language and culture but are dependant on the commitment of the individuals involved. The successful completion of this project highlights the potential of Europe - against all the odds.

Daniela Kirchner is Project Coordinator and Editor of the MAP-TV Guide.

Audio-Visual Centres in Education in the UK

The following list provides readers with a selection of audio-visual centres in academic institutions including universities, colleges of further education and a small number of schools throughout the British Isles. If you require information about similar facilities abroad contact the Information Service of the British Universities Film & Video Council (☎ 0171-734 3687).

In many cases the audio-visual centres described are prepared to accept outside work, and the key provided below is intended to summarise some of the facilities which are currently available. These can range from 1-inch video mastering to S-VHS camcorder loan, through to graphic design and desktop publishing. A brief description of each audio-visual centre is provided along with a contact name, phone number and address. Further details can be obtained from the individual named in the listing.

All the information has been obtained by direct contact with centres, but institutions which are not listed might like to send in their details which will be collated to up-date our records for future publications. The information given is correct as of March 1995.

Key

○ Outside production work accepted.
❶ Broadcast quality video (including Betacam (+SP), Hi-8, S-VHS, MII and digital formats (D1, D2, D3 etc).
❷ Other quality video (including High-band U-matic, Low-band U-matic, 1-inch etc)
❸ Film production
❹ Sound/radio production
❺ Photography
❻ Graphics

Anglia Polytechnic University (Cambridge Campus)
Media Production Division, School of Educational Services, Anglia Polytechnic University, East Road, Cambridge CB1 1PT
☎ 01223 63271 ext 2206 fax 01223 352900
Contact Roderick Macdonald
Main Activities As well as supporting the use of audio-visual media in teaching and learning throughout the University, the Department offers training and promotional video production services on a commercial basis. Clients include Logica, Bayer and Marconi, Cambridgeshire County Council and many local firms. Showreel available.
○ ❷ ❹ ❺ ❻

Anglia Polytechnic University (Essex Campus)
Media Production Department, Faculty of Educational Services, Anglia Polytechnic University, Victoria Road South, Chelmsford, Essex CM1 1LL
☎ 01245 493131 ext 3213 fax 01245 490835
Contact Don McNab
Main Activities **see above**
○ ❷ ❹ ❺ ❻

Anglo-European College of Chiropractic
Parkwood Road, Bournemouth BH5 2DF
☎ 01202 431021
Contact Brendan Johnson
Main Activities Audio-visual support, including slides and video production for academic courses.
❷ ❹ ❺ ❻

Ashridge Management College
Berkhamsted, Herts HP4 1NS
☎ 01442 843491 fax 01442 842382
Contact Ken McGlone (Media Services Manager)
Main Activities Small-scale production of video material for management training, conference coverage and CCTV use during courses in executive management training.
❷ ❹ ❺ ❻

Aston University
Continuing Education Service, Aston Triangle, Birmingham B4 7ET
☎ 0121-359 3611 ext 4342 fax 0121-359 6427
Contact John Bailey (Director)
Main Activities Produces the University's video-based distance learning postgraduate programmes as well as being sponsored by the European Commission's STRIDE programme to co-ordinate its Video Courses in Industry Unit. The Centre also hires out its video production and editing facilities.
○ ❷

BBC Open University Production Centre
Walton Hall, Milton Keynes MK7 6BH
☎ 01908 655333 fax 01908 376324
Contact Jeff Baker (Head of Resources); Clive Holloway (Head of Programmes)
Main Activities Operating a range of broadcast facilities with specialist producers, the Centre is dedicated to the production of TV, radio, video and audio over the full span of OU courses and packs. The BBC's production facility also collaborates with other training projects and offers consultancy and training.
○ ❶ ❹ ❻

Bolton Institute of Higher Education
Media Services, Chadwick Street, Bolton BL2 1JW
☎ 01204 28851 ext 3263
Contact Arun R Newell
Main Activities Media Services employs graphic designers, photographers, video specialists and educationalists. Production of educational training and promotional materials can be carried out using a wide range of media including text, graphics, photography, computers and both studio and location video.
○ ❶ ❹ ❺ ❻

The British Council
Exhibitions and Audio-Visual Unit, Design, Production and Media Department, 10 Spring Gardens, London SW1A 2BN
☎ 0171-389 4267 fax 0171-389 4366
Contact Peter R Jones
Main Activities Creates exhibitions, film, video, audio-visual and multi-media materials in support of the work of the British Council.
○ ❶ ❸ ❹ ❺

Brunel University
Department of Media Services, Uxbridge, Middx UB8 3PH
☎ 01895 274000 ext 2077/2792 fax 01895 232806 e-mail colin.burgess@brunel.ac.uk
Contact Colin Burgess (Head of Media Services); Melanie Phipps (TV Unit Producer)
Main Activities Production of educational, training, and promotional video programmes and continuing education video courses. Two-camera studio and location recording on Hi-band U-matic equipment. Hi-band U-matic and VHS editing facilities. Video production courses and presentation skills courses.
○ ❷ ❺ ❻

Buckinghamshire College
Media Services, c/o The Library, Queen Alexandra Road, High Wycombe, Bucks HP11 2JZ
☎ 01494 522141 ext 3277
Contact Peter Baker (Chief Librarian); Dorette Biggs
Main Activities Media studio facilities and support for degree-level courses.
○ ❶ ❻

Cheltenham and Gloucester College of Higher Education
Audio-Visual Unit, Pittville Campus, Albert Road, Gloucester GL2 3JG
☎ 01242 532225 fax 01242 532207
Contact Graham Bateman
Main Activities Teaching video/media production techniques to students on higher and degree-level courses including photography, fine art and graphics. In-house video production unit.
○ ❶ ❷ ❹ ❺ ❻

Dental and General Hospitals
Department of Clinical Illustration, Saint Chad's Queensway, Birmingham B4 6NN
☎ 0121-236 8611 ext 5745 fax 0121-625 8815
Contact Cheryl Parkes
Main Activities Provides a comprehensive clinical and audio-visual service using still photography, video and Apple Macintosh desktop publishing facilities to produce materials for clinical records, teaching, research and public relations activities.
○ ❷ ❺

Devon Learning Resources 21 Old Mill Road, Torquay, Devon TQ2 6AU
☎ 01803 605531 fax 01803 607127
Contact Kevin Harrodine
Main Activities Loans items including film and video equipment, and produces materials for in-service training.
○ ❷ ❸ ❹ ❺

Farnborough College of Technology Boundary Road, Farnborough, Hants GU14 6SB
☎ 01252 515511 ext 227/228
Contact Alan Harding, Principal Lecturer, Media Department
Main Activities Video training courses at various levels; commercial production facility available.
○ ❷ ❹ ❺ ❻

Glasgow Caledonian University Media Services, Cowcaddens Road, Glasgow G4 0BA
☎ 0141-331 3688 fax 0141-331 3005
Contact Gerry Doyle, (Head of Educational Development and Media Services)
Main Activities Educational development in teaching and learning. Print media and graphics services. Audio-visual television services.
○ ❶ ❻

Goldsmiths' College University of London, Department of Media and Communications, Lewisham Way, New Cross, London SE14 6NW
☎ 0181-692 7171 ext 2020 fax 0181-694 8911
Contact Ivor Gaber; John Beacham (Acting Head)
Main Activities Short courses and tailor made packages for industry and the public sector. Supporting undergraduate and postgraduate media degrees.
○ ❶ ❸ ❹ ❺ ❻

Grampian Regional Council Resources Service, Summerhill Education Centre, Aberdeen AB2 6JA
☎ 01224 321462 fax 01224 310430
Contact Colin MacKenzie (Resources Development Officer)
Main Activities Centralised educational resources service for Grampian region. Schools library service, maintenance and repair of all educational audio-visual and computer holdings; video production, graphics and reprographics, IT, exhibitions, science centre, technological studies, curriculum development, equipment and materials for special needs.
○ ❶ ❹ ❺ ❻

Hammersmith and West London College Media Services, Gliddon Road, Barons Court, London W14 9BL
☎ 0181-741 1688 ext 2108 fax 0181-741 2491
Contact Media Resources Officer
Main Activities Media Services provides a range of services to the college including graphics and desktop publishing, reprographics, photography, video and television production, audio off-air recording, audio-visual equipment loan and audio-visual presentation and production facilities.
○ ❷ ❸ ❹ ❺ ❻

Health Education Board for Scotland Woodburn House, Canaan Lane, Edinburgh EH10 4SG
☎ 0131-447 8044 ext 141 fax 0131-452 8140
Contact Steven Garrad

Main Activities	Health education videos are produced to aid training and teaching of carers and the public. Material suitable for school use is also produced. ❷ ❸
Hillcroft College	South Bank, Surbiton, Surrey KT6 6DF ☎ 0181-399 2688
Contact	Hannah Kent
Main Activities	Providing learning resources including off-air video and radio recordings for a small long-term adult residential college for women.
Imperial College of Science, Technology and Medicine	Television Studio, Level 2 Walkway, Electrical Engineering Building, Exhibition Road, London SW7 2BT ☎ 0171-594 8135 fax 0171-594 8138
Contact	Colin Grimshaw; Chris Roberts
Main Activities	Production of any type of video recording for use within Imperial College. In addition to supporting both postgraduate and undergraduate teaching, the Studio produces material for promotional purposes. ○ ❶ ❺ ❻
Keele University	Media and Communications Centre, Keele, Staffs ST5 5BG ☎ 01782 583377 fax 01782 714832
Contact	Bob Sewell; Roger Phenton
Main Activities	At present, supply of audio-visual equipment and video production. The University is adding a computer graphics facility to this centre. ○ ❶
Kent Superior Pictures (KSP)	Barton Road, Dover CT16 2ND ☎ 01304 202827 fax 01304 213824
Contact	Ian Killbery
Main Activities	Production and distribution of videos for education covering INSET and teaching materials across the curriculum; information videos for the public sector. Experienced in developing sponsored educational packages for commercial clients. ○ ❶ ❻
London Guildhall University	Calcutta House, 10 Old Castle Street, London E1 7NT ☎ 0171-320 1000 ext 1008 fax 0171-320 1117
Contact	Ian Kelso
Main Activities	Comprehensive audio-visual service, production of educational material (video, graphics and photography), publicity and promotional material, staff development. ○ ❶ ❹ ❺
Loughborough University of Technology	A/V Services, Loughborough LE11 3TU ☎ 01509 222190 fax 01509 610813
Contact	Dr David Mack (Director Audio-Visual Services)
Main Activities	Training and promotional videos and support of academic departments. ○ ❶ ❹ ❺ ❻
Manchester Royal Infirmary	University Department of Medical Illustration, Oxford Road, Manchester M13 9WL ☎ 0161-276 4670 fax 0161-273 5395

Contact	G W Rogers
Main Activities	Medical photography, video recording and video production, computer graphics.

○ ❶ ❺ ❻

Manchester University Television Productions (MUTV)

Staff Development Centre, University of Manchester, Oxford Road, Manchester M13 9PL
☎ 0161-275 2535 fax 0161-275 2529
e-mail Christine.Houghton@man.ac.uk

Contact	Ken Wrench (Head of Production); Graham McEwan (Head of Administration)
Main Activities	Produces videocassettes for education, training and information needs for both the University and outside organisations.

○ ❷ ❹ ❻

Mid-Kent College

Educational Technology Unit, Horsted, Chatham, Kent ME5 9UQ
☎ 01634 830633 ext 2237 fax 01634 830224

Contact	John Rattle
Main Activities	Audio and video production for educational and promotional ends. 3-camera studio. Training courses available in all aspects of television production.

○ ❶ ❷ ❹ ❺ ❻

Moray House College of Education

ETV-AV Service, Moray House, Holyrood Road, Edinburgh EH8 8AQ
☎ 0131-558 558 6021 fax 0131-557 3458

Contact	Robert J McCann; Norman Smith
Main Activities	Television production (studio or outside broadcast), audio-visual media production and graphics. Facilities may be hired.

○ ❶ ❺ ❻

Napier University

Video Production Unit, Colinton Road, Edinburgh EH10 5DT
☎ 0131-444 2266 ext 2690 fax 0131-452 8532

Contact	Dr F Percival; A Methven
Main Activities	Broadcast quality video production, full editing facilities and other audio-visual services.

○ ❶ ❹ ❺ ❻

North East Wales Institute of Higher Education

Media Unit, Postal Point 37 Newi, Plascoch, Mold Road, Wrexham LL11 2AW
☎ 01978 293467 fax 01244 262352

Contact	Stewart Edwards
Main Activities	The Institute's Media Unit, in collaboration with the Clwyd College of Art and Design Technology, undertakes the production of promotional, training and educational video programmes using U-matic equipment as well as photographic work and design and illustration for print.

○ ❷ ❹ ❺ ❻

Norwich City College

Learning Support Services, Ipswich Road, Norwich NR2 2LJ
☎ 01603 660011 ext 253 fax 01603 760362

Contact	Steve Phillips
Main Activities	Large library of audio-visual materials including slides and some 5000 video programmes. Video production commissions undertaken.

○ ❶

Oxford Brookes University	Educational Methods Unit, Gipsy Lane, Headington, Oxford OX3 0BP
	☎ 01865 755863 fax 01865 485723
Contact	Chris Rust
Main Activities	Supporting teaching and learning in the institution.
	○ ❷ ❹ ❺ ❻

Preston College	St Vincent's Road, Fulwood, Preston, Lancashire PR2 4UR
	☎ 01772 716511 2248/2256. fax 01772 712530
Contact	Liz Hart; Mick Gornall
Main Activities	Supporting vocational course including BTEC Media Studies, City & Guilds 770, and other television and video programmes such as A-level Film Studies, Media Studies, Adult Open College. Fully equipped digital/analogue recording studio available.
	○ ❶ ❹ ❺ ❻

Queen's University Belfast	TV Production Unit, The Science Library, Chlorine Gardens, Belfast BT9 5EQ
	☎ 01232 335493 fax 01232 382760
Contact	Alan Soutar (Director); Jonathon Brady (Producer)
Main Activities	The production of educational and corporate television programmes, audio-visual presentations and interactive video materials. Facilities include a comprehensive range of post-production facilities.
	○ ❶ ❹ ❺ ❻

St George's Hospital Medical School	Cranmer Terrace, London SW17 0RE
	☎ 0181-725 2701 fax 0181-767 4696
Contact	DJ Cleverly
Main Activities	Production of materials for patient education, staff training, student education, teaching and research using television, photographic and graphic design techniques.
	○ ❶ ❺ ❻

St Mary's University College	Television Studio, Waldegrave Road, Twickenham, Middx TW1 4SX
	☎ 0181-892 0051 ext 290 fax 0181-744 2080
Contact	Michael Murnane
Main Activities	To provide a video support service for staff and students. Teaching media/television production to drama students and students following the Diploma course in Heritage Interpretation.
	○ ❶ ❹ ❺

Sandwell College of Further and Higher Education	Media & Design Department, The Knowles Centre, Wednesbury, West Midlands WS10 9ER
	☎ 0121-556 6000 ext 8230/8222 fax 0121-556 6069
Contact	Keith Morris (Head of Media & Design); Paul Miles (Head of Television); Paul Harper (Head of Sound)
Main Activities	Television, video and audio production foundation and production courses. All television courses are run to 'skill set' competency level.
	○ ❷ ❹ ❺ ❻

Sheffield University Television	University of Sheffield, 5 Favell Road, Sheffield S3 7QX
	☎ 0114 282 6063 fax 0114 276 2106

Contact	John Stratford (Acting Director), Ros Cox (Production Co-ordinator)
Main Activities	Sheffield University Television works to full broadcast standards making a wide variety of educational material both for university departments and external clients. The unit now undertakes its own marketing of over 100 titles which reflect specific expertise in medical and scientific subjects.

○ ❷ ❹ ❻

Shropshire and Staffordshire College of Nursing and Midwifery
Royal Shrewsbury Hospital North, Mytton Oak Road, Shrewsbury, Shropshire SY3 8XQ
☎ 01743 261000 fax 01743 261061

Contact Paul Greenwood (Audio-Visual Technician)
Main Activities Library contains over 100 audio-visual resources for basic and post-basic nursing education.

Southampton University
Department of Teaching Support and Media Services, University of Southampton, Southampton S017 1BJ ☎ 01703 592330 fax 01703 593005

Contact Dr H S Mathius, Director of Teaching Support and Media Services
Main Activities Primarily serves the University of Southampton and the Wessex Health Region of the NHS.

○ ❶ ❸ ❹ ❺ ❻

Stockport College of Further and Higher Education
Media Services, Wellington Road South, Stockport SK1 3UQ
☎ 0161-958 3473 fax 0161-480 6636

Contact Brian Beardwood, Stuart Mellor
Main Activities The centre provides audio-visual support services within the College including design and production of print and video learning materials both for in-house use and under contract for external clients.

○ ❶ ❷ ❻

Thames Valley University
Media Services Department, St Mary's Road, Ealing, London W5 5RF
☎ 0181-579 5000 ext 2301 fax 0181-231 2538

Contact Course Organiser
Main Activities Runs four lens-based courses: Basic Television Production, Advanced Television Production, and Corporate Video Production.

○ ❷ ❹ ❺ ❻

Trinity and All Saints College
Educational Support Services Brownberrie Lane, Horsforth, Leeds LS18 5HD
☎ 0113 283 7100 ext 249 fax 0113 258 1148

Contact Andrew Clifford
Main Activities Media production and presentation facilities for education and commercial users which include a television studio, portable video camera units, a radio station, two sound studios and extensive graphics and desktop publishing facilities. Work up to broadcast television and radio standard is undertaken.

○ ❶ ❹ ❺ ❻

University of Birmingham
Television Services, Edgbaston Park Road, Edgbaston, Birmingham B15 2TT
☎ 0121-414 6492/6496 fax 0121-414 6999

Contact Robert Jacobs; Maureen Hutchinson
Main Activities Television programme production for both academic and commercial clients. Studio hire also available for commercial clients.

○ ❶ ❹ ❻

University of Bournemouth Library Services, Dorset House, Talbot Campus, Fern Barrow, Poole, Dorset BH12 5BB
☎ 01202 595041
Contact Lorna Kenny
Main Activities To maintain and promote the use of videotapes within the University. Collection numbers about 1000 and includes Open University programmes, commercially produced videos and off-air recordings. Production carried out by University's Media Production Department.
○ ❶ ❹

University of Brighton Media Services, Department of Learning Resources, Watts Building, Brighton BN2 4GJ
☎ 01273 642772/5 fax 01273 606093
Contact Martin Hayden; Gavin Nettleton
Main Activities Production and acquisition of video programmes and other learning materials to support University courses and research; comprehensive services in design and photography; collaborations, co-productions and distribution of generic educational and training materials.
○ ❷ ❹ ❺ ❻

University of Cambridge Audio-Visual Aids, Old Exam Hall, Free School Lane, Cambridge CB2 3RS
☎ 01223 334390 fax 01223 330475
Contact Martin Gienke (Director)
Main Activities Advisory service for purchase and utilisation of audio-visual material by University departments. Television, tape-slide, interactive multi-media, production, video-conferencing, photographic service, equipment loan, playback and teaching. The Unit is a central service complementing the many departmental audio-visual services which may include photographic facilities and small television studios.
○ ❶ ❺ ❻

University of Central Lancashire Clear Image, Department of Journalism, Lancashire Business School, Preston, Lancs PR1 2HE
☎ 01772 201201 fax 01772 892907
Contact Paul Egglestone; Mike Ward
Main Activities Corporate and training video production for clients including Leyland DAF, Lyons Biscuits, Rockwell International and Metro Rochdale.
○ ❷ ❹ ❺ ❻

University College Cork Audio-Visual Services, Cork, Eire
☎ 00 353 21 276871 fax 00 353 21 272642
Contact W A Perrott (Director)
Main Activities Photographic, graphic and video production services for teaching and publication. Provision of full conference facilities including video conferencing, simultaneous translation and interpreting. Significant medical illustration facility including photographs and video illustrations for teaching and publication.

University College Dublin Audio-Visual Centre, Belfield, Dublin 4
☎ 00 353 1 269 3244 fax 00 353 1 283 0060
Contact Micheal Foley (Director); Leo Casey (Head of Television)

Main Activities Academic support service to University College with a national role in media production in higher education in Ireland. Active in adult education television broadcasting, satellite, video conferencing, multimedia and EC programmes - Delta, Comett, Star.
○ ❷ ❹ ❺ ❻

University College Galway Audio-Visual Central Service Unit - (LIAT) - Language Centre, An Teanglann, Galway, Eire
☎ 00 353 91 24411 ext 2228 fax 00 353 91 25700
Contact Sean Macíomhair (Director); Bernadette Henchy (Secretary)
Main Activities The Unit provides a comprehensive audio-visual service for University College Galway and produces audio and video teaching and learning programmes for the College and outside bodies.
○ ❶ ❹ ❺ ❻

University College London UCL Images, 48 Riding House Street London W1P 7PL
☎ 0171-380 9327 fax 0171-580 0995
Contact Les Roberts (Producer); Antony Mangion (Studio Manager)
Main Activities Corporate and award winning medical educational video production on an international scale; surgical and medical networks across the UK and other parts of the world, using ISDN and Satellite transmission; research team for development of multimedia/ networking in universities; 'livenet'; SuperJANET. Central London studio facility used primarily for corporate media training and various productions/pack shots and commercials.
○ ❶ ❹ ❻

University College Swansea Media Resources Centre, Singleton Park, Swansea SA2 8PP
☎ 01792 295365 fax 01792 295618
Contact A H Davis
Main Activities Central Service Unit providing television, language lab, satellite reception and general audio-visual facilities. General purpose camcorder unit available for use by department as well as Hi-band and Hi-8 units.
○ ❶ ❹ ❺ ❻

University of Dundee Video Production Services, Dundee DD1 4HN
☎ 01382 344110 fax 01382 345502
Contact Peter Bartlett
Main Activities Video productions developed from concept to fully marketed package.
○ ❶

University of East Anglia Audio-Visual Centre, Norwich, Norfolk NR4 7TJ
☎ 01603 592833 fax 01603 507721
Contact Mr W Tyacke, Director
Main Activities The Audio Visual Centre is a central service unit providing technical support to teaching, conferences, public lectures, films shows, staff training and short courses. The Centre also has a video production capability centralised on the television studio which is situated under the library. Equipped with six broadcast standard cameras the studio is one of the largest non-broadcast studios in East Anglia. Four standards of video editing and recording are available: Sony High-band U-Matic SP; Sony

Low-band U-Matic; VHS and S-VHS. The studio cameras are also used as single cameras for location work. The Centre provides a wide range of equipment including camcorders, cine projectors, slide projectors, overhead projectors, television/data projectors, LCD panels, public address systems, visualisers, computer to video convertors, televisions, etc.

○ **❶ ❹ ❻**

University of Edinburgh Audio-Visual Services, 55 George Square, Edinburgh EH8 9JU
☎ 0131-650 4097 fax 0131 650 4101
Contact B G McGleave
Main Activities Production of video and audio teaching programmes. Distribution of such material. Maintenance of all television/audio-visual equipment. Design and installation of video and audio teaching facilities including advice on suitability of equipment. Provision of conference facilities.
○ **❶ ❷**

University of Essex Teaching Services, Wivenhoe Park, Colchester, Essex CO4 3SQ
☎ 01206 873220 fax 01206 873598
Contact PA Brown
Main Activities Comprehensive media services including projection television, 16 and 35mm film projection, slide-making and off-air television recording.
❶ ❷ ❹ ❺

University of Glasgow Department of Media Services, Southpark House, 64 Southpark Avenue, Glasgow G12 8LB
Contact ☎ 0141-330 4585 fax 0141-330 5674
Main Activities George Kirkland
Provision of production services in television, audio, photography, graphics and medical illustration. Installation and maintenance of equipment in lecture theatres and other areas. Advisory role, equipment loan and technical services. Training courses in television production and media presentation. Full design and production services for interactive media products in CD-ROM, CD-I and Video CD formats.
○ **❶ ❹ ❺ ❻**

University of Hertfordshire Media Services, College Lane, Hatfield, Herts AL10 9AB
☎ 01707 284471 fax 01707 284666
Contact David Coles (Manager); Mike Hare (Senior Television Technical Officer).
Main Activities Provides audio-visual service and materials production service for staff and students.
○ **❷ ❹ ❻**

University of Huddersfield Audio-Visual Services, Queensgate, Huddersfield, West Yorks HD1 3DH
☎ 01484 472079 fax 01484 516151
Contact Ian Hirstle (Head of Audio-Visual Services)
Main Activities Central audio-visual service providing teaching support.
○ **❺ ❻**

University of Leeds Audio-Visual Service, Woodhouse Lane, Leeds LS2 9JT
☎ 0113 233 2660 fax 0113 233 2655
Contact Peter Coltman

Main Activities	The unit provides services in graphics, still photography and television production, together with technical support and advice to the University. ○ ❶ ❹ ❺ ❻
University of Liverpool	Central Television and Photographic Service, PO Box 147, Liverpool L69 3BX ☎ 0151-794 2661 fax 0151-794 2221
Contact	Carl Neads (Director); David Hyde (Facilities Manager)
Main Activities	Provides television and photographic production facilities to the whole University. The Television Service produces a wide variety of teaching programmes covering medicine, dentistry, veterinary science, engineering, education and social science topics. ○ ❷ ❸ ❹ ❺ ❻
University of Luton	Pennant Productions, Park Square, Luton, Beds LU1 3JU ☎ 01582 489259 fax 01582 489259
Contact	Roy Stares; Mark Gamble
Main Activities	Support for audio-visual requirements of college and production for external commissioning agencies in video, audio, computer-generated presentation graphics and photography. ○ ❶ ❹ ❺ ❻
University of Newcastle upon Tyne	Audio-Visual Centre, Medical School, Framlington Place, Newcastle upon Tyne NE2 4HH ☎ 0191-222 6951 fax 0191-222 7696
Contact	Paul Down; Dorothy Croydon; Shirlie Hemmings
Main Activities	Wide range of programmes produced with a medical bias in studios equipped with video and computerised graphic systems. Facilities available for hire. Catalogue of current titles also available. ○ ❶ ❷ ❹ ❺ ❻
University of North London	Holloway Road, London N7 8DB ☎ 0171-753 5174 fax 0171-700 4272
Contact	John Carter
Main Activities	Production of a wide range of teaching and promotional audio-visual material for the University and for outside agencies, with emphasis on flexibility and low cost. ○ ❷ ❹ ❺ ❻
University of Nottingham	Audio-Visual Educational Services, Queen's Medical Centre, Nottingham NG7 2UH ☎ 0115 970 9357 fax 0115 970 9917
Contact	Marian Cumpstey
Main Activities	Provides a wide range of photographic, graphic and video services to the University Medical School and Nottingham Health Authority. Although specialists in medicine, the centre covers all other needs as well as undertaking outside commissions. ○ ❶ ❷ ❺ ❻
University of Oxford	Educational Technology Resources Centre, 37–41 Wellington Square, Oxford OX1 2JF ☎ 01865 270526 fax 01865 270527

Contact   Dr Miles Ellis

Main Activities   University central service (AVT Service), incorporating audio-visual loan, hire and maintenance services, television production unit, multimedia research, development and production.

○ ❶ ❹ ❺ ❻

University of Paisley   Educational Development Unit, High Street, Paisley PA1 2BE

☎ 0141-848 3820 fax 0141-848 3822

Contact   R W Rowatt (Director); W J Bell (Technical Manager)

Main Activities   Course and curriculum design for higher education. Media production in support of higher education and training. Self development and training.

○ ❶ ❷ ❹ ❺ ❻

University of Portsmouth   The Television Centre, The Rotunda, Museum Road, Portsmouth PO1 2QQ

☎ 01705 843902 fax 01705 843299

Contact   Dr Jeremy Miles (Director)

Main Activities   Acts as a production unit serving the University's teaching, research and communications activities. Also acts as a commercial production company specialising in the fields of training and distance learning, operating at broadcast standard. Uses AVID non-linear editing.

○ ❶ ❹ ❻

University of Stirling   Department of Film and Media Studies, Stirling FK9 4LA

☎ 01786 467520 fax 01786 466855

Contact   Richard Kilburn

Main Activities   **(see also below)** A wide range of academic courses are available, but practical course units are studied including television and radio journalism and documentary video production.

○ ❷ ❸ ❹ ❻

University of Stirling   Information Services, Stirling FK9 4LA

☎ 01786 473171 ext 7253 fax 01786 467249

Contact   Gordon Brewster

Main Activities   **(see also above)** Audio-visual and computer support for academic departments and courses.

○ ❷ ❸ ❹ ❺ ❻

University of Strathclyde   Audio-Visual Media Services, Alexander Turnbull Building, 155 George Street, Glasgow G1 1RD

☎ 0141-552 4400 ext 2566 fax 0141-552 5182

Contact   Sheila McNeill

Main Activities   Provides a professional service covering all aspects of audio-visual services from provision of facilities for conferences to graphics, photography and video production and multi-media.

○ ❶ ❹ ❺ ❻

University of Ulster   Coleraine, County Derry, Northern Ireland

☎ 01265 44141 fax 01265 40902

Contact   Professor Desmond Bell

Main Activities   Undergraduate and postgraduate courses in Media Studies involving integration of theoretical, critical and production elements of the discipline. Fully equipped television and radio studios available.

University of Warwick   Audio-Visual Centre, Gibbett Hill Road, Coventry CV4 7AL
                            ☎ 01203 523463 fax 01203 461606
             Contact   Terry Williams (Service Manager); Bal Dhesi (Operations Manager)
      Main Activities   A central academic service providing audio-visual support to
                            University teaching and research, provision of audio-visual equipment
                            throughout the University, administration of a video-tape library and
                            production of teaching/learning materials.
                            ○ ❷ ❸ ❹

University of the West of England   Faculty of Education, Redland Hill, Redland, Bristol BS6 6UZ
                            ☎ 0117 974 1251 fax 0117 973 2251
             Contact   Richard Egan; Paul Gilbert
      Main Activities   Video production, photography, music technology and multimedia.
                            Specialises in the video production of teacher-training and educational
                            materials.
                            ○ ❶ ❹ ❺

University of York   Audio-Visual Centre, Wentworth College, Heslington, York Y01 5DD
                            ☎ 01904 433031 fax 01904 433433
             Contact   Rob Whitton (Manager)
      Main Activities   Production facility now unavailable to customers outside the University of
                            York. The audio-visual centre now provides services to teaching and
                            visiting conferences only.

Waltham Forest Schools
Media Resource Unit   George Mitchell School, Farmer Road, London E10 5DN
                            ☎ 0181-558 3004
             Contact   Hugh Meteyard
      Main Activities   Teaching students from local schools and colleges using 3-camera studio.
                            Production of educational videos and other resource materials. Provision
                            of in-service training on video production and media education. Subtitling,
                            signing and productions in community languages also undertaken.
                            ○ ❶ ❷ ❹ ❻

Wessex Video   King Alfred's College, Winchester SO22 4NR
                            ☎ 01962 866359 fax 01962 842280
             Contact   Tony Lee; Peter Major
      Main Activities   Production of videos to support initial and in-service teacher education.
                            In addition to general teaching methodology and practice, specialises in
                            drama, special education and religious studies. Full production facilities,
                            and catalogue of programmes for sale.
                            ○ ❶ ❹

West London Institute   Media Services, Gordon House, 300 St Margarets Road, Twickenham TW1 1PT
                            ☎ 0181-891 0121 ext 2405 fax 0181-744 1441 e-mail Buckman@admin.west-
                            london-institute.ac.uk
             Contact   Keith Buckman (Media Resources Officer)
      Main Activities   An academic support service which provides video production, sound
                            recording and audio-visual services for teaching and research. Specialises
                            in the use of video in performance research.
                            ○ ❶ ❹

Education Officers in Television

The BBC   The BBC runs the Education Information Service, a telephone enquiry service (☎ 0181-746 1111) which puts callers in touch with a member of the Information Service team for education broadcast enquiries (an ansaphone service operates outside office hours).

Details of network educational programmes are given on the day of transmission on page 635 of CEEFAX.

The BBC also regularly produces a free journal *On Course: BBC Resources for Further and Adult Education* which can be obtained by contacting the Education Information Service on the number given above.

BBC Open University   BBC Open University Production Centre, Walton Hall, Milton Keynes MK7 6BH
☎ 01908 274066

Contact   The Information Officer (For leaflets send 9"x7" sae with 2nd class stamp)

Belfast   Broadcasting House, Ormeau Avenue, Belfast BT2 8HQ
☎ 01232 338435

Contact   Eric Twaddell, Senior Education Officer

Cardiff   BBC Wales Education, Broadcasting House, Cardiff CF5 2YQ
☎ 01222 572830

Contact   Dr Eleri Wyn Lewis, Education Officer

Edinburgh   BBC Broadcasting House, 5 Queen Street, Edinburgh EH2 1JF
☎ 0131-469 4261

Contact   John Russel, Senior Education Officer

Glasgow   BBC Broadcasting House, Queen Margaret Drive, Glasgow G12 8DG
0141-338 2617

Contact   David Smith, Senior Education Officer

London   BBC Education, White City, 201 Wood Lane, London W12 7TS
☎ 0181-752 5252 (Switchboard)

Contact   Jane Straw, Chief Education Officer for Continuing Education and Training
☎ 0181-752 5650

Contact   Judith Banbury, Education Officer Health and Relationships
☎ 0181-752 4844

Chris Bernthal, Education Officer Work, Business, Training, IT
☎ 0181-752 5990

Camélia Bendhaou, Assistant Manager, Languages
☎ 0181-752 5358

Gill Hind, Education Officer Personal Development and Science
☎ 0181-752 5934

Jenny Hunt, Education Officer Educational Guidance and Core Skills
☎ 0181-752 5758

Rachel Harrison, Education Officer Equal Opportunities and Further Education
☎ 0181-752 5778

Europe Singh, Education Officer Equal Opportunities and Further Education
☎ 0181-752 5786

The Independent Television Commission
33 Foley Street, London, W1P 7LB
☎ 0171-255 3000 fax 0171-306 7800
The Independent Television Commission is the public body responsible for licensing and regulating non-BBC television services provided within the UK, local delivery services and 'additional services'. Information about educational services to schools and colleges can be obtained by contacting the appropriate officer listed below.

Anglia Television
Anglia House, Norwich NR1 3JG
☎ 01603 615151 fax 01603 631032
Contact Cathy Mason, Community Education Officer

Border Television
Television Centre, Carlisle CA1 3NT
☎ 01228 25101 fax 01228 41384
Contact Gill Johnston, Personnel Officer

Carlton Television
101 St Martin's Lane, London WC2N 4AZ
☎ 0171-240 4000 fax 0171-240 4171
Contact Hardeep Kalsi, Head of Regional Affairs

Central Independent Television
Central House, Broad Street, Birmingham B1 2JP
☎ 0121-643 9898 fax 0121-616 4153
Contact Sam O'Sullivan, Community Affairs Officer

Channel Four Television
127 Horseferry Road, London, SW1P 2TX
☎ 0171-396 4444 fax 0171-306 8353
Contact Derek Jones, Editor, Support Services

Channel Television
Television Centre, St Helier, Jersey, Channel Islands JE2 3ZD
☎ 01534 68999 fax 01534 59446/24770
Contact Gillian Manning, Head of Programme Planning, Presentation and Promotion

Grampian Television
Queen's Cross, Aberdeen AB9 2XJ
☎ 01224 646464 fax 01224 635127
Contact Marian Hepworth, Community Education Officer

Granada Television
Granada Television Centre, Liverpool L23 4BA
☎ 0151-708 4217 fax 0151-708 4240
Contact Elaine Bancroft, Features Editor

HTV (Cymru) Wales The Television Centre, Culverhouse Cross, Cardiff CF5 6XJ
☎ 01222 590590 fax 01222 597183
Contact David Lloyd, Community Education Unit

HTV West The Television Centre, Bath Road, Bristol BS4 3HG
☎ 0117-977 8366 fax 0117-972 2400
Contact Gerry Dawson – Head of Education

London Weekend Television The London Television Centre, Upper Ground, London SE1 9LT
☎ 0171-261 8035 fax 0171-928 7825
Contact Helen Hewland, Community Information Coordinator, LWT Action

Meridian Broadcasting (Newbury) Hambridge Lane, Newbury, RG14 5UZ
☎ 01635 522322 fax 01635 522620
Contact Simon Theobalds, Community Liaison Officer

Meridian Broadcasting (Maidstone) West Point, New Hythe, Kent ME20 6XX
☎ 01622 882244 fax 01622 714000
Contact Elaine Johnson, Community Liaison Officer

Meridian Broadcasting (Southampton) Television Centre, Southampton SO14 0PZ
☎ 01703 222555 fax 01703 335050
Contact Helen Hayes, Community Liaison Officer

S4C Parc Ty Glas, Cardiff Business Park, Llanishen, Cardiff
☎ 0222 747444 fax 0222 754444
Contact Cenwyn Edwards, Commissioner for Factual Programming

Scottish Television Cowcaddens, Glasgow, G2 3PR
0141-332 9999 fax 0141-332 6982
Contact Brenda Little, Community Programmes Coordinator

Tyne Tees Television The Television Centre, City Road, Newcastle upon Tyne, NE1 2AL
☎ 0191-261 0181 fax 0191-261 2302
Contact Sheila Browne, Head of Education

UTV Havelock House, Ormeau Road, Belfast, BT7 1EB
01232 328122 fax 01232 246695
Contact Noel Henry, Community Education Officer

Westcountry Television Western Wood Way, Langage Science Park, Plymouth PL7 5BG
☎ 01752 333333 fax 01752 333030
Contact Stephen Lynas, Community Affairs Editor

Yorkshire Television The Television Centre, Leeds LS3 1JS
☎ 0113-243 8283 fax 0113-244 5107
Contact Barbara Siedlecki

Channel Four Schools Channel Four Schools Education Officers are contacted through:
The Educational Television Company, Leah House, 10a Great
Titchfield Street, London, W1P 7AA
☎ 0171-580 8181 (main office) ☎ 01926 433333 (information line)
fax 0171-580 9350
   Education Officers are distributed by region as follows:

Senior Education Officer, based in London
Simon Fuller
☎ 0171-580 8181

South West England
Malcolm Ward
☎ 01373 831293

South East
Adrienne Jones
☎ 0181-402 3227

Cheshire
John Austin
☎ 01270 759514

Warwickshire
Rick Hayes
☎ 01926 864719

Leeds
Liz Meenan
☎ 0113-230 5019

Northern Ireland
Peter Logue
☎ 018494 6922

Gwent
Chris Alford
☎ 01633 450596

Glasgow
Anne Fleck
☎ 0141-357 2446

Fife
Mollie Balfour
☎ 01592 622293

Aberdeen
Robert Wilson
☎ 01224 495613

Organisations

This section lists details of the aims and activities of a selection of bodies with which the BUFVC has special links or has contacted or co-operated with either for its own purposes or in response to the needs of others. The list makes no effort to be comprehensive, as other reference works such as the general *Directory of British Associations* or the specific *British Film Institute Film and Television Yearbook* fulfil this function.

Advertising Standards Authority (ASA) Brook House, 2-16 Torrington Place, London WC1E 7HN
☎ 0171-580 5555 fax 0171-631 3051
The ASA exists to make sure that advertising is legal, decent and truthful, ensuring that advertisements follow the guidelines set out in the British Code of Advertising Practice, the set of rules for what is acceptable in advertising content and what is not. The ASA checks a large number of advertisements to ensure that any that are unacceptable are corrected, but as there are around 25 million advertisements published annually in the UK it obviously cannot check them all. If you see an advertisement you think is factually wrong, misleading or offensive you can complain to the ASA.

Art Libraries Association (ARLIS) 18 College Road, Bromsgrove B60 2NE
☎ 01527 579298
Contact Sonia French, Administrator
ARLIS/UK & Ireland, the Art Libraries Society of the United Kingdom and Ireland, was founded in 1969 and has since its inception aimed to promote all aspects of the librarianship of the visual arts, including architecture and design. ARLIS is the corporate voice of art librarians in the UK and Ireland and makes their views known to the appropriate professional and educational bodies. The Society also welcomes as members all those involved in the documentation of art and design. In addition to organising courses, seminars and regular conferences, ARLIS arranges visits to libraries, publishers and other places of interest both in the UK and abroad. ARLIS is also concerned with the development of art librarianship world-wide and liaises with similar bodies abroad.

Arts Council of Great Britain 14 Great Peter Street, London SW1P 3NQ
☎ 0171-333 0100 fax 0171-973 6590
The Arts Council was formed in 1946 to continue in peacetime its work begun with government support for the encouragement of music and the arts. It operates under a revised Royal Charter granted in 1967 in which its objects are stated as: 1) to develop and improve the knowledge, understanding and practice of the arts; 2) to increase the accessibility of

the arts to the public throughout Great Britain; and 3) to advise and co-operate with departments of government, local authorities and other bodies. It is funded by the Office of Arts and Libraries.

Aslib Computer Group   Aslib – The Association for Information Management, Information House, 20-24 Old Street, London EC1V 9AP
☎ 0171-253 4488 fax 0171-430 0514

Contact   Nigel Soane, Secretary, Aslib Computer Group, University College of North Wales, Computing Building, Sackville Road, Bangor, Gwynedd LL57 1LD
☎ 0248 382962
The Computer Group is one of the special interest groups of Aslib. It was formed in 1979 as a result of the amalgamation of the Computer Information Group and the Computer Applications Group, which had been founded in 1971. Because of this amalgamation the group has two strands of interest 1) the applications of new technology in the information field, and 2) coping with information on technology, including programme libraries. The group holds about six events a year, with speakers on, and demonstrations of, specific subjects relating to the topics mentioned above.

Association of Commonwealth Universities (ACU)   John Foster House, 36 Gordon Square, London WC1H 0PF
☎ 0171-387 8572 fax 0171-387 2655
The ACU is a practical expression of the wish for co-operation on the part of universites throughout the Commonwealth and, since its foundation in 1913, has provided an administrative link between those universities, and centrally-administered services. It has 433 member universities in 32 Commonwealth countries or regions. The ACU aims to promote in various practical ways contact and co-operation between its member institutions by encouraging and supporting the movement of academic and administrative staff and students from one country of the Commonwealth to another, by providing information about universities, and by organising meetings of various kinds. The ACU publishes the *Commonwealth Universities Yearbook*.

Association of Communications, Culture and Media   Department of Literature and Languages, Nottingham Trent University, Clifton Lane, Nottingham NG11 8NS
☎ 0115 941 8418 ext 3289 fax 0115 948 6632

Contact   Georgia Stone
Launched in November 1989 (AMFIT), ACCM is a self-financed body that seeks to act as a representative and professional association for teachers and researchers in further and higher education. It currently has a membership of 150 people largely drawn from colleges and universities.

Association for Database Services in Education and Training (ADSET)   Chancery House, Dalkeith Place, Kettering NN16 0BS
☎ 01536 410500 fax 01536 414274

Contact   Andy Binns, Marketing Manager
Set up in 1990, ADSET has received support from businesses and other organisations. It aims to promote coherence and compatibility of standards for the provision of data on education and training in the UK, to develop and maintain an information service on databases for education and training in the UK, to promote the easy interchange of information between sources, to produce a code of good practice and standards

relating to the quality and integrity of information held on databases, and to accredit the service provided by members against this code.

Association for Educational and Training Technology (AETT)

Higher Millbrook, Beavor Lane, Axminster, Devon EX13 5EQ
☎ 01297 32030 fax 01297 35281

Contact Roy Winterburn, Administrator

Founded in 1962 as the Association for Programmed Learning, the AETT serves as a focus for the interests and ideas of all those involved in applying technology and systematic principles to the teaching/learning process, both in education and training. Its overall aims include: promoting the systematic application of instructional technology at all levels and in all contexts; enabling the dissemination of information to the widest international audience; providing opportunities for interested practitioners to meet, debate and discuss; establishing a contact point between members and external organisations with a mutual interest in short-term consultancy work. AETT has links with both national and international bodies. It publishes the biennial *International Yearbook of Educational and Training Technology*.

Association for Learning Technology (ALT)

ALT Administration, University of Oxford, 13 Banbury Road, Oxford OX2 6NN
☎ 01865 273281 fax 0865 273275 e-mail Alt@vax.ox.ac.uk

ALT aims to bring together all those concerned with learning technology in higher education, including researchers, developers, service providers, IT policy makers, librarians, computer manufacturers, software companies and publishers. The special membership rates for those working in UK higher educational establishments ensure a core membership of academic staff, but corporate membership is also available for companies. ALT holds an annual conference, and also organises workshops and forums.

Association for Media Education

Faculty of Education, Bretton Hall College, West Bretton, Wakefield, West Yorks WF4 4LG
☎ 0924 830261 fax 0924 830521

Contact Jeannette Ayton

The association aims to promote media education at all levels; stimulate links with and between existing media education networks and provide a forum for the dissemination of effective ideas and practice. AME is open to anyone involved in media education. It seeks to involve teachers and lecturers across all age phases as well as media professionals and cultural workers.

Association for the Study of Medical Education (ASME)

2a-4 Perth Road, Dundee DD1 4LN
☎ 01382 204006 fax 01382 204110

Contact Maureen Gyle, Administrative Secretary

ASME was founded in 1957 with the aim of creating an association in which all medical schools could share and to which any individual member, or medical teacher, could contribute. It provides a forum for communication and a focus for ideas for those concerned with medical education. Its main functions are to exchange information, organise meetings, promote research and give evidence as a representative organisation for medical education. Almost all medical schools in the UK are corporate members and there are over 600 individual members.

Audio-Visual Association Herkomer House, 156 High Street, Bushey, Watford WD2 3DD
☎ 0181-950 5959 fax 0181-950 7560

Contact Michael Simpson, Secretary
The Audio-Visual Association is the only professional body established to protect and enhance the interests of people – creative, technical, administrative and supply – involved in the non-broadcast sector of the UK audio-visual conference and multimedia industry.

British Academy of Film and Television Arts (BAFTA) 195 Piccadilly, London W1V 9LG
☎ 0171-734 0022 fax 0171-734 1792
BAFTA aims to advance the art and technique of film and television and administers the annual BAFTA Awards.

British Board of Film Classification (BBFC) 3 Soho Square, London W1V 5DE
☎ 0171-439 7961 fax 0171-287 0141
The BBFC is an independent, non-governmental body formed in 1985 from the **British Board of Film Censors** (originally formed 1912). In 1985 the BBFC was designated as the authority responsible for classifying videos under the Video Recordings Act 1984. The board issues an annual report and a guide to the implementation and practical consequences of the 1984 Video Recordings Act.

The British Computer Society (BCS) 1 Sanford Street, Swindon SN1 1HJ
☎ 0793 417417 fax 0793 480270
The BCS, incorporated by Royal Charter as the professional association for information systems engineering, became a chartered engineering institution in 1990. It represents over 34,000 computer practitioners and is concerned with maintaining and improving technical and ethical standards for the benefit of its members and society at large. It publishes a number of journals, administers training qualifications, runs specialist groups, advises Parliament and industry, lobbies Government, accredits courses and maintains a register of experts

The British Council Films, Television and Video Department, 11 Portland Place, London W1N 4EJ
☎ 0171-389 3065 fax 0171-389 3041
The British Council as a whole is an independent body promoting Britain abroad and is Britain's principal agent for cultural relations overseas. It provides a network of contacts between Government departments, universities and professional and cultural organisations in Britain and around the world. The Films, Television and Video Department is part of the Council's Arts Division. It organises film and television events and selects British entries for international film and video festivals. It maintains a film library in London and buys films and videos on behalf of the council's offices overseas. Through its work it aims to demonstrate to other countries the range and quality of British film-making, e.g. holding British film weeks.

British Federation of Film Societies (BFFS) British Film Institute, 21 Stephen Street, London W1P 1PL
☎ 0171-255 1444 fax 0171-436 0493

Contact Tom Brownley, General Secretary
The BFFS exists to promote film societies in the UK. It receives a grant from the BFI to support its work and holds events throughout the UK each year.

British Film Institute 21 Stephen Street, London W1P 1PL
☎ 0171-255 1444 fax 0171-436 0493
The BFI was founded in 1933 'to encourage the development of the art of the film, to promote its use as a record of contemporary life and manners, and to foster public appreciation and study of it'. In 1961 its memorandum of association was amended to incorporate a further aim: 'to foster study and appreciation of films for television and television programmes generally, to encourage the best use of television'. In 1983 it was incorporated by Royal Charter. The departments of the institute are: National Film and Television Archive; National Film Theatre; Library and Information Services; Stills, Posters and Designs; BFI Production; Museum of the Moving Image; BFI Distribution; Planning Unit; and BFI Research.

British Film Institute Education 21 Stephen Street, London W1P 1PL
☎ 0171-255 1444 fax 0171-436 0439
BFI Education is a department of the British Film Institute's Research and Information Division. It aims to develop knowledge and ideas about the media: film, television and video in particular. Working with people in formal education, from primary to university level, the department tries to ensure that such knowledge and ideas are spread as widely as possible.

British Interactive Multimedia Association (BIMA) 6 Washingley Road, Folksworth, Peterborough PE7 3SY
☎ 01733 242370 fax 01733 240020
BIMA is the representative body for the interactive multimedia industry. Members operate in the field of interactive design and the development of multimedia programmes for communications, learning and information management. BIMA has five objectives: to represent the multimedia industry in its relationship with customer groups and Government, to promote a wider understanding of the benefits offered by interactive multimedia, to establish professional standards for the multimedia industry and to communicate these as widely as possible, to provide a forum for the exchange of views amongst members, and to develop and maintain high standards of professional practice. The association runs the annual BIMA Awards.

British Kinematograph, Sound and Television Society (BKSTS) M6-14 Victoria House, Vernon Place, London WC1B 4DJ
☎ 0171-242 8400 fax 0171-405 3560
The BKSTS was founded in 1931 and incorporated in 1946. Its aim is to keep members abreast of current technical developments in all areas of film, sound, television, audio-visual and video. It maintains a library; publishes the monthly journal *Image Technology*; organises a regular lecture programme, a biennial conference and exhibition, and seminars and other events which give members the opportunity to meet other people in the industry and exchange information on a national and international basis.

British Screen Advisory Council (BSAC) 93 Wardour Street, London W1V 3TE
☎ 0171-413 8009 fax 0171-734 5122
The BSAC was established in its current form in 1985 as an industrial advisory body funded by the audio-visual industry. It is a unique forum bringing together the senior management of the industry, in all its forms,

to discuss issues on a regular basis under the chairmanship of Lord Attenborough. The Council aims to foster good relations between Government and Parliament on the one hand, and all aspects of the audio-visual industry on the other, providing advice through meetings and reports as appropriate.

British Videogram Association (BVA) 22 Poland Street, London W1V 3DD
☎ 0171-437 5722 fax 0171-437 0477
Contact Lavinia Carey, Director General
The BVA was established in October 1980 to give expression to and, where appropriate, to implement the collective views of the industry by promoting and protecting the interests of the copyright-owning publishers of videograms (pre-recorded videocassettes and videodiscs) in the UK. Among its activities it publishes a code of conduct, lobbies Government, operates awards, collects and publishes sales statistics, and serves as a forum for discussion.

Broadcasting Complaints Commission Grosvenor Gardens House, 35-37 Grosvenor Gardens, London SW1W 0BS
☎ 0171-630 1966
An independent statutory body set up by the Home Secretary in 1981 to consider and adjudicate upon certain specific types of complaint about radio or television programmes, the BCC's function and authority derive from the Broadcasting Act 1990. The Commission is empowered to consider complaints only if they fall within either of the following categories: 1) unjust or unfair treatment in radio or television programmes actually broadcast or included in a licensed cable or satellite programme service, and 2) unwarranted infringement of privacy in, or in connection with the obtaining of material included in, such programmes. The BCC issues an annual report.

Broadcasting, Entertainment and Cinematograph Technicians Union (BECTU) 111 Wardour Street, London W1V 4AY
☎ 0171-437 8506 fax 0171-437 8268
BECTU is the UK trade union for workers in film, broadcasting and the arts. Formed in 1991 by the merger of the ACTT and BETA, it is 42,000 strong and represents permanently employed and freelance staff in television, radio, film, cinema, theatre, and entertainment. BECTU provides a comprehensive industrial relations service based in agreements with the BBC, ITV companies, Channel 4 and others.

Broadcasting Standards Council (BSC) 7 The Sanctuary, London SW1P 3JS
☎ 0171-233 0544 fax 0171-233 0397
Established in 1988 to monitor and report on the portrayal of violence, sex, and standards of taste and decency in television or radio programmes received in the UK, the BSC undertakes research and issues a code of practice and an annual report.

Campaign for Press and Broadcasting Freedom (CPBF) 8 Cynthia Street, London N1 9JF
☎ 0171-278 4430 fax 0171-837 8868
A campaigning membership organisation established in 1979 and backed by the trade unions, the CPBF actively campaigns for fair representation of

the variety of views and peoples that make up British society and challenges censorship. It has promoted legislation on statutory right of reply and ownership and control of the media. It organises conferences and meetings and publishes the bi-monthly journal *Free Press*.

CIMTECH (National Centre for Information Media and Technology)
University of Hertfordshire, 45 Grosvenor Road, St Albans AL1 3AW
☎ 01707 284691 fax 01707 284699
CIMTECH provides impartial information about newer media and methods for originating, distributing, storing and retrieving information. It has over 900 subscribing organisations that include libraries, archives and information centres; publishers and consultants; and records management and management services departments in commerce and industry, the public sector and education. It publishes the bi-monthly journal *Information Management and Technology* and *The Information Management Document Management Yearbook*.

Combined Higher Education Software Team (CHEST)
CHEST operates from two sites: the University of Bath (specialising in deals funded centrally for the whole higher education community), and De Montfort University (specialising in educational discounts for microcomputer software).

CHEST *NISS Centre*
University of Bath, Claverton Down, Bath BA2 7AY
☎ 01225 826282 fax 01225 826176 e-mail: CHEST@bath.c.uk

CHEST *IT Services*
De Montfort University, Gateway House, Leicester LE1 9BH
☎ 01553 577151 fax 01553 577170 e-mail: B.E.B@dmu.c.uk
CHEST, initially funded largely by the Computer Board for Universities and Research Councils, was formed in 1988 in response to the need for a central body to negotiate with suppliers on behalf of the UK's Higher Education and Research Council community. Its primary aim is to arrange and administer deals with suppliers of good-quality commercially used software and datasets. CHEST now also encourages suppliers to make deals available to institutions within the further education sector. The software deals which CHEST arranges fall into three broad categories: 1) call-off deals; 2) centrally-funded deals; and 3) special offers. There are currently three main sources of information about CHEST deals: CHEST site contacts, the annual *CHEST Software Directory* and NISS on-line services.

Committee of Vice-Chancellors and Principals of the Universities of the United Kingdom (CVCP)
29 Tavistock Square, London WC1H 9EZ
☎ 0171-387 9231 fax 0171-383 5766
The CVCP was established in 1918 by the universities and is paid for by them through an annual contribution. It consists of the executive heads of all the universities in the United Kingdom. Its functions are to formulate policy on matters affecting universities in the UK; to represent UK universities in dealings with Government, Parliament, local and national institutions and other organisations and individuals world-wide; to provide information, advice and assistance to UK universities; and to provide information about UK universities to wider audiences.

Commonwealth Institute
Kensington High Street, London W8 6NQ
☎ 0171-603 4535 fax 0171-602 7374
The Commonwealth Institute is the centre for Commonwealth education

and culture. Its departments house a library, an educational resource centre and exhibition galleries. It organises exhibitions, conferences, seminars and other events.

Consortium for Drama and Media in Higher Education
British Universities Film & Video Council, 55 Greek Street, London W1V 5LR
☎ 0171-734 3687 fax 0171-287 3914 e-mail BUFVC@open.c.uk

Contact   Professor Richard Cave, Chairman, c/o Department of Drama and Theatre Studies, Royal Holloway and Bedford New College, Egham Hill, Egham, Surrey TW20 0EX
☎ 0784 434455 fax 0784 437520

Founded in June 1974 by a group of teachers from universities and other institutions of higher education with support from the British Universities Film and Video Council, the consortium is a representative body, with membership open to all institutions of higher education and other national and international bodies having an interest in its work. Its objectives are to co-ordinate the use and exchange of information on audio-visual materials for the teaching and study of drama and related topics at university or equivalent level and to facilitate the production of such materials by members through grants made from the Central Production Fund. The consortium is also concerned in representing nationally and internationally the interests of members in the documentation and availability of audio-visual materials which may be used in the study of drama, and in forming links with similar organisations overseas.

Council for British Archaeology (CBA)
Bowes Morrell House, 111 Walmgate, York, YO1 2UA
☎ 01904 671417 fax 01904 671384 e-mail 100271.456@compuserve.com

The representational role of the CBA dates back to 1944 and has always been one of its prime concerns. A continuous dialogue is maintained with Government at all levels, both independently and in association with other amenity and conservation bodies. The CBA seeks to improve the public's interest in and understanding of Britain's past and concerns itself with conservation, information, research, publishing, education and training in archaeology. Membership is available to individuals and institutions. It publishes *British Archaeology* 10 times per year and the *Council for British Archaeology Briefing* five times per year and runs, in conjunction with the BUFVC, the biennial **Channel 4 Award** for best video or film on an archaeological subject.

Department for Education (DfE)
Sanctuary Buildings, Great Smith Street, London SW1P 3BT
☎ 0171-925 5000 fax 0171-925 6000

Secretary of State   The Rt Hon Gillian P Shephard, MP

The DfE is responsible for overall Government policy for university education in the whole of the UK and for education below university level in England.

Department of National Heritage (DNH)
2 Cockspur Street, London SW1Y 5DH
☎ 0171-211 6200 fax 0171-211 6210

Secretary of State   The Rt Hon Stephen Dorrell, MP

The DNH is involved in preserving the heritage of the past and adding to that heritage for future generations, creating contemporary culture and

128

broadening opportunities for people to enjoy the benefits of their heritage and culture. It is active in the areas of the built heritage, the arts, the media, sport and recreation, and tourism. National bodies such as the British Film Institute, the Arts Council and the British Library come under the DNH's remit.

Educational Broadcasting Services Trust (EBS)

36-38 Mortimer Street, London W1N 7RB
☎ 0171-765 5714 fax 0171-580 6246
The EBS Trust exists to develop education and training resources through the technologies generally associated with broadcasting. It draws on a network of professional people throughout Britain working in education, training, television, radio and telecommunications. It uses the production and technical skills and resources of the BBC as well as commissioning independent producers. The company is financed entirely from the projects which it develops. The Trust acts as producer, consultant or broker and has consortia in which people with a common interest can work together. The Trust provides legal support for productions and arranges and commissions production and consultancy using its own specially hired staff.

Educational Recording Agency (ERA)

The Authors' Licensing and Collecting Society (ALCS), 33-34 Alfred Place, London WC1E 7DP
☎ 0171-436 4883 fax 0171-323 0486
ERA is a company limited by guarantee and created for the purpose of representing the owners, controllers and representatives of owners of copyright and similar rights in cable and broadcast programmes and works included in those programmes.
The ERA licensing scheme for off-air recording became operative with effect from 30th May 1990.

Educational Television Association (ETA)

37 Monkgate, York YO3 7PB
☎ 01904 639212 fax 01904 639212
Contact Josie Key, Administrator
The ETA aims to bring together institutions and individuals using television and other media for education and training. Its membership covers a broad spectrum of educational and training institutions and organisations, and individuals, with a wide range of interests and experience. Through its specialist subcommittees and groups it provides a forum for the exchange of advice, expertise and new ideas. Regional events give members the opportunity of attending seminars, discussion groups and demonstrations. The ETA's annual conference is held at the University of York and its annual awards are intended to stimulate the production of creative and effective video material.

Employment Department

Moorfoot, Sheffield S1 4PQ
☎ 0114-275 3275 fax 0114-259 3152
Contact Information Services
The Employment Department was established in the autumn of 1988 to replace The Training Commission and the Manpower Services Commission.

European Script Fund 39c Highbury Place, London N5 1QP
☎ 0171-226 9903 fax 0171-354 2706
Contact David Kavanagh, Director General
The European Script Fund was founded as one of the pilot projects of the Media programme. Its aims are in harmony with the other Media projects, all of which are initiatives for national audio-visual industries to extend their work beyond the borders of their own countries and to stimulate co-operation between private financiers and public funding bodies. The fund concentrates on developing fiction projects in film and television.

Federation against Software 2 Lake End Court, Taplow Road, Taplow SL6 0JQ
Theft (FAST) ☎ 01628 660377 fax 01628 660348
FAST uses the legislation of the *Copyright, Designs and Patents Act 1988* to reduce software piracy losses. It does this through enforcement co-ordination and education/awareness activities. It has over 550 members who represent the entire computer industry, both in trade associations and the majority of the leading companies. The membership has a single issue: software protection.

Federation of Commercial PO Box 422, Harrow, Middlesex HA1 3YN
Audio-Visual Libraries (FOCAL) 0181-423 5853 fax 0181-423 5853
FOCAL is the international trade association for audio-visual libraries, researchers, producers, etc. promoting the use of library footage in programming. It holds seminars and meetings and publishes a journal and directory of members.

Film Education 41-42 Berners Street, London W1P 3AA
☎ 0171-637 9932 fax 0171-637 9996
Film Education is a film industry sponsored body. Its aims are to promote the use of film in the school curriculum and to further the use of cinemas by schools. To this end it publishes a variety of free teaching materials, and organises visits, lectures and seminars.

Further Education Unit (FEU) Spring Gardens, Citadel Place, Tinworth Street, London SE11 5EH
☎ 0171-962 1280 fax 0171-962 1266
Contact Maureen Papa, Information Officer
The FEU is an advisory, intelligence and development body for further education. Its general purpose is to promote quality in further education curricula by encouraging the development of more effective, relevant and flexible learning opportunities for individual learners. Sixth-form colleges are included in the FEU's remit. The FEU initiates and manages a wide range of projects in further education and other institutions, and accepts commissions from other organisations in relevant areas of work.

Independent Television 33 Foley Street, London W1P 7LB
Commission (ITC) ☎ 0171-255 3000 fax 0171-306 7800.
The ITC replaced the Independent Broadcasting Authority and the Cable Authority in 1991. It is the public body responsible for licensing and regulating commercially funded television services provided in and from the UK. These include Channel 3 (ITV), Channel 4 and a range of cable,

local delivery and satellite services. The ITC is concerned with television services only. The regulation of independent radio services is the responsibility of the Radio Authority (see below). The ITC will not build, own or operate television or radio transmitters.

The Industrial Society Peter Runge House, 3 Carlton House Terrace, London SW1Y 5DG
☎ 0171-839 4300 fax 0171-839 3898

Contact Information Service, Robert Hyde House, 48 Bryanston Square, London W1H 7LN
☎ 0171-262 2401 fax 0171-706 1096
The Industrial Society, now in its 76th year, is the largest independent provider of advisory and training services for developing people in the world of work. Services include topical and practical training courses and conferences, in-house training and consultancy work tailored to individual needs, and a selection of publications and training videos. The membership ranges across the business, private and public sectors and includes some 12,000 organisations.

Interactive Technologies Courseware (ITC) 3 The Drive, Bishopsteignton, Devon TQ14 9SD
☎ 01626 778049 fax: 01392 264736

Contact Bruce Wright
ITC is a developer of and information source about educational applications of multimedia technologies. It specialises in low-cost, user-friendly, flexible new optical disc technologies (eg Photo CD, CD-ROM, bar-coded videodisc) and still video cameras. ITC produces an extensive set of catalogues related to optical discs and related software, courseware and hardware. ITC has gained experience on a wide range of educational research and development projects and is actively interested in promoting well designed multimedia products which reinforce, enhance, extend or replace current teaching and learning processes.

International Visual Communications Association (IVCA) Bolsover House, 5-6 Clipstone Street, London W1P 7EB
☎ 0171-580 0962 fax 0171-436 2606
The IVCA is a non-profit-making professional association representing the interests of the users and suppliers of visual communications. In particular, it pursues the interests of the producers, commissioners and manufacturers involved in the non-broadcast film, video and audio-visual market, and those of the independent facilities industry. It offers advice, special interest groups, a monthly publication *IVCA Update*, and national and regional events, including the annual IVCA Festival for which there are awards.

InterUniversity History Film Consortium (IUHFC) Department of History, Queen Mary and Westfield College, Mile End Road, London E1 4NS
☎ 0171-975 5555 ext 3388 fax 0171-975 5500

Contact Dr John Ramsden, Chairman
The IUHFC is a self-governing group of subscribing institutions of higher education which came together to enable teaching historians to make films for their own and each others' use, to foster a more scholarly approach to the use of film as visual evidence, and to arrange conferences and

publications in this field. Member institutions receive copies of all films made by the consortium and have the opportunity to make films themselves in rotation. The films are on general sale in the UK in both 16mm and video formats. Current members of the consortium are: the universities of Birmingham, Leeds, Liverpool, Nottingham, Salford and Wales; Queen Mary and Westfield College, University of London; the College of St Mark and St John, Plymouth; the College of Ripon and York St John.

Joint Academic Network (JANET) Joint Network Team, The Computer Board and Research Councils, c/o Rutherford Appleton Laboratory Chilton, Didcot OX11 0QX
☎ 01235 446737 fax 01235 445808 e-mail: S.Wood@ukerna.ac.uk

Contact Shirley Wood, User Support Manager
JANET is a computer network that links all UK universities and most research council establishments. It facilitates the use of remote computing resources and the sharing of information amongst members of the academic community. The network was instigated by the Computer Board and Research Council and continues to be funded by the board. JANET allows access to a computer at another site, sending of mail messages from one computer system to another; transfer of files from one computer system to another; submitting jobs at one computer to be run on another system.

Library Association Information The Library Association, 7 Ridgmount Street, London WC1E 7AE
Technology Group (LAITG) ☎ 0171-636 7543 fax 0171-436 7218 or 0171-636 3627
Contact Adie Scott, Secretary LAITG, Central Library, Katherine Street, Croydon CR9 1ET
☎ 0181-253 1001 fax 0181-253 1004 e-mail LBASCOTT@clip.croydon.gov.uk
The main objective of the LAITG is to bring together all members of the Library Association (LA) interested in and concerned with information technology. It aims to promote the library and information profession's role in IT; to advise the LA on IT; to provide a forum for discussion and facilities for the dissemination of ideas and experiences; to establish links with the information industry; to promote access to sources of specific expertise and interest; and to encourage the provision of appropriate education and training. It offers help and advice to its 5000-plus members on all topics ranging from the choice of which micro to buy to harnessing the power of optical discs, and has spearheaded the establishment of a database of expertise. *ITs News* is the official journal of the group.

Mechanical Copyright Protection 41 Streatham High Road London SW16 1ER
Society (MCPS) ☎ 0181-769 4400 fax 0181-769 8792
MCPS authorises on behalf of its members (composers, authors and publishers of music) use of their work in the UK and abroad by recording companies, film and video companies, background music operators and other recording bodies and individuals as well as in recordings made by radio and television organisations.

The Media Education Agency 5A Queens Parade, Brownlow Road, London N11 2DN
☎ 0181-888 4620
Contact David Lusted
The Media Education Agency is an organisation of academics, teachers,

writers, broadcasters and actors who have interests and experience in areas of film, television and the media. It offers consultancy to local education authorities and others involved in INSET and curriculum planning; organisation and delivery of INSET in media education within the national curriculum; lectures on aspects of media theory, criticism and pedagogy; speakers on subjects ranging from film stars to national broadcasting systems, from video production to desk-top publishing, and from media education in the primary school classroom to media studies at A level; broadcasters talking informally about their work as television directors and producers, and actors talking about their experiences in acting for television. The agency is a facility for educational and arts organisations, including local education authorities, INSET co-ordinators, schools and colleges, regional film theatres, arts associations, film societies and any agencies seeking specialists in any aspect of media education.

Museum of the Moving Image (MOMI) South Bank, London SE1 8XT
☎ 0171-928 3535 fax 0171-633 9323. MOMI recorded information
☎ 0171-406 2636
MOMI explores the history of cinema and television. The story is told chronologically from the earliest pre-cinema experiments to the technical wizardry of a modern television studio.

National Acquisitions Group (NAG) Westfield House, North Road, Horsforth, Leeds LS18 5HG
☎ 0113-259 1447 fax 0113-259 1447
Contact Sally Wolfe, Administrative Assistant
NAG was formally established in April 1986 at its inaugural conference in Oxford. Its aims are: 1) to bring together those concerned with library acquisitions in whole or in part, to assist them in exchanging information and comment, and by so doing to promote understanding and good practice between them; and 2) to seek to influence other organisations and individuals to adopt its opinions and standards when promulgated. It seeks, among other objectives, to provide opportunities for NAG members to bring forward acquisitions issues for discussion, to initiate discussions of acquisitions issues beyond the membership of NAG, to promote knowledge and understanding of technological developments as they relate to acquisitions, to improve awareness of producers, suppliers and librarians of the acquisitions state of the art. NAG has in membership over 500 organisations within publishing, book selling and systems supply, as well as librarians from academic, public, national, Government and special institutions.

National Association for Higher Education in Film and Video London International Film School, 24 Shelton Street, London WC2H 9HP
☎ 0171-836 9642 fax 0171-497 3718
The National Association for Higher Education in Film and Video is a forum for debate on all aspects of film, video and television education. The School fosters links with industry, the professions and Government. Represents all courses offering a major practical study in film, video or television at higher education level.

National Computing Centre (NCC) Ltd Oxford House, Oxford Road, Manchester M1 7ED
☎ 0161-228 6333 fax 0161-237 1559

Contact Gina Poole
A completely independent organisation providing expert, impartial and consultancy on every aspect of information technology. NCC provides a range of software tools, training and consultancy services, particularly in communications networking, open systems, software engineering and security. It is promoting the more effective use of information technology.

National Council for Educational Technology (NCET) Milburn Hill Road, Science Park, University of Warwick, Coventry CV4 7JJ
☎ 01203 416994 fax 01203 411418.
The NCET is an independent company set up in 1988 from an amalgamation of the Council for Educational Technology for the United Kingdom and the Microelectronics Education Support Unit. Its purpose is to implement beneficial change in the processes of learning in education and training through the development and application of educational technology. The council's governing council is drawn from education and business.

National Council for Vocational Qualifications (NCVQ) 222 Euston Road, London NW1 2BZ
☎ 0171-387 9898 fax 0171-387 0978
The Council was set up by the Government in 1986 as a registered company limited by guarantee to achieve a coherent national framework for vocational qualifications. Its main task is to design and implement a national framework of vocational qualifications and rationalise and reform the present system. NCVQ accredits awards by certifying bodies where they reflect relevant standards of competence required by industry and commerce. Awarding National Vocational Qualification (NVQ) status will raise standards, encourage more effective training and open up access to qualifications by the removal of unnecessary restrictions on methods and periods of learning, and age barriers.

National Film and Television School (NFTS) Beaconsfield Studios, Station Road, Beaconsfield HP9 1LG
☎ 01494 671234 fax 01494 674042
The NFTS provides advanced training and retraining in all major disciplines to professional standards. It offers full-time training to an NFTS Associateship in production, direction (fiction), direction (documentary), animation, screen-writing, cinematography, art direction/production design, editing, sound technique and design, and film/television music composition. Previous experience in film or a related field is expected. Assistant-level training is also available as is a wide range of short courses for industry professionals. The school is funded by a partnership of Government and industry (film, television and video), and its graduates occupy leading roles in all aspects of film and television production. It is a full member of CILECT and actively co-operates with professional bodies in the UK and abroad.

National Information Services and Systems (NISS) NISS is a split-site project, with teams based at the University of Bath (for general enquiries, NISS Gateway and NISS Bulletin Board) and the University of Southampton (for NISSWAIS).

NISS Centre Computing Services, University of Bath, Claverton Down, Bath BA2 7AY
☎ 01225 826036 fax 01225 826176 e-mail: NISS@niss.c.uk

NISS Service Computing Services, University of Southampton, Southampton SO9 5NH
☎ 01703 593697 fax 01703 593939 e-mail: NISSSOTON@niss.c.uk
NISS provides information services over the UK Joint Academic Network (JANET), and acts as a focus for computer disseminated information for the academic community. No special registration or passwords are needed in order to use NISS services. Since its creation in 1988, NISS has supported several initiatives, including the NISS Gateway, the NISS Bulletin Board and the NISS Wide Area Information Server. NISS also provides information services support for the Combined Higher Education Software Team (CHEST).

National Institute of Adult Continuing Education (England and Wales) (NIACE) 21 De Montfort Street, Leicester LE1 7GE
☎ 0116-255 1451 fax 0116-285 4514
Contact Elaine Pole, Senior Information Officer
The object of NIACE, which was formed in 1949 as the National Institute of Adult Education, is the promotion of the study and the general advancement of adult continuing education. It offers a means of consultation and co-operation for all those interested in adult continuing education. NIACE possesses a reference library of adult continuing education materials and provides information services through its yearbook, its research reports and surveys.

National Museum of Photography, Film and Television Pictureville, Bradford BD1 1NQ
☎ 01274 727488 fax 01274 723155 (Education Unit ☎ 01274 725347)
The museum looks at the past, the present and the future of photography, film and television and shows the part played by photography in all our lives through working models, equipment, dramatic reconstructions and the pictures themselves. It houses Britain's only IMAX screen.

Networking (The Film, Video and Television Organisation For Women) Vera Productions, 30-38 Dock Street, Leeds LS10 1JF
☎ 0113-242 8646 fax 0113-245 1238
Membership of Networking is open to all women interested or involved in film, video and television. It is a campaigning voice at conferences and on national and regional committees affecting women, has members throughout the UK, and maintains a directory of freelancers. Its quarterly bulletin *Networking* is distributed internationally. It offers training, courses, and advice on career opportunities. A membership directory is available.

Oral History Society British Library National Sound Archive, 29 Exhibition Road, London SW7 2AS
☎ 0171-412 7405 fax 0171-412 7441 e-mail Rob.Perks@bl.uk
Contact Dr Rob Perks
The Oral History Society encourages people of all ages to tape record or write down their own and other people's life stories. It offers practical support and advice about how to get started, what equipment to use, what techniques are best, how to look after tapes, and how to make use of what has been collected. Through journals and conferences it brings together a network of individuals and local groups from all over Britain and Europe to share ideas and problems. The society's members come from all backgrounds. It publishes the journal *Oral History* twice yearly.

Performing Rights Society (PRS) 29-33 Berners Street, London W1P 4AA
☎ 0171-580 5544 fax 0171-631 4138
The PRS is an association of composers, authors and publishers of musical works established in 1914 to administer on behalf of its members certain of the rights granted to them under copyright legislation. Two separate rights, generally referred to collectively by the single expression 'performing right', are administered by the PRS: 1) the right to perform the work in public, and 2) the right to broadcast the work or include it in a cable programme service. For a moderate annual charge the society grants blanket licences that enable the holders to comply with the provisions of the *Copyright, Designs and Patents Act 1988*. The Society is limited by guarantee, has no share capital and is non-profit making.

Press Complaints Commission (PCC) 1 Salisbury Square, London EC4Y 8AE
☎ 0171-353 1248 fax 0171-353 8355
The PCC succeeded the Press Council as the press regulatory body on 1st January 1991. It is charged to enforce a code of practice that is framed by the newspaper and periodical industry and published by the PCC.

Producers Alliance for Cinema and Television (PACT) Gordon House, Greencoat Place, London SW1 1PH
☎ 0171-233 6000 fax 0171-233 8935
The trade association and employers' body for feature film and independent television producers, PACT was formed in 1991 from the Independent Programme Producers Association and the British Film and Television Producers Association. It provides a range of services, including information and production advice, and publishes a monthly newsletter, the *Pact Magazine*, an annual members' directory and specialist guides.

The Radio Authority Holbrook House, Great Queen Street, London WC2B 5DG
☎ 0171-430 2724 fax 0171-405 7062
The Radio Authority, the regulatory and licensing body for independent radio, operates under rules contained in the Broadcasting Act 1990. It has three main tasks: 1) to widen listening choice, 2) to protect the listener, and 3) to enable independent radio broadcasters to maximise audiences and resources.

The Royal Society 6 Carlton House Terrace, London SW1Y 5AG
☎ 0171-839 5561 fax 0171-930 2170
The Royal Society is an independent learned society for the promotion of the natural sciences, including mathematics and all applied aspects such as engineering and medicine. It encourages both national and international activities in a similar way to national academies overseas. Its objectives are: to encourage scientific research and its application; to recognise excellence in scientific research; to promote international scientific relations and facilitate the exchange of scientists; to provide independent advice on scientific matters, notably to Government; to represent and support the scientific community; to promote science education as well as science understanding and awareness in the public at large; and to support research into the history of scientific endeavour.

Royal Television Society (RTS) Holborn Hall, 100 Grays Inn Road, London WC1X 8AL
☎ 0171-430 1000 fax 0171-430 0924
Founded in 1927, the RTS provides a forum for debate on the cultural and technical aspects of television. It arranges conferences, courses and symposia, publishes the monthly journal *Television* and organises the annual RTS Awards.

Schools Curriculum Assessment Authority (SCAA) Newcombe House, 45 Notting Hill Gate, London, W11 3JB
☎ 0171-229 1234 fax 0171-243 0542
The SCAA was set up under the Education Act 1993. It is responsible for advising the Secretary of State for Education on all matters relating to school examinations and assessment, and for developing the National Curriculum and its assessment arrangements at ages 7, 11, 14 and 16.

Scottish Education Department New St Andrew's House, St James Centre, Edinburgh EH1 2SY
☎ 0131-556 8400
The Scottish Education Department is responsible for the administration of public education, excluding universities, in Scotland. Is also responsible for the arts, libraries, museums, art galleries and sport.

Scottish Film Council (SFC) Dowanhill, 74 Victoria Crescent Road, Glasgow G12 9JN
☎ 0141-334 4445 fax 0141-334 8132
The SFC, originally established in 1934 and separated from the Scottish Council for Educational Technology since April 1990, is a public agency, funded mainly by Government, charged with the promotion and development of film culture in Scotland.

Society for Research into Higher Education (SRHE) 344-354 Gray's Inn Road, London WC1X 8BP
☎ 0171-837 7880
The Society for Research into Higher Education exists to stimulate and co-ordinate research into all aspects of higher education. It aims to improve the quality of higher education through the encouragement of debate and publication on issues of policy, on the organisation and management of higher education institutions, and on the curriculum, teaching and learning. Under the imprint SRHE and Open University Press, the Society is a specialist publisher of research, having over 30 titles in print. The Society also publishes *Studies in Higher Education, Higher Education Quarterly*, and *SRHE News*. In addition the Society holds regular seminars.

Training Film and Video Association (TFVA) Bolsover House, 5-6 Clipstone Street, London W1P 7EB
☎ 0171-323 1004 fax 0171-436 2606.
Contact Bridget Conneely, Administrator
The TFVA exists to discuss matters of interest to its members, in particular, the copyright, terms and conditions of sale/hire of training films and video programmes; to take joint actions to protect the interests of members; to mount any agreed promotional or public relations exercise deemed desirable by the association; to raise subscriptions to support the activities of the association; to join with other associations to further the interests of members if considered desirable; to promote the effectiveness of training programmes in the UK and overseas; and to help create a suitable environment in which to enhance the commercial activities of members.

Video Standards Council Research House, Fraser Road, Perivale, Middx UB6 7AQ
☎ 0181-566 8272 fax 0181-991 2653
The Video Standards Council was established in 1989 to set and maintain the highest standards of ethical conduct in the video industry. From July 1993 its brief was extended to cover the video and computer games industry.

Voice of the Listener 101 King's Drive, Gravesend, Kent DA12 5BQ
and Viewer (VLV) ☎ 01474 325832
Contact Jocelyn Hayes, Chairman
The VLV is a non-profit-making society with the aims of supporting high standards in broadcasting. It has no political, sectarian or commercial affiliations and speaks for listeners and viewers on the whole range of broadcasting issues and acts as the secretariat for the **European Alliance of Listeners and Viewers Associations**. It organises conferences and publishes the quarterly *Voice of the Listener and Viewer*. It has taken over responsibility for distributing the books, research findings and reports published by the **Broadcasting Research Unit** during the 10-year life of that organisation.

Wales Film Council Screen Centre, Llantrisant Road, Llandaff, Cardiff CF5 2PU
(Cyngor Ffilm Cymru) ☎ 01225 578633 fax 01225 578654
Contact Mike Sweet, Chief Executive
The Wales Film Council promotes the development of the culture of the moving image in Wales through education, exhibitions, publications and the fostering of new film-making talent. Supports and manages Wales Film and Television Archive and is actively involved in establishing a National Film School for Wales. It provides grant aid for individuals and organisations based in Wales or of Welsh extraction, for low-budget film and video production, film exhibition and education and overseas study.

Women's Audio-Visual Education London Women's Centre, 4 Wild Court, off Kingsway, London WC2B 5AU
Scheme (WAVES) ☎ 0171-430 1076
WAVES aims to promote and train women to work in the audio and visual media industries and to produce their own independent work. It also aims to forge links with existing training providers London-wide to increase women's chances of pursuing a career in the media and developing critical and analytical skills. It offers training through interrelated modular courses to allow maximum flexibility offering pre-vocational, vocational, educational, leisure and community-access opportunities. WAVES is committed to equal opportunities.

Writers and Scholars International Ltd 33 Islington High Street, London N1 9LH
☎ 0171-278 2313 fax 0171-278 1878
The Writers and Scholars Educational Trust is associated with the magazine *Index on Censorship*. It aims to help the victims of censorship, to inform the world about the issues censorship and freedom of expression, and to promote discussion and debate. The work of WSET and *Index* reaches over 110 countries.

Distributors of Film, Video and Related Media: Introduction

This guide to distributors is a thoroughly revised version of *Distributors: the Guide to Film and Video Sources for Education and Training*, published as an independent volume in 1990. Since then there have been countless changes in the distribution scene; a large number of the companies previously listed have closed down, many have moved or been taken over, and about 25% of the entries in this section are collections which, as far as we are aware, did not exist in 1990. This listing contains almost 600 different catalogues from around 550 distributors, arranged under some 100 subject sections.

Information is given on distributors who specialise in providing audio-visual materials (mainly videos, but also videodiscs, CD-ROMs with an audio or video element, computer software, films, audiocassettes, tape-slide programmes, and slide sets) for hire or sale for educational purposes. Distributors who handle computer software only are not included, as information about them is readily obtained from the CTI centres listed elsewhere in this handbook (see page 265). Almost all the distributors mentioned are based in the UK, except for a small number from Europe, Australia and the USA which have been included as they have particularly useful programmes and are prepared to supply copies in the PAL television system for use in the UK.

This is, in fact, a catalogue of catalogues, which means that only distributors who make available printed listings of their holdings, supply publicity leaflets about programmes or who hold their catalogues on disc and run off copies or printouts on demand, are included. Some of the distributors have hundreds of programmes and some very few, specialist items. Where a distributor has several separate catalogues listing programmes in distinct subject areas, these are given separate entries. Because of limitations of time and space, it has not been possible to include information on all known distributors. A selection has therefore been made on the basis of number of programmes, relevance to the academic curriculum, how readily available the programmes are, and how actively they are promoted.

Together with the distributors' catalogues themselves, several subject sections contain 'compilation' catalogues, bringing together information on all the known programmes on a specific topic, e.g. the construction industry or women and well-being, available from a wide range of sources. These have usually been assembled by a related professional body as part of its educational or information service, and contain for each programme references to the individual distributors, often with a separate index of distributors' addresses and telephone numbers.

The aim of **Distributors** is to enable teachers and lecturers, together with librarians in education, industry and professional institutions, to build up their own collections of audio-visual catalogues according to their particular subject interests. It will be helpful to film and television researchers by providing them with information on material beyond that held in stock-shot libraries, television companies and archives, with which they are already familiar. Developers of multimedia programmes are likely to find many interesting sources of material which it may be possible to incorporate into their own programmes, provided copyright laws are respected.

This listing was produced from our AVANCE database, which is being continuously revised and augmented. Distributor information is updated when we receive a new catalogue, learn of a change of name, address, telephone or fax number. As we hear of new distributors they are added to the database, and we remove details of companies which have closed down. If, therefore, you are unable to contact a distributor from the details given, please contact us to see if we have any new information.

How to use Distributors   The large 'multi-subject catalogues' section at the beginning should always be consulted. This contains distributors with large collections ranging across the whole curriculum, as well as smaller distributors who may have only a few titles, but all on different subjects. Next look at the relevant subject section. Listed there are the distributors who specialise in that particular area or who have a number of relevant programmes. Other subject sections likely to be relevant are referred to in the banner subject heading. Such cross-referencing is kept to a minimum, so if just one distributor in another section has a relevant programme, reference is made under 'other useful catalogues' at the end of the subject section.

The different media are integrated in the subject sections, but the distributors of CD-ROMs and videodiscs are all brought together in the 'multimedia distributors' section, for the convenience of those who are searching for interactive materials.

A list of organisations which offer a one-step tracing and ordering service for libraries and institutions wishing to purchase audio-visual materials from a number of producers is given in the 'library suppliers' section.

Each entry is laid out in the following order:

- Distributor's name followed by title of catalogue or list
- Year of publication or, if not known, year in which the publication was received by the BUFVC
- Number of pages or type of publication (e.g. leaflet, loose-leaf catalogue
- Price, where applicable
- Full name, address, telephone and fax number (and e-mail address if available) of distributor
- A short summary of the contents of the catalogue, pointing out programmes that might be of particular interest. When possible an indication of audience level is given
- Availability (whether the material is for hire or sale)

AMBER
SIDE

CATALOGUE
&
History of Work
since
1968

HISTORY OF AMBER/SIDE
FILM & VIDEOS
CURRENT AFFAIRS VIDEOS
TOURING EXHIBITIONS • PUBLICATIONS
LAMBTON VISUAL AIDS
ACTT WORKSHOP DECLARATION

AMBER

is a group of filmakers and photographers based in the North East of England. We have been producing films for 18 years, the last five as a franchised workshop with Channel 4. Our work has won many national and international awards – its latest being the European Community Film Prize at the Munich Film Festival 1986 for *Seacoal*.

SIDE

has a national and international reputation as a gallery for exhibiting the best of documentary photography.

AMBER/SIDE

work together as a collective
and this egalitarian base has a profound influence on
production process, the product and its usage.

THE CATALOGUE

This is the first time a complete record of all of our work has been available. This fully illustrated catalogue can be continually updated and is a must for everyone interested in film, video and photography. An invaluable guide both for reference and pleasure.

£3.50
(including P & P within UK)
Orders to

AMBER/SIDE
5 Side, Newcastle upon Tyne, NE1 3JE.

- -

Please send ＿＿ copy/copies of the AMBER/SIDE CATALOGUE

Name. ＿＿＿＿＿＿＿＿＿＿＿＿＿＿＿＿＿＿＿＿＿＿＿＿

Address. ＿＿＿＿＿＿＿＿＿＿＿＿＿＿＿＿＿＿＿＿＿＿

＿＿＿＿＿＿＿＿＿＿＿＿＿＿＿＿＿＿＿＿＿＿＿＿＿＿

＿＿＿＿＿＿＿＿＿＿＿＿＿＿＿＿＿＿＿＿＿＿＿＿＿＿

Distributors of Film, Video and Related Media

Multi-Subject Catalogues

Academy Television now trading as YITM

Video catalogue (1991 + supplements). 70 pages. 104 Kirkstall Road, Leeds LS3 1JS ☎ 0113-246 1528 fax 0113-242 9522.

Academy handles a selection of programmes broadcast by Yorkshire–Tyne Tees Television, Thames Television, Channel 4, Scottish Television, Ulster Television, HTV and WTN. The catalogue contains details of programmes relevant to the National Curriculum and for use in further and higher education. All subject areas are covered. Of particular note are the EQUINOX series and a selection of FIRST TUESDAY programmes. Sale on video.

Anglia Polytechnic University

CD-ROM and software catalogue (1993). 10 pages. Learning Technology Research Centre, Sawyers Hall Lane, Brentwood, Essex CM15 9BT ☎ 01277 200587 fax 01277 211363

A range of Macintosh-based CD-ROMs and software, some developed as part of the Renaissance Initiative in collaboration with other higher education institutions. Some materials are intended for courseware developers; others are subject-based. Includes titles on mathematics, environmental science, Shakespeare's *Twelfth Night,* Arthur Miller's *The Crucible,* and information technology in the learning environment. Sale.

AVP

Computer software and resources (1994). 24 pages. School Hill Centre, Chepstow, Gwent NP6 5PH ☎ 01291 625439 fax 01291 629671

Computer programs on English language and literature, desktop publishing and word processing. Also software for teachers. Sale only.

Educational CD-ROMs (1994). 14 pages. A wide range of CD-ROMs from various sources for the educational market. Catalogue includes INVENTORS AND INVENTIONS produced by the British Library and Yorkshire Television, a CD-ROM on fractals, and ART GALLERY, taken from the collection of the National Gallery, London. Sale.

Educational videos (1994). 28 pages. A range of educational videos from sources such as National Geographic, Team Video and the BBC, organised by subject. Sale only. Individual subject catalogues that integrate the various media for particular curriculum subject areas are available on request.

BBC Home Video

The BBC shop mail order catalogue (1994). 8 pages. BBC Enterprises Ltd, 80 Wood Lane, London W12 0TT ☎ 0181-576 2236.

Title and price list of BBC videos available for sale through retail outlets. The videos are organised in subject sections: comedy, music, science fiction, children's, drama, documentaries, wildlife and sport.

BBC Videos for Education and Training

BBC Videos for Education and Training (1994). 60 pages. 80 Wood Lane, London W12 0TT ☎ 0181-576 2415 fax 0181-576 2916

Over 500 BBC television programmes on video. Broad subject categories are anthropology, arts, business, drama, education issues, environment,

143

earth sciences and ecology, health and medicine, history and politics, natural history, and social issues. A further 2000 programmes are available on request. The range includes titles from the HORIZON and QED series as well as classic drama and business television. Sale only.

Boulton-Hawker Films　**Videos** (1993). Leaflets. Boulton-Hawker Films Ltd, Hadleigh, Ipswich IP7 5BG ☎ 01473 822235 fax 01473 824519.

In addition to individual subject catalogues for biology, physical education, personal and social education and health education, there are separate sheets for videos on careers education, home economics, physics, the earth, information technology, and geography. Sale and preview.

Bowker-Saur　**British words on cassette** (2nd edition 1992). 173 pages. Price £25.00. Bowker-Saur, Maypole House, Maypole Road, East Grinstead, West Sussex RH19 1HH ☎ 01342 330100 fax 01342 330191.

Lists over 5000 spoken word audiocassettes available for hire or sale from many sources in the UK. Includes dramatic performances, novels, poetry readings, lectures, interviews, and educational courses, with full publisher and distributor information, and author and subject indexes.

BP Video Library　**Videotape catalogue** (1992). 34 pages. BP Video Library, Unit 2, Drywall Estate, Castle Road, Murston, Sittingbourne, Kent ME10 3RL ☎ 01795 436172 fax 01795 474871.

Videos on the oil industry and associated engineering and energy conservation topics; also some more general titles on motoring and travel. Free loan.

British Film Institute　**British national film & video catalogue** (annual). Price on application. **British Film Institute**, 21 Stephen Street, London W1P 1PL ☎ 0171-255 1444 fax 0171-580 7503.

A classified catalogue giving details of 16mm films and videos released for non-theatric distribution in the UK by hundreds of different distributors during the period 1963–1991. Comprehensively indexed with subject, title and author and production indexes. *BNFVC* information from 1992 onwards is held only in electronic form on the British Film Institute's SIFT database, but quarterly publication via the British Library National Bibliographic Service is expected from early 1995.

Film & Video Library catalogue (1987 + supplements). 192 pages. Over 400 feature films and 800 shorts, documentaries and television programmes relevant to the art and history of film and television. Entries are arranged under the headings feature films, non-fiction and short fiction pre-1929, non-fiction and short fiction post-1929, and television material; also films from the BFI Experimental Film Fund and the BFI Production Board. Includes country and director indexes, an animation index, a list of film study extracts and a list of titles available on video. Hire only.

British Universities Film & Video Council

BUFVC catalogue (1990) 39 pages + 9 microfiches. Price £17.00. British Universities Film & Video Council, 55 Greek Street, London W1V 5LR ☎ 0171-734 3687 fax 0171-287 3914

Some 7000 videos, films, tape-slide programmes, audiocassettes, slide sets, computer programs and videodiscs, classified and fully described, with subject and title indexes. Many of the programmes were produced by institutions of higher education; others have been recommended for use in degree-level teaching and research. Includes television programmes from Open University courses. Appraised items are marked, as are those available for preview at the BUFVC's Audio-Visual Reference Centre. The booklet lists the addresses and telephone numbers of more than 500 UK distributors. Since 1990 the information has been updated on the BUFVC's in-house database AVANCE.

Higher Education Film and Video Library catalogue (1994) 88 pages. Price £5.00. Over 500 specialist films and videos on many subjects recommended for use in degree-level teaching. The catalogue is arranged under broad subject headings and includes programmes from organisations such as the Institut für den Wissenschaftlichen Film, Göttingen, and the Rothampstead Experimental Station. Programmes may be hired through Concord Video & Film Council, and some are available for sale from the BUFVC.

Sales catalogue (1993). 20 pages. Lists under broad subject headings some 100 videos and films suitable for use in higher education. Includes scientific programmes from the Institut für den Wissenschaftlichen Film, Göttingen, with videodiscs on cell biology and mycology. Sale only.

Cambridge CD-ROM Ltd   **The Cambridge CD-ROM catalogue** (1994). 64 pages. Cambridge CD-ROM Ltd, Combs Tannery, Stowmarket IP14 2EN
☎ 01449 774658 fax 01449 677600.
A wide range of CD-ROM titles from various producers for business, desk-top publishing and education.

CFL Vision   **CFL Vision: Directory** (1991 + supplements). 290 pages. Price £5.00. **CFL Vision**, PO Box 35, Wetherby, West Yorkshire LS23 7EX
☎ 01937 541010 fax 01937 541083.
Over 1000 titles arranged by subject in two major sections: education and general interest, and industrial training. CFL Vision is run by the Central Office of Information, and many of the programmes are of an informational nature, sponsored by government departments or bodies such as the Equal Opportunities Commission, the General Dental Council, the Building Research Establishment or the Civil Aviation Authority. The supplementary update sheets are organised by subject area. Hire or sale on film or video.

CFL Vision: Free videos for schools (1994). 17 pages. Programmes for middle and secondary schools selected from the main CFL Vision catalogue and available on free loan. Subject areas include careers, health education, renewable energy, and science and technology.

Channel Video Films   **Catalogue** (1994). 58 pages. Channel Video Films, 58 Salusbury Road, London NW6 6ND ☎ 0171-372 2025 fax 0171-372 2025
A mail-order service supplying thousands of videos from a wide range of suppliers. The catalogue lists mainly feature films, but it also covers non-fiction titles, which are organised by subject. Regular updates are issued. Sale.

145

Classroom Video	**Video catalogue** (1994). 16 pages. Classroom Video, Darby House, Bletchingley Road, Merstham, Redhill, Surrey RH1 3DN ☎ 01737 642880 fax 01737 644110 Videos aimed particularly at the National Curriculum on subjects including the environment, geography, English, social studies and history, personal development, chemistry, physics, general science, design and technology. Separate catalogues are available for the various subject areas. Sale only.
Club 50/50 Music	**CDs, tapes and videos** (1994). Leaflets. **Club 50/50 Music**, PO Box 1277, Chippenham, Wiltshire SN15 3YZ ☎ 01249 445400 fax 01249 447 691 A mail-order club for supplying videos, compact discs, cassettes and books. Approximately half the titles are music programmes and the others cover hobbies and general interest topics. Membership fee, including catalogue, is £4.99.
Cumana Ltd	**The Cumana CD-ROM portfolio for schools and colleges** (1994). 54 pages. Cumana Ltd, Pines Trading Estate, Broad Street, Guildford GU3 3BH ☎ 01483 503121 fax 01483 451371 CD-ROMs and interactive videos from various producers selected for their relevance to education. Includes the MIST series on science and technology. Sale.
CVG Promotions Ltd	**CD-ROM catalogue** (1994). 17 pages. CVG Promotions Ltd, Hassacks Business Centre, Whitecairns, Aberdeen AB23 8UJ ☎ 01358 743888 fax 01348 742713 A range of CD-ROMs for educational, business, professional and entertainment purposes. Catalogue updated regularly. Sale only.
Darvill Associates	**16mm film and video library catalogue** (1986 + supplement). 58 pages. Darvill Associates, 280 Chartridge Lane, Chesham, Buckinghamshire HP5 2SG ☎ 01494 783643 fax 01494 784873 Feature films by Scandinavian directors including Bergman, Sjoman, Sjostrom and Stiller. Also films by Tati, Borowczyk and other leading directors, Australian and Dutch features and documentaries, and the films of the Swedish Institute. Hire on film from Glenbuck; hire and sale on video from Darvill. **NIS Film Distribution catalogue** (1991 + supplements). Includes documentaries, animated films, drama, films on Holland, and children's films.
Education Distribution Service	**Catalogue** (1995). 50 pages. Education Distribution Service, Unit 2, Drywall Estate, Castle Rd, Sittingbourne, Kent, ME10 3RL ☎ 01795 427614 fax 01795 474871 This is now the only library distributing sponsored films for a range of companies, tourist boards and organisations. It has taken over many of the collections previously distributed by Viscom. Collections include those of the Post Office, BT, the German Film and Video Library, the National Trust, the Advertising Standards Authority, Lloyd's of London and many others. Hire only

Educational & Television Films
Various catalogues (1986-89, current 1994). Educational & Television Films Ltd, 247a Upper Street, London N1 1RU
☎ 0171-226 2298 fax 0171-226 8016
Feature, cartoon and puppet films from Eastern Europe and China, and documentary films from the Czech and Slovak republics, the former German Democratic Republic, the former USSR and other countries. Hire and sale.

Educational Media, Film & Video
Secondary video catalogue, Videos for primary education (1993). 40, 14 pages. Educational Media, Film & Video Ltd, 235 Imperial Drive, Rayners Lane, Harrow, Middlesex HA2 7HE ☎ 0181-868 1908 fax 0181-868 1991
Programmes in most subject areas, with a view to the National Curriculum. Includes titles formerly available from the ILEA. Hire and sale.

Educational Television Company
Resources catalogue (1994). 44 pages. Educational Television Company, PO Box 100, Warwick CV34 6TZ ☎ 01926 433333 fax 01926 450178
Videos, audiocassettes, teachers' guides, pupils' workbooks, computer software, posters and other resources produced to support Channel 4 schools programmes. Videos of some programmes broadcast by ITV Schools before Channel 4 took over the service in 1993 are also available for sale. Covers all National Curriculum subjects.

Edward Patterson Associates
Education film/video catalogue (1989, current 1994). 22 pages. **Edward Patterson Associates**, Treetops, Cannongate Road, Hythe, Kent CT21 5PT
☎ 01303 264195 fax 01303 264195.
Programmes listed by subject: art, children's films, education, geography, history, languages, literature, mathematics, religion, science, social studies, sports and recreation. Hire and sale on film; sale only on video.

Encyclopaedia Britannica
CD-ROM product and price list (1994). 6 pages. Encyclopaedia Britannica International, Education Division, Station Approach, Wallington, Surrey SM6 0DA ☎ 0181-669 4355 fax 0181-773 3631
A range of CD-ROMs from various sources, selected for use in education.
LaserDisc product and price list (1993) 5 pages.
A range of LaserDiscs from various sources.

Esso Information Service
Educational resources (1992). 36 pages. Esso Information Service, PO Box 695, Sudbury, Suffolk CO10 6YM ☎ 01787 370272 fax 01787 880866
Videos on science and technology, the environment, history, careers, business studies, art, and general interest topics. Free loan.

T C Farries & Co.
Multi media (1994). 14 pages. T C Farries & Co. Ltd, Irongray Road, Lochside, Dumfries DG2 0LH ☎ 01387 720755 fax 01387 72110
A selection of UK and US-produced CD-ROMs including encyclopaedias, reference works, educational and entertainment programmes. Sale.
Fiction audio cassettes, Non-fiction audio cassettes, Non-fiction videos (1994). 247, 194, 200 pages.
A classified listing of thousands of fiction and non-fiction audiocassettes and non-fiction videos from hundreds of sources, for supply to libraries, schools, colleges and other educational establishments, and to individuals in the UK and overseas. All subject areas are covered, and supplementary lists are issued regularly. There are showrooms in Dumfries and Hinkley,

Leicestershire, together with mobile approval collections. Full library processing including cataloguing and classification is offered. Sale.

Focal Point Audio Visual   **Video and slide programmes** (1990 + updates). 34 pages. Focal Point Audio Visual Ltd, 251 Copnor Road, Portsmouth PO3 5EE
☎ 01705 665249 fax 01705 695723.
Videos in all subject areas, selected for their relevance to the National Curriculum. The two-part main catalogue covers science and technology and arts and social sciences. Separate subject information sheets are sent out each term. These cover foreign language films, music, business studies, English and drama, biology and physics, personal and social education, art and design technology, careers, history, geography, feature films and television drama. Sale only.

Ford Motor Company   **Video loan library** (1993). 8 pages. Ford Motor Company Ltd, Audiovisual Services, 1/455, Eagle Way, Brentwood, Essex CM13 3BW
☎ 01277 252766 fax 01277 252896
Technical programmes on car design, manufacture and safety features, and programmes of a general nature on topics such as public speaking, running social and fund-raising organisations, child road safety, and the history of the Ford Motor Company. Free loan.

German Film & Video Library   **Catalogue** (1993). 69 pages. German Film and Video Library, c/o Education Distribution Service, Unit 2, Drywall Estate, Castle Road, Murston, Sittingbourne, Kent ME10 3RL ☎ 01795 427614 fax 01795 474871
Videos and a number of films on a wide range of subjects relating to Germany, including politics and history, industry, cities and regions, culture, and the full spectrum of the arts: painting, literature, music, dance, theatre and film. Many of the programmes are available in both German and English-language versions. The feature films previously distributed by the German Film Library are now handled by Glenbuck Films. Free loan.

Glenbuck Films   **Documentary, educational and animation** (1987 + updates). 65 pages. Glenbuck Films Ltd, 21 Stephen Street, London W1P 1PL
☎ 0171-957 8938 fax 0171-580 5830
Documentary features and shorts which include the work of Nick Broomfield, Felix Greene, Les Blank and Frederick Wiseman. Educational titles include the Contemporary, Walt Disney and Pyramid collections. Hire only on film and video.

Gramophone Publications   **Spoken word catalogue** (1994). 150 pages. Price £8.50. Gramophone Publications Ltd, 177-179 Kenton Road, Harrow, Middlesex HA3 0HA
☎ 0181-907 4476 fax 0181-907 4473
A comprehensive listing of currently available spoken-word and other non-music recordings of drama, literature, humour, poetry, recordings in foreign languages, children's recordings, documentaries and sound effects. Includes indexes of authors, artists and anthologies.

Granada Television International   **Programme catalogue** (1992). 80 pages. Granada Television International, Non-Theatrical Sales, 36 Golden Square, London W1R 4AH
☎ 0171-734 8080 fax 0171-494 6280

Several hundred Granada programmes selected for educational use. Includes the series HYPOTHETICALS, in which questions of crucial importance in the media, law, medicine and government are approached by those in authority; the DISAPPEARING WORLD anthropological films; the COMPASS series of journeys; and other series on science, history, geography, maths and computing. Sale only.

Holiday Brothers **Masterclass videocassettes** (1993). Leaflets. Holiday Brothers, 18 School Lane, Heaton Chapel, Stockport, Cheshire SK4 5DG
☎ 0161-442 2833 fax 0161-442 2836.
Videos for the home and leisure market. Subjects include art, gardening, health education, computing, music, drawing, dog care, sport, car maintenance, and early learning. Sale only.

Iansyst **Computer training products** (1994). 14 pages. Iansyst, United House, North Road, London N7 9DP
☎ 0171-607 5844 fax 0171-607 0187.
Video, audio, CD-ROM and computer software-based training packages for computer skills training, language learning, health and safety training, and business skills. Sale only.

Interactive Technologies Courseware **CD-ROM catalogue, Videodisc list, Courseware catalogue, Software catalogue** (1994). Loose-leaf catalogues. Interactive Technologies Courseware, Riverview, 3 The Drive, Bishopsteignton, Devon TQ14 9SD
☎ 01626 778049 fax 01392 264736.
Multimedia materials selected for educational use across most areas of the curriculum. The software catalogue lists materials to enhance the use of the videodiscs; some are of general use and some specific to particular videodiscs. Sale.

KimStacks **CD-ROM Catalogue** (1994). 78 pages. KimTec UK, Fairways House, 8 Highland Road, Wimbourne, Dorset BH21 2QN
☎ 01202 888873 fax 01202 888863.
CD-ROMs for business, development, educational and desk-top publishing purposes, produced by companies in the UK and abroad. Sale.

London Guildhall University **Educational videos from London Guildhall University** (1994). 36 pages. London Guildhall University, Educational Development and Support Service, Calcutta House, Old Castle Street, London E1 7NT
☎ 0171-320 1008 fax 0171-320 1117.
Videos on craft and design, business studies, accountancy, law, science, pilot training, retail distribution, and selection interviewing. Sale only.

Manga Entertainment Ltd (1993). Leaflets. Manga Entertainment Ltd, 40 St Peter's Road, London W6 9BD ☎ 0181-748 9000 fax 0181-748 0841.
Television programmes on video covering the environment, astronomy, and civilisation. Also programmes on study skills, the BBC ANIMATED SHAKESPEARE series and various foreign cult films.

Meckler **CD-ROMs in print** (1994). 1188 pages. Price £65.00 (print), £62.50/year (CD-ROM). Meckler, 4th Floor, Artillery House, Artillery Row, London

SW1P 1RT ☎ 0171-976 0405 fax 0171-976 0506.

An international listing of 6000 CD-ROM products arranged alphabetically by title, with subject and country indexes. Each main entry includes hardware requirements, search software, networking information, update frequency and price. There is also a company directory and an index for Macintosh-based titles, and another for both DOS and Macintosh platforms.

Mercury Educational Products   **Catalogue** (1993). 28 pages. Mercury Educational Products, 3 Primrose Mews, 1a Sharpleshall Street, London NW1 8YL ☎ 0171-483 2161 fax 0171-586 6841.
A selection of television programmes and accompanying software made for ITV Schools by Granada, Central and Anglia Television. Indications of National Curriculum level are given. Sale.

Microinfo   **CD-ROM Catalogue** (1994). 108 pages. Microinfo Ltd, PO Box 3, Omega Park, Alton, Hampshire GU34 2PG ☎ 01420 86848 fax 01420 89889.
A catalogue of scientific, medical, technical, business, educational and other professional reference services on CD-ROM from 100 sources. Sale.

National Audio Visual Library   **Videotape catalogue** (1993). Loose-leaf catalogue. Unit 16, Greenshields Industrial Estate, Bradfield Road, Silvertown, London E16 2AU ☎ 0171 474 8707 fax 0171 511 1578.
Programmes for teaching all school curriculum subjects, with educational levels indicated. Some programmes suitable for higher and further education, particularly teacher training. Hire and sale on video, some on 16mm film.

National Extension College   **Catalogue** (1994). 54 pages. National Extension College, 18 Brooklands Avenue, Cambridge CB2 2HN ☎ 01223 316644 fax 01223 313586.
A wide range of open learning resources for general education, business and vocational training, the caring professions, counselling and guidance, and teaching & training. Some courses have a video or audio element. Sale.

New Media   **Multimedia in education** (1994). Leaflets. New Media, 12 Oval Road, London NW1 7DH ☎ 0171-916 9999 fax 0171-482 4957.
CD-ROM and CD-I titles produced for use in education at primary, secondary and university level. Subject areas include chemistry, the natural world, maths, geography, learning to read, and social history. Sale.

The Open University   **Catalogue of learning resources from the undergraduate programme** (1994). 102 pages. Open University Educational Enterprises Ltd, 12 Cofferidge Close, Stony Stratford, Milton Keynes MK11 1BY ☎ 01908 261662 fax 01908 261001.

Lists by title the hundreds of videocassettes, audiocassettes, study texts and computer packages in all subject areas that form part of Open University undergraduate courses and are available for sale separately to outside institutions. Alternatively, programmes may be recorded off-air under licence from the OU. Synopses of individual programmes are given on course information sheets, which may be requested individually.

The Open University   **Open opportunities** (1994). 94 pages. Open University Learning Materials Sales Office, PO Box 188, Milton Keynes MK7 6DH ☎ 01908 652152 fax 01908 654320.
Information about registering as an Open University associate student and details of a range of study packs, many of them video-based, which may

be used for independent study in furthering leisure interests or careers. Subjects include arts, computing, environmental education, mathematics and statistics, science, social sciences, technology, education, and management. Sale.

Optech **CD-ROM product descriptions and price list** (1994). 56 pages. Koch Media Ltd, East Street, Farnham, Surrey GU9 7XX ☎ 01252 714340 fax 01252 711121. An extensive range of CD-ROMs from various sources for educational, entertainment, desk-top publishing, reference and business use.

Oxford Educational Resources **Title lists and complete catalogue on disk** (current). 3 title lists. Oxford Educational Resources, PO Box 106, Kidlington, Oxfordshire OX5 1HY ☎ 01865 842552 fax 01865 842551.
The largest distributor of medical programmes in the UK, with programmes from the collections of Camera Talks, Didactic Films, Marine Audio Visual Instruction Systems, the American Journal of Nursing, the Hospital Satellite Network and other producers world-wide. Hundreds of videos, films, tape-slide sets and software titles for medical and nursing training and health education. The complete catalogue is regularly updated and can be supplied on disk. A title list is available, and individual subject sections are printed out on request. Many language versions are available. There are also programmes in a few non-medical areas – crime prevention, language teaching, wildlife and earth sciences. Sale only.

PAVIC Publications (1993). Leaflets. PAVIC Publications, Sheffield Hallam University, 36 Collegiate Crescent, Sheffield S10 2BP ☎ 0114 253 2380 fax 0114 253 2471. Leaflets describing 11 videos on topics including using the university library, data communications, reading the formal specification language Z, using the HOST office automation system, maths in the workplace, and INSET programmes on science, human biology and bridges. Sale only.

Pennsylvania State University **Media sales catalogue** (1993). 64 pages. The Pennsylvania State University, Audio-Visual Services, Special Services Building, 1127 Fox Hill Road, University Park, PA 06803-1824, USA ☎ +1 814 865 6314 fax +1 814 863 2574. Videos suitable for use in higher education. The collection is particularly strong in anthropology and the social sciences, but most academic subjects are represented. Most programmes are available for sale to UK customers on PAL-standard videocassette.

Pergamon Open Learning **The open learning directory** (1994). 700 pages. Price £39.95. Pergamon Open Learning, Linacre House, Jordan Hill, Oxford OX3 8DP ☎ 01865 310366 fax 01865 310111.
A comprehensive listing of over 2500 open learning packages and courses, many with video support. Covers most vocational subject areas and lists support centres throughout the UK.

The Resource Base **Video lists** (1993). Leaflets. The Resource Base, Television Centre, Northam, Southampton SO9 5HZ ☎ 01703 834297 fax 01703 834363. Separate subject lists issued regularly covering all National Curriculum areas. Most of the videos are supported by teaching packs. Sale only.

Resources in Training & Education (1993). Leaflets. Resources in Training & Education, Cross Tree, Walton Street, Walton-in-Gordano, Clevedon, Bristol BS21 7AW
☎ 01275 340279 fax 01275 340327.
A wide range of videos for sale. Separate leaflets are available for anthropology, history, English, media studies, science, art and design, religious studies, geography, personal & social education, and earth sciences.

Rose Records **Audio-visual library services** (1993). Information sheets. Rose Records, The Studio, Unstable Walk, 18 Ellington Street, London N7 8PP
☎ 0171-609 8288 fax 0171-607 7851.
Rose Records is a supplier of compact discs, cassettes, records and videos to libraries in the UK and overseas. No catalogue is available, but individual lists can be printed from the database in response to specific subject requests. Videos available cover general interest, educational and feature titles, and audio programmes include spoken word and music titles and language courses. Sale.

 **Sheffield University Television** **Video catalogue** (1991). 18 pages. Sheffield University Television, Sheffield S10 2TN ☎ 0114 282 4007 fax 0114 276 2106.
Programmes on archaeology and prehistory, chemistry, computing, education, health and safety, materials, music, sociological studies, space physics, and town and regional planning. Hire and sale.

Shell Video Library **Video programmes** (1994). 66 pages. Shell Education Service, PO Box 46, Newbury, Berkshire RG14 2YX ☎ 01635 31721 fax 01635 529371.
General interest videos produced by Shell UK on the oil industry, science and engineering, the environment, history and society, music and art, motoring, and energy conservation. Sale only.

Silver Platter **Directory** (1994). 73 pages. Silver Platter Information Services, 10 Barley Mow Passage, Chiswick, London W4 4PH ☎ 0181-995 8242 fax 0181-995 5159.
CD-ROMs in the areas of business, education, food and agriculture, health and safety, health sciences, science and technology, and social sciences. Includes A-V ONLINE, the CD-ROM version of the American NICEM database of educational film and video.

The Slide Centre **Educational slides** (1994). 22 pages. The Slide Centre, Rickitt Educational Media, Great Western House, Langport, Somerset TA10 9YU
☎ 01458 253636 fax 01458 253646.
Slide sets covering all National Curriculum areas. A separate catalogue lists educational software for schools. Sale.

Steel Bank Films (1991). Leaflet. Steel Bank Film Co-op, Brown Street, Sheffield S1 2BS
☎ 0114 272 1235.
An independent production company making programmes for broadcast on Channel 4. Programmes range from investigative documentaries on topics such as genetic engineering, childhood memories and experimental music, to short comedies and full-length features. Sale.

Sussex Video (1993). Leaflets. Sussex Publications, Microworld House, 2-6 Foscote Mews, London W9 2HH ☎ 0171-266 2202 fax 0171-266 2314.

Videos, audiocassettes and computer programs from Sussex Video, Sussex Tapes and Sussex Software. The sound recordings feature discussions between leading scholars. Subjects of individual brochures are British and European history, music and art, science, the environment, social and economic studies, and languages. Sale.

TAG Developments **Software catalogue: secondary edition** (1993). 23 pages. TAG Developments Ltd, 19 High Street, Gravesend, Kent DA11 0BA ☎ 01474 357350 fax 01474 537887.
A range of software and CD-ROMs from various producers, specially selected for use in secondary education and above. Most curriculum areas are covered. A separate catalogue lists material suitable for primary education.

Team Video Productions **Catalogue** (1989 + supplements). 21 pages. Team Video Productions, 105 Canalot, 222 Kensal Road, London W10 5BN ☎ 0181-960 5536
Videos and video-based teaching packs on new technology, health and safety, pre-vocational training, business and trade union studies, nuclear power, media studies, development studies and environmental conservation. Some are accompanied by student worksheets and lesson plans. Sale only.

Teltale International **Educational video cassettes** (1992). 102 pages. Price £27.00. Teltale International, 12 Parkgrove Drive, Barnton, Edinburgh EH4 7QH ☎ 0131-336 2512 fax 0131-539 7227.
Thousands of educational videos from over 60 producers world-wide, listed alphabetically by title. Series title, production company, running time and educational level are indicated, but no synopsis is given. Sale only.

TFPL Publishing **The CD-ROM directory** (1994). 1100 pages. Price £95.00 (print), £125.00/year (CD-ROM). TFPL Publishing, 17-18 Britton Street, London EC1M 5NQ ☎ 0171-251 5522 fax 0171-251 8318.
An international guide to some 6000 CD-ROM and multimedia CD titles. Includes production company profiles and information on hardware and software. Published annually in printed form and bi-annually on CD-ROM.

Trade Service Information **Videolog** (current). Loose-leaf catalogue. Price £20.00 + £15.00 per month. Trade Service Information Ltd, Cherryholt Road, Stamford PE9 2HT ☎ 01780 64331 fax 01780 55006.
A reference catalogue intended primarily for the retail trade, reporting all the currently available pre-recorded video titles for the home video market, from a wide range of sources. It concentrates on feature films but also includes a large number of titles on drama, sport, war, hobbies and general interest subjects in broadly classified sections. Updated fortnightly.

Trumedia **Video and audio resources** (1993 + updates). Leaflets. Trumedia Ltd, PO Box 374, Headington, Oxford OX3 7NT ☎ 01865 63097 fax 01865 63097.

A wide range of videos selected for their relevance to the National Curriculum. Leaflets cover history, politics, science, technology, foreign and cult films, art, design, media studies, biology, environmental studies, chemistry, physics, and primary and middle school materials. There is a particularly good collection of classic films and adaptations of literary works. Sale only.

University of Brighton   **Video catalogue** (1990 + supplements). 28 pages. University of Brighton Media Services, Watts Building, Moulsecoomb, Brighton BN2 4GJ ☎ 01273 642778 fax 01273 606093.
Programmes on many subjects, including accountancy and banking, arts, crafts and design, business studies, chemistry, dance, education, engineering, health studies and medicine, librarianship, pharmacy and sports science. Sale only.

University of Glasgow   **Film and video catalogue** (1985, current 1994). 26 pages. University of Glasgow, Department of Media Services, Southpark House, 64 Southpark Avenue, Glasgow G12 8LB ☎ 0141-330 4611 fax 0141-330 5674
A range of videos to support teaching in all academic subject areas. Sale.

University of Leeds   **Videotape catalogue** (1994). 55 pages. University of Leeds Audio Visual Service, Leeds LS2 9JT ☎ 0113 233 2661 fax 0113 233 2655
Videos organised in subject sections: medical and nurse training, child abuse, engineering and surveying, language and literature, science, staff training and development. Sale.

University of Liverpool Television Service   **Videotape catalogue** (1994). 60 pages. University of Liverpool Television Service, Television Service, Chatham building, Chatham Street, Liverpool ☎ 0151-794 2661 fax 0151-794 2221.
Video programmes on many subjects, with dentistry, medicine and veterinary science particularly well represented. Sale only.

University of London Goldsmiths' College   (1988). Leaflets. University of London, Goldsmiths' College, Department of Media and Communications, New Cross, London SE14 6NW ☎ 0181-692 7171 fax 0181-694 8911.
Videos on digital sound sampling, early childhood education, aroma therapy, gifted children, law, offending behaviour, the city of Barcelona, Shiatsu complementary medicine, and Ukrainian folk-dancing. Sale only.

University of Newcastle upon Tyne   **AVC video catalogue** (1990). 29 pages. University of Newcastle upon Tyne Audio Visual Centre, The Medical School, Framlington Place, Newcastle upon Tyne NE2 4HH ☎ 0191-222 6633 fax 0191-222 7696
A range of programmes on medicine, surgery, obstetrics and gynaecology, general practice, education, and the use of drama in teaching. Hire and sale.

University of Southampton   **Film and video catalogue** (1988). 9 pages. , Department of Teaching Support and Media Services, South Academic Block, Southampton General Hospital, Southampton SO16, 6YD ☎ 01703 796563 fax 01703 796376
Programmes on careers, health care, medicine and surgery, industrial archaeology, safety training, biology, teacher training, and the university–industry interface. Hire and sale.

University of Strathclyde Audio Visual Services   **Film and video catalogue** (1992). 16 pages. University of Strathclyde Audio Visual Services, Alexander Turnbull Building, 15 George Street, Glasgow G1 1RD ☎ 0141-552 4400 ext. 2566 fax 0141-552 5182.
Programmes on information technology, psychology, women and work, education, serving the disabled, media studies, architecture and social geography, chemistry and pharmacy, engineering, contemporary artists, industrial archaeology, and study skills. Hire and sale on film and video.

University of Sydney **Videotape catalogue** (1991). 55 pages. University of Sydney Audiovisual Services, Central Services, Baxter's Lodge, University of Sydney, NSW 2006, Australia ☎ +61 2 692 2651 fax +61 2 692 2560.
A classified list of video programmes covering most areas of undergraduate teaching. For sale to UK customers on PAL-standard videocassette.

Video City **Catalogue** (1994). 62 pages. Video City, 117 Notting Hill Gate, London W11 3LB ☎ 0171-221 7029 fax 0171-792 9273.
Thousands of titles, mainly feature films, available for sale by mail order.

Video Plus Direct **The complete guide to what's on video** (1993). 295 pages. Price £4.95. Video Plus Direct, PO Box 190, Peterborough PE2 6UW ☎ 01733 232800 fax 01733 238966.
Mail-order company supplying over 15,000 entertainment, sport and leisure interest videos and videodisc titles to education, libraries and individuals. Catalogue is arranged alphabetically within categories and contains a brief description of each programme.

Viewtech **Disney educational productions catalogue** (1993). Loose-leaf catalogue. Viewtech Film and Video, 161 Winchester Road, Brislington, Bristol BS4 3NJ ☎ 0117 977 3422 fax 0117 972 4292.
Catalogue of mainly animated programmes intended for educational use with young people. Covers literature and arts, health and safety, science, social studies and maths and computers. Sale on video only.
Educational video and film catalogue (1989 + supplement). 64 pages. Programmes mainly from America and Australia, for use in education from primary to tertiary level. All curriculum subjects are covered. Hire or sale.
National Curriculum video finder catalogue (1993). Loose-leaf catalogue. A quick-reference guide to videos that tie in with the subjects and key stages of the National Curriculum. Arranged under subjects: primary science, science, geography, history, technology, maths, English, music, and health. Only titles and prices are given, so reference should be made to the main Viewtech catalogue for descriptions of programmes.

Wessex Video **Classified videotape list** (1987 + supplements). 40 pages. Wessex Video, King Alfred's College, Winchester SO22 4NR ☎ 01962 866359 fax 01962 842280.
A classified list of videos for use in teacher training and in classrooms on all curriculum subjects. Sale only outside the Wessex area.

World Microfilms **Educational software from Britain** (1990). 36 pages. World Microfilms Publications, Microworld House, 2-6 Foscote Mews, London W9 2HH ☎ 0171-266 2202 fax 0171-266 2314.
Combines the video, audiocassette and computer programs from Sussex Video and Sussex Tapes, Lecon Arts, Pidgeon Audio Visual and Audio-Forum. Covers most curriculum areas. Sale only.

Africa (see also anthropology, development studies)

The African Video Centre **Mail order catalogue** (1992). 50 pages. The African Video Centre, 7 Balls Pond Road, Dalston, London N1 4AX ☎ 0171-923 4224 fax 0171-275 0112.
A substantial catalogue of films and videos that depict some aspect of the black experience. Programmes are organised in categories including black film-makers, black history, drama, classic black movies, lectures, music, Rastafari, sports, travel, and wildlife. Loan to members or sale.

SOS Sahel **Audio-visual resources** (1992). 4 pages. SOS Sahel, 1 Tolpuddle Street, London N1 0XT ☎ 0171-837 9129 fax 0171-837 0856.
Two videos and three slide sets relating to the Sudan. Topics are community forestry, development theatre, land issues, and women's lives. Free loan.

Agriculture (see also development studies, veterinary science)

Council of Forest Industries **Leaflets** (1993). 3 pages. Council of Forest Industries (Canada), Tileman House, 131-133 Upper Richmond Road, London SW15 2TR
☎ 0181-788 4446 fax 0181-789 0146.
Eight programmes produced for the Council of Forest Industries of British Columbia, covering the forest industry from tree growth, harvesting, forest protection, sawmilling to end uses of the timber. Free loan on film or video.

Farming Press **Books and videos** (1993 + supplement). 16 pages. Farming Press Books and Videos, Wharfdale Road, Ipswich IP1 4LG ☎ 01473 241122 fax 01473 240501.
Videos on topics including sheep-dog training, poultry management, footcare in cattle, lamb survival, pig production, horsepower, and the history of farm mechanisation from traction engines to the present day. Sale only.

Massey Ferguson **Video index** (1993). 19 pages. Massey Ferguson Ltd, Audio Visual Services, Stareton, Kenilworth, Warwickshire CV8 2LJ ☎ 01203 531000 fax 01203 531229.
Videos on tractors, harvesting, training, and parts and implements for farm machinery. Also an archive section of older films, many transferred to video, on old machinery and working methods. Sale.

Royal Agricultural Society of England **Stansfield's Farming Studies videocassette series brochure** (1993). Leaflet. RASE Audio Visual Unit, National Agricultural Centre, Stoneleigh, Kenilworth, Warwickshire CV8 2LZ ☎ 01203 696969.
Fourteen videos on aspects of British agriculture. Sale only.

Royal Horticultural Society **Books for gardeners** (1994). 32 pages. RHS Enterprises Ltd, RHS Garden, Wisley, Woking, Surrey GU23 6QB ☎ 01483 211320 fax 01483 211003.
Includes a series of videos on gardens and plant cultivation.

University of East Anglia **Pick of the crop: a video series on European agriculture** (1993). Leaflet. University of East Anglia Audio-Visual Centre, Norwich NR4 7TJ
☎ 01603 592833 fax 01603 507721.
A series of 13 videos examining the purposes, strategies and scientific challenges of current European farming in the context of the acknowledged need to reassess the relationship between economic and environmental objectives. Sale only.

Anatomy and Physiology (see also animal research & welfare, biology, medical sciences, psychology, veterinary science)

Brain Sciences Information Project — **Films, video and teaching materials** (1991). 4 pages. BSIP, Hill House, 96 Wimbledon Hill, London SW19 7PB ☎ 0181-946 4677 fax 0181-946 4599.
Films and videos on aspects of neurology, particularly vision, movement and balance for use in the teaching of psychology and physiology. Sale.

Elsevier — **Interactive Anatomy** (1994). Leaflet. Elsevier Science BV, Department of Medical, Pharmaceutical and Biological Sciences, PO Box 181, 1000 AD Amsterdam, The Netherlands fax +31 20 5803 249.
The first programme in the INTERACTIVE ANATOMY series is a reference atlas of cross-sectional photographs and moving images covering paranasal sinuses and anterior skull bases. Available in both Philips CD-I and PC CD-ROM versions. Sale.

Oxford Educational Resources — **Title lists and complete catalogue on disk** (current). 3 title lists. Oxford Educational Resources, PO Box 106, Kidlington, Oxfordshire OX5 1HY ☎ 01865 842552 fax 01865 842551.
The largest distributor of medical programmes in the UK, with programmes from the collections of Camera Talks, Didactic Films, Marine Audio Visual Instruction Systems, the American Journal of Nursing, the Hospital Satellite Network and other producers world-wide. Hundreds of videos, films, tape-slide sets and software titles for medical and nursing training and health education. The complete catalogue is regularly updated and can be supplied on disk. A title list is available, and individual subject sections are printed out on request. Many language versions are available. There are also programmes in a few non-medical areas – crime prevention, language teaching, wildlife and earth sciences. Sale only.

Wolfe Publishing — **Complete catalogue** (1994). 152 pages. Wolfe Publishing, Mosby-Year Book Europe Ltd, Lynton House, 7-12 Tavistock Square, London WC1H 9LB ☎ 0171-388 7676 fax 0171-344 0018.
Mainly medical textbooks but also details of a significant collection of slide atlases, a video series on human anatomy, and a series of videodiscs on histology, pathology, radiology and cardiology. Sale only.

Other useful catalogues:
Boulton-Hawker (Sport and physical recreation)

Animal Research and Welfare (see also biology, veterinary science)

Advocates for Animals — **Videos** (1994). Leaflets. Advocates for Animals, 10 Queensferry Street, Edinburgh EH2 4PG ☎ 0131-225 6039 fax 0131-220 6377.
Two clandestinely made videos about activities inside medical laboratories conducting research on animals. Hire or sale.

British Union for the Abolition of Vivisection — **Videos for hire from the BUAV** (1994). 4 pages. BUAV, 16a Crane Grove, London N7 8LB ☎ 0171-700 4888 fax 0171-700 0252.
Videos on the use of animals in research, several of which include clandestinely shot footage from inside laboratories. Hire.

The National Anti-Vivisection Society	**Videos** (1994). Leaflets. The National Anti-Vivisection Society, 261 Goldhawk Road, London W12 9PE ☎ 0181-846 9777 fax 0181-846 9712. Computer programs on animal physiology, and some videos on working with animals, the use of animals in experiments, and circus animals. Free loan.
Royal Society for the Prevention of Cruelty to Animals	**Audio-visual resources catalogue** (1994). Leaflet. RSPCA, The Causeway, Horsham, West Sussex RH12 1HG ☎ 01403 64181. Videos and tape-slide programmes on the work of the RSPCA, companion animals, farm animals and wild animals. Hire.
Royal Veterinary College	**Videos for schools from the Royal Veterinary College** (1992). 4 pages. Royal Veterinary College, Unit for Veterinary Continuing Education, Royal College Street, London NW1 0TU ☎ 0171-387 2898 ext. 351 fax 0171-383 0615. Videos for the science section of the National Curriculum on animal welfare and living things. Sale only.

Anthropology (see also development studies)

Granada Television International	**Programme catalogue** (1992). 80 pages. Non-Theatric Sales, Granada Television International, 36 Golden Square, London W1R 4AH ☎ 0171-734 8080 fax 0171-494 6280. Several hundred Granada programmes selected for educational use. Includes the DISAPPEARING WORLD anthropological films and the COMPASS series on journeys. Sale only.
Royal Anthropological Institute	**Film library catalogue: Volumes 1 and 2** (1990 + supplements). 86, 92 pages. The Film Officer, RAI, 50 Fitzroy Street, London WIP 5HS ☎ 0171-387 0455 fax 0171-383 4235. Extensive details of anthropological films chosen for their educational value. Volume 2 covers films that have been added to the RAI Library since 1982. Includes programmes from THE DISAPPEARING WORLD television series. Hire; some programmes also for sale on video.
Royal Anthropological Institute	**Teacher's resource guide** (1990). 58 pages. The Film Officer, RAI, 50 Fitzroy Street, London WIP 5HS ☎ 0171-387 0455 fax 0171-383 4235. The resources section contains information about the RAI Film Library, libraries and distributors of other audio-visual anthropological material, and guides to AV-materials.
Survival International	**Resources** (1993). 9 pages. Survival International, 310 Edgware Road, London W2 1DY ☎ 0171-723 5535 fax 0171-723 4059. Includes films, videos and slides on tribal peoples and the impact of external forces on their way of life. Some of the programmes were made for television. Hire only.

Other useful catalogues:
Penn State (Social Sciences)

Archaeology (see also classical studies, history & politics)

British Museum	**Film, video and slide tape list** (1993). 9 pages. British Museum Education

Service, Great Russell Street, London WC1B 3DG ☎ 0171-323 8511.
Mainly a list of films, videos and tape-slides for showing on the museum's premises. Also some videos made by the Education Service on topics such as Sutton Hoo, the Anglo-Saxons, and Bronze Age settlements. Free loan to schools.

Council for British Archaeology   **The archaeology resource book** (1992). 146 pages. Council for British Archaeology, Bowes Morrell House, 111 Walmgate, York YO1 2UA ☎ 01904 671417 fax 01904 671384 *or* English Heritage Education Service, Keysign House, 429 Oxford Street, London W1R 2HD ☎ 0171-973 3442 fax 0171-973 3430.
Many films and videos for schools under the headings archaeological techniques, conservation and the environment, prehistory, Romans, post-medieval, and miscellaneous. Hire, free loan, and sale. Also slides, filmstrips and computer software.

English Heritage   **Resources** (1994). 16 pages. English Heritage Education Service, Keysign House, 429 Oxford Street, London W1R 2HD ☎ 0171-973 3442 fax 0171-973 3430.

Includes information on a range of videos for schools on archaeological and historical topics, which aim to encourage investigative learning by looking at the physical evidence of the past. Programmes are illustrated by historical sites and properties in the care of English Heritage. Also a series introducing aspects of the historical development of churches. Free loan or sale.

Life's Rich Tapestry   **VHS sale and hire catalogue 1994** (1994). 8 pages. Life's Rich Tapestry, Studio 1, WASPS, 22 King Street, Glasgow G1 5QP ☎ 0141-553 1716.
Videos on history, archaeology, art and social work, many with a Scottish connection. Hire and sale.

Architecture (see also arts, civil engineering & building, design)

Icarus   **Slide and microfiche catalogues** (1993). Leaflets. Icarus UK, 158 Boundaries Road, London SW12 8HG ☎ 0181-682 0900.
Slides of Italian and Spanish architecture, and slides and microfiche of European, American and Japanese prints from the British Museum. Sale.

Insite   **Videocassettes** (1994). Leaflets. Insite Video Communications Ltd, 8 Peto Place, Regent's Park, London NW1 4DT ☎ 0171-487 4848 fax 0171-224 2939.

A series of videos looking at contemporary architecture, featuring informed criticism and evaluation of architects' work and methods, as well as technical features. Particular projects are discussed, the most recent being the Waterloo International Terminal. Sale only.

Libraries Unlimited   **The slide buyers' guide: an international directory of slide sources for art and architecture** (1990). 190 pages. Libraries Unlimited Inc, PO Box 6633, Engelwood, CO 80155-6633, USA ☎ +1 303 770 1220 fax +1 303 220 8843.
A reference book listing sources of slides on architecture, art, crafts, and other arts-related subjects, with a detailed entry for each company and a substantial subject index. Regular updates are printed in the Visual Resources Association's *VRA Bulletin*.

Pidgeon Audio Visual **Architecture catalogue** (1993 + supplements). 16 pages. World Microfilms Publications, Microworld House, 2-6 Foscote Mews, London W9 2HH ☎ 0171-266 2202 fax 0171-266 2314.
Some videotapes and an extensive range of tape-slide programmes on architecture, featuring architects and other designers talking about their own work and ideas. Sale only.

Other useful catalogues:
Swingbridge Video (Social Welfare)

Art (see also arts)

Icarus **Slide and microfiche catalogues** (1993). Leaflets. Icarus UK, 158 Boundaries Road, London SW12 8HG ☎ 0181-682 0900.
Slides of Italian and Spanish architecture, and slides and microfiche of European, American and Japanese prints from the British Museum. Sale.

Libraries Unlimited **The slide buyers' guide: an international directory of slide sources for art and architecture** (1990). 190 pages. Libraries Unlimited Inc, PO Box 6633, Engelwood, Colorado 80155-6633, USA ☎ +1 303 770 1220 fax +1 303 220 8843.
A reference book listing sources of slides on architecture, art, crafts, and other arts-related subjects, with a detailed entry for each company and a substantial subject index. Regular updates are printed in the Visual Resources Association's *VRA Bulletin*.

Life's Rich Tapestry **VHS sale and hire catalogue 1994** (1994). 8 pages. Life's Rich Tapestry, Studio 1, WASPS, 22 King Street, Glasgow G1 5QP ☎ 0141-553 1716.
Videos on history, archaeology, art and social work, many with a Scottish connection. Hire and sale.

Magic Carpet Productions **Video catalogue** (1994). Leaflets. Magic Carpet Productions, 27 Richmond Hill, Richmond, Surrey TW10 6RE ☎ 0181-940 3836 fax 0181-332 6676.
Tourist guides on video for England, France and the Soviet Union, and other programmes on contemporary art and poetry. Also a range of literary audiocassettes for children and adults. Sale only.

Manchester Metropolitan University **Slide packs for the history of art and design** (1991). 9 pages. Manchester Metropolitan University, Department of History of Art and Design, The Slide Librarian, Righton Building, Cavendish Street, Manchester M15 6BG ☎ 0161-247 2000.
A series of slide packs with accompanying texts, on aspects of social and political history such as architecture, the urban and domestic environment, design, popular media, commercial art, and non-western art forms. Sale.

National Art Slide Library (1994). Leaflet. National Art Slide Library, De Montfort University, The Gateway, Leicester LE1 9BH ☎ 0116 257 7148 fax 0116 257 7170.
The national collection of art slides moved to De Montfort University from the Victoria and Albert Museum in 1992. The catalogues are currently being revised. The collection has in the past concentrated on fine and decorative arts, but it is likely that the scope will broaden. Slides are available for loan or sale.

National Gallery   **Videos available from the National Gallery** (1993). 2 pages. National Gallery Publications Ltd, 5-6 Pall Mall East, London SW1Y 5BA ☎ 0171-839 8544. Twenty-four videos made by the National Gallery to accompany exhibitions. These cover different styles and collections of paintings as well as individual artists. Also a programme on the scientific analysis of paintings. Sale. Also, a CD-ROM complied from pictures in the National Gallery collection, called ART GALLERY, is available from specialist CD-ROM suppliers (see Multimedia section).

The Roland Collection   **Catalogue** (1992 + supplement). 65 pages. The Roland Collection, Tillingham, Peasmarsh, East Sussex TN31 6XK ☎ 0179 721 421 fax 0179 721 677. Hundreds of videos on the history of art through the ages. Also programmes on applied arts and contemporary literature. Sale only.

University of Sunderland   **History of art and design slides** (1992). 7 pages. University of Sunderland, School of Art and Design, Backhouse Park, Sunderland SR2 7EG ☎ 0191-510 8585 fax 0191-565 4864.
A range of slide sets, each accompanied by detailed notes, covering contemporary and historical art, design and architecture. Topics include sculpture, garden festivals, performance art, printmaking techniques, textile art, and architecture in the Sunderland area. Individual slides may be ordered. Sale.

Other useful catalogues:
Sheila Graber (Media Studies: Short Films and Animation)

Arts (see also art, crafts, dance, drama, literature, media studies, music)

Arts Council of Great Britain Film & Video Library   **Documentaries on the arts** (1989 + supplement). 96 pages. Arts Council Film and Video Library, Arts Council of Great Britain, 14 Great Peter Street, London SW1P 3NG ☎ 0171-973 6455 fax 0171-973 6581.
Over 360 programmes on a wide range of arts topics, arranged under the headings British art, European art, American art, art and society, arts in the community, performance and video art, film and video, photography, craft and design, architecture, music, dance, theatre, poetry and literature, animation. Documentaries from television companies and overseas producers are included as well as programmes sponsored by the Arts Council. Hire and sale on video; hire only on film.

Bandung Productions   **Ten years of Bandung Films** (1994). 20 pages. Bandung Ltd, Block H, Carker's Lane, 53-79 Highgate Road, London NW5 1TL ☎ 0171-482 5045 fax 0171-284 0930.
Programmes made for the Channel 4 series BANDUNG FILE and REAR WINDOW, which cover themes in literature, cinema, music, art, architecture and the history of ideas world-wide. Sale only.

British Home Entertainment   **Catalogue** (1993). 2 pages. British Home Entertainment, 5 Broadwater Road, Walton-on-Thames, Surrey KT12 5DB ☎ 01932 228832 fax 01932 247759. Twelve video titles available through retail outlets. Subjects are mainly classic ballet, opera or theatre productions, but also two programmes on marathon running. Sale only.

Central Independent Television   **Arts, drama and music catalogue** (1993). 19 pages. Central Independent Television plc, Video Resources Unit, Broad Street, Birmingham B1 2JP ☎ 0121-643 9898 fax 0121-616 1531.
Programmes from Central Television's broadcast output selected for sale to education on video. Areas covered in this catalogue are art, design, architecture, craft, drama, literature, media education, and music.

Editions à voir   **Catalogue 1** (1993). 14 pages. Editions à voir, PO Box 53066, 1007 RB Amsterdam, The Netherlands ☎ +31 20 620 25 86 fax +31 20 638 83 19.
A European video label under which six producers from France, Belgium, the UK, Greece, and the Netherlands distribute their programmes throughout Europe. The UK producers are the Arts Council and London Video Access. The collection comprises programmes on dance, theatre, architecture, photography, design, opera, and video art. The catalogue is in English and French. London Video Access is the UK representative organisation.

Graphic Archives   **Scotland slide catalogue** (1993). Leaflet. Graphic Archives, 106 East Claremont Street, Edinburgh EH7 4JZ ☎ 0131-558 1348.
Eight sets of 50 slides each dealing with the cultural and social history of Scotland over the last 200 years. Among the subjects are the book designs of Talwin Morris, the Glasgow School of Art, and Hill House, which was designed by Charles Rennie Mackintosh.

Grey Suit   **Video for art and literature** (1993). Leaflet. Grey Suit, 21 Augusta Street, Adamstown, Cardiff CF2 1EN ☎ 01222 489565 fax 01222 489565.
A quarterly hour-long video magazine for art and literature, containing works by poets, performers, film-makers and video artists from around the world. There is also a critics' space called 'the tirade' where unorthodox opinions may be articulated. The tape also carries some archive material – work that is currently unavailable or is no longer being performed. Available by subscription only.

Institute of Contemporary Arts   **Video catalogue** (1989 + supplements). ICA Video, The Mall, London SW1Y 5AH ☎ 0171-930 0493 fax 0171-873 0051.
In addition to the WRITERS IN CONVERSATION series in which well-known writers talk about their life and work to other writers and critics, the collection has been expanded to encompass those working in the visual arts, film-making and fashion. Sale.

Oakart   **Pardon's Masterstrokes video series** (1994). Leaflet. Oakart Ltd, 5 Frederic Mews, Kinnerton Street, London SW1X 8EQ ☎ 0171-245 1049 fax 0171-823 2030.
Videos presented by the Pardon School of Specialist Decoration, showing how to achieve the decorative painting techniques of faux marbling and faux graining.

The Open University   **Catalogue of learning resources from the undergraduate programme** (1994). 102 pages. Open University Educational Enterprises Ltd, 12 Cofferidge Close, Stony Stratford, Milton Keynes MK11 1BY ☎ 01908 261662 fax 01908 261001.
Lists by title the hundreds of videocassettes, audiocassettes, study texts and computer packages in all subject areas that form part of Open University undergraduate courses and are available for sale separately to

outside institutions. Alternatively, programmes may be recorded off-air under licence from the OU. Synopses of individual programmes are given on course information sheets, which may be requested individually.

Scottish Central Film & Video Library **The arts and design on 16mm film and video** (1989). 23 pages. SCFVL, Dowanhill, 74 Victoria Crescent Road, Glasgow G12 9JN
☎ 0141-334 9314 fax 0141-334 6519.
No longer distributing.

University of Sunderland **History of art and design slides** (1992). 7 pages. University of Sunderland, School of Art and Design, Backhouse Park, Sunderland SR2 7EG
☎ 0191-510 8585 fax 0191-565 4864.
A range of slide sets, accompanied by detailed notes, covering contemporary and historical art, design and architecture. Topics include sculpture, garden festivals, performance art, printmaking techniques, textile art, and architecture in the Sunderland area. Individual slides may be ordered. Sale.

J Whiting Books **Video catalogue** (1994). 30 pages. J Whiting Books, 46 St Olaves Road, York YO3 7AL ☎ 01904 656766 fax 01904 656766.
Mail-order supplier of retail videos specialising in foreign-language feature films, literary adaptations, operas and classic feature films. Sale only.

Worshipful Company of Goldsmiths **Film list** (1992). 5 pages. Worshipful Company of Goldsmiths, Goldsmiths Hall, Foster Lane, London EC2V 6BN ☎ 0171-606 7010 fax 0171-606 1511.
Twenty-one films on the working of gold and silver, Carl Fabergé, diamonds, jewellery making, and cutlery making.

Other useful catalogues:
Life Support Productions (Education)

Astronomy and Astronautics (see also science & technology)

British Interplanetary Society **The BIS video collection** (1993). 8 pages. BIS, 27-29 South Lambeth Road, London SW8 1SZ ☎ 0171-735 3160.
Videos dealing with aspects of space technology, including the Apollo missions, Gemini, the Challenger space shuttle, the uses of satellites, and research projects. Sale only.

British Universities Film & Video Council **Physics and astronomy: video and film resources** (1989). 77 pages. Price £12.00. BUFVC, 55 Greek Street, London W1V 5LR
☎ 0171-734 3687 fax 0171-287 3914.

A classified catalogue of over 600 films and videos on physics and astronomy from many distributors, suitable for sixth form and above. Each entry contains a brief synopsis of content, production and distribution details, and an indication of appropriate course and level.

CCK Video Services **NASA videos** (1994). 4 pages. CCK Video Services Ltd, 3 Gilbert Street, London W1Y 1RB ☎ 0171-495 7005 fax 0171-409 1808.
Fifteen videos from the NASA Film Library, recording various space missions and also the history of the study of Mars, the effects of zero gravity, the possibility of life elsewhere in the universe, and an exploration of the extremes of size and time in the universe. Sale only.

The Planetarium, Armagh

Mail order list (1993). 18 pages. The Planetarium, College Hill, Armagh, Northern Ireland BT61 9DB ☎ 01861 523689 fax 01861 526187.
Videos and slides sets on space science, including material from NASA. Subjects include the solar system and moon landings. Sale only.

Other useful catalogues:
MUTV (Engineering and Manufacturing)

Austria

Austrian Institute

Video title list (1993). Leaflet. Austrian Institute, 28 Rutland Gate, London SW7 1PQ ☎ 0171-584 8653 fax 0171-225 0470.
Videos on aspects of Austrian life, literature, history and culture. Free loan.

Biology (see also anatomy & physiology, animal research & welfare, health education, science & technology)

Boulton-Hawker Films

GCSE Biology video catalogue, A-level biology video catalogue (1993). 12, 8 pages. Boulton-Hawker Films Ltd, Hadleigh, Ipswich IP7 5BG ☎ 01473 822235 fax 01473 824519.
Videos on genetics and genetic engineering, evolution, human biology and physiology, diet and nutrition, sex education, micro-organisms, botany, biotechnology, cell biology and biochemistry and immunology. Sale and preview.

British Universities Film & Video Council

Sales catalogue (1993). 20 pages. BUFVC, 55 Greek Street, London WIV 5LR ☎ 0171-734 3687 fax 0171-287 3914.
Lists under broad subject headings some 100 videos and films suitable for use in higher education. Includes scientific programmes from the Institut für den Wissenschaftlichen Film, Göttingen, with videodiscs on cell biology and mycology. Sale only.

McGraw-Hill

CD-ROMs (1994). Leaflets. McGraw-Hill Book Company Europe, Shoppenhangers Road, Maidenhead, Berkshire SL6 2QL ☎ 01628 23432 fax 01628 770244.
The PC-based MULTIMEDIA ENCYCLOPEDIA OF MAMMALIAN BIOLOGY and the MULTIMEDIA ENCYCLOPEDIA OF SCIENCE and TECHNOLOGY include text, still images, sound and full-screen-full-motion video. Sale.

The Open University

Catalogue of learning resources from the undergraduate programme (1994). 102 pages. Open University Educational Enterprises Ltd, 12 Cofferidge Close, Stony Stratford, Milton Keynes MK11 1BY ☎ 01908 261662 fax 01908 261001.
Lists by title the hundreds of videocassettes, audiocassettes, study texts and computer packages in all subject areas that form part of Open University undergraduate courses and are available for sale separately to outside institutions. Alternatively, programmes may be recorded off-air under licence from the OU. Synopses of individual programmes are given on course information sheets available separately.

Portland Press — **The Biochemical Society Biochemical Basis of Biology video series** (1995). 64 pages. Portland Press Ltd, 59 Portland Place, London WIN 3AJ ☎ 0171-580 5530 fax 0171-323 1136.
Videos on cell structure as related to energy production, and on DNA and protein synthesis, intended to complement A-level biology courses. Sale only.

Royal Society for the Protection of Birds — **Birds and wildlife on film and video** (1993). 35 pages. RSPB, Film Unit, The Lodge, Sandy, Bedfordshire SG19 2DL ☎ 01767 680551 fax 01767 692365. Wildlife films and videos for sale and hire for home, school and leisure use.

Sounds Natural — **Catalogue** (1993). 10 pages. Sounds Natural, Upper End, Fulbrook, Oxford OX8 4BX ☎ 01993 822167.
Audiocassettes, slide sets, tape-slide packs and videos on birds and birdsong, and on other wildlife and natural history topics. Sale only.

Taped Technologies — **Videos for science** (1994). Leaflet. Taped Technologies, PO Box 384, Logan, Utah 84323-0384, USA ☎ +1 801 753 6911 fax +1 801 752 5615.
Videos for the classroom and laboratory using live (not staged) recordings, with 24 videos in three series: RECOMBINANT DNA, PCR, and CELL CULTURE. For sale to UK customers on PAL-standard videocassette.

University of Portsmouth — **Vertebrate Dissection Guides** (1993). Leaflet. University of Portsmouth, Television Centre, The Rotunda, Museum Road, Portsmouth PO1 2QQ ☎ 01705 843902 fax 01705 843299.
A series of video VERTEBRATE DISSECTION GUIDES, produced with financial assistance from the European Commission, designed to both increase the success and experience of dissection, and to provide an alternative to it. The individual programmes study the functional anatomy of the dogfish, frog, pigeon and rat. Sale.

Careers Guidance (see also education)

Careers & Occupational Information Centre — **The COIC catalogue** (1991 + update). 30 pages. COIC, PO Box 348, Bristol BS99 7FE ☎ 0117 977 7199 fax 0117 972 4509.
Books, videos and software about work and job change for use in education, guidance and training. The video entries are clearly highlighted and are concerned with health and safety at work, job hunting and management skills. The CAREERS IN FOCUS series covers 26 different careers. Sale only.

Coventry Careers Service — **Higher education video catalogue** (1991). 16 pages. Coventry Careers Service, Education Department, Casselden House, Greyfriars Lane, Coventry CV1 2GZ ☎ 01203 831714.
Video prospectuses available from universities and colleges of further and higher education, as well as general videos on application procedures.

Coventry Careers Service — **Video catalogue** (1990 + updates). Unpaged. Coventry Careers Service, Education Department, Casselden House, Greyfriars Lane, Coventry CV1 2GZ ☎ 01203 831714.
Videos listed under the headings job hunting, jobspots, training schemes and further education colleges, self-employment, options and careers education, industry/education liaison, curriculum development. Free loan.

Foyles Educational   **Video careers library** (1994). Leaflet. Foyles Educational Ltd, Feldon House, Victoria Way, Burgess Hill, West Sussex RH15 9NG
☎ 01444 232797 fax 01444 247855.
A continuing series of videos entitled CAREERBEST, backed by the NCVQ and the *Times Educational Supplement*, aimed at giving young people an insight into the opportunities of a range of careers. Areas of work covered to date are the media, animal care, the food industry, the law, working in Europe, the travel industry, engineering, hotels and catering and accountancy. Sale.

Sio Communications   **Videotapes** (1992). 7 pages. Sio Communications Ltd, Georgia House, Eshe Road North, Blundellsands, Liverpool L23 8UD ☎ 0151-924 9570.
American-produced videotapes including a series on skills training for careers education. Sale only.

Trotman   **Careers guidance and educational resources** (1994). 40 pages. Trotman & Company Ltd, 12 Hill Rise, Richmond, Surrey TW10 6UA
☎ 0181-332 2132 fax 0181-332 0860.
Videos to help prospective students get into higher education and select the right course and institution for their needs. Also software packages on writing a curriculum vitae and choosing a career. Sale only.

Other useful catalogues:
General Dental Council (Dentistry)
Institution of Chemical Engineers (Chemistry and Chemical Engineering)
The Open University (Health Education)

Chemistry and Chemical Engineering (see also science and technology)

Institution of Chemical Engineers   **Safety and environmental training packages list** (1993). Leaflet. ICE, Davis Building, 165-171 Railway Terrace, Rugby CV21 3HQ
☎ 01788 578214 fax 01788 560833.
Details of videos produced by the ICE's technical section. The packages are used mainly by employers but the subject matter is suitable for university students as well. Sale only. Also, videos promoting chemical engineering as a career, i.e. BECOMING A CHEMICAL ENGINEER, PEOPLE LIKE US and MAKING THE FUTURE HAPPEN. These are available on free loan.

Royal Society of Chemistry   **Publications catalogue** (1994). 64 pages. Royal Society of Chemistry Information Services, Sales and Promotion Department, Thomas Graham House, Science Park, Milton Road, Cambridge CB4 4WF
☎ 01223 420066 fax 01223 423429.
Includes details of 12 videos produced by the University of Liverpool, designed for use at A level or for undergraduates. Topics include catalysis, liquid air, spectrometry, oxidation, chromatography, practical organic and inorganic chemistry, salt, and transitions metals. Also a continuing series of audiocassettes with accompanying workbooks, prepared and presented by leading chemists, and some interactive software for training in analytical chemistry, spectroscopy and safety. Sale only.

Civil Engineering and Building (see also architecture, health & safety, materials science)

British Cement Association
Publications and videos catalogue (1994 + supplement). 32 pages. British Cement Association, Publications Sales, Century House, Telford Avenue, Crowthorne, Berkshire RG11 6YS ☎ 01344 725704 fax 01344 727202. Includes 18 videos on concrete, concrete practice, good reinforcement practice, site management, etc. Also a video about the Spanish-born architect and engineer Santiago Calatrava. Sale.

Building Research Establishment
Catalogue (1993). BRE Bookshop, Garston, Watford WD2 7JR ☎ 01923 664444 fax 01923 664400.
Programmes on BRE research topics, which include traffic noise, wind loads, conservation of buildings, the Bradford football ground fire, fire performance of uPVC window frames, fires in the home, and fire-testing facilities. Sale on video from the BRE and free loan from CFL Vision after programmes are a year old.

CERCI Communications
A guide to audio-visual material for the construction industry (1993 + updates). 82 pages. Price £19.50. CERCI Communications, The Building Centre, 26 Store Street, London WC1E 7BT ☎ 0171-636 1802 fax 0171-436 7169. Details of over 1000 videos, films and tape-slides produced for the construction industry and available from over 100 distributors. Covers subjects as diverse as health and safety, engineering, planning, building and architecture, technology, design, and management. Hire, sale, and free loan.

College of Estate Management
Publications (1994). 19 pages. The College of Estate Management, Whiteknights, Reading RG6 2AW ☎ 01734 861101 fax 01734 755344.
A range of videos for students and practitioners of estate management on topics including building inspection, economics, air conditioning, domestic architecture, site planning and design, town and country planning and conservation. Also a series of audiotapes, the OWLION AUDIO PROGRAMMES, produced in conjunction with the Royal Institution of Chartered Surveyors, which cover business management, law and general practice relating to land and buildings, design, contracts, planning and development and rural practice. Sale only.

Construction Industry Council
Catalogue of CPD publications (1994). 4 pages. Construction Industry Council, 26 Store Street, London WC1E 7BT.
☎ 0171-627 8692 fax 0171-580 6140.
Video packages for continuing professional development in the construction industry. Sale.

Construction Industry Training Board

Publications catalogue (1994). 39 pages. CITB, Head Office, Bircham Newton, King's Lynn, Norfolk PE31 6RH ☎ 01553 776677 fax 01553 776651. Includes a number of videos on the built environment for National Curriculum technology teaching. Also videos covering careers, NVQs, bricklaying, carpentry, quality management, site management. Sale only.

Costain Group
TV and film catalogue (1992). Loose-leaf catalogue. Tandem Productions 10 Bargrove Avenue, Boxmoor, Hemel Hempstead, Herts HP1 1OP ☎ 01442 61576 fax 01442 219250.

Programmes relating to the activities of the Costain group of companies, whose civil engineering projects include the construction of a deep-water harbour, oil and gas pipelines, a dry dock and ship repair facility, a refinery, an underwater road tunnel, and the Thames Barrier. Free loan and sale on film and video.

Institution of Civil Engineers   **Audio-visual catalogue** (1994). 81 pages. Institution of Civil Engineers, Film Library, Great George Street, London SW1P 3AA ☎ 0171-222 7722 fax 0171-222 7500.
Films and videos from various sources on nuclear accidents, airport construction, tidal barriers, the Channel Tunnel, engineering careers, bridge and dam failures, desert irrigation, off-shore oil platforms, geographic information systems, quality assurance, road construction, and other topics. Free loan. The second part of the catalogue gives details of a large collection of slides available for free loan.

Longman Training   **Health and safety video catalogue** (1994). 72 pages. Training Direct, Longman House, Burnt Mill, Harlow, Essex CM20 2JE ☎ 01279 623927 fax 01279 623795.
Over 100 videos on health and safety at work, many of them dealing with the implications of specific legislation. Includes programmes produced with the Building Employers Confederation designed to promote safety awareness in the construction industry. Hire or sale.

Nottingham Trent University   **Gyrotheodolite measurements** (1993). Leaflet. Nottingham Trent University, Staff Development Service, Burton Street, Nottingham NG1 4BU ☎ 0115 941 6441.
Details of a two-part video on the processes of operation, observation and computation associated with the determination of the azimuth between two stations using a gyroscopic attachment for the theodolite. Sale.

Qi Training   **Video training modules for the construction industry** (1993). Leaflet. Qi Training Ltd, The Croft, 2 The Green, Lydiard Millicent, Swindon, Wiltshire SN5 9LP ☎ 01793 771748 fax 01793 770360.
Videos on concrete formwork, COSHH on site, sampling and testing concrete, placing and compaction, site organisation and planning, safety on site, good reinforcement practice, concrete repairs, etc. Sale only.

Royal Institution of Chartered Surveyors   **Video library catalogue** (1994). 19 pages. The Royal Institution of Chartered Surveyors, Library Information Service, 12 Great George Street, Parliament Square, London SW1P 3AD ☎ 0171-222 7000 fax 0171-334 3784.
Videos relating to building and construction, covering contracts, costs, defects, design, fire, materials, rehabilitation, surveying, conservation, planning, and professional practice. Hire.

Wimpey Films   (1993). Leaflets. George Wimpey plc, Corporate Relations Department, Hammersmith Grove, London W6 7EN ☎ 0181-748 2000 fax 0181-741 4596.
Programmes on civil engineering projects in the UK and overseas, including the design and construction of a hospital in Oman, an oil terminal, a solar evaporation system for the production of potash, and Britain's highest dam. Free loan.

Classical Studies (see also archaeology)

H A B White   **List of filmstrips and slides relating to classical studies** (1994). Leaflet. H A B White, Priory Farm, Balscote nr Banbury, Oxfordshire OX15 6JL ☎ 01295 730629.
Filmstrips and slide sets on Roman settlements in Britain, Roman and Greek sites abroad, the influence of the classics on modern life, and aspects of Greek and Roman life, e.g. flora, fauna, toys and pastimes, and books and writing materials. Sale.

Other useful catalogues:
Audio-Forum (Languages)
The Open University (Arts)
Viewtech (History and Politics)

Community Studies (see also history & politics, race relations & cultural identity, social sciences, social welfare)

A19 Film and Video   (1993). Leaflets. A19 Film & Video Ltd, 21 Foyle Street, Sunderland SR1 1LE ☎ 0191-565 5709.
Leaflets on individual video programmes about the Sunderland region, dealing with aspects of local politics or history.

Amber/Side   **Catalogue** (1987). 183 pages. Amber/Side Distribution, 5-9 Side, Newcastle upon Tyne NE1 3JE ☎ 0191-232 2000 fax 0191-230 3217.
A large collection of documentaries on current affairs and North East regional topics. Hire only on film, hire or sale on video. Also includes the Lambton Visual Aids slide collection of contemporary photographs.

Despite TV   **Tape catalogue** (1993). 10 pages. Despite TV, 113 Roman Road, London E2 0HU ☎ 0181-983 4278.
A series of video magazines produced by this East London video co-operative, dealing with local political issues, campaigns, music and events. Also single-subject programmes on the News International move to Wapping, the campaign against Clause 28, Docklands development, and an alternative view of the anti-poll-tax demonstration of March 1990. Hire or sale.

East Anglian Film Archive   **Videos you can buy** (1990). Leaflet. East Anglian Film Archive, Centre for East Anglian Studies, University of East Anglia, Norwich NR4 7IJ ☎ 01603 592664 fax 01603 58553.
A selection of films from the archive transferred to video. Subjects include industrial archaeology, farming, the seaside, Norwich, transport, rural life, industry and crafts. Sale only.

London Borough of Hammersmith & Fulham   **Video list** (1993). Leaflets. London Borough of Hammersmith & Fulham, Video and AV Unit, Hammersmith Town Hall, King Street, London W6 9JU ☎ 0181-741 3359 fax 0181-741 3359.
Videos on some of the council's services and activities organised in the borough. Also videos intended for training local authority staff. Hire.

Media Arts   **Catalogue** (1994). Loose-leaf catalogue. Media Arts, Town Hall Studios, Regent Circus, Swindon, Wiltshire SN1 1QF ☎ 01793 493451 fax 01793 490420.

Media Arts is a public media centre for watching and making videos. Programmes cover local issues such as environmental concerns, a local group for disabled children, paintings by Susan Morland, and the village of Imber, which was requisitioned for training during the war and is still a military training ground. Sale.

North West Film Archive (1993). Leaflets. North West Film Archive, Manchester Metropolitan University, Minshull House, 47-49 Chorlton Street, Manchester M1 3EU ☎ 0161-247 3097 fax 0161-247 3098.
Details of teachers' resource packs and the ongoing MOVING MEMORIES video compilation series of archive films showing popular traditions and special days. Sale only.

Northern Film and Television Archive **Catalogue of films and videotapes produced during the 1984-5 miners' strike** (1986). 32 pages. Northern Film and Television Archive, 36 Bottle Bank, Gateshead, Tyne and Wear NE8 2AR ☎ 0191-477 3601 fax 0191-478 3681.
A selection from the archive's collection of independently produced films on the 1984-5 miners' strike, available on video. Issues covered include miners' wives' support groups, the role of the police and law courts, pit closures, energy policy, and media representation. Hire and sale.

Northern Visions **Videos** (1994). Leaflets. Northern Visions, 4 Donegall Street Place, Lower Donegall Street, Belfast BT1 2FN ☎ 01232 245495 fax 01232 326608.
Northern Visions is a BECTU-franchised community workshop making videos about life in Belfast today. Topics include the use of plastic bullets, employment opportunities, issues affecting young people, women's health, the history of a local school, and daily cultural life. Sale.

Red Flannel Films (1992). Leaflets. Red Flannel Films, 3 Cardiff Road, Taffs Well, Nr Cardiff CF4 7RA ☎ 01443 401743 fax 01443 485667.
Films documenting life in the South Wales valleys as seen through the eyes of women. Specific topics include midwifery, the Welsh 'mam', and memories of sweets enjoyed in childhood.

Scottish Archive Film for Education (1989). Leaflet. Scottish Film Council, 74 Victoria Crescent Road, Glasgow G12 9JN ☎ 0141-334 4455 fax 0141-334 6519.
Compilations of extracts from films in the Scottish Film Archive on themes such as architecture, fishing, cities and social history. Sale on video.

Trilith Video **Productions** (1993). 6 pages. Trilith Video, Corner Cottage, Brickyard Lane, Bourton, Gillingham, Dorset SP8 5PJ ☎ 01747 840758
Programmes about constructive action being taken in rural communities from which others might learn, and the attitudes, outlook and experience of country-born people – a perspective which is in danger of being swamped by the enormous population changes taking place in rural areas. Sale.

Videovision Films **Video films list** (1993). 3 pages. Videovision Films, Swindon House, 160 Quay Road, Bridlington, East Yorkshire YO16 4JE ☎ 01262 605064 fax 01262 605378.

Videos relating to Yorkshire: the Brontës, Castle Howard, Burton Agnes Hall and crab fishing at Flamborough. Also a series on painting with watercolours. Sale only.

Computer Skills Training (see also information technology)

Academy Training
Video training for the PC and Macintosh (1994). 11 pages. Academy Training, 70-76 Bell Street, London NW1 6SP ☎ 0171-723 2010 fax 0171-724 7975.
A collection of over 150 videos designed for training in the use of software packages for desktop computers, at beginner, intermediate and advanced levels. Sale only.

ADC
SkillLearn video education & training courses (1994). 12 pages. ADC Education Services, 41 Whitefriars Drive, Harrow, Middlesex HA3 5HW ☎ 0181-429 2410 fax 0181-424 0415.
Video courses in the use of PC-based software packages. Many are accompanied by tutorial materials. They cover software for financial modelling, local area networking, word processing, presentation graphics and desktop publishing, operating systems, and integrated software and databases. Sale only.

Burgess Video Group
The PC software learning videos (1994). 15 pages. Burgess Video Group, Unit 6-18, Industrial Estate, Brecon, Powys LD3 8lA ☎ 01874 611633 fax 01874 625889.
Over 130 videos for training in the use of PC-based software packages, from beginner to advanced level. Sale.

Comput-Ed
A catalogue of computer-based training and videos for business and education (1993). 20 pages. Comput-Ed Ltd, Long Lane, Dawlish EX7 0QR ☎ 01703 455555 fax 01703 455544.
Video- and computer-based training programmes on management topics, concentrating on training in computing and information technology. Also, a CD-ROM entitled PROFESSOR MULTIMEDIA showing how to create a multimedia presentation. A more detailed catalogue giving a description of each programme is available free on disk.

Data-tech
Video learning packages (1994). Leaflet. Data-tech Business Resource Centre Ltd, Unit 2, Berghem Mews, Blythe Road, London W14 0HN ☎ 0171-610 4533 fax 0171 610 4535.
Self-training video packages on troubleshooting, repair and data recovery techniques for desktop computers. Packages consist of video, workbook and sometimes also tool kit and disk. Sale.

Datacal Video Library
(1994). Leaflets. Datacal Corporation UK, Publicity Centre, Hendon Road, Sunderland SR9 9XZ ☎ 01345 667766 fax 0191-510 3222.
A wide range of videos for self-instructional training in software use, covering Windows, DOS, OS/2, word processing, desktop publishing, spreadsheets, computer-aided design, accounting, databases, and Novell NetWare. Many programmes are accompanied by a tutorial disk. Sale only.

Educational Media, Film & Video
Teach Me How software training series (1994). 11 pages. Educational Media, Film and Video Ltd, 235 Imperial Drive, Rayners Lane, Harrow,

Middlesex HA2 7HE ☎ 0181-868 1908 fax 0181-868 1991.
American-produced videos for computer software training in word
processing, graphics, spreadsheets, operating systems and environments,
and system administration. Sale.

Iansyst **Computer training products** (1994). 14 pages. Iansyst, United House,
North Road, London N7 9DP ☎ 0171-607 5844 fax 0171-607 0187.
Video, audio, CD-ROM and computer software-based packages for
computer skills training, language learning, health & safety training, and
business skills. Sale only.

Learn PC **Catalog** (1994). 54 pages. Learn PC Ltd, 5 Riverview, Walnut Tree Park,
Guildford GU1 4UX ☎ 01483 456000 fax 01483 456001.
Video-based courses in computer literacy, operating systems, word
processing, databases, spreadsheets, graphics packages, electronic mail
and client-server development. Sale.

 **Sheffield** **Computer training video Leaflets** (1993). Leaflets. Sheffield University
University Television, Sheffield S10 2TN ☎ 0114 282 4007 fax 0114 276 2106.
Television Leaflets on videos with accompanying booklets, for use in computer skills
training. Packages covered are Microsoft Windows, MS-DOS, Microsoft
Word and dBASE IV. Sale.

Softvision **The Softvision learning video catalogue** (1994). 15 pages. Softvision Ltd,
47 Portsdown Hill Road, Havant, Hampshire PO9 3JU
☎ 01705 610041 fax 01705 610091.
A series of British-made, three-hour videotapes giving tuition in a
question-and-answer format on particular software packages. They cover
word processors, spreadsheets, presentation graphics, desktop publishing,
operating systems, and database management systems. Sale.

Wave Technologies **The complete technical training guide** (1994). 39 pages. Wave Technologies
UK Ltd, PO Box 1401, London W6 0WH ☎ 0181 332 0700 fax 0181-994 5611.
Mainly courses, but also details of videos on installing and operating
networks. Sale.

Dance (see also arts, drama)

Dance Books **Catalogue of books in stock** (1994). 30 pages. Dance Books Ltd, 9 Cecil
Court, London WC2N 4EZ ☎ 0171-836 2314 fax 0171-497 0473.
Includes a wide range of videos of performances and dance techniques.
Also a small number of American-produced videos in NTSC format which
are not available in the UK from other sources. Sale only.

National Resource **Dance film and video catalogue** (1992). 192 pages. Price £8.95. University
Centre for Dance of Surrey, National Resource Centre for Dance, Guildford GU2 5XH
☎ 01483 259316 fax 01483 300803 attn NRCD.
The second edition of the centre's film and video catalogue, which brings
together details of hundreds of programmes on dance available for hire or
sale from over 100 different distributors. Entries are arranged
alphabetically and indexed by choreographer, company, dancer, and
dance.

National Resource Centre for Dance **Services and publications** (1994). 14 pages. University of Surrey, National Resource Centre for Dance, Guildford GU2 5XH ☎ and fax as above.
Lists the centre's own programmes. Among the 14 videos are three on prescribed solos and set technical studies for GCSE and A/S level examinations. Also resource packs.

Other useful catalogues:
British Universities Film & Video Council (Drama)

Denmark

Royal Danish Embassy **Videos on Denmark catalogue** (1993). 16 pages. Royal Danish Embassy, Press and Cultural Section, 55 Sloane Street, London SW1X 9SR
☎ 0171-333 0200 fax 0171-333 0270.
Videos on the life, history and culture of Denmark with either English commentary or English subtitles.

Dentistry (see also health education, medical sciences)

Bristol Imaging **Bristol Biomedical Videodisc Project** (1993). Leaflet. Bristol Imaging, Royal Fort Annexe, University of Bristol, Tyndall Avenue, Bristol BS8 1UJ
☎ 0117 930 3500 fax 0117 925 5985.
A videodisc for teaching and research that holds a collection of 24,000 veterinary, medical and dental still frames, and incorporates the pathology videodisc UKPATH2. A visual database is available for detailed searches using any keyword.

Educational Dental Videos (1993). Loose-leaf catalogue. Educational Dental Videos Ltd, 2 Bank Street, Brighouse, West Yorkshire HD6 1BD ☎ 01484 715766.
Videos for patient education intended primarily for viewing in dental surgeries. Subjects include bridgework, crownwork, porcelain veneers, preventive dentistry, toothbrushing and flossing and dental health. Also children's films and cartoons. Sale only.

General Dental Council **Catalogue of dental health education material** (1993). 10 pages. General Dental Council Charitable Trust, 37 Wimpole Street, London W1M 8DQ
☎ 0171-486 2171.
Includes four health education dental videos, two for children and two for careers guidance. Free loan.

 **Sheffield University Television** **Dental video catalogue** (1991). 17 pages. Sheffield University Television, Sheffield S10 2TN ☎ 0114 282 4007 fax 0114 276 2106.
Programmes on clinical dentistry listed by subject: dental implants, general, pain and anxiety control, restorative dentistry, surgery. Hire and sale.

Design (see also architecture, art, arts, engineering & manufacturing)

Art Libraries Association **Visual resources for design** (1995). ARLIS Visual Resources Committee, c/o Jenny Godfrey, Faculty of Art, Design and Technology, Cardiff Institute of Higher Education, Howard Gardens Centre, Cardiff CF2 1SP
☎ 01222 551111 fax 01222 484970 fax 0171-925 2130.
A resource list of materials for use in the teaching of design.

Design Council | **Services and publications for secondary schools, colleges and universities** (1993). 19 pages. The Design Council, 28 Haymarket, London SW1Y 4SU ☎ 0171-839 8000.
Videos and slidepacks to support students' understanding of drawing and its application to design, engineering design, how professional designers approach projects, design practice in industry, and understanding of materials. Sale only.

Kingston University | **Design slides** (1991). Leaflets. Kingston University Library, Knights Park, Kingston-upon-Thames KT1 2QJ ☎ 0181-547 2000 fax 0181 547 7011.
Four sets of 36 slides with lecture notes on new British design, teenage consumers, British fashion textiles and assorted images. Sale.

Sio Communications | **Videotapes** (1992). 7 pages. Sio Communications Ltd, Georgia House, Eshe Road North, Blundellsands, Liverpool L23 8UD ☎ 0151-924 9570.
American-produced videotapes including the Goldscholl series on graphic design, desktop design, production art and calligraphy. Sale only.

Development Studies (see also anthropology, environmental science, race relations & cultural identity, social sciences, social welfare)

Central Independent Television | **Science, environmental issues and geography catalogue** (1993). 41 pages. Central Independent Television plc, Video Resources Unit, Broad Street, Birmingham B1 2JP ☎ 0121-643 9898 fax 0121-616 1531.
Programmes from Central Television's broadcast output selected for sale to education on video. Topics cover famine, development issues and international debt.

Christian Aid | **Catalogue** (1994). 14 pages. Christian Aid, PO Box 100, London SE1 7RT ☎ 0171-620 4444 fax 0171-620 0719.
Publications, posters, slide sets and videos illustrating the work of Christian Aid throughout the world. Includes programmes on environmental, economic, agricultural and human rights topics. Free loan or sale.

Comic Relief | **List of educational materials** (1994). 6 pages. Comic Relief, c/o Charity Projects, 1st floor, 74 New Oxford Street, London WC1A 1EF ☎ 0171-436 1122 fax 0171-436 1541.
Edited versions of broadcasts which accompanied the television appeals, showing underlying causes of poverty in Tanzania and designed for use in primary and secondary education. Also a pack on the education of disabled pupils in mainstream schools. Sale only.

Concord Video & Film Council | **Catalogue** (1993 + supplement). 273 pages. Price £3.00. Concord Video & Film Council, 201 Felixstowe Road, Ipswich IP3 9BJ ☎ 01473 715754 fax 01473 717088.
Hundreds of documentaries, animated films, and feature-length productions dealing with contemporary social issues in the UK and abroad. Concord distributes films and videos for over 350 voluntary organisations and charities. Hire and sale.

Co-operation for Development International | **Videos** (1993). Leaflet. Co-operation for Development International Ltd, 21 Germain Street, Chesham, Buckinghamshire HP5 1LB ☎ 01494 775557.

Videos about people and self-help projects in developing countries. Topics include the digging and management of a community well, disabled people in Jordan, women working for peace in South Africa, and starting small businesses in Namibia and the Middle East. Discussion notes are included. Sale only.

Humanitas   **Video series** (1994). Leaflet. Humanitas, 20 Queen Anne's Gate, London SW1H 9AA ☎ 0171-233 0278 fax 0171-233 0574.
Two series of videos focusing on the human consequences of critical problems facing the world, e.g. deforestation, disasters, famine, humanitarian intervention, human rights, refugees, indigenous peoples, modern warfare, street children. Sale from Television Trust for the Environment.

International Broadcasting Trust   **Views of the world** (1993). 24 pages. International Broadcasting Trust, 2 Ferdinand Place, London NW1 8EE ☎ 0171-482 2847 fax 0171-284 3374.
IBT-produced television and educational productions about global issues, relating particularly to development and the environment. Printed information and study guides accompany the videos. Suitable age-groups are clearly indicated in the schools section; other sections cover teacher training and sixth-form and adult audiences. There are indexes by place and topic. Videos may be hired or purchased from distribution libraries such as Concord, Academy Television and Team Video.

International Society for Ecology & Culture   **Videos** (1993). Leaflet. International Society for Ecology and Culture, 21 Victoria Square, Clifton, Bristol BS8 4ES ☎ 0117 973 1575 fax 0117 974 4853.
A programme discussing the future of the environment and development, and another on tradition and change in the Himalayan region of Ladakh. Sale.

Metro Pictures   **Film and video catalogue** (1989 + supplements). 92 pages. Metro Pictures Ltd, 79 Wardour Street, London WIV 3TH ☎ 0171-434 3357 fax 0171-287 2112.
Shorts, feature films and documentaries on development, environment, the nuclear debate, history, human rights, gay liberation, media and education, racial issues, trade unions and labour studies, and women in society. Hire on 35mm and 16mm film.

Natural Resources Institute   **Publications catalogue** (1993). 78 pages. NRI, Central Avenue, Chatham Maritime, Kent ME4 4TB ☎ 01634 880088 fax 01634 880066.
The NRI is the scientific arm of the Overseas Development Administration. Ten videos are available on the biology of leaf-cutting ants, good storage practice, rice storage in Indonesia, growing and marketing bananas, fisheries development on Lake Malawi, and other development topics. Hire or sale from CFL Vision.

Oxfam   **Audio-visual resources** (1993). 13 pages. Oxfam Information Centre, 274 Banbury Road, Oxford OX2 7DZ ☎ 01865 312449 fax 01865 312410.
Videos on economic, environmental, and social issues in development studies. Free loan or sale. A number of slide sets are also available for free loan.

Strategies for Hope   **Videos** (1994). Leaflets. Strategies for Hope, 93 Divinity Road, Oxford OX4 1LN ☎ 01865 727612 fax 01865 722203.

Books and videos for AIDS management in developing countries. Materials distributed by Teaching Aids at Low Cost. Sale.

Television Trust for the Environment **Moving Pictures 5** (1993). 40 pages. Television Trust for the Environment, TVE Centre for Environmental Communications, Prince Albert Road, London NW1 4RZ ☎ 0171-586 5526 fax 0171-586 4866.
Over 200 films and television programmes on the environment, development, health and human rights issues. Some of the best environmental films from around the world have been selected to reflect a diversity of viewpoints and cultures on the linked issues of development, poverty, inequality and environmental destruction. Programmes are available for broadcast world-wide, for free loan to non-governmental organisations and educational institutions in low- and middle-income countries, and at moderate charge to organisations in industrialised countries. The quarterly *Moving Pictures Bulletin* contains news, reviews, information about forthcoming television programmes, and listings on selected topics.

United Nations **Film & video catalogue** (1992). 71 pages. United Nations Information Centre, 20 Buckingham Gate, London SW1E 6LB ☎ 0171-630 1981 fax 0171-976 6478.
Programmes on economic concerns, human settlements, natural resources and the environment, political affairs, social issues, and the history and organisation of the United Nations itself. Free loan and sale.

Worldaware **Resources catalogue** (1993). 32 pages. Worldaware, 1 Catton Street, London WC1R 4AB ☎ 0171-831 3844 fax 0171-831 1746.
Includes videos, slides, software and teaching packs on world issues and development. The videos cover topics around the handicraft trade, life in Bangladesh, women farmers in Uganda, life in New Delhi, and general development topics. Sale. Also three videos for hire on Jamaica after Hurricane Gilbert, the developing world, and women in developing countries. Programmes were selected to use with the National Curriculum.

Other useful catalogues:
Teaching Aids at Low Cost (Health Education)

Drama (see also arts, literature, music)

Anglia Polytechnic University **CD-ROM and software catalogue** (1993). 10 pages. Anglia Polytechnic University Learning Technology Research Centre, Sawyers Hall Lane, Brentwood, Essex CM15 9BT ☎ 01277 200587 fax 01277 211363.
A range of Macintosh-based CD-ROMs and software, some developed as part of the Renaissance Initiative in collaboration with other higher education institutions. Some materials are intended for courseware developers; others are subject-based. Includes Shakespeare's *Twelfth Night* and Arthur Miller's *The Crucible*.

British Universities Film & Video Council **As you like it: audio-visual Shakespeare** (1992). 115 pages. Price £13.95. BUFVC, 55 Greek Street, London W1V 5LR ☎ 0171-734 3687 fax 0171-287 3914.
A comprehensive catalogue of 550 programmes (videos, films, slide sets, audiocassettes, computer programs, videodiscs) available for hire or sale

in the UK from 100 different distributors. Includes classic and recent feature films from various countries, recordings of stage and student productions, musical and ballet versions, as well as spin-offs and derivatives. Contains credits and synopses and is prefaced with articles addressing practicalities and issues relevant to the use of video and film in teaching Shakespeare.

Chadwyck-Healey   **Catalogue** (1992 + supplements). 94 pages. Chadwyck-Healey Ltd, The Quorum, Barnwell Road, Cambridge CB5 8SW
☎ 01223 215512 fax 01223 215513.
Includes details of the THEATRE IN FOCUS series of slide sets on the history of world theatre, produced in association with the Consortium for Drama and Media in Higher Education. Each slide set is accompanied by a monograph, and the series covers notable theatres; individual actors, directors and companies; unusual genres and styles of performance. Sale only.

Films for the Humanities & Sciences   (1994). Leaflets. Video Rights Ltd, Suites 415-416, Premier House 77 Oxford Street, London W1R 1RB ☎ 0171-439 1188 fax 0171-734 8367.
A distributor of videos for the retail market. Programmes include the English Shakespeare Company's WARS OF THE ROSES cycle and a collection of silent film classics. Sale through retail outlets.

Economics (see also development studies, management and training)

Video Rights   **Videos** (1994). Leaflets. Films for the Humanities and Sciences Inc, c/o Geoff Foster, 361 Crossley Lane, Mirfield, West Yorkshire WF14 0NU
☎ 01924 495823 fax 01924 497123.
Selected titles from this large American collection of videos and videodiscs. Includes a series comparing the economies of Japan, America and Germany. Sale.

Other useful catalogues:
United Nations (Social Sciences)
Workers Film Association (Social Sciences)

Education (see also careers guidance)

BBC Educational Developments   **Video and audio resources** (1993). 20 pages. BBC Educational Developments, White City, London W12 7TS ☎ 0181-746 1111.
A range of audio and video materials aimed at the broad educational market and available for purchase by individuals as well as schools. Subjects include helping children to read, pupil behaviour, assessment for the National Curriculum, science teaching and teacher educatio.

British Universities Film & Video Council   **BUFVC catalogue** (1990). 39 pages. + 9 microfiches. Price £17.00. BUFVC, 55 Greek Street, London WIV 5LR ☎ 0171-734 3687 fax 0171-287 3914.

Some 7000 videos, films, tape-slide programmes, audiocassettes, slide sets, computer programs and videodiscs, classified and fully described, with subject and title indexes. Many of the programmes were produced by institutions of higher education; others have been recommended for use in degree-level teaching and research. Includes television programmes from Open University courses. Appraised items are marked, as are those available for preview at the BUFVC's Audio-Visual Reference Centre. The booklet lists the addresses and telephone numbers of more than 500 UK distributors. Since 1990 the information has been updated on the BUFVC's in-house database AVANCE.

Cumana **The Cumana CD-ROM portfolio for schools and colleges** (1994). 54 pages. Cumana Ltd, Pines Trading Estate, Broad Street, Guildford GU3 3BH ☎ 01483 503121 fax 01483 451371.
CD-ROMs and interactive videos from various producers selected for their relevance to education. Includes the MIST series on science and technology. Sale.

Drake Educational Associates **Primary and middle school catalogue** (1994). 32 pages. Drake Educational Associates, St Fagans Road, Fairwater, Cardiff CF5 3AE ☎ 01222 560333 fax 01222 554909.
Computer programs, tape-slide sets and videos for teaching subjects across the National Curriculum and for teacher training. Sale only.

Dramatic Productions **Video resources for education** (1993). Leaflets. Dramatic Productions, 79 London Street, Reading RG1 4QA ☎ 01734 394170 fax 01734 394171.
Programmes for use in schools made by this independent video company managed by former teachers. Topics include discussions of general issues, multi-cultural education, special needs, school management, language development, and cross-curricular and arts initiatives. Sale only.

Educational Television Company **Resources catalogue** (1994). 44 pages. Educational Television Company, PO Box 100, Warwick CV34 6TZ ☎ 01926 433333 fax 01926 450178.
Videos, audiocassettes, teachers' guides, pupils' workbooks, computer software, posters and other resources produced to support Channel 4 schools programmes. Videos of some programmes broadcast by ITV Schools before Channel 4 took over the service in 1993 are also available for sale. Covers all National Curriculum subjects.

Focus in Education **Training resources for school-based professional development** (1993 + supplement). 12 pages. Focus in Education Productions, Focus Distribution, Q Studios, 1487 Melton Road, Queniborough, Leicester LE7 3FP ☎ 0116 260 8813 fax 0116 260 8329.
Videopacks produced in partnership with LEAs and teacher associations. Subjects are A-level marking, school governors, teacher appraisal, local management in schools, staff development, the American educational system, schools and the law, and the use of television in the primary classroom. Latest video packs are PREPARING TO BE INSPECTED, SAFELY TO SCHOOL, TEACHING IN INNER CITY CLASSROOMS, and APPRAISAL IN ACTION. Latest training resources for INSET cover total quality management in schools, classroom behaviour, high-achieving children, supporting the new teacher, and developing community schools. Sale only.

Hertfordshire Schools Library Service **Video programmes for education and training** (1993). 22 pages. Hertfordshire Schools Library Service, Hertfordshire Libraries, Arts and

178

Information, New Barnfield, Travellers Lane, Hatfield AL10 8XG
☎ 01707 281630 fax 01707 281611.
Videos made to meet specific training needs identified by LEA advisers or
college lecturers. Sale only.

Kent Educational Television   **Educational videos for schools and INSET** (1989). 19 pages. Kent
Educational Television Centre, Barton Road, Dover, Kent CT16 2ND
☎ 01304 202827 fax 01304 213824.
A range of videos produced for use as INSET material and teaching
resources across the whole curriculum. Sale only outside Kent.

Lame Duck Publishing   **Publications** (1993). 4 pages. Lame Duck Publishing, 10 Bristol Terrace,
Redland, Bristol BS6 6TG ☎ 0117 973 2881 fax 0117 973 2881.
Videos with supporting handbooks on the prevention of and reactions to
bullying, and on behaviour management in schools. Sale only.

LEAP Project   **Video training materials** (1994). Leaflets. The LEAP Office, Educational
Broadcasting Services Trust, 36-38 Mortimer Street, London W1N 7RB
☎ 0171-765 4635 fax 0171-580 6246.
A range of video-based training materials for teacher training and staff
development. Packages cover management in education, local
management in schools, appraisal in schools, quality in schools, school
inspection, and developing teaching skills. Sale.

Life Support Productions   **Educational videos** (1993). 7 pages. Life Support Productions, PO Box
2127, London NW1 6RZ ☎ 0171-723 7520 fax 0171-402 0719.
Videos on diverse topics including learning difficulties, primary and
nursery schools, suicide prevention and William Blake. Hire or sale.

National Audio Visual Library   **Videotape catalogue** (1993). Loose-leaf catalogue. National Audio Visual
Library, Unit 16, Greenshields Industrial Estate, Bradfield Road,
Silvertown, London E16 2AU ☎ 0171-474 8707 fax 0171-511 1578.
Thousands of programmes for teaching all school curriculum subjects,
with educational levels indicated. Some programmes also suitable for
further and higher education, particularly teacher training. Hire and sale
on video, also hire for some on 16mm film.

National Council for Vocational   **Publications, packs and videos** (1992). NCVQ, 222 Euston Road, London
Qualifications   NW1 2BZ ☎ 0171-728 1893 fax 0171-387 0978.
Includes information on three videos on the training revolution, aimed at
companies, managers and individuals, a training pack on NVQs for staff
development, and a video or videodisc package on assessing candidate
performance.

National Primary Centre   **Recent publications** (1994). Leaflets. National Primary Centre,
Westminster College, Oxford OX2 9AT ☎ 01865 245242 fax 01865 251847.
Several videos for teacher training. Topics are moving gymnastic
apparatus, lunchtime supervision, and behaviour management. Sale only.

Neti-Neti Theatre Company   **Resources** (1993). Leaflets. Neti-Neti Theatre Company, George Orwell
School, Turle Road,London N4 3LS ☎ 0171-272 7302.
Two packages, each consisting of script, workbook and video, on bullying

and disruptive behaviour due to bereavement or loss. The video recordings of the stage productions are available in English, Bengali or sign language. Sale only.

Northern College

Catalogue (1992). 100 pages. Northern College of Education, The Publications Unit, Gardyne Road, Broughty Ferry, Dundee DD5 1NY ☎ 01382 453433 fax 01382 455246.
Books, videos and audiocassettes on a wide range of subjects for use in education, teacher training and social work training. Sale only.

Northern Ireland Centre for Learning Resources

Quality management in schools (1993). Leaflet. Northern Ireland Centre for Learning Resources, Orchard Building, Stranmillis College, Belfast BT9 5DY ☎ 01232 664525.
An interactive video on staff development, designed for school heads of department.

Nottinghamshire Appraisal Team

Training videos (1994). Leaflet. Nottinghamshire Appraisal Team, Appraisal Office, Fairham Training Centre, Summerwood Lane, Clifton, Nottingham NG11 9AE ☎ 0115 940 5026.
Four videos on teacher appraisal: an introduction to the appraisal system, preparing for appraisal, classroom observation, and target setting. Sale.

The Open University

Professional development in education (1994). 64 pages. Open University Learning Materials Sales Office, PO Box 188, Milton Keynes MK7 6DH ☎ 01908 652152 fax 01908 654320.
Courses for professional development in education, and free-standing study packs for teachers, lecturers and others working in primary and secondary schools, further education and training. Most of the packs include a videocassette. Sale only.

Understanding British Industry

Directory of teaching materials from business and industry (1994). Price £5.95 (free to secondary schools). Understanding British Industry (UBI), Sun Alliance House, New Inn Hall Street, Oxford OX1 2QE ☎ 01865 722585 fax 01865 790014.
A directory of teaching materials listing 264 organisations that produce materials for schools free of charge or at a subsidised price. Includes an index of topics and curriculum subjects and details of how to obtain these resources.

University of Strathclyde, Faculty of Education

The Jordanhill catalogue (1994). 30 pages. University of Strathclyde, Faculty of Education, Audiovisual Services, Jordanhill Campus, 76 Southbrae Drive, Glasgow G13 1PP ☎ 0141-950 3170 fax 0141-950 3268.
Over 250 educational support titles, including books, computer software and some videos, for use in teacher training and in schools. Sale only.

Uniview

Academic videos (1993). Leaflet. Uniview Productions, 22 Mostyn Avenue, West Kirby, Wirral, Cheshire L48 3HW ☎ 0151-625 3453 fax 0151-625 3453.
A continuing series of videos about non-academic aspects of university life, designed to fill in the gaps in written prospectuses by providing a visual overview of student life in traditional universities. Covers geographic location, local town, accommodation, social amenities and study facilities. Each tape contains short sections on five different universities. Sale only.

Wessex Video **Classified videotape list** (1987 + supplements). 40 pages. Wessex Video, King Alfred's College, Winchester SO22 4NR ☎ 01962 866359 fax 01962 842280.
A classified list of videos for use in teacher training and in the classroom covering all curriculum subjects. Sale only outside the Wessex area.

Windfall Films **Videos** (1994). 2 pages. Windfall Films Ltd, 19-20 Bow Street, London WC2E 7AB ☎ 0171-379 5993 fax 0171-497 2966.
Two programmes produced for television broadcast on classroom management, and four programmes for use in schools on measurement.

Other useful catalogues:
Aston University (Physics)
Tony Jewers Productions (Film and Television Production)
National Council for Educational Technology (Information Technology)
The Open University: Community education study packs (Social Welfare)
Plymouth Medical Films (Health Education)
Television History Centre (History and Politics)

Electrical and Electronic Engineering (see also computer skills training, engineering & manufacturing, information technology, science & technology)

Institute of Electrical & Electronic Engineers **IEEE catalogue** (1994). 128 pages. IEEE, Customer Service Department, 445 Hoes Lane, PO Box 1331, Piscataway, NJ 08855-1331, USA ☎ +1 908 981 0060 fax +1 908 981 9667.
Videoconferences with experts discussing critical topics in computing, electronics and biomedical engineering. Originally broadcast live in the USA via satellite, they provide state-of-the-art information, emphasising practice rather than theory. Other series include short practical courses and video tutorials. For sale to UK customers on PAL-standard videocassette, individually or by subscription.

Institution of Electrical Engineers **IEE distance learning** (1993). Leaflet. IEE Marketing Department, Michael Faraday House, Six Hills Way, Stevenage SG1 2AY ☎ 01438 313311 fax 01438 742840.
Video- and computer-based training and educational materials for the electrical engineering, electronics and computer software industries. Intended for self-study, use by tutored groups or as resource material for company in-house training programmes. Broad subjects are codes of practice, communications, software engineering, management for engineers, and manufacturing. Sale only.

International Telecommunications Union **Catalogue of films on telecommunications and electronics** (1988 + supplement). 276 pages. ITU Film Library, Place des Nations, CH-1211 Geneva 20, Switzerland ☎ +41 22 730 5111 fax +41 22 730 5326.
Films from many countries on electronics and communications, held in the ITU library and indexed by subject, title, country, and language. Free loan.

University of Hertfordshire, Regional Electronics Centre **Distance learning packages** (1993). Leaflets. University of Hertfordshire, Regional Electronics Centre, College Lane, Hatfield AL10 9AB ☎ 01707 284455 fax 01707 284185.
Distance learning packages consisting of text and video components,

commissioned by the Department of Trade and Industry. Topics include electromagnetic compatibility, local area networks and logic cell arrays. Sale.

Energy (see also engineering & manufacturing, environmental science, science & technology)

BP Video Library
Videotape catalogue (1992). 34 pages. BP Video Library, Unit 2, Drywall Estate, Castle Road, Murston, Sittingbourne, Kent ME10 3RL ☎ 01795 436172 fax 01795 474871.
Videos on the oil industry and associated engineering and energy conservation topics. Also some more general titles on motoring and travel. Free loan.

British Coal Schools Service
Video list (1993). Leaflet. British Coal Schools Service, Public Relations Department, Room 452 Hobart House, Grosvenor Place, London SW1X 7AE ☎ 0171-235 2020.
Since the closure of the British Coal Film Unit, only five programmes are available on video for educational purposes. These deal with the origins of coal and the history of the industry. Sale only.

British Coal Television Unit
Coal on video (1993). 23 pages. British Coal Television Unit, Internal Communications Department, British Coal, Eastwood Hall, Eastwood, Nottingham NG16 3EB ☎ 01773 531313.
A large collection of videos for internal use in the coal industry. All aspects of the industry are covered including marketing, open-cast mining, safety, technology, and training. Free loan.

British Gas Video Library
Catalogue (1994). 18 pages. British Gas Video Library, Poplar Hall, Little Tey Road, Feering, Colchester CO5 9RP ☎ 01376 573292 fax 01376 573292.
Videos on the nature and uses of gas, the gas industry, pollution, energy conservation, health and safety in the home and at work, and home economics. Free loan or sale.

British Nuclear Industry Forum Education Programme
Educational resources from the UKAEA 1993-1994 (1993). 32 pages. BNIF Education Programme, AEA Technology, 329 Harwell, Didcot, Oxfordshire OX11 0RA ☎ 01235 433333 fax 01235 436548.
Videos with supporting notes, on nuclear energy issues including nuclear fission, reactors, safety, radiation and electricity. Aimed at primary and secondary schools with key words from the Programme of Study and attainment targets listed in the summary for each package. Sale only.

Electricity Association
Understanding electricity (1994). 50 pages. Electricity Association, 30 Millbank, London SW1P 4RD ☎ 0171-344 5768 fax 0171-344 5880.
Videos, wall charts and computer software for use within the science curriculum in schools, although some items are suitable for other curriculum areas such as geography, technology, and history. Includes videos on the history of electricity and domestic appliances. Free loan or sale.

Energy Technology Support Unit
Energy efficiency publications list (1994). 19 pages. Energy Technology Support Unit, Energy Efficiency Enquiries Bureau, Harwell, Didcot, Oxfordshire OX11 0RA ☎ 01235 436747.
Includes a title list of videos on topics including monitoring and targeting, combined heat and power, and heat recovery. Sale.

Esso Information Service
Educational resources (1995). 36 pages. Esso Information Service, PO Box 695, Sudbury, Suffolk CO10 6YM ☎ 01787 370272 fax 01787 880866.
Videos on science and technology, the environment, history, careers, business studies, art, and general interest topics. Free loan.

Nuclear Electric
Publications and videos (1994). Leaflet. Nuclear Electric plc, Public Relations Department, Barnett Way, Barnwood, Gloucester GL4 7RS ☎ 01452 652222 fax 01452 652776.
Videos on nuclear power generation, including related ecological aspects. Free loan and sale.

Shell Education Service
A catalogue of resources for teachers (1993). 52 pages. Shell Education Service, PO Box 46, Newbury, Berkshire RG13 2YX ☎ 01635 529371.
Resource packs, booklets, computer software, wall charts and videos developed specifically for use in schools and colleges, on topics relating to business and the oil industry. Most items are free of charge.

Shell Video Library
Video programmes (1994). 66 pages. Shell Education Service, PO Box 46, Newbury, Berkshire RG13 2YX ☎ 01635 31721 fax 01635 529371.
General interest videos produced by Shell UK on the oil industry, science and engineering, the environment, history and society, music and art, motoring, and energy conservation. Sale only.

UK Nirex
Publications list (1993). 4 pages. UK Nirex Ltd, Curie Avenue, Harwell, Didcot, Oxfordshire OX11 0RH ☎ 01235 825500 ext. 508.
Videos on the benefits of nuclear power and the safe disposal of radioactive wastes. Free loan.

Other useful catalogues:
Institution of Civil Engineers (Civil Engineering and Building)
Wimpey Films (Civil Engineering and Building)

Engineering and Manufacturing (see also civil engineering & building, electrical & electronic engineering, material science, science & technology)

American Technical Publishers
ASM International catalogue (1994). 40 pages. American Technical Publishers, 27-29 Knowl Piece, Wilbury Way, Hitchin SG4 0SX ☎ 01462 433678 fax 01462 433678.
Includes several video-based training courses covering thermal spray technology, quality, heat treating, induction heating, superalloys, composites, metallography, welding inspection, non-destructive testing, and corrosion. Sale only.

American Technical Publishers
Instrument Society of America catalogue (1994). 32 pages. American Technical Publishers, 27-29 Knowl Piece, Wilbury Way, Hitchin SG4 0SX ☎ 01462 433678 fax 01462 433678.
Includes several video-based training series on automatic and continuous process control, batch control, boiler control, industrial measurement, control technology and application, project management, instrument calibration, and control valves and actuators. Programmes are available either individually or as complete courses. Sale only.

American Technical Publishers	**Society of Manufacturing Engineers catalogue** (1994). 24 pages. American Technical Publishers, 27-29 Knowl Piece, Wilbury Way, Hitchin SG4 0SX ☎ 01462 433678 fax 01462 433678. Includes several video-based training series covering continuous improvement, die design, electronics, geometric dimensioning and tolerancing, lasers and robots, manufacturing automation, quality, and traditional machining. Programmes are available either individually or as complete courses. Sale only.
American Technical Publishers	**Technical Association of the Pulp and Paper Industry professional development catalogue** (1994). 32 pages. American Technical Publishers, 27-29 Knowl Piece, Wilbury Way, Hitchin SG4 0SX ☎ 01462 433678 fax 01462 433678. Includes several videotape-based training series covering paper manufacturing, boxplant operations, flexographic printing, statistical process control in corrugated boxplant, waste reduction and control in corrugated boxplant, finishing and converting operations, statistical process control in a paper mill, and testing strength properties. Programmes are available either individually or as complete courses. Sale only.
Audio Visual Source	**Technical training catalogues** (1994). Audio Visual Source, Item House, Beacon Road, Crowborough, East Sussex TN6 1AS ☎ 01892 668288 fax 01892 668266. A range of film and video catalogues with programmes for use in training for power plants, refinery operations, electrical and mechanical engineering techniques, and health and safety in engineering industries. Separate catalogues list interactive video-based and videodisc training programmes. Many programmes are available with Arabic commentary. Sale.
Educational Broadcasting Services Trust	**Skillbank video learning resources** (1994). 25 pages. Educational Broadcasting Services Trust, 36-38 Mortimer Street, London W1N 7RB ☎ 0171-765 5714 fax 0171-580 6246. A project supported by a consortium of further and higher education colleges, the Employment Department, the Further Education Unit and the National Council for Vocational Qualifications, aiming to provide 200 videos for skills training across the industrial and commercial sectors. Videos produced so far are in the areas of plumbing, catering, caring, construction, electrical installation, interpersonal skills and basic technology skills. Sale.
Electronic Presentation Services	**Training videos for in-house education** (1993). Leaflet. Electronic Presentation Services, 2 Fourth Avenue, Chelmsford, Essex CM1 4HA ☎ 01245 351502 fax 01245 496123. Videos for training in soldering techniques and quality control. Sale only.
Engineering Training Authority	(1991). Leaflets. Engineering Training Authority, Vector House, 41 Clarendon Road, Watford WD1 1HS ☎ 01923 238441 fax 01923 56086. Formerly the Engineering Industry Training Board. Video-based packages for designers in the engineering industry. Sale only.
Ford Motor Company	**Video loan library** (1993). 8 pages. Ford Motor Company Ltd, Audiovisual Services 1/455, Eagle Way, Brentwood, Essex CM13 3BW

☎ 01277 252766 fax 01277 252896.
Technical programmes on car design, manufacture and safety features, and a programme on the history of the Ford Motor Company. Free loan.

Institution of Mechanical Engineers (1994). 3 pages. Institution of Mechanical Engineers, 1 Birdcage Walk, London SW1H 9JJ ☎ 0171-222 7899 fax 0171-222 4557.
Videos on topics including materials technology, CAD/CAM, automation, and improving manufacturing effectiveness. Free loan.

MUTV **Spaceflight: the history and development of rockets** (1992). Leaflet. MUTV, Oxford Road, Manchester M13 9PL ☎ 0161-275 253 fax 0161-275 2529.
Two videos looking at the historical background of rocket technology from an engineering perspective. The first contrasts the predictions of science fiction with the reality of scientific fact, and the other deals with re-entry vehicles. For students of mathematics, physical sciences and engineering. Sale.

MUTV **University of Manchester, Department of Engineering** (1992). Leaflets. MUTV, Oxford Road, Manchester M13 9PL ☎ 0161-275 2535 fax 0161-275 2529.
Three series of programmes on engineering topics: engineering drawing, mechanical engineering production techniques, and engineering design. Sale only.

National Physical Laboratory **Videos and films** (1993). Leaflet. NPL Information Services, Teddington, Middlesex TW11 0LW ☎ 0181-977 3222 fax 0181-943 2155.
Videos and films on standards and measurement, including measurement by laser. The NPL also distributes the video INFORMATION TECHNOLOGY FOR THE DISABLED. Free loan and sale.

Services Ltd **Video series** (1993). Leaflet. Services Ltd, Quality and Reliability House, 82 Trent Boulevard, West Bridgford, Nottingham NG2 5BL ☎ 0115 945 5285 fax 0115 981 7137.
Video series on reliability engineering and total quality management, produced with the assistance of Professor Tony Bendell of Nottingham Trent University. Sale only.

Technical Video Library **Video list** (1992). 35 pages. TVL, Franks Hall, Horton Kirby, Dartford, Kent DA4 9LL ☎ 01322 222222 fax 01322 289953.
A loan scheme offering a wide range of videos on industrial and manufacturing materials and processes. Items are arranged under the headings design and manufacture, computerisation, electronics, process sector, and general management. Loan, by annual subscription.

Woodhead Publishing **Catalogue** (1994). 40 pages. Woodhead Publishing Ltd, Abington Hall, Abington, Cambridgeshire CB1 6AH ☎ 01223 891358 fax 01223 893694.
Includes videos from the Welding Institute on welding processes, metallurgy and materials, design and weld properties, structures and fabrication, surface engineering, health and safety, and inspection and testing. Also a range of videos on welding from the USA produced by Hellier Associates Inc and the East Coast Enterprise Training Center. Several slide sets are also available. Sale only.

Environmental Science (see also community studies, development studies, energy, geography & earth sciences, science & technology)

Central Independent Television
Science, environmental issues and geography catalogue (1993). 41 pages. Central Independent Television plc, Video Resources Unit, Broad Street, Birmingham B1 2JP ☎ 0121-643 9898 fax 0121-616 1531.
Programmes from Central Television's broadcast output selected for sale to education on video. Topics include famine, development issues, and international debt.

The Conservation Trust
Guide to resources in environmental education (1989-90). 150 pages (approx). Price £25.00. The Conservation Trust, National Environmental Education Centre, George Palmer Site, Northumberland Avenue, Reading RG2 7PW ☎ 01734 868442 fax 01734 314051.
Films, videos, books, slides, filmstrips, audiocassettes, OHPs and kits, listed under many subject headings. Films and videos are available for hire or sale from various distributors; all other materials are available for free loan to trust members and sale to non-members.

The Environment Council
Films and videos on the environment (1993). Leaflet. The Environment Council, 21 Elizabeth Street, London SW1 9RP
☎ 0171-824 8411 fax 0171-730 9941.
A guide to sources of environmental films and videos. Suppliers are listed by name and subject area.

Humanitas
Video series (1994). Leaflet. Humanitas, 20 Queen Anne's Gate, London SW1H 9AA ☎ 0171-233 0278 fax 0171-233 0574.
Two series of videos focusing on the human consequences of critical problems facing the world: deforestation, disasters, famine, humanitarian intervention, human rights, refugees, indigenous peoples, modern warfare, street children. Sale from Television Trust for the Environment.

International Broadcasting Trust
Views of the world (1993). 24 pages. International Broadcasting Trust, 2 Ferdinand Place, London NW1 8EE ☎ 0171-482 2847 fax 0171-284 3374.
IBT-produced television and educational productions about global issues, relating particularly to development and the environment. Printed information and study guides accompany the videos. Suitable age-groups are clearly indicated in the schools section; other sections cover teacher training and sixth-form and adult audiences. There are indexes by place and topic. Videos may be hired or purchased from distribution libraries such as Concord, Academy Television and Team Video.

International Centre for Conservation Education
Environmental education resources (1993). Leaflets. ICCE, Greenfield House, Guiting Power, Cheltenham GL54 5TZ ☎ 01451 5777 fax 01451 5705.
Programmes on tape-slide and video on environmental topics including pollution, wildlife, desertification, and pesticides. Sale only.

The National Trust Film & Video Library
(1994). Loose-leaf catalogue. The National Trust Film and Video Library, c/o Education Distribution Services, Unit 2, Drywall Estate, Castle Road, Murston, Sittingbourne, Kent ME10 3RL ☎ 01795 427614 fax 01795 474871.
Films and videos on National Trust properties around the country. Hire or sale on film or video.

Scottish Civic Trust   **Film and video list** (1993). Leaflet. Scottish Civic Trust, 24 George Square, Glasgow G2 1EF ☎ 0141-221 1466 fax 0141-248 6952.
A film and six videos on the work of the trust, covering the conservation of buildings and the countryside. Hire or sale.

Team Video Productions   **Catalogue** (1989 + supplements). 21 pages. Team Video Productions, 105 Canalot, 222 Kensal Road, London W10 5BN ☎ 0181-960 5536.
Videos and video-based teaching packs on new technology, health and safety, pre-vocational training, business and trade union studies, nuclear power, media studies, development studies and environmental conservation. Some are accompanied by student worksheets and lesson plans. Sale only.

Television Trust for the Environment   **Moving Pictures 5** (1993). 40 pages. Television Trust for the Environment, TVE Centre for Environmental Communications, Prince Albert Road, London NW1 4RZ ☎ 0171-586 5526 fax 0171-586 4866.
Over 200 films and television programmes on the environment, development, health and human rights issues. Some of the best environmental films from around the world have been selected to reflect a diversity of viewpoints and cultures on the linked issues of development, poverty, inequality and environmental destruction. Programmes are available for broadcast world-wide, for free loan to non-governmental organisations and educational institutions in low and middle income countries, and at moderate charge to organisations in industrialised countries. A quarterly publication, *Moving Pictures Bulletin*, features news, reviews, information about forthcoming television programmes, and listings on particular topics.

Other useful catalogues:
Team Video (Social Sciences)
United Nations (Social Sciences)

Film and Television Production

Australian Film, Television & Radio School   **Training videos and publications** (1993 + supplement). 32 pages. Australian Film, Television and Radio School, PO Box 126, North Ryde, NSW Australia 2113 ☎ +61 2 805 6454 fax +61 2 887 1030.
An extensive range of videos designed to provide a fuller understanding of all the elements involved in the creation and production of film, television and radio programmes. Intended for professionals and those involved in teaching and learning about all aspects of media and communications. For sale to UK customers on PAL-standard videocassette.

BBC Television Training   **Videos** (1992). Leaflets. BBC Television Training, Elstree Centre, Publications and Marketing, Clarendon Road, Borehamwood, Hertfordshire WD6 1JF ☎ 0181-953 6100 ext. 2588 fax 0181-207 8168.
Videos and books about television production. The videos cover editing, creative writing, electronic effects, continuity, camera mountings, filming action, design and programme production. Sale only.

Tony Jewers Productions   **Video list** (1993). Leaflets. Tony Jewers Productions, 4 Greystones Close, Colchester CO3 4RQ ☎ 01206 575788 fax 01206 44777.
Five videos on how to use a camcorder successfully. Sale only.

Metrovideo **Sony tools of the trade** (1994). Leaflet. Metrovideo, The Old Bacon Factory, 57-59 Great Suffolk Street, London SE1 0BS ☎ 0171-928 2088 fax 0171-261 0685. Three training packages sponsored by Sony Broadcast for those wishing to follow a career in the television industry. Aimed at those who have limited access to formal training. Subjects are research and scripting, production management, and post-production. Sale.

Finance and Accountancy (see also management & training)

Banking Information Service **Curriculum resource catalogue** (1994). 32 pages. Banking Information Service, Education and Careers, 10 Lombard Street, London EC3V 9AT ☎ 0171-626 9386 fax 0171-283 9655.
Resources including videos and multimedia packs, some with a video component, giving advice and information to young people, both for their personal finances and future business purposes. The multimedia packs are geared to economic areas covered in the National Curriculum. Videos available for free loan or sale, packs for sale only.

Chartered Institute of Bankers **Video leaflets** (1991). Leaflets. Chartered Institute of Bankers, Video Sales, Emmanuel House, Burgate Lane, Canterbury, Kent CT1 2XJ ☎ 01227 762600 fax 01227 763788.
Video dramatisations with support materials for teaching banking practice, accountancy and international trade finance, produced in association with the University of Brighton. Sale only.

Financial i **Films on finance** (1993). Leaflets. Financial i, Euromoney Publications plc, Nestor House, Playhouse Yard, London EC4V 5EX ☎ 0171-779 8622 fax 0171-779 8623.
Video-based training packages designed for the international banking and corporate community. Subjects include foreign exchange, currency options, the Eurobond market, futures, options, UK equities, and documentary letters of credit. Sale.

Premiere Productions **Interactive video training programmes** (1994). Leaflets. Premiere Productions, 16 Castello Avenue, London SW15 6EA ☎ 0181-785 2933 fax 0181-780 1684. Interactive video programmes for training in management, finance, and language learning.

Purple Training **Video list** (1994). Leaflets. Purple Training, 10 Barley Mow Passage, London W4 4PH ☎ 0181-742 0607 fax 0181-994 3650.
A series of videos with accompanying print material on the setting up and the financial aspects of running a small business.

Tax Training **Videos** (1994). Leaflets. Tax Training Ltd, 4 Pedlars Walk, High Street, Ringwood, Hampshire BH24 1EZ ☎ 01425 471245 fax 01425 473439.
Practical training videos on PAYE, NIC, company car provision and completing a P11D form. Sale.

University of Brighton **Video catalogue** (1990 + supplements). 28 pages. University of Brighton Media Services, Watts Building, Moulsecoomb, Brighton BN2 4GJ ☎ 01273 642778 fax 01273 606093.
A wide range of subjects including banking and business studies. Sale only.

French Studies (see also languages, media studies: feature films)

European Schoolbooks   **French catalogue** (1993). 72 pages. European Schoolbooks Ltd, The Runnings, Cheltenham GL51 9PQ ☎ 01242 245252 fax 01242 224137. Video-based language courses and individual audio and videocassettes, with supporting booklets, about cultural and social issues. Also some slide sets. Sale only.

Institut Français   **Téléthèque française** (1992). 34 pages. Institut Français du Royaume-Uni, 17 Queensberry Place, London SW7 2DT ☎ 0171-589 6211 fax 0171-581 5127. A video club allowing members to borrow French-language videos from the collection of some 200 titles on literature, cinema, drama, and other subjects.

Other useful catalogues:
BBC for Business (Management and Training)

Geography and Earth Sciences (see also development studies, environmental science, tourism)

Central Independent Television   **Science, environmental issues and geography catalogue** (1993). 41 pages. Central Independent Television plc, Video Resources Unit, Broad Street, Birmingham B1 2JP ☎ 0121-643 9898 fax 0121-616 1531. Programmes from Central Television's broadcast output selected for sale to education on video. Topics include conservation, rain forests, famine, history of science, development issues, and international debt.

Granada Television International   **Programme catalogue** (1992). 80 pages. Granada Television International, Non-Theatric Sales, Granada Television International, 36 Golden Square, London W1R 4AH ☎ 0171-734 8080 fax 0171-494 6280. Several hundred Granada programmes selected for educational use. Includes the DISAPPEARING WORLD anthropological films; the COMPASS series of journeys; and other series on science, history and geography. Sale only.

Latin America Bureau   **Rainforest resources** (1992). 23 pages. Price £2.00. Latin America Bureau, 1 Amwell Street, London EC1R 1UL ☎ 0171-278 2829 fax 0171-278 0165. Educational resources including videos on the Amazon rain forest and related issues.

Look & Learn Television   **New British-produced video resources for the National Curriculum** (1994). Leaflets. Look & Learn Television, 8 Dalby Court, Gadbrook Business Centre, Northwich, Cheshire CW9 7TN ☎ 01606 49723 fax 01606 350625. A range of videos with accompanying materials produced to support the National Curriculum in the areas of geography, science and technology. Topics include transport, map reading, bridges, structures, buildings and flight. Sale.

National Meteorological Library   **Video cassettes: title listing (public loan)** (1994). 7 pages. National Meteorological Library, London Road, Bracknell, Berkshire RG12 2SZ ☎ 01344 420242. Videos on meteorology made by companies and meteorological services around the world. Includes educational programmes on atmospheric science for secondary schools, understanding weather for primary schools, and titles on acid rain and the greenhouse effect. Hire. A separate list is also available of a wide range of slides and slide sets for loan or sale.

National Remote Sensing Centre **Video list** (1993). 8 pages. National Remote Sensing Centre Ltd, Delta House, Southwood Crescent, Southwood, Farnborough, Hampshire GU14 0NL ☎ 01252 541464 fax 01252 375016.
A title list of videos on satellite remote sensing and its applications, some of which are available for reference and others for hire. The centre also sells and hires slide sets and has an archive of over 1000 individual slides covering a wide range of topics, including imagery from the different satellites, pictures of the satellites themselves, receiving dishes, and image processing. Purchase of these for reproduction may be negotiated. The NRSC free newsletter *Albedo* contains articles, news and information on new materials.

The Open University **Catalogue of learning resources from the undergraduate programme** (1994). 102 pages. Open University Educational Enterprises Ltd, 12 Cofferidge Close, Stony Stratford, Milton Keynes MK11 1BY ☎ 01908 261662 fax 01908 261001.
Lists by title the hundreds of videos, audiocassettes, study texts and computer packages in all subject areas that form part of Open University undergraduate courses and are available for sale separately to outside institutions. Alternatively, programmes may be recorded off-air under licence from the OU. Synopses of individual programmes are given on course information sheets, which may be requested individually.

Shell Video Library **Video programmes** (1994). 66 pages. Shell Education Service, PO Box 46, Newbury, Berkshire RG13 2YX ☎ 01635 31721 fax 01635 529371.
General interest videos produced by Shell UK on the oil industry, science and engineering, the environment, history and society, music and art, motoring, and energy conservation. Sale only.

Viewtech **Humanities catalogue** (1994). 38 pages. Viewtech Film & Video, 161 Winchester Road, Brislington, Bristol BS4 3NJ ☎ 0117 977 3422 fax 0117 972 4292.
A selection of programmes from the main Viewtech catalogue in the area of humanities, covering geography, ancient civilisations, history, explorations and discovery, the 20th century, history of technology and religious studies. Sale only.

Other useful catalogues:
Attica Cybernetics (History and Politics)
Encyclopaedia Britannica (Science and Technology)

German Studies (see also languages, media studies: feature films)

European Schoolbooks **German catalogue** (1993). 58 pages. European Schoolbooks Ltd, The Runnings, Cheltenham GL51 9PQ ☎ 01242 245252 fax 01242 224137.
Video-based language courses and individual audio and videocassettes of works of German literature. Also examples of recent television advertisements and news programmes with supporting literature, and a number of programmes dealing with recent political events. Sale only.

German Film & Video Library **Catalogue** (1993). 69 pages. German Film and Video Library, c/o Education Distribution Service, Unit 2, Drywall Estate, Castle Road, Murston, Sittingbourne, Kent ME10 3RL ☎ 01795 427614 fax 01795 474871. Videos and a number of films on a wide range of subjects relating to Germany, including politics and history, industry, cities and regions, culture, and the full spectrum of the arts: painting, literature, music, dance, theatre and film. Many of the programmes are available in both German and English-language versions. The feature films previously distributed by the German Film Library are now handled by Glenbuck Films. Free loan.

Goethe-Institut **Auswahlliste: Bücher und Kassetten für den Unterricht** (1992). 96 pages. Goethe-Institut London Library, 50 Princes Gate, Exhibition Road, London SW7 2PH ☎ 0171-411 3452 fax 0171-584 3180. Audiocassettes and books for the teaching of German as a foreign language. Free loan.

Goethe-Institut **Video catalogue** (1992). 103 pages. Goethe-Institut London Library 50 Princes Gate, Exhibition Road, London SW7 2PH ☎ 0171-411 3452 fax 0171-584 3180. Video programmes, including feature films and documentaries, on all aspects of German life. The 16mm feature films previously distributed by the Goethe Institut are now handled by Glenbuck Films. Free loan.

Oxford University Press **TV und Texte on CD-ROM** (1994). Leaflet. Oxford University Press, Walton Street, Oxford OX2 6DP ☎ 01865 56767 fax 01865 56646. A video-based language-learning resource for advanced students of German. Available as a video with accompanying workbook or as a CD-ROM package. A voice-recording facility enables the learner to record and play back his or her own commentary to the film sequences. Sale.

Other useful catalogues:
BBC for Business (Management and Training)
Films for the Humanities and Sciences (Economics)

Health and Safety (see also civil engineering & building, management & training)

Aegis Healthcare **First Aid at Work** (1993). Leaflet. Aegis Healthcare Ltd, 87 Oxford Road, Waterloo, Liverpool L22 7RE ☎ 0151-920 3814 fax 0151-928 5557. FIRST AID AT WORK is a six-part video series covering resuscitation, asphyxia, bleeding and wounds, injuries, fractures, and spinal injuries. The programmes are intended to complement structured first-aid courses. Sale only.

CFL Vision **Health & Safety Executive video programme catalogue** (1993). 24 pages. CFL Vision, PO Box 35, Wetherby, West Yorkshire LS23 7EX ☎ 01937 541010 fax 01937 541083. Full details of programmes produced by the Health and Safety Executive between 1975 and 1993. Most of the programmes are directed at particular industries in response to their safety needs. A separate leaflet supplies details of Health and Safety Executive programmes for the farming and agricultural industry. Hire or sale.

Civil Aviation Authority	**Video catalogue** (1994). Leaflet. Civil Aviation Authority, Printing and Publication Services, Greville House, 37 Gratton Road, Cheltenham GL50 2BN ☎ 01242 235151 fax 01242 584139. A range of videos dealing with aviation safety. Free loan.
Consort Films International	**Catalogue** (1991 + supplement). Loose-leaf catalogue. Consort Films International, Consort House, Wesley Street, Ossett nr Wakefield WF5 9ET ☎ 01924 291440 fax 01924 291101. Films and videos on industrial and hospital fire safety and other institutional health and safety topics, as well as on motorcycle and driver training. Hire or sale.
Edward Patterson Associates Ltd	**Health and safety film/video catalogue** (1989-90). 23 pages. Edward Patterson Associates, Treetops, Cannongate Road, Hythe, Kent CT21 5PT ☎ 01303 264195 fax 01303 264195. Films and videos selected by panels of health and safety officers, from producers in the UK and the USA. Hire and sale on film; sale only on video.
Estil Tel-a-Train	**Health & safety training in Europe** (1993). Loose-leaf catalogue. Estil Tel-a-Train Ltd, Midland Road, Luton LU2 0HR ☎ 01582 23376 fax 01582 34290. Videos on chemical safety, ergonomics, and health and safety for industry and engineering. Sale only.
Factory Mutual International	**Video list** (1993). 16 pages. Factory Mutual International, FM Insurance Company Ltd, Public Relations Department, Southside, 105 Victoria Street, London SW1E 6QT ☎ 0171-828 7799 fax 0171-630 5335. A large collection of videos relating to fire safety, some involving research testing of fires in particular situations. Free loan or sale.
Fire Protection Association	**Publications catalogue** (1993). 40 pages. Fire Protection Association, 140 Aldersgate Street, London EC1A 4HX ☎ 0171-606 3757 fax 0171-600 1487. Includes four videos for training fire safety managers in industry. Sale only.
Fire Training Videos	**Training video information** (1994). Leaflet. Fire Training Videos Ltd, Video House, 42-44 Brunswick Road, Shoreham-by-Sea, West Sussex BN43 5WB ☎ 01273 461192 fax 01273 462488. Eight videos on fire prevention, fire safety and fire fighting.
H & H Scientific	**Training videos** (1994). Leaflets. H & H Scientific Consultants Ltd, PO Box MT27, Leeds LS17 8QP ☎ 0113 268 7189 fax 0113 268 7191. A series of videos on ionising radiation produced by the University of Sheffield, and one on training for radiation workers from the University of Sussex. Also a series on computing for beginners, also from the University of Sheffield. Sale only.
Health & Safety Executive	**Audiovisual resources in occupational health and safety** (1993). 182 pages. Price £11.00. HMSO, PO Box 276, London SW8 5DT ☎ 0171-873 0011 fax 0171-873 8200. Brings together details of hundreds of videos, films and tape-slide programmes available from a large number of UK distributors. Covers all occupational health and safety topics including offshore safety. Includes materials covering European and UK health and safety legislation.

Human Focus | **The ergonomics and information newsletter** (1993). 8 pages. Human Focus Ltd, Mill Green Business Park, Mill Green Road, Mitcham, Surrey CR4 4HT ☎ 0181-640 3535 fax 0181-646 8700.
Packages, most with a video component, looking at ergonomic approaches to issues of health and safety in the workplace. Topics include manual handling, VDU hazards and risk assessment and management. Sale only.

Longman Training | **Health and safety video catalogue** (1994). 72 pages. Training Direct, Longman House, Burnt Mill, Harlow, Essex CM20 2JE ☎ 01279 623927 fax 01279 623795.
Over 100 videos on health and safety at work, many of them dealing with the implications of specific legislation. Includes programmes produced with the Building Employers Confederation designed to promote safety awareness in the construction industry. Hire or sale.

Micron Video | **Video list** (1993). 24 pages. Micron Video International Ltd, Links House, Dundas Lane, Portsmouth PO3 5BL ☎ 01705 670550 fax 01705 670543.
Videos about cleanroom and contamination control procedures and good manufacturing practice in industries where control of particulates and viable organisms is essential. Available in several European languages. Sale.

Monitor Training | **Film and video training programmes** (1994). 14 pages. Monitor Training Ltd, 33 Market Place, Henley-on-Thames, Oxfordshire RG9 2AA ☎ 01491 410365 fax 01491 410105.
Videos on various aspects of health and safety training. Sale.

Royal Society for the Prevention of Accidents | **Audio visual catalogue** (1993). 16 pages. RoSPA Video Library, Cannon House, The Priory, Queensway, Birmingham B4 6BS ☎ 0121-200 2461 fax 0121-200 1254.
Videos on accident prevention and health and safety at work. Hire.

Sandown Training | **List of video packages** (1993). Leaflet. Sandown Training, Parkwood House, Painswick Road, Cheltenham GL50 2BR ☎ 01242 260056 fax 01242 260057.
Video-based resource packs on occupational hygiene, environmental protection, and health and safety. Topics are safety management, VDU safety, personal protective equipment, manual handling operations, blood pathogens, laboratory safety, and noise at work. Hire or sale.

Technical Video Sales | **Catalogue** (1994). 10 pages. TVS, Franks Hall, Horton Kirby, Dartford, Kent DA4 9LL ☎ 01322 222222 fax 01322 289953.
Industrial video training programmes for supervisors, workers and health and safety officers. Hire and sale.

Trade Films | **Health and safety video leaflet** (1993). Leaflet. Trade Films Ltd, 36 Bottle Bank, Gateshead, Tyne and Wear, NE8 2AR ☎ 0191-477 5532 fax 0191-478 3681.
HEALTH AND SAFETY: THE EUROPEAN CHALLENGE, a series of four videotapes, is an introduction to the European Community's programme for health and safety at work. Sale only.

University of Portsmouth, Occupational Health & Safety Training Unit | **Price list and order form** (1993). Leaflet. University of Portsmouth, Occupational Health and Safety Training Unit, Ravelin House, Museum Road, Portsmouth PO1 2QQ ☎ 01705 864954 fax 01705 843461.

Packages include audio- and videotapes on harmful noise: its causes, measurement and control. Also videos on industrial and commercial lighting, and on the thermal environment at work. Sale.

Other useful catalogues:
Team Video (Social Sciences)

Health Education see also dentistry, medical sciences, mental health & counselling, nursing, social welfare

Academy Television now trading as YITM

Healthwatch video catalogue (1993). 18 pages. Academy Television, Kirkstall Road, Leeds LS3 1JS ☎ 0113 246 1528 fax 0113 242 9522. Academy handles a selection of programmes broadcast by Yorkshire–Tyne Tees Television, Thames Television, Channel 4, Scottish Television, Ulster Television, HTV and WTN. This catalogue contains details of over 100 titles from the main Academy catalogue, focusing on material relating to health and social issues. The aim of the selection is to provide information and discussion material on medical advances and the social effects of illness on patients. Sale on video.

Arthritis & Rheumatism Council

(1993). Leaflets. The Arthritis and Rheumatism Council, Copeman House, St Mary's Court, St Mary's Gate, Chesterfield S41 7TD ☎ 01246 558033 fax 01246 558007. Two videos, one on arthritis and the family and the other on special gadgets and aids to mobility. Sale only.

Barony Film and Video

Distribution list (1992 + update). 16 pages. Barony Film and Television Productions Ltd, 4 Picardy Place, Edinburgh EH1 3JT ☎ 0131-558 3275 fax 0131-557 8498. Over 20 health education videos aimed at both the professional and the patient. Subjects include HIV, AIDS, young people with learning difficulties, family planning, stroke, community care, bandaging, and asthma. Sale.

Boulton-Hawker Films

Health education video catalogue (1993 + supplement). 28 pages. Boulton-Hawker Films Ltd, Hadleigh, Ipswich IP7 5BG ☎ 01473 822235 fax 01473 824519. Videos on health and hygiene, human biology, sex education and personal development. The 1994 supplement includes all the titles previously in the separate social welfare catalogue on topics such as disability, sexual harassment and abuse, and elderly people. Sale and preview.

Boulton-Hawker

Personal and social education for secondary schools video catalogue (1993). 16 pages. Boulton-Hawker Films Ltd, Hadleigh, Ipswich IP7 5BG ☎ 01473 822235 fax 01473 824519. Videos on substance abuse, sex education, personal development and relationships, communication skills, diet, and fitness. Sale and preview.

British Diabetic Association

(1993). Leaflets. British Diabetic Association, 10 Queen Anne Street, London W1M 0BD ☎ 0171-323 1531 fax 0171-637 3644. Six videos to show how people live with their diabetes. Also LOOKING AFTER YOURSELF, a video in six language versions for Asian people with non-insulin-dependent diabetes. Sale only.

British Heart Foundation   **Films and videos** (1993). Leaflet. BHF Education Department, 14 Fitzhardinge Street, London W1H 4DH ☎ 0171-935 0185 fax 0171-486 1273. A range of videos on the work of the BHF, the prevention of heart disease, and other topics for patients and their families. Free loan.

British Medical Association   **Catalogue of films and videos in the British Medical Association Library** (1993). 348 pages. Price £40.00. *Information:* BMA Library Film and Video Services, BMA House, Tavistock Square, London WC1H 9JP ☎ 0171-383 6690 fax 0171-388 2544. *Catalogue sales:* Library Association Publishing Ltd, c/o Bookpoint Ltd, 30 Milton Park, Abingdon, Oxfordshire OX14 4TD ☎ 01235 835001 fax 01235 832068.
A detailed, annotated list of the films and videos in the BMA Library. All titles have received peer review. Entries include full filmographic details, synopses and target audience. Arranged alphabetically and indexed under subject headings. Programmes available on free loan to BMA members and affiliated libraries in the UK.

British Medical Association   **Current videos for loan** (1992 + supplement). 50 pages. BMA Library Film & Video Services, BMA House, Tavistock Square, London WC1H 9JP ☎ 0171-383 6690 fax 0171-388 2544.
A collection of videos available for free loan to BMA members. The catalogue is organised under broad subject headings from abortion to urology.

Brook Advisory Centres   **Publications catalogue** (1993). 24 pages. Brook Advisory Centres, Education and Publications Unit, 153a East Street, London SE17 2SD ☎ 0171-708 1390 fax 0171-252 5622.
Videos with supporting notes on sex education topics including the gynaecological examination and sex and disability. Sale only.

Cancer Research Campaign   **Videos** (1994). Leaflet. Cancer Research Campaign, Cambridge House, 6-10 Cambridge Terrace, Regent's Park, London NW1 4JL ☎ 0171-224 1333 fax 0171-487 4310.
Two videos for health professionals on the psychological approach to cancer care and prevention and screening of melanoma in general practice, and a series of anti-smoking videos for children. Sale only.

Central Independent Television   **Health and social issues catalogue** (1993). 27 pages. Central Independent Television plc, Video Resources Unit, Broad Street, Birmingham B1 2JP ☎ 0121-643 9898 fax 0121-616 1531.
Programmes from Central Television selected for sale to education on video. Topics include women's issues, mental health and stress. Sale.

Coventry Health Promotion Services   **VHS video list** (1994). 12 pages. Coventry Health Promotion Services, Coventry and Warwickshire Hospital, Stoney Stanton Road, Coventry CV1 4FH ☎ 01203 844092.
A title listing of a wide range of videos, slides and training packs available for hire. Titles are arranged under 36 subject headings from accident prevention to women and health, with appropriate audience levels suggested.

East London and The City Health Promotion Service   **Catalogue of video programmes** (1993). 9 pages. East London and The City Health Promotion Service, Tower Hamlets Office, Bow House, 153-

159 Bow Road, London E3 2SE ☎ 0181-983 1141.
Health education videos for use with ethnic minorities on topics such as
the importance of play, dental hygiene, head lice, diet, diabetes and HIV.
Soundtracks are in Bengali, with some additionally in Cantonese, Punjabi,
Urdu, Gujerati and Hindi, with English subtitles. Sale or preview.

Educational Media, Film & Video **Health video catalogue** (1992). 44 pages. Educational Media, Film and
Video Ltd, 235 Imperial Drive, Rayners Lane, Harrow, Middlesex HA2 7HE
☎ 0181-868 1908 fax 0181-868 1991.
A large collection of videos on all aspects of health education. Also, more
specialised programmes for medical and nursing education. Sale only.

Farley's Video Library (1992). Leaflet. Farley's Video Library, PO Box 12, Nottingham NG7 2GB
☎ 0115 942 0879.
Four videos on preparation for parenthood, covering pregnancy, birth,
and the first year after having a baby. Hire.

Health Education Authority **Resource lists.** Health Education Authority, Hamilton House, Mabledon
Place, London WC1H 9TX ☎ 0171-383 3833 fax 0171-387 0550.
Resource lists including films, videos, tape-slide sets, slide sets, and
filmstrips from various distributors. There are separate lists on alcohol
education, cancer education, child development, dental health, disability,
drugs, environmental health, exercise, family planning, food safety, foot
health, HIV and AIDS, handicap, health in old age, health, social and sex
education, heart disease, home safety, nutrition education, obesity,
occupational health, personal relationships, pregnancy, radio and
television broadcasts with health education relevance for use with young
people, relationships and sexuality, sexually transmitted infections, skills
for health educators, smoking education, towards a smoke free generation,
teaching aids for children 5-8, teaching aids for children 9-13, and health
education resources for pupils with mild and moderate learning
difficulties. Individual printed lists were updated every two or three years
until the end of 1993; when supplies of these are exhausted information
will only be available through the HEA database.

Healthcare Productions **Catalogue: videos, audiocassettes, leaflets and booklets** (1994). 73 pages.
Healthcare Productions, 2 Stucley Place, Camden Lock, London NW1 8NS
☎ 0171-267 8757 fax 0171-267 4803.
A wide range of programmes for nursing and patient education. Includes
a clinical series made for the Royal College of Nursing and three
programmes from the Royal College of Midwives. Sale only.

Healthwise Productions **Catalogue of video programmes and training packs** (1993). 12 pages.
Healthwise Productions Ltd, 9 Batley Enterprise Centre, 513 Bradford
Road, Batley, West Yorkshire WF17 8JY ☎ 01924 474374 fax 01924 479597.
Videos on quality assurance, health promotion, fostering, relationships,
hospices, and health-related topics. Sale only.

Hygia Communications (1993). Leaflets. Hygia Communications Ltd, 13 Bateman St, London
W1V 6EB ☎ 0171-734 7665 fax 0171-734 7143.
Videos on various health education issues including AIDS. Sale.

Institute for the Study of Drug Dependence
Focus on drugs: a list of audio-visual materials available in Britain (1990). 14 pages. Institute for the Study of Drug Dependence, 1 Hatton Place (off St Cross Street), London EC1N 8ND ☎ 0171-430 1993.
Films and videos on drug misuse, available for hire or sale in the UK.

Leicestershire Royal Infirmary NHS Trust
(1993). Loose-leaf catalogue. Leicestershire Royal Infirmary, Health Education Video Unit, Clinical Sciences Building, Leicester Royal Infirmary, PO Box 65, Leicester LE2 7LX ☎ 0116 255 0461 fax 0116 255 0461.
Videos on substance misuse, HIV and AIDS, coronary heart disease, prevention and early detection of cancer, basic resuscitation, and cervical cancer. Also four health education videos on smoking. Sale only.

National Eczema Society
(1993). Leaflet. National Eczema Society, 4 Tavistock Place, London WC1H 9RA ☎ 0171-388 4097 fax 0171-713 0733.
Details of the video EASE THE ITCH, available for sale from the society.

The Open University

Community education study packs (1994). 20 pages. Open University Learning Materials Sales Office, PO Box 188, Milton Keynes MK7 6DH ☎ 01908 652185 fax 01908 654320.
Details of study packs for individual or group use, with the option of having one's study assessed. Designed to help people with learning that is relevant to their everyday lives and contributes to personal development. Subjects are broadly in the areas of health and lifestyle, family and school, caring for others, community issues and action, preparing for study. Packs usually consist of workbooks, course readers, video- and/or audiocassettes.

The Open University
Educational & training opportunities (1994). 44 pages. Open University, Department of Health & Social Welfare, Walton Hall, Milton Keynes MK7 6AA ☎ 01908 653743 fax 01908 654124.
Includes details of study packs suitable for individual study and in-service or college-based training but which do not lead to Open University awards. Subject areas include working and living with children and young people, ageing, disability, health studies, and social welfare.

Plymouth Medical Films
(1993). Leaflets. Plymouth Medical Films, The Barbican, 33 New Street, Plymouth PL1 2NA ☎ 01752 267711 fax 01752 222183.
Videos on language acquisition and reading, drugs and alcohol education, cancer, infant immunisations, healthy eating in later life, and a teenager's experience of being in hospital. Sale only.

Schering Health Care
List of videos (1994). 10 pages. Schering Health Care Ltd, Public Relations Department, The Brow, Burgess Hill, West Sussex RH15 9NE ☎ 01444 232323 fax 01444 244613.
Educational and promotional videos on topics including contraception, the menopause and hormone replacement therapy, diagnostic techniques, and other medical subjects. Free loan.

Scottish Health Education Group
Health education films and videos (1989 + supplements). 55 pages. SCFVL, Dowanhill, 74 Victoria Crescent Road, Glasgow G12 9JN ☎ 0141-334 9314 fax 0141-334 6519.
Films and videos for health education. Hire only.

Sickle Cell Society **Publications list** (1993). 2 pages. Sickle Cell Society, 54 Station Road, London NW10 4AU ☎ 0181-961 7765 fax 0181-961 8346.
Two videos on sickle cell anaemia. Sale only.

SMA Nutrition **Film and video catalogue** (1993). 12 pages. SMA Nutrition, Huntercombe Lane South, Taplow, Maidenhead, Berkshire SL6 0PH ☎ 01628 660633.
Videos on breast feeding, bottle feeding, weaning, cow's milk intolerance and related topics. Free loan for medical and health education purposes.

The Spastics Society **Video Library** (1993). Leaflet. Scope, Education Distribution Service, Unit 2, Drywall Estate, Castle Road, Murston, Sittingbourne, Kent ☎ 01795 427614 fax 01795 474871.
Four videos describing the society's work and aims, disability awareness, the introduction of primary and junior school children to physical disability, and antenatal care. Free loan.

The Stroke Association **Publications list** (1993). 8 pages. The Stroke Association, CHSA House, Whitecross Street, London EC1Y 8JJ ☎ 0171-490 7999 fax 0171-490 2686.
Videos on the experience of stroke, including the care of stroke patients. Hire and sale.

Teaching Aids at Low Cost **Books, slides and accessories lists** (1994). 20 pages. TALC, PO Box 49, St Albans AL1 4AX ☎ 01727 53869 fax 01727 46852.
Slide sets and two videos of a practical nature, aimed at raising standards of health care, particularly in developing countries. New items are mentioned in a regular newsletter. Sale only.

UCL Images (1994). UCL Images, University College London, 48 Riding House Street, London W1P 7PL ☎ 0171 380 9375 fax 071-580 0995.
Videos on the prevention of heart disease, the psychological preparation for heart surgery, and the removal of superficial lumps. Sale.

Video Reportage Productions (1993). Leaflets. Video Reportage Productions, 20 West Parade, Norwich NR2 3DW ☎ 01603 613879.
Details of the Kirin Davids child studies and family life videos. Sale.

Viewtech **Health and guidance film & video catalogue** (1991). 36 pages. Viewtech Film & Video, 161 Winchester Road, Brislington, Bristol BS4 3NJ ☎ 0117 977 3422 fax 0117 972 4292.
Films and videos mainly from the USA and Australia, on health education and personal development topics. Also programmes on sexual abuse, overcoming handicaps, human biology and cell biology. Hire or sale.

History and Politics (see also archaeology, community studies, development studies, military science, social sciences and under names of individual countries)

Attica Cybernetics **Multimedia CD-ROM catalogue** (1994). 17 pages. Attica Cybernetics Ltd, Unit 2, Kings Meadow, Ferry Hinksey Road, Oxford OX2 0DP ☎ 01865 791346 fax 01865 794561.
PC-based multimedia CD-ROMs including the HUTCHINSON ENCYCLOPAEDIA, THE EUROPEAN VIDEO ATLAS (with footage from ITN News), plant science, mammalian biology, the interactive periodic

table, and World War II archives (using footage and other material from the Imperial War Museum and the BBC). Sale.

The British Library   **New publications for schools** (1994). Leaflet. British Library Education Service, Great Russell Street, London WC1B 3DG ☎ 0171-323 7783. Includes CD-ROMs on inventors and inventions, British birds and medieval realms, which incorporate images, full-motion video, animation and audio commentary, designed for use in schools. Also audiocassette packs of oral history with supporting notes on survivors of the Holocaust and on the history of the steel industry. Sale.

British Universities Film & Video Council   **Postwar British history: a select list of videos and films available in the UK** (1988). 52 pages. Price £9.00. BUFVC, 55 Greek Street, London W1V 5LR ☎ 0171-734 3687 fax 0171-287 3914.

Published jointly with the Institute of Contemporary British History to encourage the study of politics and history of the period, this catalogue contains over 500 currently available films and videos from various sources selected for courses ranging from GCSE through undergraduate level.

Campaign for Press and Broadcasting Freedom   **Union views** (1990). 34 pages. Price £5.00. Campaign for Press and Broadcasting Freedom, 96 Dalston Lane, London E8 1NG ☎ 0171-923 3671. Some 300 videos either commissioned by trade unions, or about labour and union issues, available from a variety of sources. They are indexed by subject, e.g. privatisation, employment law, and by union.

Castle Communications   **International programme catalogue** (1994). 56 pages. Castle Communications, A29 Barwell Business Park, Leatherhead Road, Chessington, Surrey KT9 2NY ☎ 0181-974 1021 fax 0181-974 2674. A range of videos available for sale through retail outlets. Many programmes use archive footage, particularly those on World War II and Russian history. Other series deal with military campaigns in history, including Viking wars, Zulu wars and Agincourt, and with great figures from history, e.g. Boudicca, Alfred the Great, Henry VIII – all very much geared to the National Curriculum.

Central Independent Television   **History, politics and current affairs catalogue** (1993). 23 pages. Central Independent Television plc, Video Resources Unit, Broad Street, Birmingham B1 2JP ☎ 0121-643 9898 fax 0121-616 1531. Programmes from Central Television's broadcast output selected for sale to education on video. Topics include colonialism, civil rights, future history, traditional societies, as well as the history of particular countries and periods.

DD Video   **Video Collection** (1993). Leaflets. DD Video, 5 Churchill Court, 58 Station Road, North Harrow, Middlesex HA2 7SA ☎ 0181-863 8819 fax 0181-863 0463. Hundreds of videos for sale direct or through retail outlets, concentrating mainly on war and aviation history, but also covering motor and other sports, tourism, and hobbies.

Despite TV   **Tape catalogue** (1993). 10 pages. Despite TV, 113 Roman Road, London E2 0HU ☎ 0181-983 4278. A series of video magazines produced by this East London video co-operative, dealing with local political issues, music and events. Also single subject programmes on the News International move to Wapping, a campaign against Clause 28, Docklands development, and an alternative view of the anti-poll-tax demonstration of March 1990. Hire or sale.

East Anglian Film Archive

Videos you can buy (1990). Leaflet. East Anglian Film Archive, Centre for East Anglian Studies, University of East Anglia, Norwich NR4 7IJ ☎ 01603 592664 fax 01603 58553.
A selection of films from the archive transferred to video. Subjects include industrial archaeology, farming, the seaside, the city of Norwich, transport, rural life, industry and crafts. Sale only.

Educational & Television Films

(1986-89, current 1994). Various catalogues. Educational & Television Films Ltd, 247a Upper Street, London N1 1RU ☎ 0171-226 2298 fax 0171-226 8016. Films from Eastern Europe, China, the former USSR, Latin America and other countries, relating to their culture, history and politics. Hire and sale.

Film Archive Management & Entertainment

Films from FAME (1994). 10 pages. FAME, PO Box 608, Hailsham, Sussex BN27 3UN ☎ 01323 849186 fax 01323 840757.
Videos of classic films from British Transport Films, Inland Waterways, British Railways, London Underground and other sources dating from the 1930s onwards, showing aspects of transport and life in Britain. Sale only.

GMH Entertainments

Video title list (1994). Leaflet. GMH Entertainments, 19-23 Manasty Road, Orton Southgate, Peterborough PE2 0UP ☎ 01733 233464 fax 01733 238966. Title listing of videos on the history of war, many using original archive footage. Sale by mail order.

Hulton Deutsch Collection

(1994). Leaflets. Hulton Deutsch Collection Ltd, Unique House, 21-31 Woodfield Road, London W9 2BA ☎ 0171-266 2662 fax 0171-289 6392.
A series of CD-ROMs entitled DECADES covering the 1920s to the 1960s, with some 10,000 images from the Hulton Deutsch photographic archive. An additional PEOPLE disc contains 10,000 images of over 4000 contemporary and historical personalities. Images can be searched by keyword, name or date, and high-resolution copies of all the pictures can be obtained for commercial use.

Imperial War Museum

Film and video loans (1990). 32 pages. Imperial War Museum, Department of Film, Lambeth Road, London SE1 6HZ ☎ 0171-416 5290 fax 0171-416 5379. Actuality film relating to conflict in the 20th century from Britain and other countries. Public and educational programmes are screened in the museum's cinema; specialist groups and individual researchers may be accommodated by appointment. 16mm film and video loans are available to higher education institutions for teaching purposes. Some titles are available for sale on video.

InterUniversity History Film Consortium

Film and video material compiled by the IUHFC (1993). Leaflet. IUHFC, BUFVC, 55 Greek Street, London W1V 5LR ☎ 0171-734 3687 fax 0171-287 3914. Two series of compilation films dealing with major topics of 20th-century history, made using contemporary archival, documentary and feature film from British and foreign archives. Subjects in the BRITISH UNIVERSITIES

HISTORICAL STUDIES IN FILM series include the Munich Crisis, the Spanish Civil War, the Great Depression, Fascism, and rearmament in the 1930s. The ARCHIVE SERIES covers Neville Chamberlain, the origins of the Cold War, Stanley Baldwin, the Korean War, and relations with France 1938-40. Hire and sale on film, sale only on video.

Metro Pictures **Film & video catalogue** (1989 + supplements). 92 pages. Metro Pictures, 79 Wardour Street, London WIV 3TH ☎ 0171-434 3357 fax 0171-287 2112. Shorts, feature films and documentaries on development, environment, the nuclear debate, history, human rights, gay liberation, media and education, racial issues, trade unions and labour studies, and women in society. Hire on 35mm and 16mm film.

Museum of London **Audio-visual materials** (1993). Letter. Museum of London, Museum Shop, London Wall, London EC2Y 5HN ☎ 0171-600 3699 fax 0171-600 1058. A video about the suffragette movement, and an audiocassette-based education pack concerned with a Jewish woman's experiences of emigrating to London. Sale only.

National Maritime Museum **Publications for schools** (1993). Leaflet. National Maritime Museum, Greenwich, London SE10 9NF ☎ 0181-858 4422 fax 0181-312 6632. Videos on sea power and shipwrecks and a video-based pack entitled LEARNING THROUGH UNDERWATER ARCHAEOLOGY. Sale only.

North West Film Archive (1987-93). Leaflets. North West Film Archive, Manchester Metropolitan University, Minshull House, 47-49 Chorlton Street, Manchester M1 3EU ☎ 0161-247 3097 fax 0161-247 3098. Details of teachers' resource packs and the ongoing MOVING MEMORIES video compilation series of archive films featuring popular traditions and special days. Sale only.

Northern Film and Television Archive **Catalogue of films and videotapes produced during the 1984-5 miners' strike** (1986). 32 pages. Northern Film and Television Archive, 36 Bottle Bank, Gateshead, Tyne and Wear NE8 2AR ☎ 0191-477 3601 fax 0191-478 3681. A selection from the archive's collection of independently produced films on the 1984-5 miners' strike, available on video. Topics include miners' wives' support groups, the role of the police and law courts, pit closures, energy policy, and media representation. Hire and sale.

Past Forward **The World of the Vikings** (1993). Leaflets. Past Forward, 1 Pavement, York YO1 2NA ☎ 01904 670825 fax 01904 640029. As part of the Cultural Roots Project of the Council of Europe, Past Forward has produced videodisc and CD-ROM versions of THE WORLD OF THE VIKINGS specially designed for National Curriculum use. The Romans are the subject of a second project currently in production in this multimedia series on European history. Sale.

Platform Films **Videos** (1993). Leaflets. Platform Films, 13 Tankerton House, Tankerton Street, London WC1H 8HP ☎ 0171-278 8394. Several programmes originally produced for television. Topics include a series on 20th-century British history. Sale only.

The Post Office   **Film & video catalogue** (1995). 40 pages. The Post Office Film and Video Library, PO Box 145, Sittingbourne, Kent ME10 1NH
☎ 01795 426465 fax 01795 474871.
Programmes on the postal system, stamps and stamp collecting available on free loan or for sale. Video compilations of the classic films made by the GPO Film Unit between 1934 and 1941 are also listed.

Relay Europe   **Video list** (1994). Leaflet. Relay Europe Ltd, Enterprise Centre, 112 Malling Street, Lewes, East Sussex BN7 2RJ ☎ 01273 488666 fax 01273 488448.
A range of videos sponsored by the Commission of the European Communities on various aspects of the European Community. Free loan.

Scottish Archive Film for Education   (1989). Leaflet. SAFE, Scottish Film Council, 74 Victoria Crescent Road, Glasgow G12 9JN ☎ 0141-334 9314 fax 0141-334 6519.
Compilations of extracts from films in the Scottish Film Archive on themes such as transport, architecture, industry, fishing, rural society, cities, and social history. Hire or sale on video.

W H Smith   **Videos** (1993 + updates). Leaflets from W H Smith shops.
Information on the latest general releases on video, and details of W H Smith exclusive titles. Many of these are educational, particularly in the field of history, and some use archive footage. The CAMPAIGNS IN HISTORY series on the Civil War, Zulu wars, Waterloo, Trafalgar and Balaclava, uses reconstructions, re-enactments, period paintings and computer-mapping techniques. Sale only.

The Studio   **History Down Your Street** (1993). 2 pages. The Studio, Saltwells Education Centre, Bowling Green Road, Netherton, Dudley, West Midlands DY2 9LY
☎ 01384 634155 fax 01834 410436.
Press release about the first programme in the series HISTORY DOWN YOUR STREET, which relates the stories of ordinary people whose actions played a key role in shaping historical events.

Television History Centre   **Video leaflets** (1993). Leaflets. Television History Centre, 42 Queen Square, London WC1N 3AJ ☎ 0171-405 6627 fax 0171-242 1426.
Videos on topics in 20th-century social history, featuring first-hand accounts from the people involved. Subjects include car making at Cowley, hospitals, women and politics, the Brixton disturbances, mining in South Wales, the history of contraception, the effects of recent changes in the educational system, and pacifism. Hire and sale.

University of London, Institute of Historical Research   **Interviews with historians** (1993). Leaflet. University of London, Institute of Historical Research, Senate House, Malet Street, London WC1E 7HU
☎ 0171-636 0272 fax 0171-436 2183.
Video recordings of younger colleagues interviewing leading historians in the same field about their life, work and beliefs. Features Hugh Clegg, Geoffrey Dickens, Geoffrey Elton, Moses Finley, Margaret Gowing, Christopher Hill, Rodney Hilton, Eric Hobsbawm, Peter Laslett, Joseph Needham, Henry Pelling, Lawrence Stone, Joan Thirsk, Asa Briggs, Edward Thompson and Hugh Trevor Roper. Further videos are in preparation. Suitable for sixth form or university level. Sale.

Video Rights (1994). Leaflets. Video Rights Ltd, Suites 415-416, Premier House, 77 Oxford Street, London W1R 1RB ☎ 0171-439 1188 fax 0171-734 8367.
A distributor of videos for the retail market. Programmes include the English Shakespeare Company's WARS OF THE ROSES cycle, a series of documentaries on World War II using footage from the Soviet War Archive, and a collection of silent film classics. Sale through retail outlets.

Viewtech **Humanities catalogue** (1994). 38 pages. Viewtech Film & Video, 161 Winchester Road, Brislington, Bristol BS4 3NJ
☎ 0117 977 3422 fax 0117 972 4292.
A selection of programmes from the main Viewtech catalogue in the area of humanities, covering geography, ancient civilisations, history, explorations and discovery, the 20th century, history of technology and religious studies. Sale only.

Workers Film Association **Video and film distribution catalogue** (1989 + supplements). 36 pages. Price £1.00. Workers Film Association, 9 Lucy Street, Manchester M15 4BX
☎ 0161-848 9782 fax 0161-848 9783.
Films from various countries dealing with the economic, cultural, social and political problems of the worker. Hire only on film; hire and sale on video.

Worldwide Television News **Roving Report 1967-92** (1994). 684 pages. WTN, The Library Manager, The Interchange, Oval Road, London NW1 7EP ☎ 0171-410 5270 fax 0171-413 8327.
Catalogue of WTN's ROVING REPORTS covering major events and personalities as well as science, technology, environment, lifestyles and human-interest subjects. Entries are arranged by date and carry shot lists together with descriptions. Indexed by subject, name and country. Sale only.

Other useful catalogues:
Lancaster University Television (Literature)

Hotels and Catering (see also health education, health & safety)

Educational Broadcasting Services Trust **Skillbank video learning resources** (1994). 25 pages. Educational Broadcasting Services Trust, 36-38 Mortimer Street, London W1N 7RB
☎ 0171-765 5714 fax 0171-580 6246.
A project supported by a consortium of further and higher education colleges, the Employment Department, the Further Education Unit and the National Council for Vocational Qualifications, aiming to provide 200 videos for skills training across the industrial and commercial sectors. Videos produced so far are in the areas of plumbing, catering, caring, construction, electrical installation, interpersonal skills, and basic technology skills. Sale.

Hotel & Catering Training Company **A catalogue of books, videos, training packages and self-study workbooks to support work-based and college training** (1993). 23 pages. Hotel and Catering Training Company, International House, High Street, Ealing, London W5 4DB ☎ 0181-579 2400 fax 0181-840 6217.
Includes videos on food and drink preparation and service, health and safety, hygiene and customer relations. Hire through CFL Vision or sale direct.

Waldegrave Films **Programme list** (1994). Leaflets. Waldegrave Films, 70 Radnor Road, Twickenham, Middlesex TW1 4ND ☎ 0181-892 0078.
Videos on health and safety in the food manufacturing and catering industries, and also on food hygiene. Hire or sale.

India

High Commission of India **Catalogue of Indian documentary films on video** (1993). 4 pages. High Commission of India, Press & Information Wing, India House, London WC2B 4NA ☎ 0171-836 8484 ext. 147.
List of 52 videos on the life and culture of India. Free loan.

High Commission of India **Catalogue of Indian television programmes on video** (1992). 20 pages. High Commission of India, Press & Information Wing, India House, London WC2B 4NA ☎ 0171-836 8484 ext. 147.
Some 200 INDIA MAGAZINE programmes on the life and culture of India. Free loan.

Information Technology (see also computer skills training, electrical & electronic engineering, management & training, science & technology)

AIM Europe **Video catalogue** (1994). Leaflet. AIM Europe, The Old Vicarage, Hagley Hall, Halifax HX3 6DR ☎ 01422 368368 fax 01422 355604.
Videos on automatic identification and data collection, which explain, demonstrate and promote automatic data capture. Sale only.

Applied Learning **Multimedia training** (1994). Leaflets. Applied Learning, 1 Hogarth Business Park, Burlington Lane, London W4 2TJ ☎ 0181-994 4404 fax 0181-944 4404.
Video, CD-ROM, and computer-based training courses on topics relating to information technology, management skills, software training, and human resource development. Sale.

Aston University, Continuing Education Service **Video Courses in Industry Unit** (1992). Loose-leaf catalogue. Aston University, Continuing Education Service, Birmingham B4 7ET ☎ 0121-359 3611 ext. 4342 fax 0121-359 6427.
Some 56 video courses in microelectronics and information technology produced under the Department of Trade and Industry initiative co-ordinated at the university. Sale only.

Auriga **The fibre optic component & accessory catalogue** (1994). 225 pages. Auriga, Third Avenue, The Avant Business Centre, Denbigh West, Bletchley, Milton Keynes MK1 1DR ☎ 01908 274200 fax 01908 378998.
Includes a series of six Canadian videos with supporting workbooks on introducing fibre optics, planning and installing a fibre optic link, fibre loss testing, OTDR principles and operation, and fibre troubleshooting. Sale only.

BT Education Service **Educational resources catalogue** (1993). 24 pages. BT Education Service, BT Centre, 81 Newgate Street, London EC1A 7AJ ☎ 01800 622302.
Includes videos and computer software on telecommunications topics. Subjects of videos include how the telephone works, radio communications, pulse code modulation, satellite communications, the physics of optical communications, and satellites in education. Free loan and sale.

Comput-Ed **A catalogue of computer-based training and videos for business and education** (1993). 20 pages. Comput-Ed Ltd, Long Lane, Dawlish EX7 0QR ☎ 01703 455555 fax 01703 455544.
Video- and computer-based training programmes on management topics, concentrating on training in computing and information technology. Also, a CD-ROM entitled PROFESSOR MULTIMEDIA showing how to create a multimedia presentation. A more detailed catalogue giving a description of each programme is available free on disk.

Deja View Video **Marketing electronic information** (1994). Leaflet. Deja View Video 417 South El Dorado Street, San Mateo, CA 94402, USA ☎ +1 415 343 8899 fax +1 415 343 8974.
An eight-part series of videos on how to market electronic information on the Internet. For sale to UK customers on PAL-standard videocassettes.

Institute of Electrical and Electronic Engineers **IEEE catalogue** (1994). 128 pages. IEEE Customer Service Department, 445 Hoes Lane, PO Box 1331, Piscataway, NJ 08855-1331, USA ☎ +1 908 981 0060 fax +1 908 981 9667.
Videoconferences with experts discussing critical topics in computing, electronics and biomedical engineering. Originally broadcast live in the USA via satellite, they provide state-of-the-art information, emphasising practice rather than theory. Other series include short practical courses and video tutorials. For sale to UK customers on PAL-standard videocassette, individually or by subscription.

Look Multimedia **IT management video series** (1994). Leaflets. Look Multimedia Ltd, 1 Mortimer Street, London W1N 7RH ☎ 0171-255 2670 fax 0171-255 1995.
Videos on management issues in information technology, using interviews and location filming. Topics include outsourcing, business process re-engineering, systems integration, right-sizing, open systems, client-server computing, and building client-server systems. Sale.

Meckler **CD-ROMs in print** (1994). 1188 pages. Price £65.00 (print), £62.50/year (CD-ROM). Meckler, 4th Floor, Artillery House, Artillery Row, London SW1P 1RT ☎ 0171-976 0405 fax 0171-976 0506.
An international listing of 6000 CD-ROM products arranged alphabetically by title, with subject and country indexes. Each main entry includes hardware requirements, search software, networking information, update frequency and price. Also contains a company directory, an index for Macintosh-based titles, and another for both DOS and Macintosh platforms. Published annually in printed form and bi-annually on CD-ROM.

National Council for Educational Technology **IT resources for further education and training, IT resources for primary and secondary schools, IT resources for special educational needs** (1994). 13, 29, 13 pages. NCET, Milburn Hill Road, Science Park, Coventry CV4 7JJ ☎ 01203 416994 fax 01203 411418.
Catalogues include video-based packages for in-service teacher training in the use of information technology.

Taylor Made Films **Video lists** (1993). Leaflets. Taylor Made Films, PO Box 169, Horsham, West Sussex RH13 5YL ☎ 01403 242727 fax 01403 261555.

A video series HOW TO GET IT RIGHT IN BUSINESS, made for *Computer Weekly* in collaboration with the Department of Trade and Industry, explains the implications of information technology for business; and two series of THE SUNDAY TIMES BUSINESS VIDEO SERIES provide an introduction to the basics of computers with real-life examples of business applications. Sale.

TFPL Publishing

The CD-ROM directory (1994). 1100 pages. Price £95.00 (print), £125.00/year (CD-ROM). TFPL Publishing, 17-18 Britton Street, London EC1M 5NQ
☎ 0171-251 5522 fax 0171-251 8318.
An international guide to some 6000 CD-ROM and multimedia CD titles. Includes production company profiles and information on hardware and software. Published annually in printed form and bi-annually on CD-ROM.

UMC Sales and Marketing

Video list (1993). 6 pages. UMC Sales and Marketing, The Old Rectory, High Street, Bury, Huntingdon, Cambridgeshire PE17 1NL
☎ 01487 815300 fax 01487 710270.
Includes videos on microcomputers, business software, networks, data communications, and the Pick operating system. Sale only.

University Video Communications

Distinguished lecture series (1993 + updates). Leaflets. University Video Communications, PO Box 2666, Stanford, CA 94309, USA
☎ +1 415 327 0131 fax +1 415 813 1315.
Three series of lectures by acknowledged experts in the fields of computer science and electrical engineering. Topics include platforms, programming environments, theoretical computer science, communications, microelectronics, computer vision, RISC architecture and parallelism. For sale to UK customers on PAL-standard videocassette.

Italian Studies (see also languages, media studies, feature films)

Italian Institute

Video library list (1993). 16 pages. Italian Institute, Audio Visual Department, 39 Belgrave Square, London SW1X 8NX
☎ 0171-235 1461 fax 0171-235 4618.
A selection of videos on U-matic and VHS cassette available on free loan to educational and cultural institutions, covering a range of topics including history, arts, language teaching, literature, drama, politics, science, sport, tourism and biography.

Other useful catalogues:
Icarus (Architecture)

Japan (see also economics)

Education Matters!

Video letter from Japan (1994). Leaflet. Education Matters!, 29 High Street, Halberton, Tiverton, Devon EX16 7AF ☎ 01884 820081 fax 01884 820081.
Two series of videos showing Japanese life as seen through the eyes of the Japanese. The first is aimed at primary and secondary school pupils, and the second, JAPAN INTO THE NINETIES, is issue-based and intended for more senior students. Sale only.

Japan Foundation **Film and video library list** (1993). 21 pages. Japan Foundation, 17 Old Park Lane, London W1Y 3LG ☎ 0171-499 4726 fax 0171-495 1133.
Films and videos on Japanese life, art and culture. Subjects include archaeology, architecture and gardens, arts and crafts – ceramics, kites, lacquer, painting, paper, textiles, wood, and woodblock – contemporary society, dance, education, festivals, history, ikebana, music, natural history, performing arts, poetry, and sport. Free loan for films; videos must be viewed on the premises.

Japan Information and Cultural Centre **VHS video list** (1993). 45 pages. Japan Information and Cultural Centre, Embassy of Japan, 101-104 Piccadilly, London W1V 9FN ☎ 0171-465 6500 fax 0171-491 9347.
A wide range of videos about the Japanese people and aspects of Japanese life and culture. Topics include agriculture, business, culture, current affairs, education, technology, medical care, and transportation. Free loan.

Languages (see also french studies, german studies, italian studies, media studies: feature films, spanish studies)

Academy Television now trading as YITM **CD-ROM multimedia packages** (1993). Leaflets. Academy Television, Kirkstall Road, Leeds LS3 1JS ☎ 0113 246 1528 fax 0113 242 9522.
Five interactive CD-ROMs produced by Yorkshire Television in conjunction with Interactive Learning Productions, designed for use in education. Each package contains a CD-ROM, floppy disk, and teacher and pupil workbooks. Subjects are French, Spanish, the environment, science, and inventors and inventions. Available for Acorn Archimedes and PC with Windows 3.1.

Audio-Forum **The whole world language catalogue** (1994). 39 pages. Audio-Forum, c/o Sussex Publications, Microworld House, 2-6 Foscote Mews, London W9 2HH ☎ 0171-266 2202 fax 0171-266 2314.
Lists 238 audiocassette courses supported by texts covering 86 languages. Most full-length courses were developed by the US State Department's Foreign Service Institute. A number of foreign-language videos are also available, some in the PAL system, but most are NTSC. Sale only.

BBC English **Catalogue** (1994). Leaflets. BBC English, Bush House, The Strand, PO Box 76, London WC2B 4PH ☎ 0171-257 2851 fax 0171-430 1985.
Video and audio courses with written support materials for teaching English at beginner, intermediate and advanced levels. Separate leaflets are available listing materials for young learners, adults and young adults, and international business. Sale only.

The British Council **Publications catalogue** (1993). 52 pages. British Council, Press and Public Relations Department, 10 Spring Gardens, London SW1A 2BN ☎ 0171-389 4875 fax 0171-389 4971.
Includes a number of computer software programs and courses on audiocassette and videocassette for English language teaching. Sale only.

Cambridge University Press **Video profiles** (1993). Leaflet. Cambridge University Press, Educational Marketing Department, The Edinburgh Building, Cambridge CB2 2RU ☎ 01223 312393 fax 01223 315052.

A series of videos about young people who live in either France, Germany and Spain, designed for teaching the language and culture to 15-18-year-old pupils. Programmes accompanied by transcripts and glossaries. Sale.

Drake Educational Associates   **Modern languages catalogue** (1994). 36 pages. Drake Educational Associates, St Fagans Road, Fairwater, Cardiff CF5 3AE ☎ 01222 560333 fax 01222 554909. Audiocassettes produced by the Language Centre at the University of Exeter for teaching a wide range of modern languages up to GCSE and A level. Sale only.

Glenbuck Films   **Foreign language films** (1987-92). Loose-leaf catalogue. Glenbuck Films Ltd, 21 Stephen Street, London W1P 1PL ☎ 0171-957 8938 fax 0171-580 5830. Classic feature films from around the world. Hire only.

Grant & Cutler   **Catalogue** (1994). 350 pages. Grant & Cutler Ltd, 55-57 Great Marlborough Street, London W1V 2AY ☎ 0171-734 2012 fax 0171-734 9272.
Mainly publications for the teaching of French, German, Spanish, Italian and Portuguese, but a number of videos are included for use in language teaching. Also videos of feature film adaptations of literary works in the original language. A separate list covers French feature films on video. Sale only.

Guildsoft   **Catalogue** (1994). 32 pages. Guildsoft Ltd, The Computer Complex, City Business Park, Stoke, Plymouth PL3 4BB ☎ 01752 895100 fax 01752 894833. Computer software and CD-ROMs for education and business. Includes language-teaching programs on which the voice can be recorded and compared to native speakers. Sale.

Longman ELT   (1994). Leaflet. Longman ELT, Longman House, Burnt Mill, Harlow, Essex CM20 2JE ☎ 01279 623927 fax 01279 623795.
The LONGMAN INTERACTIVE ENGLISH DICTIONARY is a CD-ROM incorporating audio pronunciation, video, colour pictures and an 80,000-word dictionary. The LONGMAN ENGLISH WORKS is a CD-ROM-based package of self-study material for adult learners. Sale.

Macmillan   **Breakthrough languages** (1994). Leaflet. The Macmillan Press Ltd, Houndmills, Basingstoke, Hampshire RG21 2XS
☎ 01256 29242 fax 01256 28339.
The *Breakthrough* language series, covering beginner, intermediate and business levels, are complete language courses with a video element which may be purchased separately. The programmes, covering German, French and Spanish, use native speakers to make the sights and sounds of the various countries come alive. Sale. Macmillan also sells the *Harrap Shorter Dictionary* on disk or CD-ROM.

Multimedia Communication   **Catalogue of products** (1992). Leaflets. Multimedia Communication Ltd, 4 Downing Street, Farnham, Surrey GU9 7PA ☎ 01252 722707 fax 01252 710220.
A series entitled CD-LANGUES for teaching German, French, Spanish and English as a foreign language, which uses a combination of text, graphics and compact disc quality sound. Intended for those who already have a basic knowledge of the language. Sale.

Oxford University Press   **English Language Teaching: video catalogue** (1993). 16 pages. Oxford University Press, ELT Promotions, Walton Street, Oxford OX2 6DP ☎ 01865 56767 fax 01865 56646.
Video-based courses, usually with written and audio components, for teaching English at all levels, including business use. Two specialist series use news bulletin compilations and another teaches North-American English. Sale only.

Premiere Productions   **Interactive video training programmes** (1994). Leaflets. Premiere Productions, 16 Castello Avenue, London SW15 6EA ☎ 0181-785 2933 fax 0181-780 1684.
Includes interactive video programmes for language learning. Sale.

Other useful catalogues:
Longman Training (Management and Training)
J Whiting Books (Arts)

Law (see also philosophy, religion & ethics)

The Children's Society   **Video collection** (1994). 6 pages. The Children's Society, Public Relations Department, Edward Rudolf House, Margery Street, London WC1X 0JL ☎ 0171-837 4299 fax 0171-837 0211.
Videos on the work of the society covering adoption, Portage learning, runaway children, and the *guardian ad litem* role as strengthened by the 1989 Children Act. Hire or sale.

The Patent Office   **Video guides** (1993). Leaflets. The Patent Office, Marketing and Publicity Directorate, Room 1L02, Concept House, Cardiff Road, Newport, Gwent NP9 1RH ☎ 01633 813535 fax 01633 813600.
Leaflet about THE BOY'S A GENIUS, a video explaining the practical application of intellectual property rights. Also, a compilation video consisting of programmes on how to register a design, how to register a trade or service mark, and what trade marks are. Sale.

Television Education Network   (1993). Leaflet. Television Education Network Ltd, 15-17 Jockey's Fields, London WC1R 4BW ☎ 0171-753 8760 fax 0171-753 8761.
The Lawyers' Education Channel operates as a subscription service for practising lawyers. Each month a video with accompanying documentation is sent to subscribers. Tapes contain a number of 20-30 minute programmes consisting of news stories and current case law developments in the appropriate area of law, and the implications for professional practice are then discussed through interviews with experts.

20th Century Security Education   (1994). 45 pages. 20th Century Security, 274 Kingston Road, Leatherhead, Surrey KT22 7NJ ☎ 01372 374505 fax 01372 377161.
American-produced programmes on security, both of persons and property, including items on bomb threats, burglary, crisis intervention, interviewing, communication, child abuse, crime prevention, and substance abuse. Sale on video; some titles may be hired on 16mm film.

Other useful catalogues:
Campaign for Press and Broadcasting Freedom
(Social Sciences)

Library Studies (see also information technology)

Binder Vision **Videomagazine** (1993). Leaflet. Binder Vision, PO Box 146, Sevenoaks, Kent TN13 3BU ☎ 01732 454153 fax 01732 462951.
Leaflet about the quarterly magazine programme for bookbinders, collectors, archivists and conservators, which is available by subscription. Includes demonstrations of historic and modern techniques, interviews with binders and collectors, visits to important collections, and working private presses. Individual videos relating to book restoration and conservation are also available for sale.

Cable Crouch Productions (1994). Leaflet. Cable Crouch Productions Ltd, PO Box 146, Sevenoaks, Kent TN13 3BU ☎ 01732 460006.
A video showing how the Public Record Office goes about handling and preserving books, documents, photographs, textiles, film and recorded tapes, and coins and medals. Intended for home use and archivists. Sale only.

British words on cassette (2nd edition 1992). 173 pages. Price £25.00.

Literature (see also arts, drama, media studies: feature films)

Bowker-Saur Bowker-Saur, Maypole House, Maypole Road, East Grinstead, West Sussex RH19 1HH ☎ 01342 330100 fax 01342 330191.
Lists over 5000 spoken word audiocassettes available for hire or sale from many sources in the UK. Includes dramatic performances, novels, poetry readings, lectures and interviews, with full publisher and distributor information, and author and subject indexes.

British Universities Film & Video Council

As you like it: audio-visual Shakespeare (1992). 115 pages. Price £13.95.
BUFVC, 55 Greek Street, London WIV 5LR ☎ 0171-734 3687 fax 0171-287 3914.
A comprehensive catalogue of 550 programmes (videos, films, slide sets, audiocassettes, computer programs, videodiscs) available for hire or sale in the UK from 100 different distributors. Includes classic and recent feature films from various countries, recordings of stage and student productions, musical and ballet versions, as well as spin-offs and derivatives. Contains credits and synopses and is prefaced with articles addressing practicalities and issues relevant to the use of video and film in teaching Shakespeare.

T C Farries **Fiction audio cassettes** (1994). 247 pages. T C Farries & Co. Ltd, Irongray Road, Lochside, Dumfries DG2 0LH ☎ 01387 720755 fax 01387 721105.
Details of thousands of fiction audiocassettes, from hundreds of sources, for supply to libraries, schools, colleges and other educational establishments, and to individuals in the UK and overseas. Supplementary lists are issued regularly. Sale.

Green Dragon Audio Visual (1994). Green Dragon Audio Visual, St George's House, 29 St James's Road, Dudley, West Midlands DY1 3JD ☎ 01384 457669 fax 01384 455443.
Suppliers of audio-visual materials to libraries, with cataloguing and processing facilities.

Grey Suit **Video for art and literature** (1994). Leaflet. Grey Suit, 21 Augusta Street, Adamstown, Cardiff CF2 1EN ☎ 01222 489565 fax 01222 489565.
A quarterly hour-long video magazine for art and literature, containing

works by poets, performers, film-makers and video artists from around the world. There is also a critic's space called 'the tirade' where unorthodox opinions may be articulated. The tape also carries some archive material – work that is currently unavailable or is no longer being performed. Available by subscription only.

Institute of Contemporary Arts   **Video catalogue** (1989 + supplements). 38 pages. ICA Video, The Mall, London SW1Y 5AH ☎ 0171-930 0493 fax 0171-873 0051.
WRITERS IN CONVERSATION is a series of videos of writers talking about their life and work to other well-known writers and critics, recorded at events held at the ICA. Sale only.

Lancaster University Television   **Medieval videos** (1993). Leaflet. Lancaster University Television, University of Lancaster, Lancaster LA1 4YW ☎ 01524 65201 fax 01524 843087.
Five videos of performances of medieval plays and one programme on *The Bestiary* from the Bodleian Library.

Norwich Tapes   **The Critical Forum and the English Resource** (1993). 8 pages. Norwich Tapes Ltd, 10 West Street, Buckingham MK18 1HL ☎ 01424 63267.
Audiocassettes featuring academics from British universities lecturing on major works of literature, and poets and novelists reading from and talking about their work. Also recorded lectures on Chaucer and Shakespeare and a series of readings from Chaucer. Sale only.

The Poetry Library   **Audio-visual collection: items for loan** (1994). Loose-leaf catalogue. The Poetry Library, Level 5, Red Side, Royal Festival Hall, London SE1 8XX ☎ 0171-921 0943 fax 0171-921 0939
A collection of audiocassettes, records and videos of poetry readings programmes about poets. The materials are available for loan but must be collected and returned in person.

Trumedia   **Video and audio resources** (1993 + updates). Leaflets. Trumedia Ltd, PO Box 374, Headington, Oxford OX3 7NT ☎ 01865 63097 fax 01865 63097.

A wide range of videos selected for their relevance to the National Curriculum. Separate leaflets cover history and politics, science and technology, foreign and cult films, art, design and media studies, biology and environmental studies, chemistry and physics, and primary and middle school materials. There is a good collection of classic films and adaptations of literary works, and some audio recordings of readings. Sale only.

Other useful catalogues:
Brook Productions (Social Sciences)

Management and Training (see also computer skills training, finance & accountancy, health & safety, information technology)

Academy Television now trading as YITM   **Video training catalogue** (1992). 42 pages. Academy Television, Kirkstall Road, Leeds LS3 1JS ☎ 0113 246 1528 fax 0113 242 9522.
Academy handles a wide selection of programmes broadcast by Yorkshire–Tyne Tees Television, Thames Television, Channel 4, Scottish Television, Ulster Television, HTV and WTN. This catalogue contains details of over 120 titles designed to enhance the training resources of

many types of business and industry, with subjects ranging from marketing techniques to issues current in Europe. Sale on video.

Apple Television **Videos** (1994). Leaflets. Apple Television Ltd, A2 Connaught Business Centre, Hyde Estate Road, West Hendon, London NW9 6JL ☎ 0181-205 6687 fax 0181-205 0430.
Video-based training packages about time management, sales training, telephone sales, credit control and small claims court procedures. Sale.

Applied Learning **Multimedia training** (1994). Leaflets. Applied Learning, 1 Hogarth Business Park, Burlington Lane, London W4 2TJ ☎ 0181-994 4404 fax 0181-944 4404.
Video, CD-ROM, and computer-based training courses on topics relating to information technology, management skills, software training, and human resource development. Sale.

BBC for Business **Catalogue** (1995). 78 pages. BBC for Business, Woodlands, 80 Wood Lane, London W12 0TT ☎ 0181-576 2361 fax 0181-749 2867.
Videos on management skills, strategic management, health and safety, language programmes for business training. Also a series of videos on business strategy presented by professional and academic experts from European business schools. Sale only. A free brochure *BBC Resources for Training*, published twice a year, provides information on forthcoming radio and television programmes relevant to training.

Bristol Quality Centre **Training materials** (1993). Leaflets. Bristol Quality Centre, PO Box 54, Fishponds, Bristol BS16 1XG ☎ 0117 976 3932 fax 0117 958 5116.
Video-based training packages on statistical process control, problem solving, and quality improvement.

CareerTrack **Seminars & tapes** (1995). 39 pages. CareerTrack International, Drayton Road, Newton Longville, Milton Keynes MK17 0DY ☎ 01908 366544 fax 01908 368685.
A quarterly publication with details of audiocassettes and videocassettes available for sale. Topics include career development, management techniques, job skills, computers, health, finances, and communication skills.

Central Independent Television **Venture business catalogue** (1993). 18 pages. Central Independent Television plc, Video Resources Unit, Broad Street, Birmingham B1 2JP ☎ 0121-643 9898 fax 0121-616 1531.
Programmes from Central Television's award-winning VENTURE series, which examine key management issues as well as international business trends and the extent to which they will affect the UK industrial climate. Sale on video.

CFL Vision **Management, business & commerce** (1994). 13 pages. CFL Vision, PO Box 35, Wetherby, West Yorkshire LS23 7EX ☎ 01937 541010 fax 01937 541083.
Details of films and videos selected from the main CFL Vision catalogue in the areas of management, business and commerce. Hire and sale.

Connaught Training **Activities, exercises and management games catalogue** (1993). 46 pages. Connaught Training, Customer Services Department, Gower House, Croft

Road, Aldershot, Hampshire GU11 3HR ☎ 01252 331551 fax 01252 344405. Includes details of video and audio packs and an interactive video programme for management training.

Connaught Training   **Training film catalogue** (1994). Various. Connaught Training, Gower House, Croft Road, Aldershot, Hampshire GU11 3HR
☎ 01252 317711 fax 01252 344405.
Films and videos for business training, with separate catalogues for new films, empowerment, quality, communication skills, people skills, customer care, health and safety, and management skills. Sale.

The Richard Denny Organisation   **Catalogue** (1993). 8 pages. The Richard Denny Organisation, PO Box 16, Moreton in Marsh, Gloucestershire, GL56 0NH
☎ 01608 651597 fax 01608 651638.
A collection of audio- and videocassettes featuring Richard Denny, intended for training in management skills. Sale only.

Department of Trade and Industry   **M'90s videos** (1993 + supplements). 20 pages. DTI, c/o Mediascene Ltd, PO Box 90, Hengoed, Mid Glamorgan CF8 9YE
☎ 01443 821877 fax 01443 822055.
As part of its Managing the '90s programme the DTI has produced a series of videos on topics including new product design, production, purchasing and quality, and a second series of eight videos on the use of materials in industry. Free.

Educational Media, Film & Video   **Training catalogue** (1994). 12 pages. Educational Media, Film & Video Ltd, 235 Imperial Drive, Rayners Lane, Harrow, Middlesex HA2 7HE
☎ 0181-868 1908 fax 0181-868 1991.
A collection of management training videos produced by Britannica Films and AIMS Media Training in the USA. Subjects include team building, supervision, selling, leadership, communication skills and other management topics. Sale.

Entek Training Services   **Product directory** (1993). 22 pages. Entek Training Services Ltd, Southgate House, Minchenden Complex, High Street, London N14 6BJ
☎ 0181-886 0057 fax 0181-886 4112.
A collection of 3500 management and training titles from over 100 suppliers. The programmes are grouped under subject headings ranging from basic skills to training. Entek provides an information, preview and booking service.

Euromanagement   **Top management video selection** (1994). 38 pages. Euromanagement, Fellenoord 140, PO Box 2192, 5600 CD Eindhoven, The Netherlands
☎ +31 40 608899 fax +31 40 460885.
Videos of leading-edge business thinkers presenting their own ideas, many illustrated with case studies filmed on location. Those featured include Tom Peters, Sir John Harvey-Jones, Philip Kotler, Charles Handy, Harvey Mackay, and Walter Cronkite. For sale to UK customers on PAL-standard videocassette.

Eurotech   **Training programmes** (1993). Leaflets. Eurotech, Oakfield Road, East

Wittering, Chichester, West Sussex PO20 8RP
☎ 01243 672891 fax 01243 672031.
An interactive videodisc-based training package on selection interviewing and another on good manual handling practice for the prevention of back or other injuries. Hire or sale.

Fenman Training   **Resource reference guide** (1995). 47 pages. Fenman Training, Clive House, The Business Park, Ely, Cambridgeshire CB7 4EH
☎ 01353 665533 fax 01353 663644.
Training packs consisting of a video with trainer's guide on a range of management topics including body language, dealing with aggression, coaching and listening skills, and time management. Fenman Training was formerly Wyvern Training. Sale and preview.

The Industrial Society   **Books and videos** (1995). 79 pages. The Industrial Society, Quadrant Court, 49 Calthorpe Road, Edgbaston, Birmingham B15 1TH
☎ 0121-454 6769 fax 0121-456 2715.
Includes videos on business, management training, public speaking, and health and safety. Hire and sale.

Institute of Management Services   **Management Services series** (1993). Leaflet. Institute of Management Services, 1 Cecil Court, London Road, Enfield, Middlesex EN2 6DD
☎ 0181-363 7452 fax 0181-367 8149.
Series of six MANAGEMENT SERVICES videos, produced in conjunction with the British Council of Productivity Associations. Shot on location and showing real-life case studies, the series covers method study, work measurement, activity sampling, clerical work measurement, and profit improvement. Sale only.

Just Results   **Training audio and video catalogue** (1995). Leaflet. Just Results, PO Box 11, Woodstock, Oxford OX20 1SE
☎ 01993 813588 fax 01993 812074.
Video based packages for management training and marketing, some of which feature David Frost, who is involved in the company, and Brian Redhead interviewing Tom Peters and other business gurus. Sale only.

Kantola Productions   **Toastmasters International communications video series** (1993). 8 pages. Kantola Productions, c/o Conference Support International, The Old Granary, 29 Chester Road, Castle Bromwich, Birmingham B36 9DA
☎ 0121-776 7799 fax 0121-776 7447.
Four videos for teaching communication and leadership skills. Subjects are public speaking, leadership, selling, and meetings. Sale only.

Local Government Management Board   **Publications catalogue** (1994). 52 pages. Local Government Management Board, Arndale House, The Arndale Centre, Luton LU1 2TS
☎ 01582 451166 fax 01582 412525.
Books and videos for training. Videos cover aggression and the elderly, safety at work, counselling at work and grievance handling. Also an information video on the trading standards service. Sale.

Longman Training   **Skills development video catalogue** (1993). 60 pages. Training Direct,

Longman House, Burnt Mill, Harlow, Essex CM20 2JE
☎ 01279 623927 fax 01279 623795.
Details of a wide range of programmes for management and supervisory
training, including telephone techniques, sales skills, negotiating,
discipline, industrial relations, and health and safety. Hire or sale.

Longman Training **Technology-based training catalogue** (1993). 36 pages. Training Direct,
Longman House, Burnt Mill, Harlow, Essex CM20 2JE
☎ 01279 623927 fax 01279 623795.
Interactive video courses for training in assertiveness, customer care,
communication skills, conducting appraisals, sales and marketing, foreign
languages, health and safety, and finance. Sale only.

Look Multimedia **IT management video series** (1994). Leaflets. Look Multimedia Ltd,
1 Mortimer Street, London W1N 7RH ☎ 0171-255 2670 fax 0171-255 1995.
Videos on management issues in information technology, using interviews
and location filming. Topics include outsourcing, business process re-
engineering, systems integration, right-sizing, open systems, client-server
computing, and building client-server systems. Sale.

LPT Productions **Training products price list/order form** (1993). Leaflet. LPT Productions,
Unit 6, South Inch Business Centre, Shore Road, Perth PH2 8BW
☎ 01738 21189 fax 01738 21192.
Video and audiotape materials for training in leadership, management
development and communication skills. Sale only.

Melrose Film Productions **Video based training catalogue** (1995). 140 pages. Melrose Film
Productions, 16 Bromells Road, London SW4 0BL
☎ 0171-627 8404 fax 0171-622 0421.
Videos and video-based packages covering supervisory skills,
management concepts, communication and presentation, quality, customer
service, sales and marketing, computers, and accountancy. Hire and sale.

Milestone Training (1993). Leaflet. Milestone Training through Television, 51 Cliff Road,
through Television Leeds LS6 2EZ ☎ 0113 275 4988.
A range of videos for management and interpersonal skills training for the
nursing and medical professions. Hire or sale.

National Quality **Quality management on screen** (1993). 45 pages. National Quality
Information Centre Information Centre, Institute of Quality Assurance, PO Box 712, 61
Southwark Street, London SE1 1SB ☎ 0171-401 7227 fax 0171-401 2725.
A directory of videos, films and other audio-visual training aids relating to
quality management currently available from a variety of sources.

Pba Training Services **Film subject list** (1993). 8 pages. Pba Training Services, Bamfords Yard,
Turvey, Bedfordshire MK43 8DS ☎ 01234 888877 fax 01234 888878.
Lists around 350 topics in the field of management training. The company
holds thousands of programmes from most of the major management and
training distributors and offers free independent advice on the range of
materials available, preview facilities and a sales service.

Premiere Productions **Interactive video training programmes** (1994). Leaflets. Premiere

Productions, 16 Castello Avenue, London SW15 6EA
☎ 0181-785 2933 fax 0181-780 1684.
Interactive video programmes for training in management, finance, and language learning.

The Saville Group **Training videos and resources guide** (1994). 48 pages. The Saville Group, Millfield Lane, Nether Poppleton, York YO2 6PQ
☎ 01904 782782 fax 01904 782700.
Saville, with several regional offices, acts as an information, preview and booking centre for videos from most of the leading distributors of management and training programmes. The catalogue is organised by topic.

Scottish Council for Educational Technology **Training solutions for training professionals** (1993). 157 pages. SCET, 74 Victoria Crescent Road, Glasgow G12 9JN
☎ 0141-334 9314 fax 0141-334 6519.
Draws together hundreds of management training videos and packages from all the leading companies and offers them for sale and free preview in Scotland. Arranged under the broad headings of business and management, human resource development, sales and marketing, languages, health, safety and security, information technology, and quality. The larger sections have further subject subdivisions.

Services Ltd **Video series** (1993). Leaflet. Services Ltd, Quality and Reliability House, 82 Trent Boulevard, West Bridgford, Nottingham NG2 5BL
☎ 0115 945 5285 fax 0115 981 7137.
Video series on reliability engineering and total quality management, produced with the assistance of Professor Tony Bendell of Nottingham Trent University. Sale only.

Training Media Group **Management training videos** (1994). Leaflets. Training Media Group Ltd, 3a Station Parade, Ealing Road, Northolt, Middlesex UB5 5HR
☎ 0181-845 8008 fax 0181-845 9009.
Packages comprising video and support materials for management training on topics such as computer security, meetings, project management, equal opportunities, strategic planning, benchmarking, time management and health and safety. Sale.

Training Services **Catalogue** (1994). 34 pages. Training Services, Brooklands House, 29 Hythegate, Werrington, Peterborough PE4 7ZP
☎ 01733 327337 fax 01733 327337.
Videos for management training, some of them from the former Guild Training library and some of them new. Hire and sale.

TV Choice **Video catalogue** (1994). 21 pages. TV Choice Ltd, 22 Charing Cross Road, London WC2H 0HR ☎ 0171-379 0873 fax 0171-379 0263.
Videos of business case studies intended for use in education and business. Subjects include marketing, finance, small business development, quality, people in organisations, manufacturing and design, international business, computer security, and information technology. Sale only.

Video Arts Catalogue (1995). 131 pages. Video Arts Ltd, Dumbarton House, 68 Oxford Street, London WIN 9LA ☎ 0171-637 7288 fax 0171-580 8103. Programmes with support materials covering major aspects of staff development: quality, customer care, management skills, financial appreciation and sales and marketing. Also short video breaks suitable for conferences. Selected programmes are being made available in CD-i versions. Hire or sale on video.

Viewtech Business & industry catalogue (1993). 32 pages. Viewtech Film & Video, 161 Winchester Road, Brislington, Bristol BS4 3NJ ☎ 0117 977 3422 fax 0117 972 4292. American-produced management training videos, including the HARVARD BUSINESS REVIEW series. Subjects include change and innovation, quality, sales and communication skills, management development, creativity and problem solving, business ethics, and health and safety. Hire or sale.

Weightman Practical Training Products (1993). 4 pages. Weightman Practical Training Products Ltd, Meadowfield House, Ponteland Industrial Estate, Ponteland, Tyne and Wear NE20 9SD ☎ 01661 871435 fax 01661 872230. Training videos on effective meeting behaviour, discipline interviews, appraisal interviews and team briefing. Sale only.

Materials Science (see also civil engineering & building, engineering & manufacturing, science & technology)

American Technical Publishers ASM International (1994). 40 pages. American Technical Publishers, 27-29 Knowl Piece, Wilbury Way, Hitchin SG4 0SX ☎ 01462 433678 fax 01462 433678. Includes several video-based training courses on thermal spray technology, quality, heat treating, induction heating, superalloys, composites, metallography, welding inspection, non-destructive testing, and corrosion. Programmes are available individually or as complete courses. Sale only.

Council of Forest Industries (1993). 3 pages. Council of Forest Industries (Canada), Tileman House, 131-133 Upper Richmond Road, London SW15 2TR. ☎ 0181-788 4446 fax 0181-789 0146. Eight programmes produced for the Council of Forest Industries of British Columbia, covering all aspects of the forest industry from tree growth, harvesting, forest protection and sawmilling to the end uses of the timber. Free loan on film or video.

Department of Trade and Industry M'90s videos (1993 + supplements). 20 pages. DTI, c/o Mediascene Ltd, PO Box 90, Hengoed, Mid Glamorgan CF8 9YE ☎ 01443 821877 fax 01443 822055. As part of its Managing the '90s programme the DTI has produced a series of videos on topics including new product design, production, purchasing and quality, and a second series of eight videos on the use of materials in industry. Free.

The Malaysian Rubber Producers' Research Association Malaysian rubber on video (1994). Leaflet. The Malaysian Rubber Producers' Research Association, Tun Abdul Razak Laboratory,

Brickendonbury, Hertford SG13 8NL ☎ 01992 584966 fax 01992 554837.
Five videos on rubber, from production to its applications, ranging in level from general interest to technical. Free loan.

RTZ **Educational resources for schools** (1992). Leaflet. RTZ Ltd, 6 St James's Square, London SW1Y 4LD ☎ 0171-930 2399 fax 0171-930 3249.
Videos showing the world-wide activities of RTZ companies, which have interests in aluminium and its products, borax, coal, copper, diamonds, industrial and agricultural chemicals, iron ore, lead, speciality steels, tin, uranium and zinc. Other programmes deal with environmental aspects of mining, and a series of four programmes concerning decisions in industry is designed to link with GCSE technology courses. Free loan.

Woodhead Publishing Ltd **Catalogue** (1994). 40 pages. Woodhead Publishing Ltd, Abington Hall, Abington, Cambridgeshire CB1 6AH ☎ 01223 891358 fax 01223 893694.
Includes videos from the Welding Institute on welding processes, metallurgy and materials, design and weld properties, structures and fabrication, surface engineering, health and safety, and inspection and testing. Also a range of videos on welding from the USA, produced by Hellier Associates Inc and East Coast Enterprise Training Center. Several slide sets are also available. Sale only.

Zinc Development Association **Publications and films on zinc** (1991). 8 pages. Zinc Development Association, 42 Weymouth Street, London W1N 3LQ ☎ 0171-499 6636 fax 0171-493 1555.
Films and videos on galvanisation. Free loan or sale.

Mathematics

Aston University, Centre for Extension Studies **Mathematics and physics programmes catalogue** (1990). 24 pages. Aston University, Centre for Extension Studies, Aston University, Aston Triangle, Gosta Green, Birmingham B4 7ET ☎ 0121-359 3611 ext. 4590 fax 0121-359 7358.
Video lectures for INSET on A-level physics and mathematics, covering the content of school syllabuses and new approaches to teaching. Sale only.

Cap & Gown Series **Educational video tapes** (1994). Leaflets. Cap & Gown Series, PO Box 14, Penkridge, Stafford ST19 5SQ ☎ 01785 713560.
Three series of video courses for school or home to help pupils studying mathematics for National Curriculum Key Stage 3, GCSE and A level. Sale only.

The Open University

Catalogue of learning resources from the undergraduate programme (1994). 102 pages. Open University Educational Enterprises Ltd, 12 Cofferidge Close, Stony Stratford, Milton Keynes MK11 1BY ☎ 01908 261662 fax 01908 261001.
Lists by title hundreds of videocassettes, audiocassettes, study texts and computer packages in all subject areas that form part of Open University undergraduate courses and are available for sale separately to outside institutions. Alternatively, programmes may be recorded off-air under licence from the OU. Synopses of individual programmes are given on information sheets, which are available individually.

The Royal Institution   **Masterclass video series** (1993). Leaflets. The Royal Institution of Great Britain, 21 Albemarle Street, London W1X 4BS ☎ 0171-409 2992 fax 0171-629 3569.
Three lecture demonstrations with teachers' notes and workbooks. Topics are the nature of colour, geometry and perspective, and gyroscopes and boomerangs. Sale only.

Sio Communications   **Videotapes** (1992). 7 pages. Sio Communications Ltd, Georgia House, Eshe Road North, Blundellsands, Liverpool L23 8UD ☎ 0151-924 9570.
Several series of American-produced videotapes including a series on mathematics from Video Tutorial Services suitable for secondary, further, and higher education covering algebra, pre-calculus, integrated maths, differentiation, and integration. Sale only.

Media Studies (see also film & television production)

British Film Institute   **Film & Video Library catalogue** (1987 + supplements). 192 pages. British Film Institute, 21 Stephen Street, London W1P 1PL ☎ 0171-255 1444 fax 0171-436 7950.
Over 400 feature films and 800 shorts, documentaries and television programmes relevant to the art and history of film and television. Entries are arranged under the headings feature films, non-fiction and short fiction pre-1929, non-fiction and short fiction post-1929, and television material; also films from the BFI Experimental Film Fund and the Production Board. There are country and director indexes, an animation index, a film study extract list and a listing of titles available on video. Hire only.

Cinenova   **Catalogue of films & videos directed by women** (1994). 82 pages. Cinenova, 113 Roman Road, London E2 0HU ☎ 0181-981 6828 fax 0181-983 4441.
Specialist distributor of films and videos directed by women, formed from the amalgamation of the Cinema of Women and Circles distributors in 1991. Hire or sale through Glenbuck Films.

Educational & Television Films   (1986-89, current 1994). Various catalogues. Educational & Television Films Ltd, 247a Upper Street, London N1 1RU ☎ 0171-226 2298 fax 0171-226 8016.
Feature, cartoon and puppet films from Eastern Europe and China, and documentary films from the Czech and Slovak republics, the former German Democratic Republic, Vietnam, Latin America, the former USSR and other countries. Hire and sale.

Filmbank   **Film & video catalogue** (1990 + supplements). 326 pages. Price £10.00. Filmbank Distributors Ltd, Grayton House, 498-504 Fulham Road, London SW6 5NH ☎ 0171-386 5411 fax 0171-381 2405.
Thousands of feature films on 16mm film, with an increasing number of recent releases on video. Films are classified by genre: comedy, westerns, etc. Also a special-interest section containing feature-film extracts, newsreel compilations from the Pathé News Service, foreign-language films and a collection of miscellaneous short documentaries. UK distributor for Walt Disney films on 16mm film. Hire only.

Glenbuck Films   **Video catalogue** (1987 + supplements). 31 pages. Glenbuck Films Ltd, 21 Stephen Street, London W1P 1PL ☎ 0171-957 8938 fax 0171-580 5830.
Features and documentaries on video. Hire and sale.

Team Video Productions Catalogue (1989 + supplements). 21 pages. Team Video Productions, 105 Canalot, 222 Kensal Road, London W10 5BN ☎ 0181-960 5536
Videos and video-based teaching packs on new technology, health and safety, pre-vocational training, business and trade union studies, nuclear power, media studies, development studies and environmental conservation. Sale only.

Voice of the Listener and Viewer List of publications (1993). 4 pages. VLV, 101 King's Drive, Gravesend, Kent DA12 5BQ ☎ 01474 352835.
Includes audiocassettes and videocassettes of VLV lectures and seminars. Sale only.

Other useful catalogues:
Institute of Contemporary Arts (Arts)
European Schoolbooks (German Studies)
European Schoolbooks (Spanish Studies)

Media Studies: Feature Films

Artificial Eye Film catalogue (1991 + annual supplements). Artificial Eye Film Company Ltd, 13 Soho Square, London W1V 5FB ☎ 0171-437 2552 fax 0171-437 2992.
A large collection of 35mm and 16mm feature films, many by European directors, e.g. Bresson, Rohmer, Wajda, Tarkovsky. Most have original soundtrack with English subtitles. Hire through Glenbuck Films.
Video catalogue (1993 + supplements). 30 pages. Artificial Eye Film Company Ltd, 13 Soho Square, London W1V 5FB ☎ 0171-437 2552 fax 0171-437 2992.
Videos of feature films, many by European directors, e.g. Bresson, Rohmer, Wajda, Tarkovsky. Most have original soundtrack with English subtitles. For sale by mail order or through retail outlets.

British Film Institute Films on offer (1993). 245 pages. Price £12.95. British Film Institute, 21 Stephen Street, London W1P 1PL ☎ 0171-255 1444 fax 0171-436 7950.
A comprehensive list of the feature films currently available for non-theatric hire on 16mm film or VHS video from UK distributors. The films are arranged alphabetically by title and cross-indexed by director. Also includes a selection of short films.

Channel Video Films Catalogue (1995). 64 pages. Channel Video Films, 58 Salusbury Road, London NW6 6ND ☎ 0171-372 2025 fax 0171-372 2025.
A mail-order service supplying thousands of videos from a wide range of suppliers. The catalogue lists mainly feature films, but it also covers non-fiction titles, which are organised by subject. Regular updates are issued. Sale.

Connoisseur Video (1994). Leaflet. Connoisseur Video, 10a Stephen Mews, London W1P 0AX ☎ 0171-957 8957 fax 0171-957 8968.
Classic feature films from European, Japanese and American directors, available for sale on video by mail order. The companion collection Academy Video lists non-fiction material ranging from classic documentaries to experimental and avant-garde films. Both collections are administered by the British Film Institute. Sale.

Darvill Associates **16mm film and video library catalogue** (1986 + supplement). 58 pages. Darvill Associates, 280 Chartridge Lane, Chesham, Buckinghamshire HP5 2SG ☎ 01494 783643 fax 01494 784873.
Feature films by Scandinavian directors including Bergman, Sjoman, Sjostrom and Stiller. Also films by Tati, Borowczyk and other leading directors, Australian and Dutch features and documentaries, and the films of the Swedish Institute. Hire on film from Glenbuck; hire and sale on video from Darvill.

Exchange Value Video Club **Catalogue** (1991 + supplements). 80 pages. Exchange Value Video Club, Nacton, Ipswich IP10 0JZ ☎ 01473 717088 fax 01473 717088.
A mail-order sale and rental library of classic and foreign films on videocassette. Many titles no longer available for sale through retail outlets are available for hire. Regular supplements are issued.

Fast Forward (1994). 58 pages. Fast Forward, Unit 9-10 Sutherland Court, Moor Park Industrial Estate, Tolpits Lane, Watford WD1 8SP ☎ 01923 897080 fax 01923 896263.
A mail-order catalogue listing by title nearly 16,000 videos organised into 100 subject categories. Mainly feature films, but also sport and leisure-interest programmes.

Film Education (1994). Newsletters. Film Education, 41-42 Berners Street, London W1P 3AA ☎ 0171-637 9932 fax 0171-637 9996.
Several videos about the making of recent feature films and a video showreel of UIP film trailers, available free of charge to schools and education. Also the SHAKESPEARE CINEMA series of videos on Shakespeare plays, containing clips from a variety of film versions, and accompanied by study guide packs. Some items for sale and others free of charge.

Filmbank **Film & video catalogue** (1990 + supplements). 326 pages. Price £10.00. Filmbank Distributors Ltd, Grayton House, 498-504 Fulham Road, London SW6 5NH ☎ 0171-386 5411 fax 0171-381 2405.
Thousands of feature films on 16mm film, with an increasing number of recent releases on video. Films are classified by genre: comedy, westerns, etc. Also a special-interest section containing feature-film extracts, films on hobbies, newsreel compilations from the Pathé News Service, foreign-language films and a collection of miscellaneous short documentaries. Filmbank is also the UK distributor for Walt Disney films on 16mm film. Hire only.

Glenbuck Films **35mm films** (1990). 11 pages . Glenbuck Films Ltd, 21 Stephen Street, London W1P 1PL ☎ 0171-957 8938 fax 0171-580 5830.
Features and animation films on 35mm film. Hire only.
Entertainment films catalogue (1987 + updates). 154 pages. Glenbuck Films Ltd, 21 Stephen Street, London W1P 1PL ☎ 0171-957 8938 fax 0171-580 5830.
Feature films arranged under seven broad categories: action and adventure, comedy, drama and romance, mystery, thriller and suspense, sci-fi, fantasy and horror, westerns, and music. Hire only.

Glenbuck Films   **Foreign language films** (1992). Loose-leaf catalogue. Glenbuck Films Ltd, 21 Stephen Street, London W1P 1PL ☎ 0171-957 8938 fax 0171-580 5830. Classic feature films from around the world. Hire only.
German feature films (1993). 115 pages. Glenbuck Films Ltd, 21 Stephen Street, London W1P 1PL ☎ 0171-957 8938 fax 0171-580 5830.
Hundreds German feature films available for hire on 16mm film. This collection was formed from the joint holdings of the Goethe Institut London, the German Film and Video Library, and Glenbuck Films. The films are arranged chronologically (the earliest dates from 1918), with separate indexes of directors, themes and titles in both English and German. The films themselves are in German with English subtitles.

Goethe-Institut   **Video catalogue** (1992). 103 pages. Goethe-Institut London Library, 50 Princes Gate, Exhibition Road, London SW7 2PH
☎ 0171-411 3452 fax 0171-584 3180.
Videos on all aspects of German life. The feature films on 16mm film previously distributed by the Goethe Institut are now handled by Glenbuck. Free loan.

Gold Distribution   **Catalogue** (1992). 53 pages. Price £1.00. Gold Distribution, Gold House, 69 Flempton Road, Leyton, London E10 7NL ☎ 0181-556 2429 fax 0181-539 2176. A mail-order catalogue, organised by subject, with more than 11,000 video titles.

Ingram Entertainment   **Video retail catalogue** (1992). 118 pages. Ingram Entertainment plc, Bashley Road, Park Royal, London NW10 6SD
☎ 0181-965 5555 fax 0181-961 8040.
A distributor of videos mainly for the rental and sell-through markets. Library accounts are welcomed. Feature films predominate, and titles are arranged under the headings children, features, music, special interest and sport, with a combined title index. New-release supplements appear bi-monthly.

Mr Benson's Video Collection   (1994 + monthly updates). 70 pages. Price £2.00. Mr Benson's Video Collection, 375 Harrow Road, London W9 3BR
☎ 0181-960 4868 fax 0181-969 7211.
Around 17,000 video titles covering feature films, sport and leisure interests, available for sale by mail order. Includes CD-I and videodisc versions.

Polish Cultural Institute   **Video cassettes lending library catalogue** (1993). 21 pages. Polish Cultural Institute, 34 Portland Place, London W1N 4HQ
☎ 0171-636 6032 fax 0171-637 2190.
Some 400 videos in the following categories: feature films (Polish language only), feature films (Polish language with English subtitles), Polish films for children, theatre, general culture including music and dance, folk, and miscellaneous. Free loan.

Rose Records   **Audio-visual library services** (1993). Information sheets. Rose Records, The Studio, Unstable Walk, 18 Ellington Street, London N7 8PP
☎ 0171-609 8288 fax 0171-607 7851.
Rose Records is a supplier of compact discs, cassettes, records and videos

to libraries in the UK and overseas. No catalogue is available, but individual lists can be printed from the database in response to specific subject requests. Videos available cover general interest, educational and feature titles, and audio programmes include spoken word and music titles and language courses. Sale.

Tartan Video **Around the world in eighty films** (1994). 24 pages. Tartan Video Ltd, Metro Tartan House, 79 Wardour Street, London W1V 3TH
☎ 0171 494 1400 fax 0171-439 1922.
Videos of recent and classic feature films arranged by country of origin. Sale by mail order or through retail shops.

Trade Service Information **Videolog** (current). Loose-leaf catalogue. Price £20 + £15 monthly. Trade Service Information Ltd, Cherryholt Road, Stamford PE9 2HT
☎ 01780 64331 fax 01780 55006.
A reference catalogue intended primarily for the retail trade, reporting all the currently available pre-recorded video titles for the home video market, from a wide range of sources. It concentrates on feature films but includes also a large number of titles on drama, sport, war, hobbies and general interest subjects in broadly classified sections. Updated fortnightly.

Twentieth Century Movies **16mm entertainment catalogue** (1987 + supplement, current 1994). 104 pages. Price £7.00. Twentieth Century Movies, 120 Queen Margaret Drive, Glasgow G20 8NZ ☎ 0141-946 1121
Hundreds of popular feature films and films of sporting events, particularly football and boxing. Hire on 16mm film.

Video City **Catalogue** (1994). 62 pages. Video City, 117 Notting Hill Gate, London W11 3LB ☎ 0171-221 7029 fax 0171-792 9273.
Many thousands of titles, mainly feature films, available for sale by mail order.

Video Plus Direct **The complete guide to what's on video** (1993). 295 pages. Price £4.95. Video Plus Direct, PO Box 190, Peterborough PE2 6UW
☎ 01733 232800 fax 01733 238966.
Mail-order company supplying over 15,000 entertainment, sport and leisure interest videos and videodisc titles to education, libraries and individuals. Catalogue is arranged alphabetically within categories and contains a brief description of each programme.

Video Rights (1994). Leaflets. Video Rights Ltd, Suites 415-416, Premier House, 77 Oxford Street, London W1R 1RB ☎ 0171-439 1188 fax 0171-734 8367.
A distributor of videos for the retail market. Programmes include the English Shakespeare Company's WARS OF THE ROSES cycle, a series of documentaries on World War II using footage from the Soviet War Archive, and a collection of silent film classics. Sale through retail outlets.

Other useful catalogues:
British Universities Film & Video Council (Literature)
Institut Français (French Studies)
Metro Pictures (History and Politics)

Media Studies: Independent and Experimental Film and Video

British Film Institute   **Production catalogue 1951-94** (1994). 68 pages. British Film Institute, 21 Stephen Street, London W1P 1PL ☎ 0171-255 1444 fax 0171-436 7950.
A complete list of available films from the BFI Production Board's 40-year history. Includes fiction and non-fiction titles with title and director indexes. Hire or sale from the BFI Film and Video Library.

London Filmmakers Co-op   **Catalogue** (1993). 182 pages. Price £20.00. LFC, 42 Gloucester Avenue, London NW1 8JD ☎ 0171-586 4806 fax 0171-483 0068.
The first comprehensive catalogue from the LFC in over 10 years. Over 1500 experimental and avant-garde films ranging from European classics of the 1920s and classic American and British titles, to an international range of work being produced by film-makers exploring the radical possibilities of the film medium. Hire only.

London Electronic Arts   **Catalogue** (1991 + supplements). 136 pages. Price £12.00. London Video Access, 5-7 Buck Street, London NW1 8NJ ☎ 0171-284 4588 fax 0171-267 6078.
Several hundred videos portraying artistic experiments, subjective allegories, reflections on political activism or questions of identity and sexuality. Hire or sale.

Visionary Communications   **Mail order catalogue** (1993). 10 pages. Visionary Communications Ltd, PO Box 30, Lytham St Anne's FY8 1RF ☎ 01253 712453 fax 01253 712362.
A mail-order library specialising in cult music videos, art and experimental films, and New Age and gay films. Sale only.

Media studies: Short Films and Animations

British Film Institute   **Animation catalogue** (1993). 96 pages. Price £2.50. British Film Institute, 21 Stephen Street, London W1P 1PL ☎ 0171-255 1444 fax 0171-436 7950.
Lists hundreds of animation films from the earliest period to the present day, which are distributed by the BFI Film & Video Library. The films are listed under the following categories: early animated film, early work by artists, the avant-garde, sponsored films, Norman McLaren, National Film Board of Canada, animation in the UK, Eastern European animation, animation in Western Europe, American independents, computer animation, and other films. Hire on film, some for sale on video.

Glenbuck Films   **Documentary, educational & animation** (1987 + updates). 65 pages. Glenbuck Films Ltd, 21 Stephen Street, London W1P 1PL ☎ 0171-957 8938 fax 0171-580 5830.
Documentary features and shorts that include the work of Nick Broomfield, Felix Greene, Les Blank and Frederick Wiseman. Educational titles include the Contemporary, Walt Disney and Pyramid collections. Hire on film and video.
Films for young audiences (1987). 31 pages. Glenbuck Films Ltd, 21 Stephen Street, London W1P 1PL ☎ 0171-957 8938 fax 0171-580 5830.
Films from the Children's Film and Television Foundation. Hire only.

Sheila Graber   **Animated films catalogue** (1985, current 1994). 24 pages. Sheila Graber Animated Films, 50 Meldon Avenue, South Shields, Tyne and Wear NE34 0EL ☎ 0191-455 4985.

Animated 16mm films on art (Michelangelo, Blake, Mondrian, expressionism), evolution, a television news station, women in the North East, and many fiction subjects. Sale.

Halas & Batchelor Animation (1993). Leaflets. Halas & Batchelor Animation, 6 Holford Road, London NW3 1AD ☎ 0171-435 8674 fax 0171-431 6835.
A collection of classic animation films made by Halas & Batchelor. Also the series MASTERS OF ANIMATION representing the best of animation from 11 different countries, and two compilation programmes of computer animation from around the world. Sale only.

Leeds Animation Workshop (1994). Leaflets. Leeds Animation Workshop, 45 Bayswater Row, Leeds LS8 5LF ☎ 0113 248 4997.
Animated films made by this women's collective on subjects such as the shortage of women in senior management positions, stress, environmental issues, international debt, and homelessness. Hire or sale on film or video.

The Short Film Index (1993). 146 pages. Price £14.95. The Short Film Index, Leeds Design Innovation Centre, 46 The Calls, Leeds LS2 7EY ☎ 0113 266 2454 fax 0113 242 3687.
A reference guide to hundreds of fiction, experimental, animation and documentary 16mm and 35mm short films made in the UK and Ireland since 1990. Organised by the above four genres with a breakdown by film durations of 0-10, 10-20, 20-60 minutes. Full distribution information is given.

Viewtech **Disney educational productions catalogue** (1993). Loose-leaf catalogue. Viewtech Film & Video, 161 Winchester Road, Brislington, Bristol BS4 3NJ ☎ 0117 977 3422 fax 0117 972 4292.
Mainly animated programmes intended for educational use with young people. Covers literature and arts, health and safety, science, social studies and maths and computers. Sale on video only.

Other useful catalogues:
British Universities Film & Video Council (Literature)
Institut Français (French Studies)
Metro Pictures (History and Politics)

Medical Sciences (see also anatomy & physiology, health & safety, health education, mental health & counselling, nursing, science & technology)

Bristol Imaging **Bristol Biomedical Videodisc Project** (1993). Leaflet. Bristol Imaging, Royal Fort Annexe, University of Bristol, Tyndall Avenue, Bristol BS8 1UJ ☎ 0117 930 3500 fax 0117 925 5985.
A videodisc for teaching and research that holds a collection of 24,000 veterinary, medical and dental still frames, and incorporates the pathology videodisc UKPATH2. A visual database is available for detailed searches using any keyword.

British Medical Association **Catalogue of films and videos in the British Medical Association Library** (1993). 348 pages. Price £40.00. *Information:* BMA Library Film & Video Services, BMA House, Tavistock Square, London WC1H 9JP ☎ 0171-383 6690 fax 0171-388 2544. *Catalogue sales:* Library Association Publishing Ltd,

c/o Bookpoint Ltd, 30 Milton Park, Abingdon, Oxfordshire OX14 4TD
☎ 01235 835001 fax 01235 832068.
A detailed, annotated list of the films and videos in the BMA Library. All titles have received peer review. Entries include full filmographic details, synopses and target audience. Arranged alphabetically and indexed under subject headings. Programmes available on free loan to BMA members and affiliated libraries in the UK.
Current videos for loan (1992 + supplements). 50 pages. BMA Library Film & Video Services, BMA House, Tavistock Square, London WC1H 9JP ☎ 0171-383 6690 fax 0171-388 2544.
A collection of videos available for free loan to BMA members. The catalogue is organised under broad subject headings from abortion to urology.

Chadwyck-Healey　**CD-ROM publications** (1994). 28 pages. Chadwyck-Healey Ltd, The Quorum, Barnwell Road, Cambridge CB5 8SW ☎ 01223 215512 fax 01223 215513.
Includes *The UK National Medical Slide Bank on Videodisc*, with 12,440 images of diseases, injuries, medical treatment and healthcare practice.

Cystic Fibrosis Trust　**Publications and video catalogue** (1993). 6 pages. Cystic Fibrosis Trust, Research, Support and Education, Alexandra House, 5 Blythe Road, Bromley, Kent BR1 3RS ☎ 0181-464 7211 fax 0181-313 0472.
Videos on the nature and management of cystic fibrosis and the problems of cystic fibrosis sufferers. Free loan or sale.

Down's Syndrome Association　**Literature list** (1992). 12 pages. Down's Syndrome Association, 155 Mitcham Road, London SW17 9PG ☎ 0181-682 4001 fax 0181-682 4012.
Includes three videos on Down's syndrome: HELEN'S STORY, ONE OF US, and EARLY INTERVENTION: PHYSIOTHERAPY FOR BABIES. Sale.

Educational Media, Film & Video　**Health video catalogue** (1992). 44 pages. Educational Media, Film & Video Ltd, 235 Imperial Drive, Rayners Lane, Harrow, Middlesex HA2 7HE ☎ 0181-868 1908 fax 0181-868 1991.
A large collection of videos on all aspects of health education and more specialised programmes for medical and nursing education. Sale only.

Geistlich　**Videos** (1993). Leaflet. Geistlich Sons Ltd Pharmaceuticals, Newton Bank, Long Lane, Chester CH2 3QZ ☎ 01244 347534 fax 01244 319327.
Four videos on infection control, wound healing, and haemofiltration, as well as a computer program covering parenteral nutrition design and appropriate pharmacy labelling procedures.

Glaxo Pharmaceuticals　**Video library alphabetical listing** (1993). 24 pages. Glaxo Pharmaceuticals UK Ltd, Records Management Department, Stockley Park West, Uxbridge, Middlesex UB11 1BT ☎ 0181-990 9000 fax 0181-990 4321.
Computer printout of some 1300 items on pharmaceutical topics, including proceedings of meetings and symposia held in various countries, workshop items, conference inserts, and advertisements. Sale only.

Graves Medical Audiovisual Library　**Catalogue** (1993). Loose-leaf catalogue. Graves Medical Audiovisual Library, c/o Concord Video & Film Council, 201 Felixstowe Road, Ipswich

IP3 9BJ ☎ 01473 714754 or 01473 726012 fax 01473 274531.
A large collection of videos, tape-slide programmes, audiotapes, computer software and booklets on medical subjects. Entries are arranged by subject and include descriptions and suggested audience levels. There are subject, title, author and numerical indexes. Hire and sale.

Dr M. A. Hutson **Orthopaedic medicine** (1993). Leaflets. Dr M. A. Hutson, The Park Row Clinic, 30 Park Row, Nottingham NG1 6GR ☎ 0115 941 1544.
Details of videos produced in association with the Institute of Orthopaedic Medicine. Subjects are strains and sprains, manipulation of the spine, lumbar instability, and the painful shoulder. Free loan through the BMA Library.

Imperial Cancer Research Fund **Educational video programmes**(1993). Leaflet. ICRF Public Relations Department, PO Box 123, Lincoln's Inn Fields, London WC2A 3PX ☎ 0171-242 0200 fax 0171-831 6264.
Videos on the prevention of cancer in women, skin cancer, cutting the risk of developing cancer, cervical cancer, and cancer in children. Hire and sale.

Leicestershire Royal Infirmary NHS Trust **Health Education Video Unit** (1993). Loose-leaf catalogue. Leicestershire Royal Infirmary, Health Education Video Unit, Clinical Sciences Building, Leicester Royal Infirmary, PO Box 65, Leicester LE2 7LX ☎ 0116 255 0461 fax 0116 255 0461.
Videos on substance abuse, HIV and AIDS, coronary heart disease, prevention and early detection of cancer, basic resuscitation, and cervical cancer. Also four health education videos on smoking. Sale only.

Medical Education Services **Video library** (1993). Leaflets. Medical Education Services, The Laurels, Porthycarne Street, Usk, Gwent NP5 1RY ☎ 01291 672625 fax 01291 672604.
The PRIMARY MEMBERSHIP VIDEO SERIES consists of videotaped lectures designed to help candidates prepare for MRCP (Part 1) examinations. Also video series on basic and advanced electrocardiology, depression in general practice, epilepsy, AIDS, a revision anatomy course for FRCS candidates, and current topics in cardiology. Sale only.

MUTV **Understanding and treating incontinence** (1994). Leaflet. MUTV, Oxford Road, Manchester M13 9PL ☎ 0161-275 2535 fax 0161-275 2529.
Seven videos for doctors and nurses on the causes and management of urinary and faecal incontinence, with accompanying booklets. Sale.

Napp Laboratories (1993). Leaflets. Napp Laboratories, Cambridge Science Park, Milton Road, Cambridge CB4 4GW ☎ 01223 424444 fax 01223 424441.
Videos on head lice, scabies, arthritis, and cancer pain and care. Free loan.

National Council for Child Health **Video list** (1993). Leaflet. National Council for Child Health, 311 Gray's Inn Road, London WC1X 8PT ☎ 0171-837 0623 fax 0171-713 0809.
Videos on the immunisation for children, covering rubella and the MMR vaccine. RUBELLA is aimed primarily at Asian women, with Hindi and Bengali language versions. Sale only.

National Society for Epilepsy **Publications list** (1993). Leaflet. National Society for Epilepsy, Chalfont St Peter, Gerrards Cross SL9 0RJ ☎ 01494 873991 fax 01494 871927.
Includes videos for nurses and teachers on recognising, describing and

managing epileptic fits in adults and children, as well as videos for
doctors on the diagnosis and treatment of epilepsy and on understanding
anti-epileptic drugs. Sale only.

Oxford Educational Resources

Title lists and complete catalogue on disk (current). 3 title lists. Oxford
Educational Resources, PO Box 106, Kidlington, Oxfordshire OX5 1HY
☎ 01865 842552 fax 01865 842551.
The largest distributor of medical programmes in the UK, with
programmes from the collections of Camera Talks, Didactic Films, Marine
Audio Visual Instruction Systems, the American Journal of Nursing, the
Hospital Satellite Network and other producers world-wide. Hundreds of
videos, films, tape-slide sets and software titles for medical and nursing
training and health education. The complete catalogue is regularly updated
and can be supplied on disk. A title list is available, and individual subject
sections are printed out on request. Many language versions are available.
There are also programmes in a few non-medical areas – crime prevention,
language teaching, wildlife and earth sciences. Sale only.

Royal Pharmaceutical Society

Catalogue (1993). 95 pages. Royal Pharmaceutical Society of Great Britain,
Department of Pharmaceutical Sciences, 1 Lambeth High Street, London
SE1 7JN ☎ 0171-735 9141 fax 0171-735 7629.
Videos, audiocassettes, and tape-slide lectures on drugs and their
applications in diseases available to pharmacists only. Subjects cover the
gastro-intestinal system, cardiovascular system, respiratory system,
central nervous system, endocrine system, malignant diseases and
immunosupression, skin diseases, biotechnology, drug and substance
abuse, the practice of pharmacy, poisoning and British poisonous plants,
and the training and education of pharmacists.

Royal Society of Medicine

Film and Television Unit: Video list (1993). 3 pages. Royal Society of
Medicine Services Ltd, 1 Wimpole Street, London W1M 8AE
☎ 0171-408 2119 fax 0171-355 3198.
Videos on fallopian tube surgery, doctor–patient encounters, heart disease,
hearing therapy, surgical techniques and other medical topics. Sale only.

Schering Health Care

List of videos (1994). 10 pages. Schering Health Care Ltd, Public Relations
Department, The Brow, Burgess Hill, West Sussex RH15 9NE
☎ 01444 232323 fax 01444 244613.
Educational and promotional videos on topics including contraception,
the menopause and hormone replacement therapy, diagnostic techniques,
and other medical subjects. Most are intended for medical audiences but
some for patient education. Free loan.

 **Sheffield
University
Television**

Medical video catalogue (1991 + supplements). 25 pages. Sheffield
University Television, Sheffield S10 2TN ☎ 0114 282 4007 fax 0114 276 2106.
Videos listed by subject: anaesthesia, anatomy and physiology, clinical
oncology, community medicine, health and safety, obstetrics and gynaecology,
paediatrics, pathology, psychiatry, rheumatology, surgery. Hire and sale.

**Smiths Industries
Medical Systems**

Portex film library (1993). Leaflet. Smiths Industries Medical Systems, 1
High Street, Hythe, Kent CT21 5AB ☎ 01303 260551.

Title list of videos on medical topics including chorionic villi sampling and epidural techniques.

Tuberous Sclerosis Association (1993). Leaflet. Tuberous Sclerosis Association of Great Britain, c/o Mrs J Medcalf (Secretary), Barnsley Farm, Bromsgrove B61 0NQ ☎ 0191-668 5717. Details of a video and a tape-slide presentation on tuberous sclerosis.

University of Newcastle upon Tyne AVC Video catalogue (1990). 29 pages. University of Newcastle upon Tyne Audio Visual Centre, The Medical School, Framlington Place, Newcastle upon Tyne NE2 4HH ☎ 0191-222 6633 fax 0191-222 7696. A wide range of programmes on medicine, surgery, obstetrics and gynaecology and general practice. Hire and sale.

University of Southampton Film and video catalogue (1988). 9 pages. University of Southampton, Department of Teaching Support & Media Services, Southampton SO16 6YD ☎ 01703 796563 fax 01703 796376. Includes programmes on health care, medicine and surgery, safety training and biology. Hire and sale.

Upjohn Audio-Visual Library Catalogue (1990). 8 pages. Upjohn Ltd, The Audio-Visual Librarian, Fleming Way, Crawley, West Sussex RH10 2LZ ☎ 01293 531133 fax 01293 548850. Includes video and tape-slide programmes on various medical topics and related drug therapy. Free loan.

Wellcome Trust Medicine, biomedical science and history (1994). 54 pages. The Wellcome Trust, Audio-Visual Resources Department, 210 Euston Road, London NW1 2BE ☎ 0171-611 8888 fax 0171-611 8545.

Some 50 films and videos on contemporary and historical aspects of tropical medicine and parasitology, immunology, physiology and pharmacology, cardiology, clinical neurology, obstetrics, and veterinary medicine. Sale only.

Wolfe Publishing Complete catalogue (1994). 152 pages. Wolfe Publishing, Mosby-Year Book Europe Ltd, Lynton House, 7-12 Tavistock Square, London WC1H 9LB ☎ 0171-388 7676 fax 0171-344 0018. Mainly medical textbooks, but also includes details of a significant collection of slide atlases, a series of videos on human anatomy, and a series of videodiscs on histology, pathology, radiology and cardiology. Sale only.

Other useful catalogues:
Lawrence Erlbaum (Psychology)
Granada Television (Philosophy, Religion and Ethics)
Institute of Electrical & Electronic Engineers (Electrical and Electronic Engineering)

Mental Health and Counselling (see also health education, psychology, social welfare)

British Association for Counselling Audio-visual aids catalogue (1994). 8 pages. Price £1.50. British Association for Counselling, 1 Regent Place, Rugby CV21 2PJ ☎ 01788 578328 fax 01788 562189. Programmes mainly from the USA on assertiveness training, encounter groups, transactional analysis and related topics for the training of counsellors. Hire or sale from Concord Video & Film Council.

Creative Vision **Video list** (1993). 3 pages. Creative Vision Services Ltd, 38c Torrington Park, North Finchley, London N12 9TP ☎ 0181-446 4187 fax 0181-959 0275. Videos made for the National Association of Citizens Advice Bureaux on counselling and training skills. Hire or sale.

Films for the Humanities & Sciences **Videos** (1994). Leaflets. Films for the Humanities & Sciences Inc, c/o Geoff Foster, 361 Crossley Lane, Mirfield, West Yorkshire WF14 0NU ☎ 01924 495823 fax 01924 497123.
Selected titles from this large American collection of videos and videodiscs. Includes a series on the assessment and treatment of psychological disorders. Sale.

Institute of Counselling **Training videos** (1994). Leaflet. Institute of Counselling, Resources Department, 6 Dixon Street, Glasgow G1 4AX ☎ 0141-204 2230.
Six training videos designed for trainers and students of counselling, showing counselling models, principles and skills, and live counselling sessions using the person-centred approach. Sale.

Institute of Family Therapy **Teaching tape catalogue** (1994). 16 pages. Institute of Family Therapy, 43 New Cavendish Street, London W1M 7RG ☎ 0171-935 1651 fax 0171-224 3291. Videos on aspects of family and marital therapy, some showing actual clients, some using role play, and some lectures. Hire.

Macmed **Videos** (1988). Leaflet. Macmed, 6 Douglas Terrace, Dundee DD3 6HN. Videos with teaching notes on systemic family therapy, the impact of chronic disability on the family, and child sexual abuse. Sale only.

Mencap **Catalogue** (1993). 110 pages. Mencap Books, The Mencap Shop, 123 Golden Lane, London EC1Y 0RT ☎ 0171-696 5569 fax 0171-608 3254. Includes six videos designed for people with learning disabilities, their families and professional carers. Hire.

Mental Health Media **Ability & disability video directory** (1993). 66 pages. Price £6.00. MHM, 356 Holloway Road, London N7 6PA ☎ 0171-700 8129 fax 0171-700 0099. A comprehensive list of videos on disability available for hire or sale from around 100 different distributors. Topics include specific disabilities, family perspectives, independent living, education, and educating the community.

Mental Health Media **Coping with bereavement directory** (1993). 30 pages. Price £6.00. MHM, 356 Holloway Road, London N7 6PA ☎ 0171-700 8129 fax 0171-700 0099. A comprehensive list of videos on death and bereavement available for hire or sale from around 70 different distributors. Topics include communication, cultural identity, euthanasia, facing death, near-death experience, palliative care and hospice care. Video directories on other subject areas in mental health and well-being are also available.

Mental Health Media **Mental distress directory** (1994). 42 pages. Price £4.00. MHM, 356 Holloway Road, London N7 6PA ☎ 0171-700 8129 fax 0171-700 0099. Hundreds of videos relating to mental distress available for hire or sale from various sources. Programmes are arranged under topic headings such as day care, depression, electro-convulsive therapy, housing, law, self-help. Video directories on other subject areas in mental health and well-being are also available.

Mental Health Media **Stress & stress management video directory** (November 1993). 30 pages. Price £4.00. MHM, 356 Holloway Road, London N7 6PA
☎ 0171-700 8129 fax 0171-700 0099.
A comprehensive list of the videos on stress made after 1980 and available for hire or sale from various distributors.

Mental Health Media **Videos** (1993). Leaflets. MHM, 356 Holloway Road, London N7 6PA
☎ 0171-700 8129 fax 0171-700 0099.
Three videos produced and distributed by the MHMC: an employers' guide to mental health issues and recruitment, a programme on advocacy, empowerment and mental health, and a programme to help people coming off tranquillisers. Sale only.

Routledge **Health & social welfare catalogue** (1994). 68 pages. Routledge Videotapes, 11 New Fetter Lane, London EC4P 4EE
☎ 0171-583 9855 fax 0171-583 0701.
Previously Tavistock Videos. Includes four pages of videos depicting encounters between health professionals and a variety of patients or clients, to help trainees become aware of the importance of interpersonal skills in medical practice. Subjects include art therapy, family therapy, group psychotherapy, working with sexually abused children, interviewing in general practice, teaching communication skills, social work practice, and behavioural psychotherapy. Sale only.

Scottish Association for Mental Health **Video list** (1993). Leaflet. Scottish Association for Mental Health, Atlantic House, 38 Gardner's Crescent, Edinburgh EH3 8DQ
☎ 0131-229 9687 fax 0131-229 3558.
Videos on aspects of mental health and well-being. Hire.

Turnip Video Services **Catalogue** (1993). 11 pages. Turnip Video Services, 36 Eton Road, Datchet, Berkshire SL3 9AY ☎ 01753 543889.
Videos on anorexia nervosa, behavioural psychotherapy and psychological defence mechanisms. Sale only.

University of Leicester (1993). Leaflets. University of Leicester Audio Visual Services, PO Box 138, Medical Sciences Building, University Road, Leicester LE1 9HN
☎ 0116 255 2917 fax 0116 252 3993.
Videos for counselling training on the initial interview, a subsequent interview with the same client, the person-centred approach for the new client and for the long-term client, introductory skills, pitfalls in the process, and issues of race and culture in counselling settings. Hire and sale.

Other useful catalogues:
Brook Productions (Philosophy, Religion and Ethics)
Local Government Management Board (Management and Training)

Middle East (see also development studies)

Greenpark Productions

(1992). Leaflets. Greenpark Productions, St Wilfrid's, 101 Honor Oak Park, London SE23 3LB ☎ 0181-699 7234 fax 0181-699 1223.
Videos on Qatar, the Queen visiting Arabia, Royal Jordan, calligraphy in the Qur'an, Islam and the sciences, and the history of advertising. Sale only.

United Nations Relief and Works Agency for Palestine Refugees in the Near East

Audio-visual catalogue (1993). 11 pages. UNRWA, Public Information Office, PO Box 700, A-1400 Vienna, Austria
☎ +43 222 211310 fax +43 222 2307487.
Videos, 16mm films, tape-slide programmes and slide sets dealing with the welfare of Palestine refugees and the Middle East conflict. Soundtracks available in several languages. Sale only.

Military Science (see also history and politics)

Castle Communications

International programme catalogue (1994). 56 pages. Castle Communications, A29 Barwell Business Park, Leatherhead Road, Chessington, Surrey KT9 2NY ☎ 0181-974 1021 fax 0181-974 2674.
A range of videos available for sale through retail outlets. Many programmes use archive footage, particularly those on World War II and Russian history. Other series deal with military campaigns in history, including Viking wars, Zulu wars and Agincourt, and with great figures from history, e.g. Boudicca, Alfred the Great – all very much geared to the National Curriculum.

DD Video

Video Collection (1995). Leaflets. DD Video, 5 Churchill Court, 58 Station Road, North Harrow, Middlesex HA2 7SA ☎ 0181-863 8819 fax 0181-863 0463.
Hundreds of videos for sale direct or through retail outlets, concentrating mainly on war and aviation history.

GMH Entertainments

Video title list (1994). Leaflet. GMH Entertainments, 19-23 Manasty Road, Orton Southgate, Peterborough PE2 0UP ☎ 01733 233464 fax 01733 2838966.
Title listing of videos on the history of war, many using original archive footage. Sale by mail order.

Services Sound & Vision

The Joint Services catalogue of military training films and videos (1994). 90 pages. Services Sound & Vision Corporation, Chalfont Grove, Narcot Lane, Chalfont St Peter, Gerrards Cross SL9 8TN
☎ 01494 871737 fax 01494 872982.
Exclusive distribution of Ministry of Defence training films and videos. The catalogue contains details of Navy, Army and Air Force programmes. Sale.

Other useful catalogues:
Media Arts (Community Studies)

Music (see also arts and under names of individual countries)

Club 50/50 Music

CDs, tapes & videos (1994). Leaflets. Club 50/50 Music, PO Box 1277, Chippenham, Wiltshire SN15 3YZ ☎ 01249 445400 fax 01249 447691.
A mail-order club for supplying videos, compact discs, cassettes and books. Approximately half the titles are music programmes and the others cover hobbies and general interest. Membership fee, including catalogue, is £4.99.

Entertainment Direct **Opera, ballet and classical music on video** (1991). 24 pages.
Entertainment Direct, 1 Redicap Trading Estate, Sutton Coldfield, West
Midlands B75 7BU ☎ 0121-311 2808.
Videos on classical music, opera and ballet from various suppliers
available for sale by mail order.

K-Jazz **Jazz on video** (1989). 6 pages. K-Jazz, 29 May Road, Rochester, Kent ME1
2HY ☎ 01634 405698 fax 01634 403732.
Famous jazz and blues artists on video. Sale.

Rose Records **Audio-visual library services** (1993). Information sheets. Rose Records,
The Studio, Unstable Walk, 18 Ellington Street, London N7 8PP ☎ 0171-609
8288 fax 0171-607 7851.
Rose Records is a supplier of compact discs, cassettes, records and videos
to libraries in the UK and overseas. No catalogue is available, but
individual lists can be printed from the database in response to specific
subject requests. Videos available cover general interest, educational and
feature titles, and audio programmes include spoken word and music
titles and language courses. Sale.

TCB Releasing **Jazz & blues films** (1989, current 1994). 11 pages. TCB Releasing, Stone
House, Rudge, Frome, Somerset ☎ 01373 830769.
16mm films of performances by jazz and blues musicians including Count
Basie, Duke Ellington, Charlie Parker and Mahalia Jackson. Hire only.

Other useful catalogues:
British Universities Film & Video Council (Drama)

The Netherlands

NIS Film Distribution **Catalogue** (1994). 110 pages. NISS Film Distribution, Anna
Paulownastraat 76, 2518 BJ The Hague The Netherlands
☎ +31 70 356 4205 fax +31 70 362 5464.
Includes documentaries, animated films, drama, films on Holland, and
children's films.

NIS Film Distribution **Documentaries on the Netherlands** (1993). 20 pages. NISS Film
Distribution, Anna Paulownastraat 76, 2518 BJ The Hague The
Netherlands
☎ +31 70 356 4205 fax +31 70 362 5464.
Videos distributed on behalf of the Netherlands Ministry of Foreign
Affairs on tourism, geography, art and culture, hydraulic engineering,
social welfare and education, and commerce, industry and technology.
Free loan.

Norway

National Audio Visual Library **Films on Norway** (1994). 5 pages. National Audio Visual Library, Unit 16,
Greenshields Industrial Estate, Bradfield Road, Silvertown London E16 2AU
☎ 0171 474 8707 fax 0171-511 1578.
Films, videos and slide sets on Norway and its culture. Free loan plus
charge for postage.

Nursing (see also health education, medical sciences, mental health & counselling, social welfare)

Aegis Healthcare
First Aid at Work (1993). Leaflet. Aegis Healthcare Ltd, 87 Oxford Road, Waterloo, Liverpool L22 7RE ☎ 0151-920 3814 fax 0151-928 5557.
FIRST AID AT WORK is a six-part video series covering resuscitation, asphyxia, bleeding and wounds, injuries, fractures, and spinal injuries. The programmes are intended to complement structured first-aid courses. Sale only.

British Medical Association
Catalogue of films and videos in the British Medical Association Library (1993). 348 pages. Price £40.00. *Information:* BMA Library Film & Video Services, BMA House, Tavistock Square, London WC1H 9JP ☎ 0171-383 6690 fax 0171-388 2544. *Catalogue sales:* Library Association Publishing Ltd, c/o Bookpoint Ltd, 30 Milton Park, Abingdon, Oxfordshire OX14 4TD ☎ 01235 835001 fax 01235 832068.
A detailed, annotated list of the films and videos in the BMA Library. All titles have received peer review. Entries include full filmographic details, synopses and target audience. Arranged alphabetically and indexed under subject headings. Programmes available on free loan to BMA members and affiliated libraries in the UK.

British Medical Association
Current videos for loan (1992 + supplement). 50 pages. BMA Library Film & Video Services, BMA House, Tavistock Square, London WC1H 9JP ☎ 0171-383 6690 fax 0171-388 2544.
A collection of videos available for free loan to BMA members. The catalogue is organised under broad subject headings from abortion to urology.

Educational Media, Film & Video
Health video catalogue (1992). 44 pages. Educational Media, Film & Video Ltd, 235 Imperial Drive, Rayners Lane, Harrow, Middlesex HA2 7HE ☎ 0181-868 1908 fax 0181-868 1991.
A large collection of videos on all aspects of health education and more specialised programmes for medical and nursing education. Sale only.

ENB Publications
The nursing of children: a resource guide (1994). Loose-leaf catalogue. Price £12.50. ENB Publications, Victory House, 170 Tottenham Court Road, London W1P 0HA. ☎ 0171-391 6314 fax 0171-383 4031.
Along with articles relevant to the subject, the guide contains annotated listings of multimedia resources that have been recommended by members of the children's nursing profession. Includes appraisals of these materials and suggestions on how they may be used.

Graves Medical Audiovisual Library
Catalogue (1993). Loose-leaf catalogue. Graves Medical Audiovisual Library, c/o Concord Video & Film Council, 201 Felixstowe Road, Ipswich IP3 9BJ ☎ 01473 714754 ☎ 01473 726012 fax 01473 274531.
A large collection of videos, tape-slide programmes, audiotapes, computer software and booklets on medical subjects. Entries are arranged by subject and include descriptions and suggested audience levels. There are subject, title, author and numerical indexes. Hire and sale.

Healthcare Productions

Catalogue: videos, audiocassettes, leaflets and booklets (1993). 73 pages. Healthcare Productions, 2 Stucley Place, London Camden Lock, NW1 8NS ☎ 0171-267 8757 fax 0171-267 4803.

A wide range of programmes for nursing and patient education. Includes a clinical series made for the Royal College of Nursing and three programmes from the Royal College of Midwives. Also some health programmes made for Channel 4. Sale only.

Milestone Training through Television

(1993). Leaflet. Milestone Training through Television, 51 Cliff Road, Leeds LS6 2EZ ☎ 0113 275 4988.

A range of videos for management and interpersonal skills training for the nursing and medical professions. Hire or sale.

Oxford Educational Resources

Title lists and complete catalogue on disk (current). 3 title lists. Oxford Educational Resources, PO Box 106, Kidlington, Oxfordshire OX5 1HY ☎ 01865 842552 fax 01865 842551.

The largest distributor of medical programmes in the UK, with programmes from the collections of Camera Talks, Didactic Films, Marine Audio Visual Instruction Systems, the American Journal of Nursing, the Hospital Satellite Network and other producers world-wide. Hundreds of videos, films, tape-slide sets and software titles for medical and nursing training and health education. The complete catalogue is regularly updated and can be supplied on disk. A title list is available, and individual subject sections are printed out on request. Many language versions are available. There are also programmes in a few non-medical areas – crime prevention, language teaching, wildlife and earth sciences. Sale only.

South Bank University

Catalogue (1993). 15 pages. South Bank University, Distance Learning Centre, South Bank Technopark, 90 London Road, London SE1 6LN ☎ 0171-928 8989 fax 0171-815 7899.

A range of distance- and open-learning courses for nurses, midwives and health visitors for use in pre- and post-registration courses. Sale only.

Philosophy and Religion

British Humanist Association

(1992). Leaflet. British Humanist Association, 14 Lamb's Conduit Passage, London WC1R 4RH ☎ 0171-430 0908.

Details of a video on non-religious ethics, specifically on humanist values and morality. Sale.

Brook Productions

Programmes from Brook (1993). 40 pages. Brook Productions, 21-24 Bruges Place, Randolph Street, London NW1 0TF ☎ 0171-482 6111 fax 0171-284 0626.

Six series of discussion programmes from the VOICES series, first shown on Channel 4: KNOWLEDGE IN CRISIS, WRITERS & POLITICS, MODERNITY & ITS DISCONTENTS, PSYCHOANALYSIS, and THE TROUBLE WITH TRUTH. In another discussion series, FIN DE SIECLE, international writers and thinkers voice their preoccupations as we approach the year 2000. Also a series of psychodramas entitled THE SESSION, and individual programmes on mental health. Sale only.

Central Independent Television   **Religious catalogue** (1993). 29 pages. Central Independent Television plc, Video Resources Unit, Broad Street, Birmingham B1 2JP ☎ 0121-643 9898 fax 0121-616 1531.

Programmes from Central Television's broadcast output on issues relating to religion, selected for sale to education on video. Includes titles from the award-winning VIEWPOINT series. Individual programmes look at ethical issues such as abortion, animal rights, black people in Britain, charities, euthanasia, and poverty.

The Church Army   **Video catalogue** (1993). 16 pages. Church Army Resource Centre, Independents Road, Blackheath, London SE3 9LG, 081 318 1226 ext. 240. Videos on aspects of Christianity organised under headings that include ministry, children, family, testimonies, and young people. Hire or sale.

CTVC   **Video programme catalogue** (1995). 19 pages. CTVC Video Library, Hillside, Merry Hill Road, Bushey, Watford WD2 1DR ☎ 0181-950 4426 fax 0181-950 6694.

Titles from world-wide sources with ethical and/or Christian themes. Includes children's programmes, lectures and teaching programmes, discussion starters, documentaries, profiles and testimonies, and some fiction films. Sale only.

Granada Television International   **Programme catalogue** (1992). 80 pages. Granada Television International, Non-Theatric Sales, Granada Television International, 36 Golden Square, London W1R 4AH ☎ 0171-734 8080 fax 0171-494 6280.

Several hundred Granada programmes selected for educational use. Includes the series HYPOTHETICALS, in which questions of crucial importance in the media, law, medicine and government are approached by those in authority. Sale only.

Humanitas   **Video series** (1994). Leaflet. Humanitas, 20 Queen Anne's Gate, London SW1H 9AA ☎ 0171-233 0278 fax 0171-233 0574.

Two series of videos focusing on the human consequences of critical problems facing the world, e.g. deforestation, disasters, famine, humanitarian intervention, human rights, refugees, indigenous peoples, modern warfare, street children. Sale from Television Trust for the Environment.

Kensington Church Videos   (1993). Leaflet. Kensington Church Videos, PO Box 5031, London W12 9ZR ☎ 0181-740 0173 fax 0181-995 8599.

Videos for religious education in schools and parishes. GOD'S HOUSE, GOD'S FAMILY examines the link between the church building and the church community and visits various Christian churches. Other videos explore the significance of baptism, marriage and Holy Communion.

Pathway Productions   **Catalogue** (1994). 26 pages. Pathway Productions, 22 Colinton Road, Edinburgh EH10 5EQ ☎ 0131-447 3531 fax 0131-452 8745.

A department of the Church of Scotland producing videos on religious and social welfare topics for hire. Several tape-slide and audiocassette programmes are also available.

Viewtech **Humanities catalogue** (1994). 38 pages. Viewtech Film & Video, 161 Winchester Road, Brislington, Bristol BS4 3NJ
☎ 0117 977 3422 fax 0117 972 4292.
A selection of programmes from the main Viewtech catalogue in the area of humanities, including programmes suitable for religious studies. Sale only.

Physics (see also astronomy & astronautics, energy, information technology, science & technology)

Aston University, Centre for Extension Studies **Mathematics and physics programmes catalogue** (1990). 24 pages. Aston University, Centre for Extension Studies, Aston University, Aston Triangle, Gosta Green, Birmingham B4 7ET ☎ 0121-359 3611 ext. 4590 fax 0121-359 7358.
Video lectures for INSET on A-level physics and mathematics, covering the content of school syllabuses and new approaches to teaching. Sale only.

British Universities Film & Video Council **Physics & astronomy: video & film resources** (1989). 77 pages. Price £12.00. BUFVC, 55 Greek Street, London W1V 5LR
☎ 0171-734 3687 fax 0171-287 3914.

A classified catalogue of over 600 films and videos on physics and astronomy from many distributors, suitable for sixth-form level and above. Each entry contains a brief synopsis of content, production and distribution details, and an indication of appropriate course and level.

National Physical Laboratory **Videos and films** (1993). Leaflet. NPL Information Services, Teddington, Middlesex TW11 0LW ☎ 0181-977 3222 fax 0181-943 2155.
Videos and films on standards and measurement, including measurement by laser. Free loan and sale.

University of Iowa **The mechanics of fluids** (1992). Leaflet. University of Iowa, AVC Marketing, 215 Seashore Center, Iowa City, IA 52245-1402, USA
☎ +1 319 335 2555 fax +1 319 335 2507.
Six videos on the basic principles of fluid mechanics and their application, shown through experiments and animation. For sale to UK customers on PAL-standard videocassette either individually or as a series. Printed scripts provided with each programme.

Other useful catalogues:
National Meteorological Library (Geography and Earth Sciences)
National Physical Laboratory (Engineering and Manufacturing)

Poland

Polish Cultural Institute **Video cassettes lending library catalogue** (1993). 21 pages. Polish Cultural Institute, 34 Portland Place, London W1N 4HQ
☎ 0171-636 6032 fax 0171-637 2190.
Some 400 videos in the following categories: feature films (Polish language only); feature films (Polish language with English subtitles); Polish films for children; theatre; general culture, including music and dance; folk, and miscellaneous. Free loan.

Psychology (see also mental health & counselling, science & technology, social sciences)

Brain Sciences Information Project **Films, videos and teaching materials** (1991). 4 pages. BSIP, Hill House, 96 Wimbledon Hill, London SW19 7PB ☎ 0181-946 4677 fax 0181-946 4599. Films and videos on aspects of neurology, particularly vision, movement and balance, for use in the teaching of psychology and physiology. Sale.

British Psychological Society **Teaching psychology: information and resources** (1993). 261 pages. Price £29.99. British Psychological Society, St Andrew's House, 48 Princess Road East, Leicester LE1 7DR ☎ 0116 254 9568 fax 0116-247 0787.
A handbook of resources for teachers of psychology. A chapter on audio-visual aids lists the main distributors of psychology material and a selection of programmes. Another chapter on psychology and the cinema discusses the use of feature films in the teaching of psychology and gives examples of films to illustrate particular themes e.g. adolescence, disability, women. Other chapters cover literature, psychological tests, software, and laboratory equipment.

Lawrence Erlbaum **Cognitive, developmental and neuropsychology** (1993). 84 pages. Lawrence Erlbaum Associates Ltd, 27 Palmeira Mansions, Church Road, Hove, East Sussex BN3 2FA ☎ 01273 207411 fax 01273 205612.
Includes a series of five videos on cognitive neuropsychology covering dyslexia, agnosia and attentional dysfunction, and another series of three videos on visual neglect after a stroke. Sale.

Psychology News **Video sales** (1993). Leaflet. Psychology News, 17a Great Ormond Street, London WC1N 3RA ☎ 0171-831 3385 fax 0171-404 7072.
A small range of videos originally made for ITV and Channel 4 on topics of social and psychiatric interest, such as memory, how children abuse other children, Soviet psychiatric hospitals, eye conditions and their treatment, and mental health in Japan. Sale only.

Turnip Video Services **Catalogue** (1993). 11 pages. Turnip Video Services, 36 Eton Road, Datchet, Berkshire SL3 9AY ☎ 01753 543889.
Videos on topics including anorexia nervosa, behavioural psychotherapy and psychological defence mechanisms. Sale only.

Uniview **The psychology series** (1994). Leaflet. Uniview Productions, 22 Mostyn Avenue, West Kirby, Wirral, Cheshire L48 3HW ☎ 0151-625 3453 fax 0151-625 3453.
A continuing series of videos on cognitive psychology for students from GCSE to first-year undergraduate level. Topics covered so far are attention and cognitive development. Sale only.

Race Relations and Cultural Identity (see also community studies, development studies, social sciences)

The African Video Centre **Mail order catalogue** (1992). 50 pages. The African Video Centre, 7 Balls Pond Road, Dalston, London N1 4AX ☎ 0171-923 4224 fax 0171-275 0112.
A substantial catalogue of films and videos that depict some aspect of the black experience. Programmes are organised in categories including biography,

black film-makers, black history, drama, classic black movies, lectures, music, Rastafari, sports, travel, and wildlife. Loan to members or sale.

Bandung Productions   **Ten years of Bandung Films** (1994). 20 pages. Bandung Ltd, Block H, Carker's Lane, 53-79 Highgate Road, London NW5 1TL
☎ 0171-482 5045 fax 0171-284 0930.
Programmes made for the Channel 4 series BANDUNG FILE and REAR WINDOW, which cover themes in literature, cinema, music, art, architecture and the history of ideas world-wide. Sale only.

British Film Institute   **Black & Asian film/video list** (1988). 200 pages. Price £4.20. British Film Institute, 21 Stephen Street, London W1P 1PL
☎ 0171-255 1444 fax 0171-436 7950.
Some 600 feature films and documentaries dealing with arts culture, politics and history in a black and Asian context. With descriptions, production details and distribution information. Hire and sale.

Ceddo   **Film and video list** (1993). 2 pages. Ceddo Film & Video Workshop, 63-65 Coburg Street, London N22 6UB ☎ 0181-889 7654.
A collection of videos, some of which have been broadcast, exploring the effect of social issues on the cultural development of individuals and groups in the UK and in Third World countries. Hire or sale.

Mental Health Media   **Cultural identity & racism video directory** (1993). 53 pages. Price £6.00. MHM, 356 Holloway Road, London N7 6PA ☎ 0171-700 8129 fax 0171-700 0099.
A comprehensive list of videos on cultural identity and racism available for hire or sale from around 100 different distributors. Topics include culture, education, employment, family relationships, media representations, and sexuality. Video directories on other subject areas in mental health and well-being are also available.

Penumbra Productions   **Film and television productions** (1987). 4 pages. Penumbra Productions Ltd, 21a Brondesbury Villas, London NW6 6AH
☎ 0171-328 4550 fax 0171-328 3844.
Videos on the South Asian sub-continent and about South Asians living in Britain. Sale only.

Runnymede Trust   **Anti-racist resources: a guide for adult & community education** (1989). 91 pages. Price £5.95. Runnymede Trust, 11 Princelet Street, London E1 6QH
☎ 0171-375 1496.
Includes films and videos from many distributors for use in teaching about issues of race and anti-racism, and for integrating an anti-racist perspective into education generally.

Science and Technology (see also chemistry & chemical engineering, civil engineering & building, electrical & electronic engineering, energy, engineering & manufacturing, information technology, physics)

Academy Television   **CD-ROM multimedia packages** (1993). Leaflets. Academy Television,
now trading as YITM   Kirkstall Road, Leeds LS3 1JS ☎ 0113 246 1528 fax 0113 242 9522.
Five interactive CD-ROMs produced by Yorkshire Television in conjunction with Interactive Learning Productions, designed for use in

education. Each package contains a CD-ROM, a floppy disk, and teacher and pupil workbooks. Subjects are French, Spanish, the environment, science, and inventors and inventions. Available for Acorn Archimedes and PC with Windows 3.1.

Academy Television now trading as YITM — **Equinox catalogue** (1994). 20 pages. Academy Television, Kirkstall Road, Leeds LS3 1JS ☎ 0113 246 1528 fax 0113 242 9522.
Details of all programmes in the Channel 4 EQUINOX series broadcast in the last five years (Series 4 onwards). These cover a wide range of topics in the areas of engineering, science, design and technology. Programmes are available for sale on video immediately after broadcast.

Atlas Copco — **Compressed air video library** (1993). Leaflet. Atlas Copco Compressors Ltd, Communications Department, Swallowdale Lane, Hemel Hempstead HP2 7HA ☎ 01442 61201.
Eight videos selected to give an initial understanding of the fundamentals of compressed air and compressor installations, from how compressed air is produced, through drying and refrigeration to basic installation principles and heat recovery. Sale only.

Atlas Copco — **Video programmes available from Airpower** (1993). 20 pages. Atlas Copco Compressors Ltd, Communications Department, Swallowdale Lane, Hemel Hempstead HP2 7HA ☎ 01442 61201.
Videos on air compressors, listed in chronological order and covering types, ancillary equipment, sales and service, basic techniques and technical fundamentals. Sale only.

Attica Cybernetics — **Multimedia CD-ROM catalogue** (1994). 17 pages. Attica Cybernetics Ltd, Unit 2, Kings Meadow, Ferry Hinksey Road, Oxford OX2 0DP ☎ 01865 791346 fax 01865 794561.
PC-based multimedia CD-ROMs including the HUTCHINSON ENCYCLOPAEDIA, the EUROPEAN VIDEO ATLAS (with video profiles created from ITN news footage), plant science, mammalian biology, the interactive periodic table, and World War II archives (using footage and other material from the Imperial War Museum and the BBC).

BBC Videos for Education and Training — (1994). 60 pages. BBC Videos for Education & Training, BBC Enterprises Ltd, 80 Wood Lane, London W12 0TT ☎ 0181-576 2415 fax 0181-576 2916.
Over 500 BBC television programmes on video. Broad subject categories are anthropology, arts, business, drama, education issues, environment, earth sciences and ecology, health and medicine, history and politics, natural history, and social issues. A further 2000 programmes are available on request. The range includes titles from the HORIZON and QED series as well as classic drama and business television. Sale only.

British Gas — (1994). 36 pages. British Gas Education Service, 326 High Holborn, London WC1V 7PT ☎ 0171-242 0789 ext. 3452.
Resource packs, some video or software-based, designed to link in with National Curriculum work in science, technology and geography. Sale only.

The British Library — **New publications for schools** (1994). Leaflet. British Library Education

Service, Great Russell Street, London WC1B 3DG ☎ 0171-323 7783.
Includes CD-ROMs on inventors and inventions, British birds and
medieval realms, which incorporate images, full-motion video, animation
and audio commentary, designed for use in schools. Also audiocassette
packs of oral history with supporting notes on survivors of the Holocaust
and on the history of the steel industry. Sale.

British Nuclear Fuels   **Primary and secondary educational resources** (1993). Leaflets. British Nuclear
Fuels, Risley, Warrington, Cheshire WA3 6AS ☎ 01925 832000 ext. 255.
Includes a range of educational resources, some of them video-based, on
the theme of living with technology. Sale only.

British Universities   **Discovery & invention: a review of films & videos on the history of**
Film & Video Council   **science and technology** (1988). 74 pages. Price £7.00. BUFVC, 55 Greek
Street, London WIV 5LR ☎ 0171-734 3687 fax 0171-287 3914.

283 films and videos, from various distributors, recommended for use in
teaching the history of science, with reviewers' comments included.
Topics are the philosophy of science, social relations, industrial
archaeology, transport, medicine, and the main scientific and
technological disciplines.

British Universities   **Higher Education Film and Video Library catalogue** (1994). 88 pages.
Film & Video Council   Price £5.00. BUFVC, 55 Greek Street, London WIV 5LR
☎ 0171-734 3687 fax 0171-287 3914.

Over 500 specialist films and videos on many subjects recommended for
use in degree-level teaching. The catalogue is arranged under broad
subject headings and includes programmes from organisations such as the
Institut für den Wissenschaftlichen Film, Göttingen, and the Rothampstead
Experimental Station. Programmes may be hired through Concord Video
and Film Council, and some are available for sale from the BUFVC.

Central Independent Television   **Science, environmental issues and geography catalogue** (1993). 41 pages.
Central Independent Television plc, Video Resources Unit, Broad Street,
Birmingham B1 2JP ☎ 0121-643 9898 fax 0121-616 1531.
Programmes from Central Television's broadcast output selected for sale
to education on video. Topics in this catalogue include famine, history of
science, development issues, international debt, etc.

Classroom Video   **Video catalogue** (1994). 16 pages. Classroom Video, Darby House,
Bletchingley Road, Mertsham, Redhill, Surrey RH1 3DN
☎ 01737 642880 fax 01737 644110.
Videos aimed particularly at the National Curriculum. Subjects include the
environment, geography, English, social studies and history, personal
development, chemistry, physics, general science, and design and technology.
Separate catalogues are available for the various subject areas. Sale only.

Cumana   **The Cumana CD-ROM portfolio for schools and colleges** (1994). 54
pages. Cumana Ltd, Pines Trading Estate, Broad Street, Guildford GU3
3BH ☎ 01483 503121 fax 01483 451371.
CD-ROMs and interactive videos from various producers selected for their
relevance to education. Includes the MIST series on science and technology.

241

Encyclopaedia Britannica **Laserdisc product & price list** (1993). 6 pages. Encyclopaedia Britannica International Ltd, Education Division, Station Approach, Wallington, Surrey SM6 0DA ☎ 0181-669 4355 fax 0181-773 3631.
Five series of interactive videodiscs for science teaching, covering physics, earth science and biology. A separate catalogue lists CD-ROMs of various reference works. Sale only.

Guildsoft **Catalogue** (1994). 32 pages. Guildsoft Ltd, The Software Centre, East Way, Lee Mill Industrial Estate, Ivybridge nr Plymouth PL21 9PE ☎ 01752 895100 fax 01752 894833.
Computer software and CD-ROMs for education and business. Includes CD-ROMs on the body, UFOs and science topics, which use full-motion video and 3-D images. Sale.

H & H Scientific **Training videos** (1994). Leaflets. H & H Scientific Consultants Ltd, PO Box MT27, Leeds LS17 8QP ☎ 0113 268 7189 fax 0113 268 7191.
Videos on ionising radiation produced by the University of Sheffield, and one on training for radiation workers from the University of Sussex. Sale only.

Philip Harris **Catalogue** (1994). 742 pages. Philip Harris Education, Lynn Lane, Shenstone, Lichfield, WS14 0EE ☎ 01543 480077 fax 01543 480068.
Includes audio-visual materials and equipment, including a range of videos for teaching biology, chemistry and physics from primary to tertiary level.

Institut für den Wissenschaftlichen Film **Scientific films** (1983). 166 pages. IWF, c/o BUFVC, 55 Greek Street, London WIV 5LR ☎ 0171-734 3687 fax 0171-287 3914.
Over 250 university-level films with English commentaries, chosen from the IWF library for their usefulness in English-speaking countries. Subjects include biology, physics, biophysics, chemistry, meteorology, engineering, medicine, veterinary medicine, psychology, and ethnology. 78 of these films are available for hire or sale from the BUFVC and may be previewed there free of charge.

Look & Learn Television **New British produced video resources for the National Curriculum** (1994). Leaflets. Look & Learn Television, 8 Dalby Court, Gadbrook Business Centre, Northwich, Cheshire CW9 7TN ☎ 01606 49723 fax 01606 350625.
A range of videos with accompanying print materials produced to support the National Curriculum geography, science and technology. Topics include transport, map reading, bridges, structures, buildings, flight, child development and the life cycle of a frog. Sale.

McGraw-Hill **CD-ROMs** (1994). Leaflets. McGraw-Hill Book Company Europe, Shoppenhangers Road, Maidenhead, Berkshire SL6 2QL ☎ 01628 23432 fax 01628 770244.
The PC-based MULTIMEDIA ENCYCLOPEDIA OF MAMMALIAN BIOLOGY and the MULTIMEDIA ENCYCLOPEDIA OF SCIENCE & TECHNOLOGY. Sale.

The Open University **Catalogue of learning resources from the undergraduate programme** (1994). 102 pages. Open University Educational Enterprises Ltd, 12 Cofferidge Close, Stony Stratford, Milton Keynes MK11 1BY ☎ 01908 261662 fax 01908 261001.

Lists by title the hundreds of videocassettes, audiocassettes, study texts and computer packages in all subject areas that form part of Open University undergraduate courses and are available for sale separately to outside institutions. Alternatively, programmes may be recorded off-air under licence from the OU. Synopses of individual programmes are given on course information sheets, which may be requested individually.

The Royal Institution   **Masterclass video series** (1993). Leaflets. The Royal Institution of Great Britain, 21 Albemarle Street, London W1X 4BS
☎ 0171-409 2992 fax 0171-629 3569.
Three lecture demonstrations with teachers' notes and workbooks. Topics are the nature of colour, geometry and perspective, and gyroscopes and boomerangs. Sale only.

Science & Engineering Research Council   **Video catalogue** (1992). 8 pages. SERC, Public Relations Unit, Polaris House, North Star Avenue, Swindon, Wiltshire SN2 1ET ☎ 01793 444000.
Videos about various SERC research projects and facilities including CERN, the Ariel VI programme, sub-nuclear particle physics, computer-simulated engineering, microfabrication facilities, the Royal Greenwich Observatory, the British National Space Centre, the working of a transputer for parallel computing, and particulate technology research. Free loan.

Scottish Council for Educational Technology   **Unilever catalogue** (1985). 12 pages. SCET Training Resources, Dowanhill, 74 Victoria Crescent Road, Glasgow G12 9JN ☎ 0141-337 5000.
Science programmes commissioned by Unilever in the 1960s and early 1970s.

The Standing Conference on Schools Science and Technology   **Technology publications** (1994). Leaflet. SCSST, Technology in Context Publications, 76 Portland Place, London W1N 4AA
☎ 0171-278 2468 fax 0171-753 5200.
SCSST is an independent national organisation established to promote the development of science and technology in schools. The TECHNOLOGY IN CONTEXT series of videos, multimedia and text resources is designed to help teachers of technology, showing how technology is important for many aspects of everyday life. Sale.

UMC Sales and Marketing   **Video list** (1993). 6 pages. UMC Sales and Marketing, The Old Rectory, High Street, Bury, Huntingdon, Cambridgeshire PE17 1NL
☎ 01487 815300 fax 01487 710270.
Over 40 videos in the TECHNOLOGY SOLUTIONS series which serve to illustrate how new technology is influencing the way markets do business. Subjects include construction, the motor trade, hotels and catering, premises management, energy management, retailing, wholesaling, distribution, warehousing, and logistics. Also generic titles on microcomputers, business software, networks, data communications, and the Pick operating system. Sale only.

Windfall Films   **Videos** (1994). 2 pages. Windfall Films Ltd, 19-20 Bow Street, London WC2E 7AB ☎ 0171-379 5993 fax 0171-497 2966.
Two programmes made for television that deal with classroom management and a series of four programmes on measurement produced for use in schools.

Scotland

Graphic Archives

Scotland slide catalogue (1993). Leaflet. Graphic Archives, 106 East Claremont Street, Edinburgh EH7 4JZ, Scotland ☎ 0131-558 1348
Eight sets of 50 slides each dealing with the cultural and social history of Scotland over the last 200 years. Among the subjects are the book designs of Talwin Morris, the Glasgow School of Art, and Hill House, which was designed by Charles Rennie Mackintosh.

Life's Rich Tapestry

VHS sale & hire catalogue 1994 (1994). 8 pages. Life's Rich Tapestry, Studio 1, WASPS, 22 King Street, Glasgow G1 5QP ☎ 0141-553 1716.
Videos on history, archaeology, art and social work, many with a Scottish connection. Hire and sale.

Scottish Archive Film for Education

(1989). Leaflet. Scottish Film Council, 74 Victoria Crescent Road, Glasgow G12 9JN ☎ 0141-334 4455 fax 0141-334 6519.
Compilations of extracts from films in the Scottish Film Archive on themes such as architecture, fishing, cities, and social history. Sale on video.

Scottish Civic Trust

(1993). Leaflet. Scottish Civic Trust, 24 George Square, Glasgow G2 1EF ☎ 0141-221 1466 fax 0141-248 6952.
Title list of six videos and a film on the conservation work of buildings, including church buildings, and the countryside. Hire or sale.

Social Sciences (see also community studies, development studies, economics, history & politics, law, mental health & counselling, psychology, race relations & cultural identity, social welfare, women's studies)

Albany Video Distribution

Catalogue (1986 + supplements). 48 pages. Albany Film & Video Distribution, Television Centre, Battersea Studios, Thackeray Road, London SW8 3TW ☎ 0171-498 6811 fax 0171-498 1494.
Videos by community-based workshops on topics that include racism, women's issues, handicap, old people, homelessness, AIDS, community action, media, Northern Ireland, youth, black representation, incest, and the law. Hire or sale.

British Film Institute

Lesbian & gay catalogue (1994). 48 pages. Price £2.50. British Film Institute, 21 Stephen Street, London W1P 1PL ☎ 0171-255 1444 fax 0171-436 7950.
Films and videos available from BFI Distribution that are likely to be of particular interest to compilers and audiences of programmes on gay and lesbian themes. Includes shorts, features, video, 35mm and 16mm film. Hire.

Brook Productions

Programmes from Brook (1993). 40 pages. Brook Productions, 21-24 Bruges Place, Randolph Street, London NW1 0TF ☎ 0171-482 6111 fax 0171-284 0626.
Six series of discussion programmes from the VOICES series, first shown on Channel 4: KNOWLEDGE IN CRISIS, WRITERS & POLITICS, MODERNITY & ITS DISCONTENTS, PSYCHOANALYSIS, and THE TROUBLE WITH TRUTH. In another discussion series, FIN DE SIECLE, international writers and thinkers voice their preoccupations as we approach the year 2000. Also a series of psychodramas entitled THE SESSION, and individual programmes on mental health. Sale only.

Campaign for Press & Broadcasting Freedom

Union views (1990). 34 pages. Price £5.00. Campaign for Press & Broadcasting Freedom, 96 Dalston Lane, London E8 1NG ☎ 0171-923 367. Some 300 videos either commissioned by trade unions, or about labour and union issues, available from a variety of sources. They are indexed by subject, e.g. privatisation, employment law, and by union name.

Concord Video and Film Council

Catalogue (1993 + supplement). 273 pages. Price £3.00. Concord Video & Film Council, 201 Felixstowe Road, Ipswich IP3 9BJ ☎ 01473 715754 fax 01473 717088.
Hundreds of documentaries, animated films, and feature-length productions dealing with contemporary social issues in the UK and abroad. Concord distributes films and videos for over 350 voluntary organisations and charities. Hire and sale.

Leeds Animation Workshop

(1994). Leaflets. Leeds Animation Workshop, 45 Bayswater Row, Leeds LS8 5LF ☎ 0113 248 4997.
A range of animated films made by this women's collective on subjects such as the shortage of women in senior management positions, stress, environmental issues, international debt, and homelessness. Hire or sale on film or video.

Metro Pictures

Film & video catalogue (1989 + supplements). 92 pages. Metro Pictures Ltd, 79 Wardour Street, London WIV 3TH ☎ 0171-434 3357 fax 0171-287 2112.
Shorts, feature films and documentaries on development, environment, the nuclear debate, history, human rights, gay liberation, media and education, racial issues, trade unions and labour studies, and women in society. Hire on 35mm and 16mm film.

The Open University

Catalogue of learning resources from the undergraduate programme (1994). 102 pages. Open University Educational Enterprises Ltd, 12 Cofferidge Close, Stony Stratford, Milton Keynes MK11 1BY ☎ 01908 261662 fax 01908 261001.
Lists by title the hundreds of videocassettes, audiocassettes, study texts and computer packages in all subject areas that form part of Open University undergraduate courses and are available for sale separately to outside institutions. Alternatively, programmes may be recorded off-air under licence from the OU. Synopses of individual programmes are given on course information sheets, which may be requested individually.

Out on a Limb

Catalogue (1993). 25 pages. Out on a Limb Film & Video Distribution, Television Centre, Battersea Studios, Thackeray Road, London SW8 3TW ☎ 0171-498 9643 fax 0171-498 1494.
Videos and films on lesbian and gay themes. Section headings are features, documentaries, experimental and short fiction, the films of Monika Treut, responses to HIV and AIDS, and archive material. Hire and sale.

Pennsylvania State University

Media sales catalogue (1993). 64 pages. The Pennsylvania State University, Audio-Visual Services, Special Services Building, 1127 Fox Hill Road, University Park, PA 06803-1824, USA ☎ +1 814 865 6314 fax +1 814 863 2574.
A sizeable collection of videos suitable for use in higher education. The collection is particularly strong in anthropology and the social sciences,

but most academic subjects are represented. Most programmes are available for sale to UK customers on PAL-standard videocassette.

Scottish Central Film & Video Library

Social subjects on 16mm film & video (1989). 52 pages. SCFVL, Downanhill, 74 Victoria Crescent Road, Glasgow G12 9JN
☎ 0141-334 9314 fax 0141-334 6519.
No longer available.

Team Video Productions

Catalogue (1989 + supplements). 21 pages. Team Video Productions, 105 Canalot, 222 Kensal Road, London W10 5BN ☎ 0181-960 5536.
Videos and video-based teaching packs on new technology, health and safety, pre-vocational training, business and trade union studies, nuclear power, media studies, development studies and environmental conservation. Some are accompanied by student worksheets and lesson plans. Sale only.

United Nations

Film & video catalogue (1992). 71 pages. United Nations Information Centre, 20 Buckingham Gate, London SW1E 6LB ☎ 0171-630 1981 fax 0171-976 6478.
Films on economic concerns, human settlements, natural resources and the environment, political affairs, social issues, and the history and organisation of the United Nations itself. Free loan and sale.

Workers Film Association

Video and film distribution catalogue (1989 + supplements). 36 pages. Price £1.00. Workers Film Association, 9 Lucy Street, Manchester M15 4BX ☎ 0161-848 9782 fax 0161-848 9783.
Films from various countries dealing with the economic, cultural, social and political problems of the worker. Hire only on film; hire and sale on video.

Social Welfare (see also development studies, health education, mental health & counselling, social sciences)

Academy Television now trading as YITM

Healthwatch video catalogue (1993). 18 pages. Academy Television, Kirkstall Road, Leeds LS3 1JS ☎ 0113 246 1528 fax 0113 242 9522.
A selection of programmes broadcast by Yorkshire–Tyne Tees Television, Thames Television, Channel 4, Scottish Television, Ulster Television, HTV and WTN. This catalogue contains details of over 100 titles from the main Academy catalogue, focusing on material relating to health and social issues. The aim of the selection is to provide information and discussion material on medical advances and the social effects of illness on patients. Sale on video.

Barnardo's

Child care publications list (1993). 14 pages. Barnardo's Child Care Publications, Tanners Lane, Barkingside, Ilford, Essex IG6 1QG
☎ 01268 520224 fax 01268 520230.
Videos illustrating Barnardo's child care services, including fostering, work with handicapped children, youth and community projects, learning skills, speech and language development, and the history of child care. Hire or sale.

Boulton-Hawker Films

Health education video catalogue (1993 + supplement). 28 pages. Boulton-Hawker Films Ltd, Hadleigh, Ipswich IP7 5BG
☎ 01473 822235 fax 01473 824519.

Videos on health and hygiene, human biology, sex education and personal development. The 1994 supplement includes all the titles previously in the separate social welfare catalogue on topics such as disability, sexual harassment and abuse, and elderly people. Sale and preview.

Central Council for Education & Training in Social Work
Community Care Database (quarterly). 64 pages. CCETSW, Derbyshire House, St Chad's Street, London WC1H 8AD
☎ 0171-278 2455 fax 0171-278 2934.
A quarterly bulletin with materials, events and networks related to training in community care. Includes a substantial number of videos, available from a range of sources.

Central Independent Television
Health and social issues catalogue (1993). 27 pages. Central Independent Television plc, Video Resources Unit, Broad Street, Birmingham B1 2JP
☎ 0121-643 9898 fax 0121-616 1531.
Programmes from Central Television's broadcast output selected for sale to education on video. Topics include women's issues, mental health and stress, physical handicap, healthcare, and social issues. Sale.

The Children's Society
Video collection (1994). 6 pages. The Children's Society, Public Relations Department, Edward Rudolf House, Margery Street, London WC1X 0JL
☎ 0171-837 4299 fax 0171-837 0211.
Videos on the work of the society covering adoption, Portage learning, runaway children, and the *guardian ad litem* role as strengthened by the 1989 Children Act. Hire or sale.

Comic Relief
List of educational materials (1994). 6 pages. Comic Relief, c/o Charity Projects, 1st floor, 74 New Oxford Street, London WC1A 1EF
☎ 0171-436 1122 fax 0171-436 1541.
Edited versions of broadcasts that accompanied the television appeals, showing underlying causes of poverty in Tanzania. Designed for use in primary and secondary education. Also a pack on the education of disabled pupils in mainstream schools. Sale only.

Concord Video and Film Council
Catalogue (1993 + supplement). 273 pages. Price £3.00. Concord Video & Film Council, 201 Felixstowe Road, Ipswich IP3 9BJ
☎ 01473 715754 fax 01473 717088.
Hundreds of documentaries, animated films, and feature-length productions dealing with contemporary social issues in the UK and abroad. Concord distributes films and videos for over 350 voluntary organisations and charities. Hire and sale.

DMP Video Productions
(1993). Leaflet. DMP Video Productions, 14 Oakfield Road, Roath, Cardiff CF2 3RD ☎ 01222 499745.
Training videos for health and social work education. Sale only.

Institute for the Study of Drug Dependence
Focus on drugs (1990). 14 pages. Institute for the Study of Drug Dependence, Waterbridge House, 32-36 Lomon Street, London SE1 0EE ☎ 0171-928 1221.
Films and videos on drug misuse that are available for hire or sale in the UK.

Mental Health Media
Ability & disability video directory (1993). 66 pages. Price £6.00. MHM, 356 Holloway Road, London N7 6PA ☎ 0171-700 8129 fax 0171-700 0099.

A comprehensive list of videos on disability available for hire or sale from around 100 different distributors. Topics include specific disabilities, family perspectives, independent living, education, and educating the community. Video directories on other subject areas in mental health and well-being are also available.

Mental Health Media   **Community care video directory** (1992). 42 pages. Price £6.00. MHM, 356 Holloway Road, London N7 6PA ☎ 0171-700 8129 fax 0171-700 0099.
A comprehensive list of videos on community care available for hire or sale from around 100 different distributors. Topics include carers' perspectives, day services, educating the community, health and safety, learning difficulties, older people, and work. Video directories on other subject areas in mental health and well-being are also available.

National Foster Care Association   **Training list** (1995). Leaflet. National Foster Care Association, Leonard House, 5-7 Marshalsea Road London SE1 1EP, London SW1P 1DE ☎ 0171-828 6266 fax 0171-357 6668.
Two training videos which introduce the concept and explain the process of fostering to prospective carers, and also give the point of view of young people whose parents are carers. Topics include child development, emotional problems, abuse, children with disabilities, children in hospitals and institutions, AIDS, anti-racism, sex education, substance abuse, young people, elderly people, and legal matters.

Northern College   **Catalogue** (1992). 100 pages. Northern College of Education, The Publications Unit, Gardyne Road, Broughty Ferry, Dundee DD5 1NY ☎ 01382 453433 fax 01382 455246.
Books, videos and audiocassettes on a wide range of subjects for use in education, teacher training and social work training. Sale only.

The Open University    **Community education study packs** (1994). 20 pages. Open University Learning Materials Sales Office, PO Box 188, Milton Keynes MK7 6DH ☎ 01908 652185 fax 01908 654320.
Details of study packs for individual or group use, with the option of having one's study assessed. Designed to help people with learning that is relevant to their everyday lives and contributes to personal development. Subjects are broadly in the areas of health and lifestyle, family and school, caring for others, community issues and action, preparing for study. Packs usually consist of workbooks, course readers, video- and/or audiocassettes.

The Open University   **Educational & training opportunities** (1994). 44 pages. Open University, Department of Health & Social Welfare, Walton Hall, Milton Keynes MK7 6AA ☎ 01908 653743 fax 01908 654124.
Details of study packs suitable for individual study and in-service or college-based training but which do not lead to Open University awards. Packs usually consist of workbooks, course readers and video- and/or audiocassettes. Areas covered include working and living with children and young people, ageing, disability, health studies, and social welfare.

Pavilion Publishing **Catalogue** (1994). 32 pages. Pavilion Publishing (Brighton) Ltd, 8 St George's Place, Brighton BN1 4GB ☎ 01273 623222 fax 01273 625526. Training materials for the caring services. Includes video-based packs and videos on decision-making for people with learning difficulties, safer sex for people with learning difficulties, the experience of mentally ill people living in the community, better communication with old people, reminiscence with the elderly, and QUARTZ quality reviews. Sale.

PLANET'S Resource Database **Video list** (1993). 92 pages. Price £6.50. PLANET, c/o Harperbury Hospital, Harper Lane, Radlett, Hertfordshire WD7 9HQ ☎ 01923 854861 ext. 4384. Currently available videos from the PLANET Resource Centre database listing more than 230 videos from various distributors on aspects of disability.

Project Icarus **Videos** (1993). 2 pages. Project Icarus, 214a Havant Road, Drayton, Portsmouth PO6 2EH ☎ 01705 324248.
A range of videos on drug, alcohol and solvent abuse. Hire or sale.

Re-Solv (1994). Leaflets. Re-Solv, 30a High Street, Stone, Staffordshire ST15 8AW ☎ 01785 817885 fax 01785 813205.
Videos with supporting literature on the prevention of solvent and substance abuse. Sale.

Rolf Harris Video **Educational and training programmes** (1993). Leaflets. Rolf Harris Video, 183 Drury Lane, London WC2B 5QF ☎ 0171-240 8777 fax 0171-240 8779. Videos for schoolchildren and their teachers on personal safety, divorce, the family problems caused by unemployment, and water safety. Some programmes are supported by teaching notes. Sale only.

Royal National Institute for the Blind **Some films on blindness** (1993). 35 pages. Price £2.00. RNIB, 224 Great Portland Street, London W1N 6AA ☎ 0171-388 1266 fax 0171-388 2034. A wide range of videos and other audio-visual materials relating to blindness and visual impairment, available from various distributors.

Scottish Council for Single Parents **Tape-slide programmes and videos** (1993). 4 pages. Scottish Council for Single Parents, 13 Gayfield Square, Edinburgh EH1 3NX ☎ 0131-556 3899. Videos and tape-slide programmes about single-parent families. In addition to using documentary footage several of the programmes employ humour and drama to make their points. Hire.

Scottish Women's Aid **List of audio-visual resources** (1993). Leaflet. Scottish Women's Aid, 12 Torpichen Street, Edinburgh EH3 AHQ ☎ 0131-221 0401 fax 0131-221 0402. Videos and audiotapes on the experiences of battered women and their children, and how men can take responsibility for their violence through self-help groups. Hire or sale.

Swingbridge Video **Tapes** (1994). Leaflets. Swingbridge Video, Norden House, 41 Stowell Street, Newcastle upon Tyne NE1 4YB ☎ 0191-232 3762. A workers' co-operative producing videos on topics such as drug abuse, social control through architecture, community care, survivors of the Holocaust, poverty, police powers, racism, and housing. Hire or sale.

Trust for the Study of Adolescence **Tapes about teenagers** (1994). Leaflets. TSA Publishing Ltd, 23 New Road, Brighton BN1 1WZ ☎ 01273 680281 fax 01273 679907.
Audiocassettes discussing problems and experiences for the parents and families of adolescents. Sale.

Twentieth Century Vixen **Videos** (1994). Leaflets. Twentieth Century Vixen, 13 Aubert Park, London N5 1TL ☎ 0171-359 7368.
Videos looking at issues including disability, the changing role of women in Japan, conductive education, child abuse, and bringing up children with learning and behavioural problems. Sale.

Other useful catalogues:
BBC Educational Developments (Education)
Pathway Productions (Philosophy, Religion and Ethics)

Spanish Studies (see also languages, media studies: feature films)

Encyclopaedia Britannica **Laserdisc product & price list** (1993). 6 pages. Encyclopaedia Britannica International Ltd, Education Division, Station Approach, Wallington, Surrey SM6 0DA ☎ 0181-669 4355 fax 0181-773 3631.
Includes an interactive videodisc programme for Spanish language teaching. Sale only.

European Schoolbooks **Spanish & Portuguese catalogue** (1993). 34 pages. European Schoolbooks Ltd, The Runnings, Cheltenham GL51 9PQ ☎ 01242 245252 fax 01242 224137.
A number of video-based language courses and individual audio- and videocassettes of works of Spanish literature. Also examples of recent television advertisements with supporting literature. Sale only.

Spanish Tourist Office **Videos available on loan** (1993). Leaflet. Spanish Tourist Office, 57 St James's Street, London SW1A 1LD ☎ 0171-499 0901 fax 0171-629 4257.
Title list of an extensive range of videos on topics relating to Spanish culture available on free loan.

Other useful catalogues:
BBC for Business (Management and Training)
Icarus (Architecture)

Sport and Physical Recreation

Boulton-Hawker Films **Physical education video catalogue** (1994). 12 pages. Boulton-Hawker Films Ltd, Hadleigh, Ipswich IP7 5BG ☎ 01473 822235 fax 01473 824519.
Videos on sports science, anabolic steroids, fitness and exercise, anatomy and physiology, personal hygiene, diet and nutrition, drug education, and self-defence for women. Sale and preview.

Burgess Video Group **Marine video catalogue** (1994). 16 pages. Burgess Video Group, Unit 6-18, Industrial Estate, Brecon, Powys LD3 8IA ☎ 01874 611633 fax 01874 625889.
Videos covering all aspects of marine sport, including techniques, navigation, maintenance, accident prevention and instrumentation. Also separate leaflets on diving and classic cars. Sale.

The Central Council of Physical Recreation — (1993). Leaflet. CCPR, Francis House, Francis Street, London SW1P 1DE ☎ 0171-828 3163 fax 0171-630 8820.
Includes three videos on CCPR training awards. Sale only.

Chrisfilm and Video — **Catalogue** (1993). 15 pages. Chrisfilm & Video Ltd, Glasshouses Mill, Pateley Bridge, Harrogate HG3 5QH ☎ 01423 711310 fax 01423 712271.
Instructional videos on a range of outdoor sports, and recordings of outstanding events and expeditions. Sale only.

Coachwise — **Annual catalogue** (1994). 22 pages. 114 Cardigan Road, Headingley, Leeds LS6 3BJ ☎ 0113 274 3889 fax 0113 231 9606.
Includes seven videotapes on the art and science of coaching, a series on great moments in various sports, and individual videos on training in volleyball, plyometrics, weight training, and nutrition for sport. Sale only.

Duke Marketing — **Powersport video news** (1994). 24 pages. Duke Marketing Ltd, PO Box 46, Milbourn House, St George's Street, Douglas, Isle of Man IM99 1DD ☎ 01624 623634 fax 01624 629745.
Hundreds of videos on car and motorbike racing. Sale by mail order.

Human Kinetics — **Annual catalogue** (1994). 140 pages. Human Kinetics (Europe), PO Box IW14, Leeds LS16 6TR ☎ 0113 278 1708 fax 0113 278 1709.
Includes videos on basketball, tennis, athletics, skiing, swimming and diving, volleyball, juggling, and movement activities for children. Sale.

National Coaching Foundation — **Action Replay** (1990). 119 pages. Price £20.00. The National Coaching Foundation, 4 College Close, Beckett Park, Leeds LS6 3QH ☎ 0113 274 4802 fax 0113 275 5019.
A joint publication between the National Coaching Foundation and the Sports Library and Information Centre, produced from the NCF audio-visual database. Contains details of over 900 videos on sport and leisure, ranging from athletics to yoga, available for sale in the UK.

Sports Council — **Videos held in the Information Centre** (1993). 14 pages. Sports Council Information Centre, 16 Upper Woburn Place, London WC1H 0QP ☎ 0171-388 1277 fax 0171-383 5740.
Videos on a range of sports, all available for viewing by prior appointment at the Sports Council Information Centre. Also gives distribution information.

Twentieth Century Movies — **16mm entertainment catalogue** (1987 + supplement, current 1994). 104 pages. Price £7.00. Twentieth Century Movies, 120 Queen Margaret Drive, Glasgow G20 8NZ ☎ 0141-946 1121.
Hundreds of popular feature films and films of sporting events, particularly football and boxing. Hire on 16mm film.

Other useful catalogues:
British Home Entertainment (Arts)
DD Video (History and Politics)

Switzerland

Swiss National Tourist Office — **List of videocassettes** (1992). 5 pages. Swiss National Tourist Office, Swiss Centre, Swiss Court, London W1V 8EE ☎ 0171-734 1921.

Videos dealing with summer and winter holiday locations, customs and traditions, sport, history, geography and all forms of transport. A separate list covers 16mm films. Hire.

Taiwan

Taipei Representative Office

Film title list (1993). 11 pages. Taipei Representative Office in the UK, 50 Grosvenor Gardens, London SW1W 0EB ☎ 0171-396 9152.
Lists 260 titles on many subjects, most of which are in Chinese. Free loan.

Tourism (see also under names of individual countries)

Audience Planners

Catalogue of services to the travel industry (1993). 16 pages. Audience Planners, 107 Power Road, Chiswick, London W4 5PL ☎ 0181-742 0400 fax 0181-742 0200.
Videos on tourism in many countries around the world. Free loan.
Audience Planners Guide (1993). 20 pages. Audience Planners, 107 Power Road, Chiswick, London W4 5PL ☎ 0181-742 0400 fax 0181-742 0200.
A video and photographic library for the travel industry, sponsored by tourist boards and travel companies. Videos on visits and expeditions (mountain climbing, trekking, cycling, rafting, etc.) to many countries around the world (including Britain), on underground railways of the world, and on wildlife conservation on the continent of Africa. Free loan.

Education Distribution Service

Catalogue (1995). 50 pages. Education Distribution Service, Unit 2, Drywall Estate, Castle Road, Sittingbourne, Kent ME10 2RL ☎ 01735 427614 fax 01735 474871.
This is now the only library distributing sponsored films for a range of companies, tourist boards and organisations. It has taken over many of the collections previously distributed by Viscom. Collections include those of the Post Office, BT, the German Film and Video Library, the National Trust, the Advertising Standards Authority and many others. Hire only.

International Video Network

Video visits catalogue (1993). 14 pages. International Video Network, 107 Power Road, Chiswick, London W4 5PL ☎ 0181-742 2002 fax 0181-995 7871.
A range of travel videos covering areas of the United Kingdom and destinations world-wide. Sale.

Magic Carpet Productions

Video catalogue (1994). Leaflets. Magic Carpet Productions, 27 Richmond Hill, Richmond, Surrey TW10 6RE ☎ 0181-940 3836.
A range of tourist guides to England, France and the Soviet Union. Sale only.

Travel Television

Video travel guides (1994). Leaflets. Travel Television, PO Box 60, Hindhead, Surrey GU26 6XL ☎ 01428 607213 fax 01248 604673.
Some 40 videos on popular holiday destinations abroad. Sale only.

Other useful catalogues:
DD Video (History and Politics)

Transport (see also energy, science & technology)

Ian Allan

Videos (1994). 8 pages. Ian Allan Publishing, c/o Bookpoint Ltd, 39 Milton

252

Park, Abingdon, Oxfordshire OX14 4TD ☎ 01235 831700.
A catalogue of books and videos about various aspects of railways and
steam trains, and a series of videos on learning to fly a plane. Sale.

Paul O'Connor   **Video list** (1992). 4 pages. Paul O'Connor, 25 Dickinson Drive, Sutton
Coldfield, West Midlands, B76 8FP ☎ 0121-378 5668 fax 0121-329 2629.
Videos showing Land Rovers and Range Rovers, their history and
specialised uses. Sale.

**Road Transport Industry Training
Board**   **Learning materials & training services** (1993). 27 pages. RTITB, High
Ercall, Telford, Shropshire TF6 6RB ☎ 01952 770441.
Training packages, some containing a video or audio component, covering
industrial and commercial skills such as electronics, automotive glazing,
driver training and forklift truck training. Sale.

**Transport & Road
Research Laboratory**   **Video and film catalogue** (1991). 39 pages. TRRL Information Services,
Crowthorne, Berkshire RG45 ☎ 01344 773131 fax 01344 770193.
The TRRL is part of the Department of Transport and carries out research
to help set standards for highways, vehicles, traffic and safety. The 140
films and videos are records of these research projects. Hire and sale.

Other useful catalogues:
Film Archive Management & Entertainment (History and Politics)

Veterinary Science (see also anatomy & physiology, animal research & welfare, biology, science & technology)

**Allan White Memorial
Video Library**   **catalogue** (1993). 12 pages. Allan White Memorial Video Library, Marjorie
Taylor, 101 Higher Lane, Rainford, St Helens, Lancashire WA11 8BQ
☎ 01744 883409.
Videos produced by American universities on veterinary subjects,
including animal handling and restraint, diagnosis, surgery,
ophthalmology, and radiography. Hire only.

Bristol Imaging   **Bristol Biomedical Videodisc Project** (1993). Leaflet. Bristol Imaging,
Royal Fort Annexe, University of Bristol, Tyndall Avenue, Bristol BS8 1UJ
☎ 0117 930 3500 fax 0117 925 5985.
A videodisc for teaching and research that holds a collection of 24,000
veterinary, medical and dental still frames, and incorporates the pathology
videodisc UKPATH2. A visual database is available for detailed searches
using any keyword.

Royal Veterinary College   **Audio visual programmes for equine veterinarians** (1993). 24 pages. Royal
Veterinary College, Unit for Veterinary Continuing Education, Royal
College Street, London NW1 0TU ☎ 0171-387 2898 ext. 351 fax 0171-383 0615.
Includes video, tape-slide and audio programmes under the headings
anatomy of the limbs, bandaging, colic, examination, grass sickness,
lameness, locomotion, manipulation, parasites, radiology, reproduction,
restraint, surgery. Hire and sale.
Catalogue of audio visual programmes for farm animal veterinarians
(1993). 32 pages. Royal Veterinary College, Unit for Veterinary Continuing
Education, Royal College Street, London NW1 0TU ☎ 0171-387 2898 ext.

351 fax 0171-383 0615.

Includes video, tape-slide and audio programmes under the headings cattle, deer, goats, pigs, sheep, welfare, and farming. Hire and sale.

Catalogue of audio-visual programmes for small animal veterinarians (1993). 44 pages. Royal Veterinary College, Unit for Veterinary Continuing Education, Royal College Street, London NW1 0TU ☎ 0171-387 2898 ext. 351 fax 0171-383 0615.

Video, tape-slide and audio programmes under headings including anatomy, behaviour, dermatoses, diagnostic techniques, practice management, reptiles, and zoonoses. Hire and sale.

Catalogue of audio visual programmes for veterinary nurses (1993). 32 pages. Royal Veterinary College, Unit for Veterinary Continuing Education, Royal College Street, London NW1 0TU ☎ 0171-387 2898 ext. 351 fax 0171-383 0615.

Programmes on anaesthesia, anatomy, bandaging, bees, bone diseases, cardiology, dermatoses, horses, infectious and parasitic diseases, radiography, reptiles, restraint, small animals, surgery, and animal welfare. Hire and sale.

Extending education (1994). 24 pages. Royal Veterinary College, Unit for Veterinary Continuing Education, Royal College Street, London NW1 0TU ☎ 0171-387 2898 ext. 351 fax 0171-383 0615.

A catalogue bringing together books and all audio-visual programmes made by the UVCE. Listings are by title only; for further information on individual programmes the appropriate UVCE catalogue should be consulted. Sale.

University of Cambridge Department of Clinical Veterinary Medicine   **Teaching videotapes for sale** (1994). Leaflet. University of Cambridge, Department of Clinical Veterinary Medicine, Madingley Road, Cambridge CB3 0ES ☎ 01223 337733 fax 01223 337610.

Nine programmes on clinical veterinary medicine concerned with horses, dogs and cattle. Sale only.

University of Sydney   **Videotape catalogue** (1991). 55 pages. University of Sydney Audiovisual Services, Central Services, Baxter's Lodge, University of Sydney, NSW 2006, Australia ☎ +61 2 692 2651 fax +61 2 692 2560.

Includes programmes on small animal soft tissue surgery, equine medicine and surgery, canine surgery, clinical procedures for dogs and cats, and material specific to racing greyhounds. For sale to UK customers (PAL VHS).

Women's Studies (see also development studies, health education, medical sciences, social sciences)

British Film Institute   **Women's film list** (1989). 211 pages. Price £6.50. British Film Institute, 21 Stephen Street, London W1P 1PL ☎ 0171-255 1444 fax 0171-436 7950.

Hundreds of films, mainly features, but also dramas, drama-documentaries and animated films, from various distributors and concerned with themes of particular interest to women, listed alphabetically from abortion and contraception to work.

Cinenova **Catalogue of films & videos directed by women** (1994). 82 pages. Cinenova, 113 Roman Road, London E2 0HU
☎ 0181-981 6828 fax 0181-983 4441.
Specialist distributor of films and videos directed by women, formed from the amalgamation of the Cinema of Women and Circles distributors in 1991. Fiction and non-fiction films are arranged under broad subject headings. Hire or sale through Glenbuck Films.

Mental Health Media **Women & well-being video directory** (1993). 64 pages. Price £6.00. MHM, 356 Holloway Road, London N7 6PA
☎ 0171-700 8129 fax 0171-700 0099.
A comprehensive list of videos on women's health available for hire or sale from around 100 different distributors. Includes programmes on health, social and political issues. Video directories on other subject areas in mental health and well-being are also available.

Out on a Limb **Catalogue** (1993). 25 pages. Out on a Limb Film & Video Distribution, Television Centre, Battersea Studios, Thackeray Road, London SW8 3TW
☎ 0171-498 9643 fax 0171-498 1494.
Videos and films on lesbian and gay themes. Section headings are features, documentaries, experimental and short fiction, the films of Monika Treut, responses to HIV and AIDS, and archive material. Hire and sale.

Red Flannel Films (1992). Leaflets. Red Flannel Films, 3 Cardiff Road Taffswell, Nr Cardiff CF4 7RA
☎ 01222 813086 fax 01222 813086.
Films documenting life in the South Wales valleys as seen through the eyes of women. Specific topics include midwifery, the Welsh 'mam', and memories of sweets enjoyed in childhood.

Scottish Women's Aid **List of audio-visual resources** (1993). Leaflet. Scottish Women's Aid, 12 Torpichen Street, Edinburgh EH3 8JQ ☎ 0131-221 0401 fax 0131-221 0402.
Videos and audiotapes about the experiences of battered women and their children, and how men can take responsibility for their violence through self-help groups. Hire or sale.

Other useful catalogues:
Central Independent Television (Social Welfare)
Leeds Animation Workshop (Media Studies: Short Films and Animation)
Television History Centre (History and Politics)
Twentieth Century Vixen (Social Welfare)

NEW *in* 1995

BRITISH NATIONAL FILM AND VIDEO GUIDE

CLASSIFIED SUBJECT ARRANGEMENT

AUTHORITATIVE CATALOGUE RECORDS

CONCISE SUMMARY OF CONTENT

COMPREHENSIVE DISTRIBUTORS LIST

INTENDED AUDIENCE INFORMATION

FULL SUBJECT INDEX

A unique guide to all films and videos available for screening to non-fee-paying audiences within the UK such as colleges, businesses and special interest groups.

Over 500 educational and training films, feature films, documentaries and television programmes will be listed in every issue.

PUBLISHED QUARTERLY AND CUMULATED ANNUALLY

FIRST ISSUE AVAILABLE APRIL 1995

For further information and a sample issue contact:
Brenda Jackson-Hill
British Library National Bibliographic Service
Boston Spa, Wetherby, W.Yorkshire LS23 7BQ
Tel: 01937 546160 Fax: 01937 546586
E-mail: brenda.jackson-hill@bl.uk

THE BRITISH LIBRARY
NATIONAL BIBLIOGRAPHIC SERVICE
The world's leading resource for scholarship, research and innovation

Sources of Multimedia Materials

Multimedia Catalogues

The following are distributors of multimedia teaching programmes (videodiscs, CD-ROMs incorporating audio or video, CD-I). They are listed additionally in their respective subject sections.

Academy Television now trading as YITM   **CD-ROM multimedia packages** (1993). Leaflets. Academy Television, Kirkstall Road, Leeds LS3 1JS ☎ 0113 246 1528 fax 0113 242 9522.
Five interactive CD-ROMs produced by Yorkshire Television in conjunction with Interactive Learning Productions, designed for use in education. Each package contains a CD-ROM, a floppy disk and teacher & pupil workbooks. Subjects are French, Spanish, the environment, science, and inventors & inventions. Available for Acorn Archimedes and IBM-compatibles running Windows 3.1.

Anglia Polytechnic University   **CD-ROM & software catalogue** (1993). 10 pages. Anglia Polytechnic University Learning Technology Research Centre, Sawyers Hall Lane, Brentwood, Essex CM15 9BT ☎ 01277 200587 fax 01277 211363.
A range of Macintosh-based CD-ROMs and software, some developed as part of the Renaissance Initiative in collaboration with other higher education institutions. Some materials are intended for courseware developers; others are subject-based. Includes titles on mathematics, environmental science, Shakespeare's *Twelfth Night,* Arthur Miller's *The Crucible,* and IT in the learning environment.

Applied Learning   **Multimedia training** (1994). Leaflets. Applied Learning, 1 Hogarth Business Park, Burlington Lane, London W4 2TJ ☎ 0181-994 4404 fax 0181-944 4404.
Video, CD-ROM, and computer-based training courses on topics relating to information technology, management skills, software training, and human resource development.

Attica Cybernetics   **Multimedia CD-ROM catalogue** (1994). 17 pages. Attica Cybernetics Ltd, Unit 2, Kings Meadow, Ferry Hinksey Road, Oxford OX2 0DP ☎ 01865 791346 fax 01865 794561.
PC-based CD-ROMs including the HUTCHINSON ENCYCLOPAEDIA, the EUROPEAN VIDEO ATLAS, plant science, mammalian biology, the interactive periodic table, and World War II archives.

AVP   **Educational CD-ROMs** (1994). 14 pages. AVP, School Hill Centre, Chepstow, Gwent NP6 5PH ☎ 01291 625439 fax 01291 629671.

A wide range of CD-ROMs from various sources for the educational market. Catalogue includes INVENTORS AND INVENTIONS produced by the British Library and Yorkshire Television and ART GALLERY, taken from the collection of the National Gallery, London.

The British Library   **New publications for schools** (1994). Leaflet. British Library Education Service, Great Russell Street, London WC1B 3DG ☎ 0171-323 7783.
Includes CD-ROMs on inventors and inventions, British birds and medieval realms, which include multimedia sequences and commentary designed for use in schools.

British Universities Film & Video Council   **Sales catalogue** (1993). 20 pages. BUFVC, 55 Greek Street, London WIV 5LR ☎ 0171-734 3687 fax 0171-287 3914.
Includes videodiscs on cell biology and mycology from the Institut für den Wissenschaftlichen Film, Göttingen.

Cambridge CD-ROM   **catalogue** (1994). 64 pages. Cambridge CD-ROM Ltd, Combs Tannery, Stowmarket IP14 2EN ☎ 01449 774658 fax 01449 677600.
A wide range of CD-ROM titles from various producers for business, desktop publishing and educational purposes.

Chadwyck-Healey   **CD-ROM publications** (1994). 28 pages. Chadwyck-Healey Ltd, The Quorum, Barnwell Road, Cambridge CB5 8SW ☎ 01223 215512 fax 01223 215513.
A range of CD-ROMs covering news and business information, literature, bibliographies, official publications, statistics, cartography, and climate. Includes *The UK National Medical Slide Bank on Videodisc*, with 12,440 images of diseases, injuries, medical treatment and healthcare practice.

Comput-Ed   **A catalogue of computer-based training and videos for business and education** (1993). 20 pages. Comput-Ed Ltd, Long Lane, Dawlish EX7 0QR ☎ 01703 455555 fax 01626455544.
Catalogue includes PROFESSOR MULTIMEDIA CD-ROM on how to create a multimedia presentation.

Cumana   **The Cumana CD-ROM portfolio for schools and colleges** (1994). 54 pages. Cumana Ltd, Pines Trading Estate, Broad Street, Guildford GU3 3BH ☎ 01483 503121.
CD-ROMs and interactive videos selected for their relevance to education. Includes the MIST series on science and technology. Sale.

CVG Promotions   **CD-ROM catalogue** (1994). 17 pages. CVG Promotions Ltd, Hassacks Business Centre, Whitecairns, Aberdeen AB23 8UJ ☎ 01358 743888.
CD-ROMs for educational, business, professional and entertainment.

Elsevier   **Interactive Anatomy** (1994). Leaflet. Elsevier Science BV, Department of Medical, Pharmaceutical & Biological Sciences, PO Box 181, 1000 AD Amsterdam, The Netherlands fax +31 20 5803 249.
The first programme in the INTERACTIVE ANATOMY series is a reference atlas of cross-sectional photographs and moving images covering paranasal sinuses and anterior skull bases. For Philips CD-I and PC CD-ROM systems.

Encyclopaedia Britannica   **CD-ROM product & price list** (1994). 6 pages. Encyclopaedia Britannica

International Ltd, Education Division, Station Approach, Wallington, Surrey SM6 0DA ☎ 0181-669 4355 fax 0181-773 3631.
A range of CD-ROMs from various sources, selected for use in education.

Encyclopaedia Britannica   **Laserdisc product & price list** (1993). 6 pages. Encyclopaedia Britannica International Ltd, Education Division, Station Approach, Wallington, Surrey SM6 0DA ☎ 0181-669 4355 fax 0181-773 3631.
Five series of interactive videodiscs for science teaching, covering physics, earth science and biology. Also an interactive videodisc programme for Spanish language teaching. A separate catalogue lists CD-ROM reference works.

Eurotech   **Training programmes** (1993). Leaflets. Eurotech, Oakfield Road, East Wittering, Chichester, West Sussex PO20 8RP ☎ 01243 672891 fax 01243 672031.
An interactive videodisc-based training package on selection interviewing and another on good manual handling practice for the prevention of back or other injuries. Hire or sale.

T C Farries   **Multi media** (1994). 14 pages. T C Farries & Co. Ltd, Irongray Road, Lochside, Dumfries DG2 0LH ☎ 01387 720755 fax 01387 721105.
A selection of UK and US-produced CD-ROMs, including encyclopaedias, reference works, educational and entertainment programmes.

Guildsoft   **Catalogue** (1994). 32 pages. Guildsoft Ltd, The Computer Complex, City Business Park, Stoke, Plymouth PL3 4BB ☎ 01752 895100.
Computer software and CD-ROMs for education and business. Includes language-teaching programs on which the voice can be recorded and compared to native speakers.

Hulton Deutsch Collection   (1994). Leaflets. Hulton Deutsch Collection Ltd, Unique House, 21-31 Woodfield Road, London W9 2BA ☎ 0171-266 2662 fax 0171-289 6392.
A series of CD-ROMs entitled DECADES covering the 1920s to the 1960s, with some 10,000 images from the Hulton Deutsch photographic archive. An additional PEOPLE disc contains 10,000 images of over 4000 contemporary and historical personalities. Images can be searched by keyword, name or date, and high-resolution copies of all the pictures can be obtained for commercial use.

Iansyst   **Computer training products** (1994). 14 pages. Iansyst, United House, North Road, London N7 9DP ☎ 0171-607 5844 fax 0171-607 0187.
Video, audio, CD-ROM and computer software-based training packages for computer skills training, language learning, health & safety training and business skills.

KimStacks   **CD-ROM Catalogue** (1994). 78 pages. KimTec UK, Fairways House, 8 Highland Rd, Wimbourne, Dorset BH21 2QN ☎ 01202 888873 fax 01202 888863.
A wide range of CD-ROMs produced by companies in the UK and abroad.

Longman ELT   (1994). Leaflet. Longman ELT, Longman House, Burnt Mill, Harlow, Essex CM20 2JE ☎ 01279 623927 fax 01279 623795.
The LONGMAN INTERACTIVE ENGLISH DICTIONARY is a CD-ROM incorporating audio pronunciation, video, colour pictures and an 80,000-

word dictionary. The LONGMAN ENGLISH WORKS is a CD-ROM-based package of self-study material for adult learners.

Longman Training — **Technology-based training catalogue** (1993). 36 pages. Training Direct, Longman House, Burnt Mill, Harlow, Essex CM20 2JE ☎ 01279 623927 fax 01279 623795.
Interactive video courses for training in assertiveness, customer care, communication skills, conducting appraisals, sales and marketing, foreign languages, health & safety and finance.

McGraw-Hill — **CD-ROMs** (1994). Leaflets. McGraw-Hill Book Company Europe, Shoppenhangers Road, Maidenhead, Berkshire SL6 2QL ☎ 01628 23432.
The PC-based MULTIMEDIA ENCYCLOPEDIA OF MAMMALIAN BIOLOGY and the MULTIMEDIA ENCYCLOPEDIA OF SCIENCE & TECHNOLOGY.

Meckler — **CD-ROMs in print** (1994). 1188 pages. Price £65.00 (print), £62.50/year (CD-ROM). Meckler, 4th Floor, Artillery House, Artillery Row, London SW1P 1RT ☎ 0171-976 0405 fax 0171-976 0506.
An international listing of 6000 CD-ROM products arranged alphabetically by title, with subject and country indexes. Each main entry includes hardware requirements, search software, networking information, update frequency and price.

Melrose Film Productions — **Video based training catalogue** (1994). 96 pages. Melrose Film Productions, 16 Bromells Road, London SW4 0BL ☎ 0171-627 8404.
Videos and video-based packages covering supervisory skills, management concepts, communication and presentation, quality, customer service, sales and marketing, computers, and accountancy. CD-I versions of several programmes are available. Hire and sale.

Microinfo — **CD-ROM Catalogue** (1994). 108 pages. Microinfo Ltd, PO Box 3, Omega Park, Alton, Hampshire GU34 2PG ☎ 01420 86848 fax 01420 89889.
Scientific, medical, technical, business, educational and other professional reference services on CD-ROM from 100 sources.

Multimedia Communication — **Catalogue of products** (1992). Leaflets. Multimedia Communication Ltd, 4 Downing Street, Farnham, Surrey GU9 7PA ☎ 01252 722707 fax 01252 710220.
A series entitled CD-LANGUES for teaching German, French, Spanish and English as a foreign language. Intended for those who already have a basic knowledge of the language. Uses a combination of text, graphics and compact disc-quality sound.

National Council for Vocational Qualifications — **Publications, packs and videos** (1992). NVCQ, 222 Euston Road, London NW1 2BZ ☎ 0171-728 1893 fax 0171-387 0978.
Includes a videodisc-based package on assessing candidate performance.

Northern Ireland Centre for Learning Resources — **Quality management in schools** (1993). Leaflet. Northern Ireland Centre for Learning Resources, Orchard Building, Stranmillis College, Belfast BT9 5DY ☎ 01232 664525.
An interactive video on staff development, designed for school heads of department.

Optech   **CD-ROM product descriptions and price list** (1994). 56 pages. Koch Media Ltd, East Street, Farnham, Surrey GU9 7XX ☎ 01252 714340 fax 01252 711121.
An extensive range of CD-ROMs from various sources for educational, entertainment, desk-top publishing, reference and business use.

Oxford University Press   **TV und Texte on CD-ROM** (1994). Leaflet. Oxford University Press, Walton Street, Oxford OX2 6DP ☎ 01865 56767 fax 01865 56646.
A video-based language-learning resource for advanced students of German. Available as a video with accompanying workbook, or as a CD-ROM-based package.

Past Forward   **The World of the Vikings** (1993). Leaflets. Past Forward, 1 Pavement, York YO1 2NA ☎ 01904 670825 fax 01904 640029.
As part of the Cultural Roots Project of the Council of Europe, Past Forward has produced videodisc and CD-ROM versions of THE WORLD OF THE VIKINGS specially designed for National Curriculum use. The Romans are the subject of a second project currently in production.

Premiere Productions   **Interactive video training programmes** (1994). Leaflets. Premiere Productions, 16 Castello Avenue, London SW15 6EA ☎ 0181-785 2933 fax 0181-780 1684.
Interactive video programmes for training in management, finance, and language learning.

Silver Platter   **Directory** (1994). 73 pages. Silver Platter Information Services, 10 Barley Mow Passage, Chiswick, London W4 4PH ☎ 0181-995 8242 fax 0181-995 5159.
CD-ROMs in the areas of business, education, food and agriculture, health and safety, health sciences, science & technology and social sciences.

TAG Developments   **Software catalogue: secondary edition** (1993). 23 pages. TAG Developments Ltd, 19 High Street, Gravesend, Kent DA11 0BA ☎ 01474 357350 fax 01474 537887.
A range of software and CD-ROMs from various producers, specially selected for use in secondary education and above. Most curriculum areas are covered.

TFPL Publishing   **The CD-ROM directory** (1994). 1100 pages. Price £95.00 (print), £125.00/year (CD-ROM). TFPL Publishing, 17-18 Britton Street, London EC1M 5NQ ☎ 0171-251 5522 fax 0171-251 8318.
An international guide to some 6000 CD-ROM and multimedia CD titles. Includes production company profiles and information on hardware and software. Published annually in printed form and bi-annually on CD-ROM.

Video Arts   **Catalogue** (1994). 115 pages. Video Arts Ltd, Dumbarton House, 68 Oxford Street, London WIN 9LA ☎ 0171-637 7288 fax 0171-580 8103.
Programmes with support materials covering major aspects of staff development: quality, customer care, management skills, financial appreciation and sales & marketing. Hire or sale on video.

Wolfe Publishing   **Complete catalogue** (1994). 152 pages. Wolfe Publishing, Mosby-Year Book Europe Ltd, Lynton House, 7-12 Tavistock Square, London WC1H 9LB ☎ 0171-388 7676 fax 0171-344 0018.
Mainly medical textbooks but includes a series of videodiscs on histology, pathology, radiology and cardiology.

Library Suppliers of Audio-Visual Materials

The following organisations offer a one-step tracing and ordering service for libraries and institutions wishing to purchase material from a number of producers. Some offer a similar service to individuals.

Channel Video Films **Catalogue** (1994). 58 pages. Channel Video Films, 58 Salusbury Road, London NW6 6ND ☎ 0171-372 2025 fax 0171-372 2025.
A mail-order service supplying thousands of videos from a wide range of suppliers. The catalogue lists mainly feature films, but it also covers non-fiction titles, which are organised by subject. Regular updates are issued.

Exchange Value Video Club **Catalogue** (1991 + supplements, current 1994). 80 pages. Exchange Value Video Club, Nacton, Ipswich IP10 0JZ ☎ 01473 717088 fax 01473 717088.
A mail-order sale and rental library of classic and foreign films on videocassette. Many titles no longer available for sale through retail outlets are available for hire. Catalogue cost is refunded on the first rental.

T C Farries **Fiction audio cassettes, Non-fiction audio cassettes, Non-fiction videos** (1994). 247, 194, 200 pages. T C Farries & Co. Ltd, Irongray Road, Lochside, Dumfries DG2 0LH ☎ 01387 720755 fax 01387 721105.
A classified listing of thousands of fiction and non-fiction audiocassettes and non-fiction videos from hundreds of sources, for supply to libraries, schools, colleges and other educational establishments, and to individuals in the UK and overseas. All subject areas are covered, and supplementary lists are issued regularly. There are showrooms in Dumfries and Hinkley, Leicestershire, together with mobile approval collections. Full library processing including cataloguing and classification is offered.

Fast Forward (1994). 58 pages. Fast Forward, Unit 9-10 Sutherland Court, Moor Park Industrial Estate, Tolpits Lane, Watford WD1 8SP
☎ 01923 897080 fax 01923 896263.
A mail-order catalogue listing by title nearly 16,000 videos organised into 100 subject categories. Mainly feature films, but also sport and leisure-interest programmes.

Gold Distribution **Catalogue** (1992). 53 pages. Price £1.00. Gold Distribution, Gold House, 69 Flempton Road, Leyton, London E10 7NL ☎ 0181-556 2429 fax 0181-539 2176.
A mail-order catalogue, organised by subject, with more than 11,000 video titles.

Ingram Entertainment **Video retail catalogue** (1992). 118 pages. Ingram Entertainment plc, Bashley Road, Park Royal, London NW10 6SD ☎ 0181-965 5555 fax 0181-961 8040.
A distributor of videos mainly for the rental and sell-through markets. Library accounts are welcomed. Feature films predominate, and titles are

arranged under the headings children, features, music, special interest and sport, with a combined title index. New-release supplements appear bi-monthly.

Mr Benson's Video Collection (1994 + monthly updates). 70 pages. Price £2.00. Mr Benson's Video Collection, 375 Harrow Road, London W9 3BR ☎ 0181-960 4868 fax 0181-969 7211.
Around 17,000 video titles covering feature films, sport and leisure interests, available for sale by mail order. Includes CD-I and videodisc versions.

Rose Records **Audio-visual library services** (1993). Information sheets. Rose Records, The Studio, Unstable Walk, 18 Ellington Street, London N7 8PP ☎ 0171-609 8288 fax 0171-607 7851.
Rose Records is a supplier of compact discs, cassettes, records and videos to libraries in the UK and overseas. No catalogue is available, but individual lists can be printed from the database in response to specific subject requests. Videos available cover general interest, educational and feature titles, and audio programmes include spoken word & music titles and language courses.

Video City **Catalogue** (1994). 62 pages. Video City, 117 Notting Hill Gate, London W11 3LB ☎ 0171-221 7029 fax 0171-792 9273.
Many thousands of titles, mainly feature films, available for sale by mail order.

Video Plus Direct **The complete guide to what's on video** (1993). 295 pages. Price £4.95. Video Plus Direct, PO Box 190, Peterborough PE2 6UW ☎ 01733 232800 fax 01733 238966.
Mail-order company supplying over 15,000 entertainment, sport and leisure interest videos and videodisc titles to education, libraries and individuals. Catalogue is arranged alphabetically within categories and contains a brief description of each programme.

Computers in Teaching Initiative (CTI) Centres

The Computers in Teaching Initiative (CTI) was established in 1986 as part of a joint initiative of the University Grants Committee and Computer Board on computers in university teaching. Each centre is staffed by subject specialists with expertise in computer based learning.

Computers in Teaching Initiative Support Service (CTISS) University of Oxford, 13 Banbury Road, Oxford OX2 6NN
☎ 01865 273273 fax 01865 273275 e-mail: ctiss@vax.ox.ac.uk
Contact Jonathan Darby, Joyce Martin
The aims of the CTI are 1) to encourage the development of computer-assisted teaching and learning in UK universities, 2) to evaluate the educational potential of information technology in UK universities, and 3) to promote an awareness of the potential of information technology among lecturers and students in all disciplines. CTISS coordinates the work of the CTI centres and acts as a focal point for activities relating to the use of information technology in university teaching in the UK. It publishes *Active Learning* twice a year.

CTI Centre for Accounting, Finance and Management School of Information Systems, University of East Anglia, Norwich NR4 7TJ
☎ 01603 592312 fax 01603 507720 e-mail: ctiac@uea.ac.uk
WWW = http://www.sys.uea.ac.uk/cti/CTI-AFM.HTM
Contact Ailsa Nicholson
Serves as an information source and disseminator through the journal Account, which includes articles on the use of computers in teaching, software news and reviews, updates on relevant TLTP projects and information on conferences. Runs workshops, seminars and an annual conference. Disseminates through a World Wide Web page and mailbase discussion lists cti-acc-business, cti-acc-audit and cti-acc-marketing.

CTI Centre for Biology Donnan Laboratories, University of Liverpool, PO Box 147, Liverpool L69 3BX
☎ 0151-794 5118 fax 0151-794 4401 e-mail: ctibiol@liverpool.ac.uk
WWW = http://www.liv.ac.uk/ctibiol.html
Contact Éamonn Twomey
Promotes the effective use of computers in teaching of tertiary-level biology, including the applied and pre-clinical disciplines; provides support for academics who are using, or wish to use, computers in teaching; presents lectures, seminars and demonstrations in departments and at scientific meetings of learned societies; publishes the newsletter *Life Sciences Educational Computing* and a resource directory; reviews relevant software; organises and participates in workshops and conferences on the use of computers in teaching; maintains a range of electronic services

accessible via JANET and the Internet, including a World Wide Web server, Gopher and FTP archive.

CTI Centre for Chemistry
Donnan Laboratories, University of Liverpool, PO Box 147, Liverpool, L69 3BX
☎ 0151-794 3576 fax 0151-794 3586 e-mail: ctichem@liverpool.ac.uk
WWW = http://www.liv.ac.uk/ctichem.html
Contact Roger Gladwin
Aims 'to enhance the quality of teaching and learning of chemistry through the use of appropriate technology'. Produces and distributes an annually updated guide to software sources; produces and distributes the journal Software Reviews and the newsletter CacheFile twice a year; maintains an electronic bulletin board at NISS and a World Wide Web site; evaluates software for chemistry teaching by the staff of the centre and by a team of external academics; attends lectures and conferences concerned with computer-aided learning; and organises a series of workshops on the use of computers in teaching chemistry.

CTI Centre for Computing
Faculty of Informatics, University of Ulster at Jordanstown, Newtownabbey, County Antrim, Northern Ireland BT37 0QB
☎ 01232 365131 ext 3020 fax 01232 362803 e-mail: cticomp@ulster.ujvax.ac.uk
WWW = http://www.uist.ac.uk/cticomp/index.html
Contact Sylvia Alexander
Publishes NewsSheet.

CTI Centre for Computing in Economics
Department of Economics, University of Bristol, 8 Woodland Road, Bristol BS8 1TN
☎ 0117-928 8478 fax 0117-928 8577 e-mail: cticce@bristol.ac.uk
WWW = http://www.bristol.ac.uk/deptsctice/home.htm
Contact Mike Emslie
Organises workshops and visits to other economics departments. The information base is available via the World Wide Web on JANET. Publishes a Catalogue of Economics Software and Cheer: Computers in Higher Education Economics Review. Enquiries are welcomed.

CTI Centre for Engineering
Department of Mechanical Engineering, Queen Mary and Westfield College, Mile End Road, London E1 4NS
☎ 0171-975 5528 fax 0171-975 5500 e-mail: ctieng@qmw.ac.uk
Contact Mukesh Bhatt

CTI Centre for Geography (with Geology) (CTICG)
Department of Geography, University of Leicester, University Road, Leicester, LE1 7RH
☎ 0116-252 3824 fax 0116-252 3854 e-mail: cti@le.ac.uk
WWW = http://www.le.ac.uk/cti/
Contact John Castleford
Publishes Geocal magazine, which contains articles on computer-assisted learning in the geography curriculum, reports on the centre's TLTP project, details of new products, product reviews and software developments. Involved in developing courseware and disseminating TLTP materials; is setting up a World Wide Web server whereby news and information about the CTICG can be assessed via the Internet; publishes a

newsletter with information on new products, courses and seminars. CTI-GEOG is the mailbase e-mail distribution list.

CTI Centre for History   University of Glasgow, 1 University Gardens, Glasgow G12 8QQ
☎ 0141-330 4942 fax 0141-330 5518 e-mail: ctich@glasgow.ac.uk
WWW = http://www.arts.gla.ac.uk/www/ctich/homepage.html

Contact   Donald Spaeth, Trish Cashen
Supports and encourages the introduction of computers in the teaching of history and archaeology and facilitates links between research and teaching. Most services are free of charge to lecturers. Holds information on courses which use computers, as well as datasets, copies of software, books and articles on computer topics. Arranges visits for lecturers to use the resources. Publishes A Guide to Software for Historians (a new edition will cover art history and archaeology also), runs training courses for academic staff and postgraduates, and publishes the newsletter Craft. Organises seminars visits to art, history and archaeology departments. Workbooks are available for purchase.

Archaeology Consortium   10 The Square, Glasgow G12 8QQ
☎ 0141-339 8855 ext 8313 fax 0141-307 8044 e-mail: tltparch@dish.gla.ac.uk
WWW = http://www. arts.gla.ac.uk/www/ctich/homepage.html

Contact   Dr Ewan Campbell
Aims to improve the quality and efficiency of teaching and learning in higher education by providing a set of high-quality interactive hypermedia computer-assisted learning packages and resources for archaeology undergraduates, which will be distributed free to UK higher education institutions.

Core Resources for Historians: the
History Courseware Consortium   University of Glasgow, 1 University Gardens, Glasgow G12 8QQ
☎ 0141-339 8855 ext 6953 fax 0141-330 5518 e-mail: tltphist@dish.gla.ac.uk
WWW = gopher://gopher.arts.gla.ac.uk

Contact   Dr Astrid Wissenburg
Develops source-based tutorials on computer to help academics teach the large number of history students in higher education more efficiently and effectively. Tutorials and bibliographies will address important historical topics taught at many institutions, with the current focus on the coming of mass politics, the industrial revolution and post-industrialism; medieval and pre-modern themes will be addressed in the second year of the project.

CTI Centre for Human Services   Department of Social Work Studies, University of Southampton, Southampton SO9 5NH
☎ 01703 592779 fax 01703 592779 e-mail: ctihums@soton.ac.uk

Contact   Jackey Rafferty, Suki Sitaram
Publishes New Technology in the Human Services: the Journal of the CTI Centre for Human Services and a regular newsletter. Disseminates information via workshops, conferences and a bulletin board. Collects, reviews and catalogues suitable software for teachers in the human services. Explores computer-based methods of teaching and maintains a database of individuals in the UK, Europe and North America interested in the use of computers in the field.

CTI Centre for Land Use and Environmental Studies	William Guild Building, University of Aberdeen, Aberdeen AB9 1UB 01224 273754 fax 01224 273752 e-mail: cticlues@aberdeen.ac.uk WWW = http://www.clues.abdn.ac.uk:8080/cti.html
Contact	Jacqui Nicol Provides practical support and training for staff and is developing computer-assisted learning courseware. Promotes and discusses the effective use of information technology in teaching, publishes a newsletter and organises a programme of workshops, talks and software demonstrations. Also publishes the Directory of Resources for Computer-Based Learning in Land Use and Environmental Sciences.
CTI Centre for Law	School of Law, University of Warwick, Coventry CV4 7AL ☎ 01203 523294 fax 01203 524105 e-mail: ctilaw@warwick.ac.uk WWW = http://www.csv.warwick.ac.uk:8001/default.html
Contact	Colin Shaw, Centre Manager
CTI Centre for Library and Information Studies	Department of Information and Library Studies, Loughborough University of Technology, Loughborough LE11 3TU ☎ 01509 223057 fax 01509 223053 e-mail: ctilis@lut.ac.uk WWW = http://info.lut.ac.uk/departments/dils/cti/cti.html Fytton Rowland Contributes information to the Bulletin Board for Libraries (BUBL) on JANET, and maintains a Janet e-mail mailing list for up-to-date information. Issues a newsletter every two months, organises workshops and publishes the Resources Guide, which aims to provide information on packages and datasets.
CTI Centre for Mathematics	Centre for Computer-Based Learning, University of Birmingham, Edgbaston, Birmingham B15 2TT ☎ 0121-414 4800 fax 0121-414 6267 e-mail: ctimath@bham.ac.uk WWW = http://www.bham.ac.uk/citmath/
Contact	Pam Bishop
CTI Centre for Statistics	Department of Statistics, University of Glasgow, University Gardens, Glasgow G12 8QW ☎ 0141-330 4873 fax 0141-330 4814 e-mail: ctistat@stats.gla.ac.uk
Contact	Susan MacInnes Authoritative source of information about computer-based material appropriate for teaching mathematics and statistics, provided as a service to the UK higher education sector. Publishes the resource guide Maths & Stats: Guide to Software for Teaching, which provides details of software packages and other available materials, and the quarterly newsletter Maths & Stats, which contains articles and reviews of software as used in teaching. Also organises regular workshops and conferences, commissions reviews of software, runs several electronic discussion lists which provide a forum for exchanging information, and encourages the exchange of teaching materials. Information sheets, reviews and reports are available in written form and on the World Wide Web server. Anonymous ftp server contains courseware materials and demo versions of commercial packages.

CTI Centre for Medicine	Royal Fort Annex, University of Bristol, Tyndall Avenue, Bristol, BS8 1UJ ☎ 0117-928 7492 fax 0117-925 5985 e-mail: cticm@bristol.ac.uk
Contact	Dr Adrian Longstaffe, Director; Sue Furber, Academic Manager

Encourages and supports the use of computers in medical education, with services generally free to medical teachers in universities. Also serves as information provider for computer-based teaching materials. Visits to the centre can be arranged. Establishes and maintains a database of courseware and other resources for computer-aided learning, which includes multimedia and details of current projects and developments in the field, with the information published in the Guide to Software and Resources for Computer-Based Learning in Medicine, Dentistry and Veterinary Science. General information can be found in newsletters, including CTICM Update. Organises conferences, workshops, talks and demonstrations, arranges reviews and assessment of software and course material and advises on the hardware in the specialised area of interactive video and multimedia. Also has contact with commercial organisations.

CTI Centre for Modern Languages (with Classics)	School of European Languages and Cultures, University of Hull, Cottingham Road, Hull HU6 7RX ☎ 01482 465872 fax 01482 473816 e-mail: cti.lang:hull.ac.uk
Contact	Jenny Parsons, June Thompson

Established to 'support and encourage the use of computers in the teaching of modern languages in the UK higher education sector'. Publishes the ReCALL Journal, ReCALL Newsletter and the ReCALL Software Guide. Lead site of the TELL Consortium and headquarters of EUROCALL.

CTI Centre for Music	Department of Music, Lancaster University, Lancaster LA1 4YW ☎ 01524 593776 fax 01524 593939 e-mail: ctimusic@lancaster.ac.uk WWW = http://www.lancs.ac.uk/music/research/CTI.html
Contact	Lisa Whistlecroft

Gathers information on computer applications that might be of use to university musicians and musicologists in their teaching and has a library of music software. Publishes the journal Musicus and the newsletter CTImusic News, and disseminates information electronically via the World Wide Web. Staff will visit university music departments to demonstrate software and/or discuss the integration of computer-assisted learning into curricula. Visits to the centre can be arranged.

CTI Centre for Physics	Department of Physics, University of Surrey, Guildford GU2 5XH ☎ 01483 259329 fax 01483 259501 e-mail: ctiphys@ph.surrey.ac.uk WWW = http://www.ph.surrey.ac.uk
Contact	Margaret Millington

Publishes a quarterly newsletter Computers in Physics Education and an annual couseware catalogue listing software applicable to teaching physics/engineering in physics departments in UK universities.

CTI Centre for Psychology	Department of Psychology, University of York, Heslington, York, Y01 5DD ☎ 01904 433156 fax 01904 433181 e-mail: ctipsych@york.ac.uk

WWW = http://ctipsych.york.ac.uk/ctipsych.html

Contact   Annie Trapp

CTI Centre for Sociology and the Policy Sciences (SocInfo)

Department of Applied Social Science, University of Stirling, Stirling FK9 4LA
☎ 01786 467703 fax 01786 466880 e-mail: ctisoc@stirling.ac.uk
WWW = http://lorne.stir.ac.uk:80/departments/cti_centre

Contact   Ms Millsom Henry, Director

Researches the social implications of new technologies. Offers a comprehensive consultancy, research and training service to social science academics. Publishes annually a software catalogue and three newsletters containing articles, software reviews, reports and general news. Organises events on related topical issues.

CTI Centre for Textual Studies

Oxford University Computing Services, 13 Banbury Road, Oxford OX2 6NN
☎ 01865 273221 fax 01865 273275 e-mail: ctitext@vax.ox.ac.uk

Contact   Lorna Hughes, Stuart Lee

Aims to cover all text-based subjects: philosophy, logic, theology, and theatre arts and drama. Has the responsibility of the Office for Humanities Communication, which conducts research on matters of current concerns; disseminates information by organising conferences and meetings; and produces printed and on-line newsletters such as Computers and Texts. Produces the on-line bulletin board HUMBUL on computing in the humanities. Undertakes major surveys. Is also involved in other publications, for example, a discussion of the use of computers in literary studies (Deegan, Lee, and Mullings, 1992). Has strong links with other departments of UK universities. Publishes a Resources Guide, with reviews and descriptions of software packages which are available for demonstration at the centre.

Equipment Suppliers and Services

The following is a selected list of equipment manufacturers and service suppliers. The list is not intended to be comprehensive. It should be regarded as a starting point for prices and advice. The companies listed have either been used by the British Universities Film & Video Council in the past or have been recommended to us. If you are a member of the BUFVC we will be happy to try to answer enquiries concerning possible sources of specialised equipment or services (☎ 0171-734 3687).

The list includes suppliers of specialised equipment and services, such as *microscopes and image processing* and *high-speed camera systems*, which may only rarely be required in the course of producing film or television material for teaching. The Council can also advise on possible sources of help in specialist fields for one-off events or productions.

Computer Accessories Inmac, Stuart Road, Manor Park, Runcorn, Cheshire WA7 1TH
☎ 0181-740 9540 fax 01800 611116

Computer Data and Graphics Displays Gordon Audio-Visual Ltd, Symes Mews, 37 Camden High Street, London
(including OHP LCD tablets) NW1 7JE
☎ 0171-387 3399 fax 0171-383 7411

Inmac, Stuart Road, Manor Park, Runcorn, Cheshire WA7 1TH
☎ 0181-740 9540 fax 01800 611116

Diazochrome Materials Gordon Audio-Visual Ltd, Symes Mews, 37 Camden High Street, London
NW1 7JE
☎ 0171-387 3399 fax 0171-383 7411

Equipment Cases Case Design, Chiltern Hill, Chalfont St Peter, Bucks SL9 9UQ
☎ 01753 889969 fax 01753 889855

Light Alloy Ltd, Dales Road, Ipswich, Suffolk IP1 4JR
☎ 01473 740445 fax 01473 240002

Oakleigh Cases Ltd, 10 The Summit Centre, Summit Road, Potters Bar,
Herts EN6 3JN
☎ 01707 655011 fax 01707 646447

Equipment Stands Bretford Manufacturing Ltd, Shirley Lodge, 470 London Road, Slough SL3 8QY

Unicol Engineering, Green Road, Headington, Oxford OX3 8EU
☎ 01865 66000 fax 01865 67676

Film Animation Rostrums Neilson Hordell, Unit 18, Central Trading Estate, Staines, Middx TW18 4XE
☎ 01784 456456 fax 01784 459657

Film and Video Editing Supplies PEC, 4 Dean Street, London W1V 5RN
(gloves, spacer, tape, spools etc) ☎ 0171-437 4633 fax 0171-287 0492

Philip Rigby and Sons Ltd, 14 Creighton Avenue, Muswell Hill, London N10 1NU
☎ 0181-883 3703 fax 0181-444 3620

Topham Film Supplies, 316-318 Latimer Road, London W10 6QN
☎ 0181-960 0123 fax 0181-969 3714

Film Stock Manufacturers Agfa-Gevaert Ltd, 27 Great West Road, Brentford, Middx TW8 9AX
and Suppliers ☎ 0181-231 4310 fax 0181-231 4315

The Film Stock Centre, 70 Wardour Street, London W1V 3HP
☎ 0171-494 2244 fax 0171-494 2645

Fuji Photo Film (UK), Fuji Film House, 125 Finchley Road, London NW3 6JH
☎ 0171-586 5900 fax 0171-722 4259

Keith Johnson and Pelling, 93-103 Drummond Street, London NW1 2HJ
☎ 0171-380 1144 fax 0171-387 3354

Kodak Ltd, Kodak House, PO Box 66, Station Road, Hemel Hempstead, Herts HP1 1JU
☎ 01442 61122 fax 01442 41656

Film and Slide Projectors Edric Audio Visual, 34-36 Oak End Way, Gerrards Cross, Bucks SL9 8BR
☎ 01753 884646 fax 01753 887163

Gordon Audio-Visual Ltd, Symes Mews, 37 Camden High Street, London NW1 7JE
☎ 0171-387 3399 fax 0171-383 7411

Hanimex Audio-Visual, 22-23 Westmead, Swindon, Wilts SN5 7YT
☎ 01793 526211 fax 01793 544814

Hargreaves, Cavendish House, Orrel Mount, Hawthorne Road, Liverpool L20 6PX
☎ 0151-922 9922 fax 0151-922 1504

Jessop of Leicester, Jessop House, 98 Scudamore Road, Leicester LE3 1TZ
☎ 0116 2320033 fax 0116 2320060

Keith Johnson and Pelling, 93-103 Drummond Street, London NW1 2HJ
☎ 0171-380 1144 fax 0171-387 3354

Metro Presentation Hire, 57-59 Great Suffolk Street, London SE1 0BS

☎ 0171-928 2088 fax 0171-261 0685

Film Cleaning and Checking Equipment   RTI (UK) Ltd, Unit 6, Swan Wharf Business Centre, Waterloo Road, Uxbridge, Middx UB8 2RA
☎ 01895 252191 fax 01895 274692

Film Laboratories   Filmatic Laboratories, 16 Colville Road, London W11 2BS
☎ 0171-221 6081

Metrocolour London Ltd, 91-95 Gillespie Road, London N5 1LS
☎ 0171-226 4422 fax 0171-359 2353

Rank Film Laboratories Ltd, North Orbital Road, Denham, Uxbridge, Middx UB9 5HQ
☎ 01895 832323 fax 01895 832446

Soho Images, 8-14 Meard Street, London W1V 3HR
☎ 0171-437 0831 fax 0171-734 9471

Film Restoration and Treatment   The Film Clinic, c/o Soho Images, 8-14 Meard Street, London W1V 3HR
☎ 0171-734 9235 fax 0171-734 9471

High-Speed Camera Systems (for slow motion and technical analysis)   (LoCam, HiCam and Fastax importers) Gordon Audio-Visual Ltd, Symes Mews, 37 Camden High Street, London NW1 7JE
☎ 0171-387 3399 fax 0171-383 7411

Hadland Photonics Ltd, Newhouse Laboratories, Newhouse Road, Bovingdon, Hemel Hempstead, Herts HP3 0EL
☎ 01442 832525 fax 01442 833733

Photosonics International Ltd, 5 Thame Park Business Centre, Wenman Road, Thame, Oxon OX9 3FR
☎ 01844 260600 fax 01844 260126

(Videodisc analysis system) Sammy's, 21 Derby Road, Metropolitan Centre, Greenford, Middx UB6 8UJ
☎ 0181-578 7887 fax 0181-578 2733

Interactive Video Equipment   LaserMedia UK Ltd, Media House, Arundel Road, Walberton, Arundel, West Sussex BN18 0QP
☎ 01243 555005 fax 01243 555025

Mar-Com Systems Ltd, Marcom House, 1 Heathlands, Heath Gardens, Twickenham, Middx TW1 4BP
☎ 0181-891 5061 fax 0181-892 9028

Metro Multimedia, 57-59 Great Suffolk Street, London SE1 0BS
☎ 0171-928 2088 fax 0171-261 0685

Philips Interactive Media Systems, 188 Tottenham Court Road, London W1P 9LE
☎ 0171-911 3000 fax 0171-911 3040

Saville Group Ltd, Millfield Lane, York YO2 6PQ
☎ 01904 782782 fax 01904 782700

Sony Broadcast and Communications, Jays Close, Viables, Basingstoke, Hants RG22 4SB
☎ 01256 55011 fax 01256 474585

Interactive Videodisc Test Pressings
Microvitec plc, Futures Way, Bolling Road, Bradford BD4 7TU
☎ 01274 390011 fax 01274 734944

VideoTime Ltd, 22-24 Greek Street, London W1V 5LG
☎ 0171-439 1211 fax 0171-439 7336

Interactive Videodisc Mastering and Pressing
Metro Multimedia, 57-59 Great Suffolk Street, London SE1 0BS
☎ 0171-928 2088 fax 0171-261 0685

Philips and Du Pont Optical (PDO), Philips Road, Blackburn BB1 5RZ
☎ 01254 52448 fax 01254 54729

Telemedia (London), c/o Mohn UK Ltd, 26-27 Conduit Street, London W1R 9TA
☎ 0171-499 5330 fax 0171-493 7244

Laser Pointers
Gordon Audio-Visual Ltd, Symes Mews, 37 Camden High Street, London NW1 7JE
☎ 0171-387 3399 fax 0171-383 7411

Lenses and Accessories (Film and Video)
Optex, 22-26 Victoria Road, New Barnet, Herts EN4 9PF
☎ 0181-441 2199 fax 0181-449 3646

Library Storage and Display Units
Ateka Tape Racks, 8 Station Road Industrial Estate, Hailsham, East Sussex BN27 2ER
☎ 01323 845580 fax 01323 843366

BGU Manufacturing, Meadow Lane, London Road, Nottingham NG2 3JQ
☎ 01602 862460 fax 01602 862522

Bieb System, 95-97 Canterbury Road, Croydon, Surrey CR0 3HH
☎ 0181-665 6311 fax 0181-665 6425

Don Gresswell, Bridge House, Vera Avenue, Grange Park, London N21 1RB
☎ 0181-360 6622 fax 0181-360 9231

Librex Educational Company, Colwick Road, Nottingham NG2 4BG
☎ 01602 504664 fax 01602 586683

Point Eight Ltd, Shaw Road, Dudley, West Midlands DY2 8TP
☎ 01384 238282 fax 01384 455746

Low-Cost Computer Graphics Systems for Television/Video
G2 Systems, 5 Mead Lane, Farnham, Surrey GU9 7DY
☎ 01252 737147 fax 01252 737147

Microscopes and Image Processing Systems

Carl Zeiss Jena (JenaOptic) Ltd, PO Box 43, 1 Elstree Way, Borehamwood, Herts WD6 1NH
☎ 0181-953 1688 fax 0181-953 9456

Carl Zeiss (Oberkochen) Ltd, PO Box 78, 15-20 Woodfield Road, Welwyn Garden City, Herts AL7 1LU
☎ 01707 331144 fax 01707 373210

Leica Cambridge Ltd, Clifton Road, Cambridge CB1 3QH
☎ 01223 411411 fax 01223 412776

Linkam Scientific Instruments Ltd, 8 Epsom Downs Metro Centre, Waterfield, Tadworth, Surrey KT20 5HT
☎ 01737 363476 fax 01737 363480

Olympus Optical Co (UK) Ltd, 2-8 Honduras Street, London EC1Y 0TX.
☎ 0171-250 0179 fax 0171-490 7880

Optivision (Yorkshire) Ltd, Ahed House, Dewsbury Road, Ossett, West Yorks WF5 9ND
☎ 01924 277727 fax 01924 280016

Synoptics Ltd, 271 Cambridge Science Park, Milton Road, Cambridge CB4 4WE
☎ 01223 423223 fax 01223 420040

Mini Video Cameras

Metrovideo, 57-59 Great Suffolk Street, London SE1 0BS
☎ 0171-928 2088 fax 0171-261 0685

Vista Vision Systems (Levanroy Ltd), Levanroy House, Deanes Close, Steventon, Oxon OX13 6SR
☎ 01235 834466 fax 01235 832540

PAL Encoders and Genlock Systems (for computer images to video)

CED, 40 The Ridgeway, London N11 3LJ
☎ 0181-368 9417 fax 0181-368 8099

Screens

Audio-Visual Material, AVM House, Hawley Lane, Farnborough, Hants GU14 8EH
☎ 01252 540721 fax 01252 549214

Gordon Audio-Visual Ltd, Symes Mews, 37 Camden High Street, London NW1 7JE
☎ 0171-387 3399 fax 0171-383 7411

Harkness Screens Ltd, The Gate Studios, Station Road, Borehamwood, Herts WD6 1DQ
☎ 0181-953 3611 fax 0181-207 3657

Slide and Photograph Storage Systems

DW Viewpacks Ltd, Unit 7/8 Peverel Drive, Granby, Milton Keynes MK1 1NL
☎ 01908 642323 fax 01908 640164

Nicholas Hunter Ltd, Unit 8, Oxford Business Centre, Osney Lane, Oxford

OX1 1TB
☎ 01865 727292 fax 01865 200051

Metrovideo, 57-59 Great Suffolk Street, London SE1 0BS
☎ 0171-928 2088 fax 0171-261 0685

Subtitling and Translation Services (Video)
Essential Pictures Ltd, 222 Kensal Road, London W10 5BN
☎ 01813-969 7017 fax 0181-960 8201

Tape Erasers and Degaussers
RTI (UK) Ltd, Unit 6, Swan Wharf Business Centre, Waterloo Road, Uxbridge, Middx UB8 2RA
☎ 01895 252191 fax 01895 274692

Tape-Slide Projectors
Gordon Audio-Visual Ltd, Symes Mews, 37 Camden High Street, London NW1 7JE
☎ 0171-387 3399 fax 0171-383 7411

Tape/Videocassette Suppliers
Carousel Tapes, Magnetic Media Distributors, Unit D, Inchbrook Trading Estate, Nailsworth, Gloucestershire GL5 5EY
☎ 01453 83 5500 fax 01453 835508

Professional Magnetics Ltd, Cassette House, 329 Hunslet Road, Leeds LS10 1NJ
☎ 01532 706066 fax 01532 718106

Stanley Productions, 147 Wardour Street, London W1V 3TB
☎ 0171-494 4545 fax 0171-437 2126

Transco Audio and Video Trade Sales, Transco Mastering Services Ltd, 7 Soho Square, London W1V 5DD
☎ 0171-287 3563 fax 0171-494 3583

Television Receiver/Monitors for Education
Hitachi Denshi (UK) Ltd, 13-14 Garrick Industrial Centre, Irving Way, London NW9 6AQ
☎ 0181-202 4311 fax 0181-202 2451

JVC Professional Products, Alperton House, Bridgewater Road, Wembley, Middx HA0 1EG
☎ 0181-902 8812 fax 0181-900 0941

Sony Broadcast and Communications, Jays Close, Viables, Basingstoke, Hants RG22 4SB
☎ 01256 55011 fax 01256 474585

Tyne Professional Television, Unit 2, The Townsend Centre, Blackburn Road, Houghton Regis, Dunstable, Beds
☎ 01582 606266 fax 01582 606266

Video/Film Camera Shutter Controllers
Broadcast Video Engineering, 13 Riverside Park, Dogflood Way, Farnham GU9 7UG

☎ 01252 710 030 fax 01252 710 058

Video Camera Supports Metrovideo, 57-59 Great Suffolk Street, London SE1 0BS
☎ 0171-928 2088 fax 0171-261 0685

W Vinten Ltd, Western Way, Bury St Edmunds, Suffolk IP33 3TB
☎ 01284 752121 fax 01284 750560

Optex (Sachtler supplier), 22-26 Victoria Road, New Barnet, Herts EN4 9PF
☎ 0181-441 2199 fax 0181-449 3646

Video Production Equipment DPL Video Services*, Unit 6, Wembley Park Business Centre, North End
(*denotes second-hand Road, Wembley, Middx HA9 0AG
and new equipment) ☎ 0181-900 1866 fax 0181-903 5448

Hitachi Denshi (UK) Ltd, 13-14 Garrick Industrial Centre, Irving Way,
London NW9 6AQ
☎ 0181-202 4311 fax 0181-202 2451

Horizon Video, Unit 11, Progress Business Park, Progress Way, Croydon
CR0 4XA
☎ 0181-688 4430 fax 0181-688 3010

IEC Cinema House, 93 Wardour Street, London W1V 3TE
☎ 0171-413 8003 fax 0171-494 3576

JVC Professional Products, Alperton House, Bridgewater Road, Wembley,
Middx HA0 1EG
☎ 0181-902 8812 fax 0181-900 0941

Sony Broadcast & Communications, Jays Close, Viables, Basingstoke, Hants
☎ 01256 55011 fax 01256 474585

Videocassette Labels BGU Manufacturing Company, Meadow Lane, London Road, Nottingham
(printed sleeve labels and NG2 3JQ
self-adhesive cassette labels) ☎ 01602 862460 fax 01602 862522

Videocassette Boxes BGU Manufacturing Company, Meadow Lane, London Road, Nottingham
NG2 3JQ
☎ 01602 862460 fax 01602 862522

Librex Educational Company, Colwick Road, Nottingham NG2 4BG
☎ 01602 504664 fax 01602 586683

Quality Plastic Supplies Ltd, Unit C, 2 Endeavour Way, Durnsford Road
Industrial Estate, London SW19 8UH
☎ 0181-946 8388 fax 0181-947 8909

Stanley Productions, 147 Wardour Street, London W1V 3TB
☎ 0171-494 4545 fax 0171-437 2126

Transco Audio and Video Trade Sales, Transco Mastering Services Ltd, 7
Soho Square, London W1V 5DD

☎ 0171-287 3563 fax 0171-494 3583

Videotape Cleaning and Checking   RTI (UK) Ltd, Unit 6, Swan Wharf Business Centre, Waterloo Road, Uxbridge, Middx UB8 2RA
☎ 01895 252191 fax 01895 274692

Video Printers
(to produce hard-copy
pictures from video sources)   Mitsubishi Electric UK Ltd, Security Equipment Group, Electronics Division, Travellers Lane, Welham Green, Hatfield, Herts AL10 8XB
☎ 01707 278760 fax 01707 278755

Seikosha (UK) Ltd, Unit 14, Poyle 14, Newlands Drive, Colnbrook, Berks SL3 0DX
☎ 01753 685873 fax 01753 682036

Sony Broadcast and Communications UK, Jays Close, Viables, Basingstoke RG22 4SB
☎ 01256 55011 fax 01256 474585

Video Projectors   Barco Cameron Ltd, Communicate House, 50 Sutton Park Avenue, Reading, Berks RG6 1AZ
☎ 01734 664611 fax 01734 267716

Metrovideo, 57-59 Great Suffolk Street, London SE1 0BS
☎ 0171-928 2088 fax 0171-261 0685

Sarner International Ltd, 32 Woodstock Grove, London W12 8LE
☎ 0181-743 1288 fax 0181-749 7699

Sharp Electronics UK Ltd, Sharp House, Thorp Road, Newton Heath, Manchester M40 5BE
☎ 0161-205 2333 fax 0161-205 7076

Sony Broadcast and Communications UK, Jays Close, Viables, Basingstoke, Hants RG22 4SB
☎ 01256 55011 fax 01256 474585

Video Rostrum/Presentation Stands   Sony Broadcast and Communications UK, Jays Close, Viables, Basingstoke, Hants RG22 4SB
☎ 01256 55011 fax 01256 474585

Metro Video, 57-59 Great Suffolk Street, London SE1 0BS
☎ 0171-928 2088 fax 0171-261 0685

Hanimex Audio-Visual, 22-23 Westmead, Swindon, Wilts SN5 7YT
☎ 01793 526211 fax 01793 544814

Media Legislation
and Reports

This anotated bibliography comprises mainly Government publications but also diverse reports published by industry bodies, trade unions and independent pressure groups.

1909 *Cinematograph Act, 1909,* 6 pages HMSO, 1909.
Sets out the law concerning the licensing of cinema premises by local authorities and fire safety.

1923 *Broadcasting Committee Report,* Chairman: Sir Frederick Sykes. (Cmd. 1951). 46 pages HMSO, 1923.
The earliest comprehensive review of the scope and potentialities of broadcasting.

1926 *Report of the Broadcasting Committee, 1926,* Chairman: Earl of Crawford and Balcarres. (Cmd. 2599). 22 pages HMSO, 1926.
The Committee was appointed to advise on arrangements subsequent to the expiring of the British Broadcasting Company's licence in 1926. It recommended that the broadcasting service should be conducted by a public corporation.

1927 *Cinematograph Films Act 1927,* ii, 24 pages HMSO, 1927.
An Act to restrict blind booking and advance booking of cinematograph films, and to secure the renting and exhibition of a certain proportion of British films, and for purposes connected therewith.

1932 *The film in national life: being the report of an enquiry conducted by the Commission on Educational and Cultural Films into the service which the cinematograph may render to education and social progress.* Chairman: B S Gott. xii, 204 pages George Allen and Unwin, 1932.
The principal recommendation of the report, 'that a National Film Institute be set up in Great Britain financed in part by public funds...', led to the founding of the British Film Institute.

1935 *Report of the Television Committee.* Chairman: Lord Selsdon. (Cmd. 4793). 27 pages HMSO, 1935.
The Committee was appointed in 1934 to consider the development of television and to advise the Postmaster General on the relative merits of the several systems and the conditions under which any public service of television should be provided.

1936 *Report of the Broadcasting Committee, 1935.* Chairman: Viscount Ullswater.

279

(Cmd. 5091). 77 pages HMSO, 1936.
A report on conditions generally within the broadcasting service.

Report of a Committee appointed by the Board of Trade to consider the position of British films. Chairman: Lord Moyne. (Cmd. 5320). 41 pages HMSO, 1936.
A pre-war view of the industry and of the protective use of the Quota.

'A statistical survey of the cinema industry in Great Britain in 1934' by S Rowson. In *The Journal of the Royal Statistical Society.* vol. 99, part 1, 1936. pages 67-129.
Gives figures on cinema seats available, films passed by censor, film supply and distribution, etc.

1938   *Cinematograph Films Act, 1938.* iii, 48 pages HMSO, 1938.
An Act to make further provision for securing the renting and exhibition of a certain proportion of British cinematograph films, and for restricting blind booking and advance booking of cinematograph films.

1944   *Tendencies to monopoly in the cinematograph film industry: Report of a Committee appointed by the Cinematograph Films Council.* Chairman: Albert Palache. 41 pages HMSO, 1944.
Discusses the value of the industry to the nation, the strength of the big circuits, the position of the independent producer, barring practices, etc.

1945   *Report of the Television Committee, 1943.* Chairman: Lord Hankey. (29054). 25 pages HMSO, 1945.
The report of the committee appointed in 1943 to prepare plans for the reinstatement and development of the television service after the Second World War.

1947   *The Factual Film: a survey sponsored by the Dartington Hall Trustees.* 260 pages PEP (Political and Economic Planning on behalf of the Arts Enquiry of the Dartington Hall Trustees), 1947.
The Factual Film is the second report of the Arts Enquiry initiated in autumn, 1941. Deals with British documentary film, newsfilm, films of record, and the use of film in education. Appendices cover the British feature film industry, film censorship and the educational film movement in Scotland.

1948   *Report of the Committee on the British Film Institute.* Chairman: Sir Cyril J Radcliffe. (Cmd. 7361). 13 pages HMSO, 1948.
The Committee was appointed in 1947. Discusses the functions and purposes of the Institute.

Report of the Film Studio Committee. Chairman: G H Gater, 17 pages HMSO, 1948.
The Committee was appointed by the President of the Board of Trade to consider and review the suggestion that a studio, owned and/or managed by the State might make an important contribution to solving the difficulties of independent producers.

1949   *Distribution and exhibition of cinematograph films: Report of the Committee of Inquiry appointed by the President of the Board of Trade.* Chairman: Sir Arnold Plant. (Cmd. 7837). 63 pages HMSO, 1949.
Completes the picture of the industry in the 1940s begun in the Palache Report, q.v.

Report of the Working Party on film production costs. Chairman: Sir George Gater. 32 pages HMSO, 1949.
Discusses problems of labour relations and analyses the costs of film making.

1950   *The film industry in Great Britain: some facts and figures.* vi, 41 pages The British Film Academy, 1950.
A report of the facts and figures which were made available by others. Contains information on production, distribution, sponsorship, Quota regulations, etc. The booklet was originally compiled for the convenience of the British Film Academy staff and was later given wider distribution.

1951   *Report of the Broadcasting Committee, 1949.* Chairman: Lord Beveridge. (Cmd. 8116). 327 pages HMSO, 1951.
The Committee was appointed in 1949 to consider the constitution, control, finance and other general aspects of the sound and television broadcasting services of the UK and to advise on the conditions under which these services and wire broadcasting should be conducted after 31 December 1951.

Report of the Broadcasting Committee, 1949: Appendix H Memoranda submitted to the Committee. (Cmd. 8117). viii, 583 pages HMSO, 1951.
Evidence presented by most organisations and individuals is included. The lengthy BBC submission is followed by evidence from Government departments, BBC Advisory bodies; 'disinterested outsiders' (e.g. The British Film Institute and the Labour Party); 'minorities with a message'; 'inside interests' (e.g. ACTT and BBC Staff Association); 'outside interests' (e.g. Paramount Pictures and Granada theatres); and commercial broadcasting.

Broadcasting memorandum on the Report of the Broadcasting Committee, 1949. (Cmd. 8291). 12 pages HMSO, 1951.
Comment by the Attlee Government on the Report.

1952   *The British film industry: a report on its history and present organisation, with special reference to the economic problems of British feature film production.* 307 pages PEP (Political and Economic Planning), 1952.
The results of a study carried out at the suggestion of the British Film Institute. Aims to give a comprehensive account of the development, organisation and problems of the British film industry.

Broadcasting: memorandum on the Report of the Broadcasting Committee, 1949. (Cmd. 8550). 10 pages HMSO, 1952.
Recommendations by the Churchill Government for the renewal of the BBC's Charter. Includes the Government's conclusion that, in the expanding field of television, provision should be made to permit some element of competition.

Cinematograph Act, 1952. 6 pages HMSO, 1952.
Sets out the law concerning the licensing of cinema premises by local authorities and fire safety. See also the 1909 Act.

1953   *Broadcasting: memorandum on television policy.* (Cmd. 9005). 7 pages HMSO, 1953.
Statement by the Churchill Government redefining the policy stated in the Memorandum of 1952 and outlining proposals for the setting up of an independent television authority.

1954   *Television Act, 1954.* 21 pages HMSO, 1954.
An Act to make provision for television broadcasting services in addition to those provided by the British Broadcasting Corporation, and to set up a special authority for that purpose.

1956   *Copyright Act, 1956.* iii, 92 pages HMSO, 1956.
Part 2, 13, deals with copyright in cinematograph films and Part 2, 14, with copyright in television broadcasts and sound broadcasts.

1957   *Cinematograph Films Act, 1957.* ii, 12 pages HMSO, 1957. Deals with the Levy and the mandate of the National Film Finance Corporation.

1958   'The British Film Industry'. In *PEP (Political and Economic Planning)*, vol. 24, no. 424. Planning. 23 June 1958. pages 131-170.
In two sections. Section 1 discusses decline in cinema attendance, films on television, impact of wide screens, the Government and the industry. Section 2 discusses exhibition, quota regulations, distribution, production, etc.

1960   *Films Act, 1960.* iii, 33 pages HMSO, 1960.
Consolidates the earlier Acts and sets out the principal laws governing film business.

1962   *Report of the Committee on Broadcasting, 1960.* Chairman: Sir Harry Pilkington. (Cmnd. 1753). xii, 342 pages HMSO, 1962.
The Committee was appointed to consider the future of the broadcasting services in the United Kingdom, the dissemination by wire of broadcasting and other programmes, and the possibility of television for public showing; to advise on the services which should in future be provided in the UK by the BBC and the ITA.

1963   *Television Act, 1963.* 25 pages HMSO, 1963.
The Act extended the period for which the ITA was to provide television services.

1964   *Report of the Departmental Committee on the Law on Sunday Observance.* Chairman: Lord Crathorne. (Cmnd. 2528). v, 81 pages HMSO, 1964.
Part 2, Chapter 5, pages 18-21; Part 4, Chapter 17, pages 58-59 and

Appendix C, page 72, deal specifically with cinemas and conditions of Sunday employment in cinemas.

Recommendations of the Cinematograph Films Council. Chairman of the Cinematograph Films Council: Sir Sydney C Roberts. (Cmnd. 2324). 31 pages HMSO, 1964.
Discusses the decline in cinema admissions, the changing patterns of attendance, and the distribution circuits. Includes the 'Roberts Committee Report of the Structure and Trading Practices Sub-Committee of the Cinematograph Films Council', which detailed the complaints of independent exhibitors and independent producers and assessed the solutions proposed.

Television Act, 1964. ii, 37 pages HMSO, 1964.
Consolidates the Television Acts of 1954 and 1963.

Survival or extinction? A policy for British films. 47 pages Association of Cinematograph, Television and allied Technicians, 1964.
Includes the 'Roberts Committee Report of the Structure and Trading Practices Sub-Committee of the Cinematograph Films Council' which detailed the complaints of independent exhibitors and independent producers and assessed the solutions proposed.

1966 *Broadcasting.* (Cmnd. 3169). 11 pages HMSO, 1966.
Conclusions reached by the Government on the finances of the BBC, the future fourth television service, local sound radio, etc.

Films: a report on the supply of films for exhibition in cinemas. Chairman: Ashton Roskill. (House of Commons paper, 206). v, 113 pages HMSO, 1966.
The Monopolies Commission's report.

1967 *National Film School: report of a committee to consider the need for a national film school.* 49 pages London: HMSO, 1967.
The Committee, under the Chairmanship of Lord Lloyd of Hampstead, was appointed by Jennie Lee in October 1965 with the following terms of reference - 'To consider the need for a National Film School and to advise, if necessary, on the objects and size of such a school, its possible location and form of organisation, and the means by which it might be financed'. The Committee decided that a National Film School 'should be established at the earliest possible moment'. (The School opened in 1971.)

1971 *ITV2: a submission to the Minister of Posts and Telecommunications by the Independent Television Authority.* 24 pages ITA, 1971.
Gives the Authority's views about the use of the fourth television channel.

1972 *Report of the Television Advisory Committee, 1972.* Chairman: Sir Robert Cockburn. 21 pages HMSO, 1972.
The Committee was appointed to advise the Minister on questions on the technical development of television and sound broadcasting and related matters.

Sound Broadcasting Act, 1972. 20 pages HMSO, 1972.
Extended the functions of the ITA, renamed the Independent
Broadcasting Authority, so as to include the provision of local sound
broadcasting services.

1973 *Television Advisory Committee, 1972: papers of the Technical Sub-Committee.*
ix, 87 pages HMSO, 1973.
Deals with matters relating to the extension of the 625-line service and the
closure of the 405-line service.

Independent Broadcasting Authority Act, 1973. ii, 52 pages HMSO, 1973.
Consolidates the Television and Sound Broadcasting Acts 1964 and 1972.

Nationalising the film industry: Report of the ACTT Nationalisation Forum. 59
pages Association of Cinematograph, Television and allied Technicians, 1973.
An ACTT special publication in two sections with appendices. Section 1,
'The film industry today' analyses the position of the British film industry
in the early 1970s: Section 2, 'A publicly owned film industry', lays down
guidelines for the creation, structure and operation of a nationalised
industry. The appendices assemble the statistical material and research data.

*Television in Wales: the fifth channel solution: a policy document on the future of
television in Wales.* 29 pages Association of Cinematograph, Television
and allied Technicians, HTV Cardiff Shop, 1973.
Supports a separate Welsh language television channel for Wales.

1974 *Independent Broadcasting Authority Act, 1974.* 11 pages HMSO, 1974.
An Act to make further provision as to the payments to be made to the
Independent Broadcasting Authority by television programme contractors.

Report of the Committee on Broadcasting Coverage. Chairman: Sir Stewart
Crawford. (Cmnd. 5774). v, 96 pages HMSO, 1974.
Investigation into the broadcasting needs of Scotland, Wales, Northern
Ireland and rural England.

1975 *Report of the Working Party on a Fourth Television Service in Wales: Adroddiad
y Gweithgor ar Bedwerydd Gwasanaeth Teledu yng Nghymru.* Chairman: J W
N Siberry. (Cmnd. 6209). v, 143 pages HMSO, 1975. (English text to page
69, Welsh text, pages 70-143.)
The Working Party was appointed to work out arrangements required to
provide a fourth television service in Wales, including timing and
estimates of cost, on the basis of the Report of the Crawford Committee on
Broadcasting Coverage.

1976 *Future of the British Film Industry: Report of the Prime Minister's Working
Party.* Chairman: Mr John Terry. (Cmnd. 6372). v, 33 pages HMSO, 1976.
The Working Party was established in 1975 to consider the requirements
of a viable and prosperous British film industry over the next decade with
special reference to scale of production, financial needs and resources, and
the desirability of a closer integration between the cinematograph and

television industries in respect of the resources and the film entertainment and information which they can afford. Recommended that a new public body, to be called the British Film Authority, should be created to assume responsibility for film functions fulfilled up to that time, in the main, by two Government Departments.

Support for the Arts in England and Wales: a report to the Calouste Gulbenkian Foundation by Lord Redcliffe Maud. 201 pages Calouste Gulbenkian Foundation, UK and Commonwealth Branch, 1976.
The enquiry was initiated in 1974 by the Foundation at the request of the Standing Conference of Regional Arts Associations and the Arts Council of Great Britain to study the future pattern of national, regional and local patronage of the arts in England and Wales, including the work of regional arts associations and the role of local authorities. Chapter 3, pages 76-80, discusses the funding of the British Film Institute.

1977   *Copyright and Designs Law: Report of the Committee to consider the Law on Copyright and Designs.* Chairman: The Honourable Mr Justice Whitford. (Cmnd. 6732). xiv, 272 pages HMSO, 1977.
The Committee was appointed in 1974 to consider and report whether any, and if so what, changes were desirable in the law relating to copyright as provided in particular by the Copyright Act 1956 and the Design Copyright Act 1968, including the desirability of retaining the system of protection of industrial designs provided by the Registered Designs Act 1949. Chapter 5, pages 75-84, discusses audio and video recording. Chapter 19, pages 224-229, discusses cinematography films and broadcasts.

Report of the All-Industry Committee (convened by the Association of Independent Producers) of the Film Industry 1977. Chairman: Robert Bolt. 12 pages Association of Independent Producers, 1977.
The report of an *ad hoc* body, comprising people directly and currently working in the British film industry and drawn from every branch of it, in the light of the proposals of the Terry Committee.

Report of the Committee on the Future of Broadcasting. Chairman: Lord Annan. (Cmnd. 6753). xv, 522 pages HMSO, 1977.
The Committee was appointed in 1974 to consider the future of the broadcasting services in the United Kingdom, including the dissemination by wire of broadcast and other programmes and of television for public showing; to consider the implications for present of any recommended additional services or new techniques; and to propose what constitutional, organisational and financial arrangements and what conditions should apply to the conduct of all these services.

Report of the Committee on the Future of Broadcasting. Chairman: Lord Annan. Appendices E-I: Research papers commissioned by the Committee. (Cmnd. 76753-1). iii, 168 pages HMSO, 1977.
Contents. J G Blumler: The intervention of television in British politics. J D Halloran and P Croll: Research findings on broadcasting. B V Hindley: The profits of advertising-financed television broadcasting. G B G

Lomas: The population of Great Britain, 1961-1991. A Smith: The relationship of management with creative staff.

1978   *AIP Report: recommendations to the Government following the Prime Minister's Working Party Report on the future of the British Film Industry and the Interim Action Committee's Report on the setting up of a British Film Authority.* 31 pages Association of Independent Producers, 1978.
Analyses the UK production industry and the involvement of Government and states the AIP's proposals for change.

Broadcasting. (Cmnd. 7294). 71 pages HMSO, 1978.
A White Paper setting out the Government's proposals for the future constitution, structure and organisation of broadcasting in the UK. The proposals, among which was one for establishing an Open Broadcasting Authority, were the result of the Callaghan Government's consideration of the 'Report of the Committee on the Future of Broadcasting' under the chairmanship of Lord Annan, and of the many comments received on the Committee's recommendations.

The FOCUS report: recommendations to the Government following the Prime Minister's Working Party Report on the Future of the British Film Industry and the Interim Action Committee's Report on the setting up of a British Film Authority. 49 pages FOCUS, 1978.
FOCUS (Film Conservation and Utilisation Society) is a consumer group for filmgoers. Its report covers marketing, monopoly, cinema admissions, and programming.

Proposals for the setting up of a British Film Authority. Report of the Interim Action Committee on the Film Industry. Chairman: Sir Harold Wilson. (Cmnd. 7071). iv, 14 pages HMSO, 1978.
The Committee was appointed to advise, among other things, on the achievement of a viable and prosperous British film industry over the ensuing decade, and in doing so, to make a closer study of the appropriate constitution and operating role of the British Film Authority recommended by the Terry Report, to assist in identifying the statutory requirements when legislation could be introduced.

Report of the Working Party on the Welsh Television Fourth Channel Project: Adroddiad y Gweithfor ar y Cynllun Pedwaredd Sianel i Gymru. Chairman: D J Trevelyan (to Jan. 1978) Mrs S Littler (from Jan. 1978 to May 1978). iv, 99 pages HMSO, 1978. (English text to page 48: Welsh text, pages 51-99).
The Working Party was appointed in 1977 to consider how progress might be made with the project for a fourth television channel in Wales, taking into account the Siberry Working Party Report and the recommendations on the framework of broadcasting generally and the fourth channel in particular which are made in the report of the Annan Committee so that, once money is available, an immediate start could be made.

1979   *The financing of the British film industry. Second Report of the Interim Action Committee on the Film Industry.* Chairman: Sir Harold Wilson. (Cmnd.

7597). iv, 13 pages HMSO, 1979.
Deals with the financial background, state support for film production and the effect of taxation on the industry.

Report of the Committee on Obscenity and Film Censorship. Chairman: Bernard Williams. (Cmnd. 7772). vii, 270 pages HMSO, 1979.
The Committee was appointed in 1977 to review the laws concerning obscenity, indecency and violence in publications, displays and entertainment in England and Wales, except in the field of broadcasting, and to review the arrangements for film censorship in England and Wales; and to make recommendations.

1980 *A Bill to amend and supplement the Independent Broadcasting Authority Act 1973 in connection with the provision by the Independent Broadcasting Authority of a second television service and otherwise in connection with the functions of the Authority; to establish a Broadcasting Complaints Commission; to require consultation between the British Broadcasting Corporation and the Authority about the scheduling of television programmes in Welsh; and for connected purposes.* (Bill 139). vi, 30 pages HMSO, 1980.

Statistics, technological developments and cable television: third report of the Interim Action Committee on the Film Industry. Chairman: Sir Harold Wilson. (Cmnd. 7855). iv, 24 pages HMSO, 1980.
Looks at technological developments (video reproduction, satellite broadcasting, etc.) and cable television.

A Bill to provide for the televising of the proceedings of the House of Commons and its committees and to establish a Parliamentary Television Unit to control the televising, provide feeds and recordings to outside organisations and maintain an electronic Hansard. (Bill 134). iv, 2 pages HMSO, 1980.

Broadcasting Act, 1980. 37 pages HMSO, 1980.
An Act to amend and supplement the Independent Broadcasting Authority Act 1973 in connection with the provision by the IBA of a second televising service...; to make provision as to the arrangements for the broadcasting of television programmes for reception in Wales...; to establish a Broadcasting Complaints Commission; and for connected purposes.

Broadcasting Act, 1981. iv, 81 pages HMSO, 1981.
An Act to consolidate the Independent Broadcasting Authority Acts 1973, 1974 and 1978 and the Broadcasting Act 1980.

1981 *Direct broadcasting by satellite: reports of a Home Office study.* vi, 100 pages HMSO, 1981.
A study, initiated by the Home Secretary, of the implications of establishing a UK DBS service by about 1985 or 1990. Covers technical, financial and resource implications for the UK broadcasting system. Also considers European aspects of DBS.

Film and television co-operation: fourth report of the Interim Action Committee on the Film Industry. Chairman: Sir Harold Wilson. (Cmnd. 8227). iv, 5

pages HMSO, 1981.
Makes recommendations for encouraging investment in production, whether of TV features, film for TV, or feature films intended for showing first in cinemas and subsequently by other means, including television.

National Film Finance Corporation Act 1981. 12 pages HMSO, 1981.
An Act to consolidate the Cinematograph Film Production (Special Loans) Acts 1949 to 1980 and to repeal, as spent, certain enactments relating to the National Film Finance Corporation.

A Bill to prohibit the sale and setting on hire of videocassettes of adult category to children and young persons. (Bill 46). 2 pages HMSO, 1981.

1982 *Broadcasting in the Welsh language and the implications for Welsh and non-Welsh speaking viewers and listeners. Second report from the Committee on Welsh Affairs, session 1980-81.* Home Office and Welsh Office. (Cmnd. 8469). 24 pages HMSO, 1982.
Observations by the Secretary of State for the Home Department and the Secretary of State for Wales, the BBC, IBA and the Welsh Fourth Channel Authority.

The cable broadcast debate: More channels – more choice? Implications of the proposals of the Hunt inquiry: the views of the Independent Broadcasting Authority. 8 pages Independent Broadcasting Authority, 1982.

The cable debate: the BBC's response to the Hunt Report. 43 pages British Broadcasting Corporation, Information Division, 1982.
Contains four essays by members of the BBC Directorate with an appendix giving the BBC's evidence to the Hunt inquiry.

Cinematograph (Amendment) Act, 1982. 14 pages HMSO, 1982. Extends and amends the Cinematograph Acts 1909 and 1952.

The distribution of films for exhibition in cinemas and by other means: fifth report of the Interim Action Committee on the Film Industry. Chairman: Sir Harold Wilson. (Cmnd. 8530). iv, 29 pages HMSO, 1982.
Deals with distribution and exhibition of films, making reference to the significant technological advances that were made from the time the Committee was first set up.
The handling of the press and public information during the Falklands conflict. First report from the Defence Committee, House of Commons. Volume I: Report and minutes of proceedings. Session 1982-83. Chairman: Sir Timothy Kitson. lxxviii pages HMSO, 1982.
Considers the problems bearing in mind two principles about the reporting of the war – the public's right to information and the Government's duty to withhold information for reasons of operational security.

The handling of the press and public information during the Falklands conflict. First report from the Defence Committee, House of Commons. Volume II: Minutes of evidence. Session 1982-83. Chairman: Sir Timothy Kitson. viii, 493 pages HMSO, 1982.

Minutes of evidence taken on 21, 22, 27, 28 July, 20, 27 October, 9, 10 November.

Public and private funding of the arts: interim report on the nitrate problem at the National Film Archive. Together with a memorandum. Fourth report from the Education, Science and Arts Committee, House of Commons. Chairman: Christopher Price. v, 6 pages HMSO, 1982.
Examines with some urgency the situation developing at the NFA with regard to its holdings on nitrate film stock.

Public and private funding of the arts: together with the minutes of evidence and appendices. Eighth report from the Education, Science and Arts Committee, House of Commons. Volume I. Chairman: Christopher Price. cxli pages HMSO, 1982.
Report of a Select Committee. Investigates methods by which the arts are funded. Chapter xii deals with the media arts and commercial provision and includes proposals for the creation of a single ministry to be responsible for all the performing arts.

Public and private funding of the arts: together with the minute of evidence and appendices. Eighth report from the Education, Science and Arts Committee, House of Commons. Volume II: Minutes of evidence. Session 1980-81. Chairman: Christopher Price. xxi, pages 1-485. HMSO, 1982.

Public and private funding of the arts: together with the minute of evidence and appendices. Eighth report from the Education, Science and Arts Committee, House of Commons. Volume III: Minutes of evidence. Session 1981-82. Chairman: Christopher Price. xxi, pages 486-933. HMSO, 1982.

Report of the Broadcasting Complaints Commission 1982. v, 29 pages HMSO, 1982.
The first report of the Commission recommended by the Annan Committee and set up under the Broadcasting Act 1980. Covers the period 1 June 1981 to 31 March 1982 and considers 23 complaints. During the period under review 114 complaints were received, 91 of which were considered to be outside the Commission's jurisdiction.

Report of the inquiry into cable expansion and broadcasting policy. Chairman: Lord Hunt of Tanworth. (Cmnd. 8679). vi, 46 pages HMSO, 1982.
The Home Secretary announced on 22 March 1982 that this Inquiry was to be established with the following terms of reference:-
'To take as its frame of reference the Government's wish to secure the benefits for the UK which cable technology can offer and its willingness to consider an expansion of cable systems which would permit cable to carry a wider range of entertainment and other services (including when available services of direct broadcasting by satellite), but in a way consistent with the wider public interest, in particular the safeguarding of public service broadcasting; to consider the questions affecting broadcasting policy which would arise from such an expansion, including in particular the supervisory framework; and to make recommendations by 30 September 1982.'

Report on Cable systems. Cabinet Office: Information Technology Advisory

Panel. 54 pages HMSO, 1982.
Considers the potential role of cable systems in the UK and the desirability of a major programme of cable installation.

A Bill (as amended on report) intituled an Act to extend and amend the Cinematograph Acts 1909 and 1952. (194). 14 pages HMSO, 1982.
Intended to bring under the cinema licensing system any form of moving picture exhibition other than BBC and IBA television transmissions, licensed cable relays and private performances.

1983   *A Bill to make provision for regulating the distribution of video recordings and for connected purposes.* (Bill 14). iv, 16 pages HMSO, 1983.

A Bill intituled an Act to provide for the establishment and functions of a Cable Authority and to make other provisions with respect to cable programme services; to amend the Broadcasting Act 1981 and to make further provision with respect to broadcasting services; and for connected purposes. (83). viii, 55 pages HMSO, 1983.

Choice by cable; the economics of a new era in television. by C G Veljanovski and W D Bishop. 115 pages Institute of Economics Affairs, 1983. (Hobart Paper 96).
Chapter 7 is devoted to a critique of the Hunt Report.

Copyright (Amendment) Act 1983. 4 pages HMSO, 1983.
An Act to amend section 21 of the Copyright Act 1956 so as to provide new penalties for offences relating to infringing copies of sound recordings and cinematograph films; and to provide for the issue and execution of search warrants in relation to such offences.

The development of cable systems and services. Home Office and Department of Industry. (Cmnd. 8866). 90 pages HMSO, 1983.
Sets out the Government's proposals for a framework for the development of cable systems and services.

Films: a report on the supply of films for exhibition in cinemas. Monopolies and Mergers Commission. (Cmnd. 8858). v, 123 pages HMSO, 1983.
The first report on the supply of films in Britain since 1966.

Intellectual property rights and innovation, by the Chief Scientific Officer, Cabinet Office. (Cmnd. 9117). x, 46 pages HMSO, 1983.
Considers how best to support the commercialisation of ideas and in particular how to help small but enterprising firms. Recommends a number of changes to the intellectual property rights system.

The protection of military information: report of the study group on censorship. Chairman: General Sir Hugh Beach. (Cmnd. 9112). viii, 92 pages HMSO, 1983.
Considers, in the light of the Falklands conflict, how the Government should protect military information immediately prior to or during the conduct of operations.

Report of the Broadcasting Complaints Commission 1983. v, 59 pages HMSO, 1983.

The second report of the Commission. Covers the period 1 April 1982 to 31 March 1983. 234 complaints were received of which 188 were outside and 46 fell within the Commission's jurisdiction.

1984 *A Bill intituled an Act to provide for the establishment and functions of a Cable Authority and to make other provision with respect to cable programme services; to amend the Broadcasting Act 1981 and to make further provision with respect to broadcasting services; and for connected purposes.* (Bill 127). vii, 54 pages HMSO, 1984.

Film Policy. (Cmnd. 9319). 27 pages HMSO, 1984.
White Paper outlining the Government's plans for investing in the British Film Industry (through a privatised version of the National Film Finance Corporation) to the end of the 80s.

Public and private funding of the arts: observations by the Government on the eight report from the Education, Science and Arts Committee. Session 1981-82. Office of Arts and Libraries. (Cmnd. 9127). 26 pages HMSO, 1984.
Chapter 6, Film and Television and the British Film Institute, deals with the recommendations concerned with films and television, including the Committee's consideration of the activities of the BBC and the independent television companies.

Video Recordings Act, 1984. 17 pages HMSO, 1984.
Makes provision for regulating the distribution of video recordings.

Report of the Broadcasting Complaints Commission 1984. vi, 85 pages HMSO, 1984.
Third report of the Commission covering the period 1 April 1983 to 31 March 1984; 228 complaints were received of which 181 were outside and 47 fell within the Commission's jurisdiction.

1985 *The protection of military information: Government Response to the Report of the Study Group on Censorship.* (Cmnd. 9499). 10 pages Ministry of Defence, 1985.
The response to the 1983 Beach Report (Cmnd. 9112).

Report of the Broadcasting Complaints Commission 1985. vi, 78 pages HMSO, 1985.
Fourth report of the Commission covering the period 1 April 1984 to 31 March 1985; 218 complaints were received of which 185 were outside and 33 fell within the Commission's jurisdiction.

The recording and rental of audio and video copyright material: a consultative document. Department of Trade and Industry. (Cmnd. 9445). iv, 14 pages HMSO, 1985.
Green Paper inviting comments on the proposition that 'copyright holders are entitled to payment for the home taping of their material and that a levy on blank audio and video tape is the only practicable way of providing such payment'. Discusses also the recording of broadcasts for educational purposes.

1986   *Intellectual property and innovation.* Department of Trade and Industry. (Cmnd. 9712). iv, 78 pages HMSO, 1986.
White Paper. Response to 'Intellectual property and innovation' (Cmnd. 9117, 1983) and other reports on copyright.

Report of the Broadcasting Complaints Commission 1986. vi, 79 pages HMSO, 1986.
Fifth report of the Commission covering the period 1 April 1985 to 31 March 1986; 208 complaints were received of which 161 were outside and 47 fell within the Commission's jurisdiction.

Report of the Committee on Financing the BBC. Chairman: Professor Alan Peacock. (Cmnd. 9824). xx, 219 pages HMSO, 1986.
The Home Secretary announced on 27 March 1985 that this Committee was to be established with the following terms of reference: 'To assess the effect of the introduction of advertising or sponsorship on the BBC's Home Services, either as an alternative or a supplement to the income now generated through the licence fee.'

1987   *A Bill intituled an Act to restate the law of copyright, with amendments; to make fresh provision as to the rights of performers and others in performances; to confer a design right in original designs; to amend the Registered Designs Act 1949; to make provision with respect to patent agents and trade mark agents; to confer patents and designs jurisdiction on certain county courts; to amend the law of patents; to make fresh provision penalising the fraudulent reception of programmes; to make the fraudulent application or use of a trade mark an offence; to enable financial assistance to be given to certain international bodies; and for connected purposes.* (HL Bill 12). xxviii, 192 pages HMSO, 1987.

Report of the Broadcasting Complaints Commission 1987. vi, 74 pages HMSO, 1987.
Sixth report of the Commission covering the period 1 April 1986 to 31 March 1987. 222 complaints were received of which 174 were outside and 48 fell within the Commission's jurisdiction.
Broadcasting in the '90s: Competition, Choice and Quality Home Office. (Cm. 517) iv, 46 pages HMSO, 1988.
White Paper setting out the Government's proposals for broadcasting in the UK in the 1990s. Includes proposals for satellite broadcasting, radio and programme standards.

1988   *Copyright, Designs and Patents Act 1988.*
ix, 238 pages HMSO, 1988.
An Act to restate the law of copyright, with amendments; to make fresh provision as to the rights of performers and others in performances; to confer a design right in original designs; to amend the Registered Designs Act 1949; to make provision with respect to patent agents and trade mark agents; to confer patents and designs jurisdiction on certain county courts; to amend the law of patents; to make provision with respect to devices designed to circumvent copy-protection of works in electronic form; to

make fresh provision penalising the fraudulent reception of transmissions; to make the fraudulent application or use of a trade mark an offence; to make provision for the benefit of the Hospital for Sick Children, Great Ormond Street, London; to enable financial assistance to be given to certain international bodies; and for connected purposes.

Report of the Broadcasting Complaints Commission 1988. HMSO, 1988. Seventh report of the Commission covering the period 1 April 1987 to 31 March 1988. 152 complaints were received of which 93 were outside the Commission's jurisdiction and 59 fell within it.

3rd Report: the future of broadcasting Volume II. Minutes of evidence and appendices. Home Affairs Committee. (*House of Commons Paper 262-II*). x, 372 pages HMSO, 1988.
(*Volume I, House of Commons Paper 262-I*, Session 1987-88, also gives minutes of evidence.)

1989 *A Bill to make new provision with respect to the provision and regulation of independent television and sound programme services and of other services provided on television or radio frequencies; to make provision with respect to the provision and regulation of local delivery services; to amend in other respects the law relating to broadcasting and the provision of television and sound programme services; to make new provision relating to the Broadcasting Complaints Commission; to provide for the establishment and functions of a Broadcasting Standards Council; to amend the Wireless Telegraphy Acts 1949 to 1967 and the Marine, &c., Broadcasting (Offences) Act 1967; and for connected purposes.* [Bill 9]. viii, 159 pages HMSO, 1989.

Broadcasting Standards Council Annual Report and Code of Practice 1988-89. 56 pages London: Broadcasting Standards Council, 1989.
First annual report of the Council which was set up 'to consider the portrayal of violence, of sex, and matters of taste and decency in broadcast and video works.' Its code of practice is printed as an appendix.

Report of the Broadcasting Complaints Commission 1989. vi, 139 pages HMSO, 1989
Eighth report covering the period 1 April 1988 to 31 March 1989; 348 complaints were received, more than twice as many as the preceding year. Of those within the Commission's jurisdiction formal decisions on 89 were made, 39 being full adjudications.

Study of privatisation options for the terrestrial broadcasting transmission networks [by Price Waterhouse, Department of Privatisation Services]. Home Office/Department of Trade and Industry. 62 pages HMSO, 1989. The jointly-commissioned report takes account of the views of Government departments, other public sector bodies, selected television and radio programme companies, and equipment manufacturers. The BBC and IBA also co-operated.

The Windlesham/Rampton Report on 'Death on the Rock'. 146 pages Faber & Faber, 1989.

The report commissioned by Thames Television from Lord Windlesham and Richard Rampton, QC, on the controversial THIS WEEK special 'Death on the Rock'. The Government had attempted to have the screening postponed until after the inquest into the shooting by the security forces of three IRA members.

1990   *Broadcasting Act 1990.* x, 291 pages HMSO, 1990.
An Act to make new provision with respect to the provision and regulation of independent television and sound programme services and of other services provided on television or radio frequencies; to make provision with respect to the provision and regulation of local delivery services; to amend in other respects the law relating to broadcasting and the provision of television and sound programme services and to make provision with respect to the supply and use of information about programmes; to make provision with respect to the transfer of the property rights and liabilities of the Independent Broadcasting Authority and the Cable Authority and the dissolution of those bodies; to make new provision relating to the Broadcasting Complaints Commission; to provide for the establishment and functions of a Broadcasting Standards Council; to amend the Wireless Telegraphy Acts 1949 to 1967 and the Marine, &c., Broadcasting (Offences) Act 1967; to revoke a class licence granted under the Telecommunications Act 1984 to run broadcast relay systems; and for connected purposes.

Broadcasting Standards Council Annual Report 1989-90. 59 pages London: Broadcasting Standards Council, 1990.
Second annual report of the Council.

The European initiative: the business of television and film in the 1990s. ii, 40 pages British Screen Advisory Council, 1990.
Examines the business of television and film in the 1990s. Based upon a seminar held in January 1990, attended by producers, directors and others from eight European countries. Distils the main arguments emerging from that seminar.

High Definition Television (HDTV): the potential for non-broadcast applications. Department of Trade and Industry. vii, 31 pages HMSO, 1990.
Discusses the technology and its potential; criteria for assessing the potential of markets, convergence of HDTV and the computer.

Report of the Broadcasting Complaints Commission 1990. iv, 151 pages HMSO, 1990.
Ninth report covering the period 1 April 1989 to 31 March 1990; 550 complaints were received compared to 348 the previous year. Most were outside the Commission's jurisdiction. Formal decisions on 94 complaints were made, of which 44 were the subject of full adjudications.

1991   *Enquiry into standards of cross media promotion: report to the Secretary of State for Trade and Industry* by John Sadler. (Cm 1436). iv, 134 pages HMSO, 1991.
The terms of reference required the author to consider to what extent it was proper for media companies to promote their own, or any associate's

interests in the provision of media services or products and, where such behaviour was found to be improper and, taking into account the effect on the relevant markets, to consider what remedies might be appropriate. The evidence received was mainly about three specific examples of cross media promotion: 1) the promotion of Sky Television in newspapers owned by News International, 2) the promotion on BBC Television of magazines published by the BBC, and 3) the promotion of premium rate telephone services by national newspapers which had direct or indirect financial interests in such services.

Report of the Broadcasting Complaints Commission 1991. vi, 179 pages HMSO, 1991.
Tenth report covering the period 1 April 1990 to 31 March 1991; 930 complaints were received compared to 550 the previous year. Of these, 127 were within the jurisdiction of the Commission. 44 went to adjudication and a further 65 were under consideration at the end of the year.

Television licence fee: a study for the Home Office: management summary [by Price Waterhouse]. Home Office, 14 pages HMSO, 1991.
Report by Price Waterhouse Management Consultants who were commissioned by the Home Office in October 1990 to advise how future increases in the television licence fee from April 1991 could be set below the level of inflation measured by the Retail Price Index (RPI). The consultants were asked to examine the consequences of a range of formulae for such increases while having regard to the need to maintain the BBC's cornerstone role in British broadcasting.

1992 *Independent Television Commission Report and Accounts 1991.* London: Independent Television Commission, 1992.
First annual report of the ITC. For earlier reports and accounts of the independent television controlling authorities consult those published by the Independent Television Authority (later Independent Broadcasting Authority) for the years 1954-1990.

Report of the Broadcasting Complaints Commission 1992. vii, 204 pages HMSO, 1992.
Eleventh report covering the period 1 April 1991 to 31 March 1992; 1,048 complaints were received compared to 930 the previous year. Of these, 928 were outside the Commission's jurisdiction and 120 fell within it. With the 65 complaints before the Commission at the beginning of the year the latter total amounted to 185. Decisions were given in 130 of these complaints. The remaining 55 were awaiting decision on 31 March 1992.

Towards a national arts and media strategy. vi, 172 pages National Arts and Media Strategy Monitoring Group, 1992.
Comprises a brief 'strategic framework' of principles, priorities and action points, and a comprehensive set of 'draft strategies' including a summary of conclusions and recommendations. A draft document offered for final consultation, comment and suggested amendment.

Paying for broadcasting: the handbook, by Andrew Graham, Gavyn Davies, Brian Sturgess and William B Shew. London: Routledge, 1992. 256 pages. Commissioned by the BBC to inform debate in the run-up to the 1966 Charter renewal. Drawing on examples from Britain and other world-wide broadcasting markets, the authors project future possibilities for the revenues available from different sources - advertising and sponsorship, subscription, programme sales and co-production, and various kinds of public funding.

The future of the BBC: a consultation document. Department of National Heritage. (Cmd 2098), 43 pages London: HMSO, 1992.
A document intended to raise discussion about the future of the BBC after the Corporation's present Charter comes to an end in 1996.

Extending choice: the BBC's role in the new broadcasting age. 88 pages London: BBC, 1992.
Intended by the BBC to open up public discussion in the Charter renewal debate.

1993 *ITC Annual Report & Accounts 1992: Licensing and Regulating Commercial Television.* London: Independent Television Commission, 1993.
Second annual report of the ITC. The Commission noted that it had received 3,602 complaints about programmes - 1,460 of them relating to the proposed scheduling change of the religious series *Highway*. It had also dealt with 3,504 complaints about television advertising - 742 of them relating to sanitary protection - and upheld complaints against 47 advertisements.

1994 *Home Affairs Committee: Fourth Report - Video Violence and Young Offenders* (HC 514). xiv, 69 pages HMSO, 1994.
As a contribution to the public debate on the impact of violent films on children, the Home Affairs Committee interviewed witnesses and sought opinion from experts as to the effect of videotapes such as *Child's Play 3*. In its report the Committee voiced its concerns about the "corrupting influence" of violent films, but added that "the possibility...that a child might accidentally see a few minutes of a video being watched by his or her parents...is not in our view sufficient reason for banning the sale or rent of all such videos even to adults."

ITC Report & Accounts 1993: Licensing and Regulating Commercial Television. London: Independent Television Commission, 1994.
Third annual report, in which the ITC noted that it had received 4,463 programme complaints - 450 of them about the decision not to network the soap opera *Take the High Road*. It had also dealt with 2,581 complaints about television advertising, and upheld those against 44 advertisements. The report also contains annual performance reviews for Channels 3 and 4, as required under the Broadcasting Act 1990.

European Audio-Visual Projects

MEDIA Programme (The Commission of the European Communities) Director General Audiovisual, Information, Communication, Culture, 120 Rue de Treves, 1040 Brussels, Belgium
☎+32 2 299 9436 fax +32 2 299 9214

Head of Programme Holde Lhoest

The MEDIA Programme consists of projects supporting various aspects of the film and television industries. The MEDIA Programme was originally created for a period of five years (1991 – 1995) and sought to encourage the establishment of cross-border networks. Officially, these projects come to an end in 1995 however, the European Commission has already adopted proposals for MEDIA II to begin in 1996 and run until the year 2000. The focus of MEDIA II will be development, distribution and training. The structure of MEDIA II will be confirmed by the end of 1995. Enquiries about the projects and the type of support available should, in the first instance, be directed to:

UK MEDIA Desk British Film Institute, 21 Stephen Street, London W1P 1PL
☎ 0171-255 1444 fax 0171-436 7950

Contact Susanne Knepscher
The MEDIA Desk informs UK professionals about the MEDIA Programme through seminars, workshops, individual consultancy and documentation. It is designed to help the UK industry benefit from European support. Publishes *MEDIA Action UK*, the newsletter of the UK MEDIA Desk, three times yearly.

Other UK points of contact:

MEDIA Antenna Glasgow c/o Scottish Film Council, 74 Victoria Crescent Road, Glasgow G12 9JN
☎ 0141-334 4445 fax 0141-334 8132

Contact Margaret O'Connor

MEDIA Antenna Cardiff c/o Screen Wales, Screen Centre, Llantrisant Road, Cardiff CF5 2PU
☎ 01222 578370 fax 01222 578654

Contact Robin Hughes

The 19 projects are:

Broadcasting Across the Barriers of European Language (BABEL) c/o European Broadcasting Union, Case Postale 67, 1218 Grand Saconnex, Geneva, Switzerland
☎+41 22 717 21 11 fax +41 22 798 58 97
Christian Clausen, Co-ordinator
The aim of BABEL is to promote the wider distribution of television

programmes by providing financial support for dubbing and/or subtitling of programmes and contributing to the development of multi-lingualism in all its forms. Priority given to productions in less widely spoken languages for transfer into majority languages. The range of BABEL's activities includes training in the multilingual audio-visual sphere and research into new technologies.

CARTOON 418 Boulevard Lambermont, B-1030 Brussels
☎+32 22 45 12 00 fax +32 22 45 46 89
Contact Marc Vandeweyer, General Secretary
CARTOON provides support to the European animation industry. Its activities are directed towards developing projects and the production capacity of European animation studios in Europe.

DOCUMENTARY 29A Skindergade, DK-1159 Copenhagen K
☎+45 33 15 00 99 fax +45 33 15 76 76
Contact John Marshall, Secretary General
Documentaries are respected in both film and television, but coexistence with TV- journalism and information films has caused a growing confusion. This part of the MEDIA programme has been established to re-define and stimulate the genre on the basis of its own qualities.

European Audio-Visual Entrepreneurs (EAVE) 14 rue de la Presse, B-1000 Brussels
☎+32 22 19 09 20 fax +32 22 23 00 34
Raymond Ravar, Managing Director
EAVE acts as a training tool for producers and has, since 1988, trained around 250 European cinema and television producers in the area of European co-production.

European Film Distribution Office (EFDO) 14-16 Friedensalle D-22765 Hamburg
☎+49 40 390 90 25 fax +49 40 390 62 49
Contact Ute Schneider, Secretary General
In Europe, 80 per cent of all films do not cross the borders of their country of origin. EFDO aims to assist the distribution of European films from the 12 EU countries as well as Austria, Finland, Iceland, Norway, Sweden, Poland and Hungary.

MEDIA Investment Club 4 Avenue de l'Europe, F-94366 Bry-Sur-Marne Cedex
☎+33 14 983 28 63 fax +33 14 983 26 26
Contact Patrick Madelin, General Secretary
The MEDIA Investment Club's objective is to promote audio-visual creation and production using advanced technologies. It intervenes in three main areas.
• applications in the audio-visual field of digital and computer techniques (digital video computer graphics, computer-aided animation, special effects, virtual reality);
• the production of interactive multimedia programmes (CD-I and CD-ROM);
• the development of interactive television programmes.
• it also funds training, including courses in new media.

Euro MEDIA Garanties	66 Rue Pierre Charron, F-75008 Paris
	☎+33 14 359 88 03 fax +33 14 563 85 58
Contact	Sylvie Depondt, Co-ordinator

Because film and television productions, especially larger budget productions, require proper finance, Euro MEDIA Garanties has been founded to provide financial guarantees across Europe to link up the financial sector with the audio-visual production sector. The scheme is for European independent producers and the financial institutions providing loans for audio-visual productions.

European Association for an Audio-Visual Independent Market (EURO AIM)	210, Avenue Winston Churchill, B-1180 Brussels
	☎+32 23 46 15 00 fax +32 23 46 38 42
Contact	Nicolas Steil, General Director

EURO AIM is a service and support structure for the financing and promotion of European independent productions which ensures a profile of independent companies at major markets such as MIP-TV and MIPCOM. Access to these markets, at reasonable rates, includes a group stand and a range of services including: contact base, message box, screening booths, promotional material display sites and free access to a team of marketing and distribution consultants. EURO AIM also ensures the presence of European independents at other major trade events on the continent and operations are set up according to each event. Other EURO AIM services include:

- **Production Database** of more than 13,000 European independent productions designed to facilitate buyers and distributors searching for programmes on a wide range of parameters.
- **Producers Mediabase** offering profiles of more than 1,300 European independent production companies, established to assist producers in finding the most appropriate potential partners in Europe.
- **Projects Mediabase** to allow financiers to have a real-time follow up of production process.
- **Ad Scheme** to help producers and distributors in their advertising campaigns, by reimbursing up to 50 % of the cost of promotional material and/or placements in the trade press.
- **Rendez-Vous Services** offers producers year-round expertise in the area of international project financing.

Europa Cinémas	10 rue Auber, F-75009 Paris
	☎+33 1 42 71 53 70 fax +33 1 42 71 4755

Created to broaden the programming of European films in key cities of the European Union and to increase their audience by improving the conditions in which they are presented. Europa Cinémas is for competitive first release cinemas situated in capital and key cities which will: undertake to programme a majority of new European films; ensure coherence and diversity in their programming policy; give priority to the screening of films in their original version; regularly take initiatives to promote European films. The scheme provides exhibitors with technical and financial support so they can develop their programming, promotion and in-house activities.

European Script Fund   39c Highbury Place, London N5 1QP
☎+44 171 226 9903 fax +44 171 354 2706
Contact   David Kavanagh, Director General
The European Script Fund makes loans to independent producers,
broadcasters and writers for the development of film and television fiction
projects. Projects are supported by sharing information and guiding the
film or television programme towards the right people across Europe who
can put it into production.

Espace Vidéo Européen (EVE)   6 Eustace Street, Dublin 2 Ireland
☎+35 31 679 5744 fax +35 31 679 9657
Contact   John Dick, Chief Executive
EVE's object is to establish and promote systems to encourage the
publication and distribution of European audio-visual productions on all
platforms for use in the home video market (ie video, laser-disc, CD-I and
ROM etc). The need for action is due to the small market share of
European production and to the structural imbalances inherent to the
development of the European home video industry. The scheme operates
by way of:
• **EVE Loan Scheme** offering financial support to video publishers who
  are releasing on the home video market.
• **EVE Company Development Scheme** which invests directly into the
  distribution infrastructure with a special emphasis on cross-border
  activity.
• **Mediabase and Information Services and Conference** database,
  publications and consultancy service which encourages all sectors to
  exploit the home video market to its best advantage. Hosts the annual
  European Video Perspective in co-operation with the Media Business
  School and local partners.

Groupment Européen pour la   32 Widenmayerstrasse D-80538 München
Circulation des Oeuvres (GRECO)   ☎+49 89 21 21 48 48 fax +49 89 21 21 48 49
Contact   Maritta von Uechtritz
GRECO aims to promote the circulation of high quality television fiction
in Europe and throughout the world. The fund allows producers to face
development, distribution and marketing overcosts in a better way. The
scheme aims to strengthen independent producers and broadcasters by
allowing them to secure the creation of a catalogue of lasting distribution
rights. Applicants must have secured the contribution of at least three
broadcasts from three different linguistic zones and must possess the
distribution rights to supported works. These can be for periods beyond
the rights acquired by the initial broadcasters or for areas other than those
of the initial broadcasters.

Lumière Project Association   Rua Bernardo Lima, 35-5° P-1000 Lisboa
☎+35 11 57 08 25 fax +35 11 57 06 67
Contact   Jose Manuel Costa, President
This project is concerned with the rescue and survival of the European
film heritage and its most important objective is the permanent

300

preservation of films whose survival is in danger, in order to make them visible and give them new life. It is intended to help European film archives whose main goal is the protection and preservation of the film heritage. The project also has the following aims: to research and publish a European filmography; to create a database of the holdings of European film archives; to identify and search for lost films; to promote and present restored films.

Memory Archives Programmes TV (MAP-TV) 1 Place de Bordeaux, F-670051 Strasbourg, Cedex
☎+33 88 56 68 47 fax +33 88 56 68 49
Contact JJ Lemoine/AJ Hindhaugh
A programme for independent producers looking for European partners to co-produce archive-based programmes and broadcasters interested in these programmes. Archive holders wishing to publicise their holdings may also join the programme. MAP-TV acts like a club facilitating communication among its members and circulating their programme proposals, allowing them to set up co-productions. It also provides development loans for projects incorporating a minimum of 20 % archive material.

MEDIA Business School (MBS) 10 Torre Galindo, E-28016 Madrid
☎+34 1 359 0247 fax +34 1 345 7606
Contact Fernando Labrada, General Manager
The MEDIA Business School aims to provide the European audio-visual sector with formulae and strategies designed to help it take advantage of the opportunities offered by the single European Market. Projects are designed to target different areas of film, television and video and professionals can submit training projects or participate in existing activities which focus on the financial, technical, legal and commercial aspects of the audio-visual industry.

MEDIA Salles 2 Via Soperga I-20127 Milano
☎+39 2 66 98 44 05 fax +39 26 698 1574
Contact Elisabetta Brunella, General Secretary
MEDIA Salles, in collaboration with national and international associations of European cinema exhibitors, aims to reinforce the action of the MEDIA Programme in the field of film distribution. MEDIA Salles carries out initiatives to promote the cinema as a service to the local community as a major means to disseminate film, especially European films. The initiative concentrates on promotion, information and training, especially in marketing skills and initiatives to increase young people's interest in films.

Small Countries Improve Their Audio-Visual Level in Europe (SCALE) Rua Dom Joah V, 8 -r/c -Dto P-1200 Lisboa
☎+35 11 386 06 30 fax +35 11 386 06 47
Contact Artur Castro Neves, General Secretary
Established to support the audio-visual industry in 'smaller countries', and has established a resource centre which provides incentives which have the effect of improving the volume and the quality of audio-visual production and distribution. The resource centre will provide incentives

for development pools, co-production pools, marketing pools and information and research.

Stimulating Outstanding Resources for Creative European Screenwriting

92 Jan Luykenstraat NL-1071 CT Amsterdam
☎+31 20 672 0801 fax +31 20 672 0399

Contact Dick Willemsen, Secretary General

The aim of SOURCES is to contribute to a higher standard of European film and television production by means of script-development workshops for professional screenwriters and other activities to stimulate and improve the craft of writing in Europe.

Courses and Events

The following pages list selected courses and events which may be of interest to those involved in film and television for education. Further information on relevant events can be found in *Viewfinder* magazine or *Screen Digest*. More courses are listed in three British Film Institute publications: *Film and Television Training*, *Studying Film and Television*, and *Directions*.

BBC Milton Keynes EDTV BBC Milton Keynes, the production centre for the Open University, offers training and consultancy in making programmes for educational purposes, with courses being held in the summer of each year. Courses include lectures, exercises, seminars, and programme evaluations with an emphasis on practical work in a professional environment, using broadcast standard equipment. The final exercises are broadcast quality radio and television productions. The EDTV group also offers consultancy both within the UK and abroad. The courses do not teach specialist craft or technical skills but concentrate on production methods, directing, and educational script writing.
For further details contact: John Jaworski, Director of EDTV, BBC Milton Keynes, The Open University Production Centre, Walton Hall, Milton Keynes MK7 6BH.
☎ *01908 655442 fax 01908 655300 e-mail EDTV@oupc.bbc.co.uk*

British Universities Film & Video Council Each year the BUFVC holds a series of one-day courses, seminars and screenings. They are of particular interest to teachers and audio-visual librarians. Courses on research and locating audio-visual materials in particular subjects such as history, chemistry, and drama are regularly held. The Council also holds seminars on access to film archive holdings and workshops on technology for librarians.
For further information contact: The Administrator, BUFVC, 55 Greek Street, London W1V 5LR
☎ *0171-734 3687 fax 0171-287 3914*

Granada Centre for Visual Anthropology With sponsorship from Granada Television, the Granada Centre for Visual Anthropology at the University of Manchester was established to promote the use of film, video and visual media in anthropology.
Starting in October each year, the Centre offers a 13-month programme of post-graduate study leading to the degree of MA(Econ) in Visual Anthropology. In association with the Department of Social Anthropology, supervision is also provided for students working towards a PhD incorporating the use of visual materials.
For further information contact: Paul Henley, The Granada Centre for Visual Anthropology, Roscoe Building, University of Manchester, Manchester M13 9PL
☎ *0161-275 3999 fax 0161-275 4023*

International Federation of Film Archives (FIAF)

The International Federation of Film Archives will be holding their next summer school in 1996 hosted and organised by the National Film Archive at the J Paul Getty Jr Conservation Centre, Berkhamsted, Hertfordshire.

The aim of the summer school is to provide an intensive three-week training course for film archivists from all over the world who have some experience of film handling and archival practices. The focus of the course is mainly technical, with an emphasis on the preservation of moving images, but it also embraces the history and philosophy of film archiving, together with guidance on essential activities such as acquisition, cataloguing, access and programming.

For an application form or further information contact: Clyde Jeavons, Curator, NFA (London), 21 Stephen Street, London W1P 1PL
☎ *0171-255 1444 fax 0171 580 7503*

BFI South Bank Education

BFI on the South Bank hosts evening seminars, study days, workshops and exhibitions to encourage the understanding and enjoyment of cinema and television. The events cover a wide range of themes, with 1995/96 focusing on cinema history in celebration of the Centenary.

For further details contact: Carol Walker, BFI South Bank Education, Museum of the Moving Image, South Bank, Waterloo, London SE1 8XT
☎ *0171-815 1418 fax 0171 928 7938*

National Short Course Training Programme (NSCTP)

The National Short Course Training Programme (NSCTP) operates as a separate unit within the National Film and Television School in Beaconsfield. Created to help those in the film and television industry who need retraining and updating in new technology, the programme offers a range of short courses in camera, sound, editing, production, direction, design and special effects.

For further information contact: Lisa Ash or Emma Lovett, NSCTP, The National Film and Television School, Beaconsfield HP9 1LG
☎ *01494 677903 fax 01494 674042*

Oxford University Department for Continuing Education (OUDCE)

Oxford University Department for Continuing Education (OUDCE) organises an Undergraduate Certificate course in film studies, open to both extra-mural and Open University students. It consists of two modules each requiring a year of part-time study. Students successfully completing both modules will also be eligible for the award of two Open University credits.

For more information regarding entry in January 1996 contact: The Manager of Public Programmes, OUDCE, Rewley House, 1 Wellington Square, Oxford OX1 2JA
☎ *01865 270360 fax 01865 270309*

University of East Anglia MA in Film Archiving

This full-time one-year course is the only specialist training programme for film archivists to be offered anywhere at graduate level. It is taught jointly by the Film Studies department in the School of English and American Studies, and by staff of the East Anglian Film Archive, which is located in the same building. The primary purpose of the course is to equip students for jobs in film archives both in Britain and abroad; many of its former students now occupy such posts.

For a prospectus and further details contact: Graduate Studies Secretary, School of English and American Studies, University of East Anglia, University Plain, Norwich NR4 7TJ
☎ *01603 592798 fax 01603 507728*

Conferences and Screenings

British Universities Film & Video Council

The BUFVC organises an annual conference which takes place in March/April each year. In 1994 the theme was *Putting Movies on Computer* and was held at the Scientific Society Lecture Theatre in London. In 1995 the Council will be organising a conference entitled *Learning from Television* which will be held at the National Film Theatre.
Further details from BUFVC Conference, BUFVC, 55 Greek Street, London W1V 5LR
☎ *0171-734 3687 fax 0171-287 3914*

Educational Television Association

The ETA organises an annual conference in the spring at the University of York. The programme includes ETA awards presentations and the conference has an associated technical exhibition.
For further details contact Josie Key, Administrator, ETA, 37 Monkgate, York YO3 7PB
☎ *01904 639212*

International Visual Communications Association Convention

The International Visual Communications Association, which represents producers, distributors, sponsors and technical facilities involved with commercial, industrial and training films, organises an annual convention in July. The three day convention offers formal sessions as well as an opportunity to view the winning entries to the IVCA Festival.
Further details from IVCA, Bolsover House, 5/6 Clipstone Street, London W1P 7EB
☎ *0171-580 0962 fax 0171 436 2606*

Festivals and Awards

Awards are made at various festivals and conferences to educational film and video productions. Listed below is a selection of annual and biennial awards schemes.

British Archaeological Film and Video Awards

Sponsored by Channel Four Television and presented at the British Archaeological Awards ceremony held every other year in November, this award is made for the best British video or film production on an archaeological subject released into general distribution. The five categories for submissions are 1) non-broadcast educational videos or films, 2) programmes made for television, 3) single-site or site-specific videos or films, 4) conservation videos or films, and 5) promotional videos or films.
For entry details and other information contact: Cathy Grant, Hon. Secretary, CBA/BUFVC AV Media Working Party, BUFVC, 55 Greek Street, London W1V 5LR
☎ *0171-734 3687 fax 0171-287 3914*

British Interactive Multimedia Association Awards

The annual British Interactive Multimedia Association awards are variously sponsored. Awards are given in a number of categories, including bespoke training for the best programmes that provide a

training function and education, for interactive multimedia programmes that have been produced primarily for use within a school, college or higher education institution.
For entry details and further information contact: Jane Callaghan, BIMA, 6 Washingley Road, Folksworth, Peterborough PE7 3SY
☎ *01733 245700 fax 01733 240020*

British and International Short Film and Video Festival

New short films and video productions are screened each year at the British and International Short Film and Video Festival, sponsored by British Petroleum. Entries are accepted from British and international students as well as from anyone who has completed a programme within the last 12 months which has not been produced commercially or already broadcast.
For entry details and further information contact: Cinema Department, BP EXPO, Riverside Studios, Crisp Road, London W6 9RL
☎ *0181-741 2251*

British Medical Association Awards

The British Medical Association presents gold, silver and bronze awards each year to outstanding video and film programmes for health education, professional education and patient education. They are given on the basis of accurate treatment of the subject, educational effectiveness, and creativity. In addition there are certificates for educational merit and the 'Medicine in the Media' awards given to productions originally made for television.
For entry details and other information contact: Mary Last, British Medical Association, BMA House, Tavistock Square, London WC1H 9JP
☎ *0171-387 4499 fax 0171-388 2544*

Co-operative Retail Society's Young People's Film Festival

In October each year Mental Health Media judges make two awards at the Co-operative Retail Society's Young People's Film and Video Festival for the film and video productions that most contribute to an understanding of other people. The festival also accepts entries from sixth-form colleges, schools and individuals from all over the country.
For entry details and other information contact: Russell Gill, Co-operative Retail Society, Corporate Affairs, 29 Dantzic Street, Manchester M4 4BA
☎ *0161-832 8152 fax 0161-950 0411*

Educational Television Association Awards

Each year at its international conference, the Educational Television Association presents five major awards and five craft awards. A Premier Award is made for the video material which has most effectively exploited the resources available to meet a specific educational need. Craft Awards are judged in relation to their contribution towards the educational effectiveness of an entry. The awards aim to stimulate the production of creative and effective educational video material and give recognition, publicity and critical evaluation to producer and technicians whose work deserves acknowledgement.
For entry details and other information contact: Josie Key, ETA, 37 Monkgate, York Y03 7PB
☎ *01904 639212*

Festival International du Film Médical de Mauriac

The main objective of this festival is to promote training and information in health matters, thus creating a truly international meeting place for members of the professions involved in health, medical and scientific research, film industry, manufacturing industry, education and environment. The festival was created in 1987 by members of the medical health professions who shared on enthusiasm for audio-visual resources. Since then the festival has been extended to include health education and environmental health films. For each section presentations are made for the main festival award, special jury award, award for the best audio-visual quality, award for the best educational quality and special jury distinction. There is also a public award selected by participants at the festival.

For entry details and other information contact: Secretariat du Festival; 14 Place Georges Pompidou, BP 53 - 15200 Mauriac, France
☎ *+33 71 67 37 37 fax +33 71 68 10 00*

International Association of Media in Science (IAMS) Accreditation

IAMS holds a congress and festival every two years to promote the production, documentation and preservation of scientific and educational film and video material. IAMS accreditation is awarded to programmes which deal with higher education, research and popular science subjects. The festival also makes two special awards: the Chevtchenko Award, which recognises a production made in conditions of great danger, and the Nat Taylor Award, which recognises a production that explains a complicated concept clearly and with style and humour.

For entry details and further information contact: Michael J Clark, Audiovisual Resources Manager, Wellcome Trust, 183 Euston Road, London NW1
☎ *0171-611 8596 fax 0171-611 8545*

International Film and Television Festival Awards

The International Film and Television Festival held each November in New York makes awards in three categories for 1) commercials, 2) industrial and educational films, and 3) filmstrips and shorts. A trophy is awarded, together with gold, silver and bronze medals in each category.

For entry details and further information contact: IFTF of New York, 5 West 37th Street, New York NY 10018, USA

International EMMA Awards

Launched in 1992 as the European Multimedia Awards, the scheme has been expanded to include international entries for the first time in 1995. Category classifications aim to reflect all areas of multimedia and include Education, Information and Reference, Interactive Literature, Multimedia Art, Museums and Exhibitions, Music, News and Current Affairs, Science and Natural History, and Technological Innovation. Special Awards include Best International Product, Best Visuals and Best Audio.

For entry details and further information contact: EMMA International Limited, Rayner House, 23 Higher Hillgate, Stockport SK1 3ER
☎ *0161-429 9448 fax 0161-429 9568*

International Visual Communications Association Awards

The IVCA awards are the only UK awards for effectiveness and artistic merit in the use of visual communications for suppliers of non-broadcast film and video. All award-winning and finalist programmes are shown at the annual International Visual Communications Association Festival. Best Category awards are made to programmes in each of 16 categories. In addition, discretionary Awards of Excellence are made to programmes

which have demonstrated the highest possible standard of creativity, production values and technical quality. A Grand Prix is made to the winner from those programmes which have won Gold Awards of Excellence. All category winners then compete in the International ITVA Festival.
For entry details and other information contact: Kim Belcher, IVCA Festival, Bolsover House, 5-6 Clipstone Street, London W1P 7EB
☎ *0171-580 0962*

Mental Health Media Awards
First awarded in 1994, the Mental Health Media Awards are made to television or radio programmes which increase public understanding of mental health. There are categories for non-factual television, factual television and radio.
For entry details and other information contact: Mental Health Media, The Resource Centre, 356 Holloway Road, London N6 6PA
☎ *0171-700 0100 ext 204   fax 0171-700 0099*

National Schools and Colleges Video Programme Awards
A new educational project organised by educational publishers Trotman and Co Ltd in association with Thames Valley University. The awards aim to encourage creative video-making, develop team skills, add value in media and communication studies, foster links between students and teachers and reward the best entries with valuable prizes.
For entry details and other information contact: Trotman and Co Ltd, 12 Hill Rise, Richmond, Surrey TW10 6UA
☎ *0181-940 5668   fax 0181-948 9267*

Panda Awards
Formerly the Green Oscars, the Panda Awards are presented biennially to acknowledge and encourage creative and technical excellence in programmes about the natural world made for general audiences. The awards are intended to increase public awareness of the issues involved in conservation and environmental management. Awards include the WWF Golden Panda for the production judged to best express the aims of the festival by means of outstanding creative and technical qualities.
For entry details and further information contact: The Wildscreen Trust, 15 Whiteladies Road, Bristol BS8 1PB
☎ *0117 9733082 fax 0117 9239416*

Recontres Internationales de l'Audiovisuel Scientific - Image et Science
The *raison d'être* of the *Recontres* is to provide a focus for concentrated critical reflection on all issues involving the audio-visual arts and new communications technologies, seen as aids both to research and to scientific information and culture. Three awards are made encompassing television, creativity in programme making, and multimedia.
For entry details and further information contact: Image et Science, 27 rue Paul Bert 94204 Ivry s/Seine France
☎ *+33 1 49 60 41 20 fax +33 1 49 60 41 56*

Ronda Popular Science Film Festival
The Ronda festival is a festival of scientific films produced during the previous two years with trophies awarded for the three best films from research, higher education and popular science categories. A prize of honour and special mentions are also made.
For entry details and further information contact: Centro de Medios

Audiovisuales, Avenida Carlos Haya, 25 -29010 Malaga, Spain
☎ *+34 52 30 68 94 fax +34 52 61 57 61*

Royal Anthropological Institute Awards
The Royal Anthropological Institute International Film Festival, held every two years in Manchester, represents ethnographic film production world-wide. There are awards in three film/video categories: the JVC Students Prize for student films, the RAI Prize for the most outstanding film on anthropology or archaeology, and the Basil Wright prize, which recognises the evocative power of a film and its concern for humanity.
For entry details and other information contact: Jonathan Benthal, Royal Anthropological Institute, 50 Fitzroy Street, London W1P 5HS
☎ *0171-387 0455 fax 0171-383 4235*

Royal Television Society Awards
Each year the Royal Television Society's Scottish Centre makes an award to the best student programme. Entries are considered from primary and secondary schools, as well as from colleges of further and higher education and universities. Programmes entered for the award should have been made for non-broadcast use.
For entry details and other information contact: George Kirkland, University of Glasgow, Southpark House, 64 Southpark Avenue, Glasgow G12 8LB
☎ *0141-339 8855*

It should also be noted that details of awards and prizes presented at major international film and video festivals can be found in the *Directory of International Film and Video Festivals*, published by the British Council (latest edition 1995/96).

BUFVC Membership, Activities, Publications and Information Service

The British Universities Film & Video Council (BUFVC) was first established as the British Universities Film Council in 1948 by a group of university teachers who were pioneering the use of film for higher education and research. At the time 16mm film was a relatively new medium which, for the first time, made moving pictures available to teachers and researchers for use in their work.

The Council received its first grant support in 1968 when a full-time secretary was appointed. The organisation then became a grant-in-aid body of the British Film Institute. Between 1968 and 1975 the Council's staff grew to seven full-time personnel.

In 1983 the Council moved away from the British Film Institute into separate offices, and from that time has been entirely independent, funded with a grant directly from the Department of Education and Science. Since 1993 the Council has been supported by a grant from the Higher Education Funding Council for England (HEFCE) received via the Open University.

While the Council receives a substantial grant it also generates its own income from membership subscriptions, publishing, services, sponsorship, advertising, conferences and courses.

Membership

The Council exists to promote the production, study and use of film, television, video and other audio-visual media for higher education and research. There are four types of membership: Ordinary, Associate, Corporate, and Schools.

Ordinary Membership is open to all universities and university colleges in Great Britain and Northern Ireland. All members of staff of an Ordinary Member institution may use the services of the Council. Each institution appoints one or two representatives who act as the focus for the distribution of Council information.

Associate Membership is open to overseas universities and colleges, to colleges of higher and further education in the UK, and to non-profit-making bodies associated with university education either in the UK or abroad. All members of staff of an Associate Member institution may use the Council's services.

Corporate Membership is open to commercial organisations which have an interest in the work of the BUFVC. All members of staff of a Corporate Member organisation may use the Council's services.

Schools Membership is open to all secondary schools and sixth-form colleges (from both independent and public sectors) with an interest in the work of the Council.

Other grades of membership are available to **individuals** in member institutions (those people who wish to receive their own copies of publications and mailings direct) and to individual **researchers**.

Publications

Viewfinder

Viewfinder is the BUFVC magazine. It explores the production, study and use of film, television and related media for higher education and research through up-to-the-minute articles and other information and comment. Other sections include BUFVC news, film and video catalogues, events, new equipment, courses, subject news, multimedia and reviews of books and film/video productions.

The main representative in each member institution receives free copies of *Viewfinder* for distribution to colleagues. Alternatively, individual subscriptions are available.

ISSN 0265 4444 Published three times/year (February, May and November).

Price Free to BUFVC members through their representatives
£10.00 in UK

Overseas price £15.00 (European destinations)
£18.00 (Destinations outside Europe)

Film and Television in Education: The Handbook of the BUFVC

The *BUFVC Handbook* features articles by practitioners working in different audio-visual and related fields, a directory of sources of audio-visual materials, equipment suppliers, film and video organisation, etc. The *Handbook* is designed for teachers and trainers in tertiary, secondary, vocational and further education and for trainers in industry and commerce.

ISBN 1-857130-16-2

Price £24.99 (Discount available to BUFVC members)
One copy free to each BUFVC Member Institution.

Higher Education Film and Video Library Catalogue

The Higher Education Film and Video Library is a collection of nearly 500 films for use in teaching and research in higher education. It is maintained as a service of the British Universities Film & Video Council and contains many archival films which have been kept in circulation because they are not available elsewhere.

The films concentrate on science and social science topics, although the arts and humanities are well represented. Entries in the catalogue are arranged under 35 subject headings ranging from agriculture and American studies to town planning and zoology. Sources include the Institut für den Wissenschaftlichen Film in Göttingen, the City University of New York, Rothamsted Experimental Station, the National Research Council of Canada, and many others. A separate historical section lists films that have been retained because they are becoming increasingly valuable as records of historical events or of pioneering scientific experiments.

Programmes are available for hire from the Higher Education Film and Video Library by contacting: Concord Video and Film Council, 201 Felixstowe Road, Ipswich, IP3 9BJ ☎ 0473 715754 fax 0473 717088

Some titles are available for sale on videocassette. Contact the Assistant Director at the British Universities Film & Video Council for details.

Price £5.00 (inc. postage & packing)

Research Publications

British Newsreels Issue Sheets 1914-1970 on Microfiche

The newsreels, precursors of the television news bulletins of today, began in Britain in the second decade of the 20th century and reached their zenith in the 1930s and 1940s. They were supplanted by television news in the mid-1950s, although two reels continued producing into the 1970s. Today, the film shot by the different companies over 60 years forms a fascinating record of events and personalities in Britain and abroad.

In the 1970s the Slade Film History Register obtained copies of all the extant issue sheets (with the exception of those of the early *Topical Budget* which later came to light – and held them for use by researchers. Issue sheets are the lists prepared by the newsreel companies showing the 'stories', or topics, covered in each edition.

With the co-operation of the newsreel companies the complete collection has been reproduced on microfiche by the BUFVC in order to make this invaluable historical resource more widely accessible. The microfiche edition (275 fiches 1984) will enable researchers to discover which newsreel company covered a particular event and what prominence was given to the story. Most of the film material is still accessible through newsreel libraries and archives although a small percentage has been lost through deterioration and wartime damage.

Historians, social scientists, archivists and librarians will require this convenient and illuminating record of the visual history of the 20th century covering as it does the tumultuous events that have changed all our lives.

Price £245.00 plus VAT in UK
£195.00 plus VAT to BUFVC members
Overseas: £245 plus mailing costs.
Overseas: £195 plus mailing costs to BUFVC members.
Customers should specify whether airmail or surface mail is required.

The Researcher's Guide to British Film and Television Collections

This is the fourth edition of this *Guide*, completely revised and updated since the last three. The *Guide* documents the existence of film and television materials in the UK that are not normally available for viewing outside the premises where they are held, i.e., collections of an archival nature (but including stock shot, newsreel and production libraries).

There are some 60 new entries, from collections as diverse as the British Library National Sound Archive, Ivo Peters' Railway Film Archive and the Methodist Church Overseas Division. The subjects covered by the *Guide* range from Aberdeen to zoology.

Nine new articles cover film archives, copyright, video standards, HDTV, the independent television franchises, amateur film, specialist archive holdings, film archive training, and research in foreign archives.

The *Guide* has already proved its value to professional researchers working in the media. This new edition will also be of interest to postgraduates whose research involves film and television records, archivists, reference librarians, teachers and media workers.

ISBN 0 901299 64 2. (Paperback 226 pages) 1993.

Price £18.95 in UK
£11.95 to BUFVC members and students

The Researcher's Guide to British Newsreels Vols I, II and III The twofold concern of this publication in three volumes is to act as a guide to the literature of the British newsreel and cinemagazine and to serve as a reference document for the film researcher. The *Guide* draws together 317 items that have been abstracted from books, journals and articles, spanning the years 1901 to 1982, written by the newsreel makers themselves, their critics and historians. Volume II contains an additional 184 items covering the period from 1920 to 1988. The holdings of the major newsreel libraries, archives and documentation centres are indicated. In addition, a chronological chart has been devised to show the period covered by the newsreels.

The *Guide* is a companion volume to the *Researcher's Guide to British Film and Television Collections*, and is a further indication of the Council's long-standing interest in film and history.

The primary audience for the Guide will be postgraduates in film and/or media studies, and professional researchers working on film and television productions. Archivists, reference librarians and others working in the media will also find the book valuable.

ISBN 0 901299 32 4 (Vol I Paperback 119 pages) 1983.
0 901299 57 X (Vol II Paperback 47 pages) 1988.
0 901299 65 0 (Vol III Paperback 86 pages) 1993.

Price Vol III £13.50 (£9.50 to BUFVC members)
Vols I & II £16.50 (£12.00 to BUFVC members)
Vols I, II & III £27.00 (£20.00 to BUFVC members)

As You Like It – AudioVisual Shakespeare This list of over 380 programmes is designed to bring together, for students and teachers of Shakespeare, information on material which is available for hire or sale within the UK.

The catalogue includes full-length performances and critical studies with sections on acting, directing, stage design and theatre history. Dance, musical and ballet versions of the plays are covered as are films inspired by the plots and characters created by Shakespeare, so that alongside Orson Welles' *Macbeth* there is Kurosawa's *Throne of Blood*; next to Zeffirelli's *Romeo and Juliet*, *West Side Story* and the Fonteyn/Nureyev ballet.

ISBN   0 901299 63 4 (3rd edition, paperback, 115 pages)

Price   £13.95
£9.95 (to BUFVC members and members of the Consortium for Drama and Media in Education)

First copies of BUFVC publications are provided without charge to members. Further copies are available to members at the special rates indicated after each entry. For full details write to: BUFVC Publications, 55 Greek Street, London W1V 5LR

Information Service

At the heart of the Council's operation is the Information Service which employs four full-time staff who manage a book collection, a computerised database – *AVANCE*, specialist information on archives and television transmissions, and a comprehensive collection of film and video catalogues from around the world.

The Information Service assists member television researchers and production companies as well as members from the academic community. It can locate and advise on the availability of specialist film and video productions. There is a researcher's desk which can be used, by appointment, by members.

Production/Viewing Facilities

The Council's viewing facilities include a small screening room, capable of seating up to 20 people and equipped to run 16mm film, U-matic Hi- and Lo-band, Betacam, VHS, S-VHS, Betamax, Philips 1500 (for archival copies) and LaserVision videodisc (active play). It provides preview facilities for our members' productions. Facilities can be rented out to members, at special rates, and to other organisations.

Editing facilities for both video (two-machine Betacam and Hi-band U-matic) and 16mm film are available and the film cutting room is equipped with a 35mm Steenbeck and a six-plate Steenbeck with Compeditor.

Events

The Council organises conferences, courses and screenings. There is usually an annual conference in the UK which provides an opportunity for members to meet and discuss selected issues. Recent conferences have had the following titles: *Using Learning Technology (1992)*, *The Role of Media in Education (1993), Putting Movies on Computer (1994) and Learning from Television (1995).*

The Council carries out administrative work organising events on behalf of other related organisations: the InterUniversity History Film Consortium and the Consortium for Drama and Media in Higher Education (see page 325). The Council also runs the British Video History Trust in partnership with the BBC.

To Apply for Membership
All applications for membership should be made by letter to the Director of the BUFVC. This will be formally approved by the BUFVC's Executive Committee. The letter should come from the registrar, director or principal of the company or institution and should, if possible, name the representative proposed. This is the person to whom correspondence and publications will be sent.

Please note that the subscription year runs from 1st April to 31st March.

For full details of the current membership rates contact: British Universities Film & Video Council, 55 Greek Street, London W1V 5LR ☎ 0171-734 3687

BUFVC Related
Organisations

The British Video History Trust British Universities Film & Video Council, 55 Greek Street, London
W1V 5LR ☎ 0171-734 3687 fax 0171-287 3914 e-mail BUFVC@open.ac.uk

Contact Murray Weston or Geoffrey O'Brien

In 1984 BBC Television's Documentary Features Department produced a
series of programmes with the title ALL OUR WORKING LIVES. Using
oral history and archive film the series examined the recent history of
work in Britain in 11 different industries. In the course of production it
became apparent that the rarest material held in film archives and private
collections was film records of everyday activities – people at work and
going about their normal lives.

This was precisely the source material which the producers required
and which was the most valuable historically. The paucity of this record
was frustrating to the programme makers, but of rather more concern was
the realisation that, even with the enormous increase in the recording of
film and television in recent years, there had been little attempt to record
moving images of everyday life in Britain to be kept for future study.

This was the spur that brought together staff of the BUFVC and staff of
the BBC TV Documentary Features Department to establish a group which
would provide high-quality equipment and facilities to record people and
places in Britain for archiving. A committee was formed under the
chairmanship of Will Wyatt (BBC) which comprised Sir Roger Cary (BBC),
Secretary; David Renwick (BBC), Treasurer; Elizabeth Oliver (BUFVC);
Murray Weston (BUFVC); Angela Holdsworth (BBC) and Mark Patterson
(BBC); with historical advisers Angus Calder (Open University, Scotland)
and John Roberts (University of Oxford). This group formed the British
Video History Trust under the trusteeship of the BBC and the BUFVC.

Early on, the Trust's committee established a set of policies
underpinning its activities. Firstly, it would aim only to support the
recording of raw material intended for study and programme making in
the future; it would not support the 'making of programmes'. It was
intended that the recordings would comprise sights and sounds of
everyday activities, and interviews. Some of these interviews might be
oral history, others would be interviews exploring the present day.

Secondly, it would aim to create an archive of broadcast-standard
recordings with equipment being provided to undertake this work.

Thirdly, the agenda for the Trust's activities would be set by the general
public - projects would be proposed, and carried out, by any individuals
or groups who could present a focused proposal to the Trust.

Fourthly, the Trust would retain all broadcast rights to the material recorded, and any income from sales of footage would be fed back into the maintenance of the archive and the recording equipment. Individuals or groups making the recordings would have access to the camera master material, in addition to receiving VHS copies of their project to edit into programmes for non-theatric use.

The Trust's committee then set about the task to obtain funding and sponsorship support. Its plan to put valuable broadcast equipment into the hands of untrained individuals or groups to make recordings was obviously fraught with problems. Would the project groups be able to make useful recordings? How much training would be required to get them started? What about insurance? How would one deal with breakage and repairs?

Some of the broadcast-trained staff of companies which were approached for support visibly winced as they heard of the Trust's plans. Despite this initial reaction, interest was shown in the proposal. After all, the BBC had shown in the past that useful material could be recorded by members of the public with very little training. One example at that time was the Mick Burke awards scheme and then, more recently, the results of the BBC Community Programme Unit's VIDEO DIARIES.

Sony Broadcast Ltd provided the Trust with Betacam equipment, on loan, for a pilot project to find out whether it was really feasible for local groups to produce useful recordings after a minimal amount of training. The project chosen for this pilot was run by a group at the community centre on the Isle of Dogs, London. They spent a day interviewing local people – ex-lightermen, barge builders and dockers – about the changes in London's Docklands. They also recorded the Docklands' wharves from a boat travelling down-river from Tower Bridge. The pilot project showed that high-quality recordings could be made by members of the public on this equipment.

Shortly afterwards Sony Broadcast donated a single-tube Betacam camcorder, microphones and power supplies to the Trust. Later, W Vinten Ltd donated a Vision 10 camera support; Rank Electric donated a lighting kit; MTV Europe provided once-used Betacam tape stock and British Gas provided other tape stock to be used for the Trust's work. In addition, BBC Television made a cash donation of £10,000 to the Trust's bank account. These donations meant that the Trust's work could start in earnest.

In the plans it was intended ultimately to obtain three recording units and other support equipment, but the Trust decided to start making the recordings on the single camcorder it had acquired as soon as possible. The Trust was therefore launched at a press conference at the National Film Theatre in London in July 1988.

Posters, leaflets and project application forms were distributed to public libraries, associations and groups around the country. Local radio stations carried features on the Trust's work and a substantial number of groups came forward with project proposals.

Applicants were asked to fill in a simple form to describe the aims of their project and to enable the Trust's committee to judge whether they had a properly focused project. The committee also needed to decide whether proposals coincided with the aims of the Trust. The variety of projects proposed was quite startling. Subjects ranged from documenting a coven of witches and their rituals to recording the work of a primary school; from interviewing people who were imprisoned in the 1960s for rioting to recording the work of locksmiths working in the Black Country.

Some of the applications came from organised community groups. Quite a number were from individuals who had a special interest in a subject and simply wished to make a recording for posterity. Other applications were plainly from people who wanted free access to broadcast standard equipment solely to promote their careers as television producers with only a minor interest in the aims of the Trust. Care therefore had to be taken in selection not least because the Trust was proposing to loan, free of charge and without supervision, some £30,000 worth of equipment to people previously unknown to it, for periods of up to three weeks.

The Trust was also conscious that the applications were from a mixed-ability group. Some had experienced cameramen and sound recordists to help them, others had no experience whatsoever. It was therefore decided to issue all applicants with a small handbook when their project was accepted. This provided a reminder of the aims of the Trust, a simplified guide to the operation of the equipment, a list of 'dos and don'ts' and a summary of how to conduct an interview. When they came to collect the equipment they would receive a half-day of basic training and have an opportunity to view past work (good and bad) before finally being let loose to record their project. On completion, recordings are returned to the Trust where they are immediately transferred to VHS for viewing purposes, and a complete copy is given to the project group to keep. Copies of the original material can also be made on Hi-band and Lo-band U-matic format, or S-VHS format for editing purposes.

In July 1994, the Trust was able to increase its recording capacity with the loan of three Hi-8 Viewcam liquid crystal camcorders from Sharp Electronics (UK) Ltd. It was felt that these cameras would not only be more user-friendly, but also enable longer recordings to be made, as cassettes had the ability to record for up to 90 minutes each.

The Trust has completed 47 projects and two of these have already contributed to the making of television programmes. One for the BBC's Community Unit was transmitted in March 1990. Entitled WE'RE STILL HERE, it was about the people of Folkestone, Kent, who were at the centre of a riot in the town in 1969. The other was for one of Channel Four's CRITICAL EYE series. OPERATION SOLSTICE, transmitted in November 1991, examined the clash between the police and New Age travellers at Stonehenge in Wiltshire.

Listed on the following pages are some of the projects which have been undertaken so far.

Ralph Bond – Film Maker Ralph Bond, the documentary film-maker was best known for his films TODAY WE LIVE and THE NORTH SEA. A staunch supporter of the film union ACTT, he was recorded by a group from the Co-operative Society shortly before his death.

Farming and Estate Management This project looks at a Northampton farm/estate and at its management during the seasons of autumn, winter, spring and summer.

Folkestone Riots Interviews with the group of people who were involved in the civil riots in 1969 at Folkestone, Kent. Shots of Folkestone town and harbour.

The Jewellery Quarter of Birmingham Interviews with people in different occupations in the jewellery manufacturing business in Birmingham. Also many scenes of craftsmen at work.

The Bailies of Benaghie Interviews with crofters and dry-stone wallers in northern Scotland in the region of Benaghie.

Military Embroiderers Hobson and Sons, the military embroiderers and manufacturers of regimental colours and military badges, moved to new London premises. This recording shows the company at work before the move.

Savile Row Tailor Interviews with a Savile Row tailor and shots of him making a suit.

Bespoke Tailor – Alfred Frost Sequences show Alfred Frost, a tailor in Manchester, making a suit by hand. The interview with him underlines how his business is part of a dying trade.

Portland Foundry, Brighton A working foundry, under threat of development, shown at work. Interviews with the foreman and demonstrations of casting and fettling.

Hampshire Coal Man Recorded two days before an independent coal man gave up his business of delivering coal from door to door. There are interviews with him and scenes of delivery, collection and coal yard activities.

Locksmiths of the Black Country One of the last businesses to manufacture locks by hand in the Black Country. Interviews and shots of the processes.

Lighthouse Keepers of Lundy Scenes of Lundy and its lighthouse plus interviews with the keepers. This lighthouse was one of the last manned lights and has now become automatic.

Paediatric Care and Care of the Elderly in the West Country Interviews with doctors, midwives, health visitors and nurses about the changes in the practice of care in a service with a rural catchment.

Printing and Publishing Trade Interviews Interviews with personnel employed in different operations in the publishing process. Scenes of present day computer-based typesetting and printing.

Tough's River Boatyard Tough's boatyard on the river Thames was one of the collection points for the little ships which went to Dunkirk. The yard itself was a well known Thames river business building and repairing tugs, barges and pleasure boats. It had to close because of dwindling orders and the redevelopment of the town centre in Kingston-upon-Thames.

Butler's Wharf Warehouse The last working wharf in London's Docklands which handled sacked cargoes, mainly juniper berries. The wharf has now closed.

Launching *Peter P* Views of one of the last dry-dock operations on the north bank of the river Thames. Shows the taking in and then the slipping of *Peter P*.

John Perry's Wallpaper John Perry's company is a small factory in north London which makes hand-printed wallpaper using blocks with a technique used in the 18th century. Scenes show the manufacturing process in addition to some interviews.

Hoover Factory The Hoover factory, which moved to the Merthyr Valley in south Wales in 1948, faces closure. Interviews with some of the early workers recall memories of those early days. Scenes show the manufacture of washing machines inside the factory.

People of Bacup, Manchester Interviews with people in Bacup, a close-knit community based around long-established factories in Manchester. Shows the manufacture of textiles and shoes.

Freddy McKay A recording of the experiences of Freddy McKay – craftsman, political activist and notable amateur performer of Irish songs and monologues. His songs and monologues reflect, and attempt to bridge, the sectarian divisions in Ulster.

Comyns – The Silversmith One of the few remaining silversmiths in Britain receives a prize order to manufacture a massive wine cistern. This has enabled a company with eleven chasers, polishers, spinners, and smiths to remain in business in what is a declining trade. Interviews with the silversmiths, and illustrations of them at work, in addition to an interview with the owner.

Animal Hospital An account of everyday situations at the Sir Harold Harmsworth Memorial Hospital for animals. Interviews with people who have taken their animals for treatment plus shots of ambulance staff responding to emergency calls, and operations taking place inside the hospital.

New Age Travellers Interviews with people who are current or ex-travellers. Sequences illustrate the different life-styles with their distinctive attitudes, situations and cultures. Shots show travellers living in vehicles both in urban and greenlanes sites; in a 'tepee village' in south Wales; and with a travellers' school bus at a winter site.

International Brigade A series of interviews with veterans of the International Brigade who fought alongside the Republicans during the Spanish Civil War. Previously unheard stories are told about the social and political background which led them to become volunteers for Spain. Shots include a reunion of two veterans after a 30-year gap, and an IBA Commemorative Day.

Montague Street Records stories of people in their 60s and 70s who were bombed out of their homes during World War Two and who were placed in requisitioned property.

Life on the River Crouch Documents life on the River Crouch in Essex. Includes interviews with the farming community and people from old established businesses that relied on the river's existence for their survival.

Surrey Street Market A visual record of the market trading and of the buildings in Surrey Street, Croydon, Surrey, which have been on the site since 1279. The redevelopment of the town centre will mean the loss of the local market from its historic site.

The Sylvia Dale School of Dance Sylvia Dale taught children the art of ballet and tap dance from the early 1920s until quite recently. The recording shows Sylvia Dale training children for both the music hall and variety show numbers, together with her comments.

Pie and Mash Shops There are only two eel, pie and mash shops remaining in inner London which, for decades, formed part of its life-style. Shots show eels prepared and displayed for sale; kitchen staff making the pie and mash dishes; and meals being served to customers in the restaurant. Interviews with owner and customers.

Scuba Divers Divers describe their experiences of, and their attitudes to, the various developments in the use of diving equipment and how it has progressed from the early snorkel to today's deep-water apparatus. Interviews include oil-rig divers and World War Two frogmen.

English National Opera Scenes show the day-to-day running of the English National Opera plus shots of the elaborate architecture inside the London Coliseum, the setting of the stage, and the Royal Box with its retiring room. Interviews with the managing director, the conductor, the stage manager and some of the artists.

Chinese People in Britain Interviews with the Chinese people who have migrated to Britain from Hong Kong. Some express their fears about the change of political power in 1997, while others explain how they have adjusted to a new life-style in Britain.

Stone Walling Scenes illustrate the different types of stone wall and the various features which can be incorporated in its construction. The history and skills involved in the ancient craft of dry-stone walling are explained in training courses. A stone walling competition is followed from start to finish. Interviews with two brothers, each a master craftsman, and the Duchess of Devonshire, who hosts the annual stone-walling competition.

Village Corner Shops Scenes of local village corner shops in Surrey. Their owners explain how most of the shops have been run by the same family for many years. They express their fears about how they are struggling to keep their businesses going in the face of supermarket competition. Scenes include a baker's shop in Tadworth, a family butcher's shop in Dorking, a haberdasher in Leatherhead, and a toy shop in Epsom.

Deptford Coal-Power Station A record of the memories and working practices of a community whose life-style came to a halt when the Deptford coal-power station was closed and demolished. Shots include rescued old documents relating to the day-to-day running of the power station, some dating back to 1913.

Campanology Records the diverse activities of ringing bells. Scenes show the use of the bell to announce impending church services. The working of bells is shown in detail, in particular the trajectory on the swing of the bell. A vicar is interviewed about his belief in the importance of maintaining a bell-ringing facility to call people to church. Other scenes show bell ringing in a different form – the teaching of hand-bell ringing at a local pub. The publican is interviewed.

Street Sports Interviews with youngsters from different age groups and backgrounds, in Bath, Avon, who practise skateboarding and roller-skating as a street-sport pastime. There are extensive cutaways of skaters in action.

Hand Milking Records the story of the last dairy farm at West Haddon in the Midlands where cows are still milked by hand. The head of the family describes the benefits to the cows of such a practice whilst he is milking.

Hillsborough Community Interviews with the people of Hillsborough, Sheffield, record the stories and memories of the area, known as Sheffield 6, about how the quality of life has been improved by the introduction of much-needed services and facilities in the community.

England's Oldest Borough The building of a new downstream bridge in Barnstaple, Devon, changes the landscape of one of the oldest boroughs in England. Interviews with owners of the town's family businesses describe how these changes are likely to affect their lives. Scenes show Barnstaple's old buildings, with their architectural features, traditional street names and their unique paving stones, and a typical antiques shop.

Quarrymen and Sculptors A record of the event of *'winning the stone'* where blocks of stone are cut and won, by masons and quarrymen using traditional hand-quarrying techniques, from the working face of Tout Quarry on the island of Portland, Dorset. Scenes show the men at work, combined with interviews of retired quarrymen and masons about their earlier quarrying days recalling the myths and legends associated with the art.

The committee of the British Video History Trust currently comprises:
Asa Briggs – President
Will Wyatt (BBC) – Chair
David Renwick (BBC) – Treasurer
Hugh Purcell (Café Productions) – Secretary
Mark Patterson (Border TV)
Murray Weston (BUFVC)
Martin Parry (Western Film Archive)
Geoffrey O'Brien (BUFVC)
Vicki Wegg-Prosser (Flashback Productions)

Historical Advisers:
Peter Catterall
Nicholas Hiley
Kate Morris

If you would like to receive further information and an application form to put a project proposal to the Trust, please send a stamped self-addressed envelope to the Trust c/o the British Universities Film & Video Council.

Film Archive Forum   British Universities Film & Video Council, 55 Greek Street, London
W1V 5LR ☎ 0171-734 3687 fax 0171-287 3914 e-mail BUFVC@open.ac.uk

Contact   Dr Nicholas Hiley, Chairman

Following an initiative by Elizabeth Oliver, the former BUFVC Director,
and with the support of David Francis, the former Curator of the National
Film Archive, the Film Archive Forum was established in 1987 with the
object of fostering an informal network of British film archives. Four
archives sent representatives to the first meeting, but the Forum now
contains nine institutional members, representing all the national and
regional film archives of the UK. Ms Oliver chaired the Forum until her
departure from the Council in 1989, when responsibility for convening
and chairing the Forum passed to the BUFVC Head of Information. Full
membership remains institutional, although others can be invited to
attend Forum meetings as Observing Members.

The Forum has taken an interest in all the archival aspects of the moving
image, and has particular interest in the preservation of nitrate film,
acetate film, and videotape; the training of archivists, acquisitions policy,
standards for archives, copyright, co-operation with film laboratories, and
contacts with foreign archives. In 1988 it gave its backing to the BUFVC
conference *Moving Images: Preservation and Access*, held at the RAF
Museum in Hendon. A workshop, Moving Images: Working With a Small
Collection, was organised by the Forum itself at the East Anglian Film
Archive in the same year.

From the outset the Forum was particularly eager to establish a
postgraduate course in film archiving at an institution of higher education
in the UK. After much hard work, and with major sponsorship from
Studio Film and Video Laboratories Ltd and the British Film Institute, this
became a reality in 1990 with the start of two one-year pilot courses at the
University of East Anglia, leading to an MA degree. These pilot courses
were a great success, and in 1992 the one-year MA in Film Archiving was
formally recognised by the University of East Anglia. The annual intake is
10-12 students, who are taught the practical and administrative elements
of archiving by David Cleveland, Curator of the East Anglian Film
Archive and by his assistant, Jane Alvey. Placements are also arranged at
the National Film Archive, the Imperial War Museum and other regional
archives. For further details of the course see Section **Courses and Events**.

The Forum has always been concerned to maintain the highest
standards of film archiving, and in 1990 it agreed the following set of
guidelines for the establishment of regional or specialist film archives:

• Identify the remit of the archive and adopt an active policy of
  researching sources of film with a view to its acquisition for long-term
  archival purposes, either in their collection or in a suitable repository
  elsewhere.
• Undertake the preservation of the images in the recommended manner
  to archival standards, i.e. preservation negatives or master material or,
  failing that, the best surviving copy.

- Address the particular problem of the preservation of nitrate stock.
- Provide suitable storage conditions for archival film.
- Catalogue, index and compile data on the content and provenance of each title, and make the information accessible for research and study.
- Provide access to the collection where possible, providing preservation needs have first been satisfied. Be aware of copyright and preserve the rights of copyright owners and donors.
- Have at the disposal of the archive, staff who have a thorough understanding and knowledge of the area or subject covered, and technical expertise in the specialised techniques of archival film repair and handling.

Since 1990 the concept of a film archive has expanded to include all forms of audio-visual transmission, from regional television to video games. However, the Forum's commitment to the long-term preservation of the the UK's audio-visual heritage is still strong, and the Forum is closely involved in the establishment of new regional archives, whose staff may be invited to attend as Observing Members pending their Full Membership. The BUFVC continues to act as convenor of the Forum, whose Full Membership currently comprises the East Anglian Film Archive, the Imperial War Museum, the National Film and Television Archive, the North West Film Archive, the Scottish Film Archive, the Wales Film and Television Archive, and the Wessex Film Archive, with the TSW Film and Television Archive for the South West and the Yorkshire Film Archive as Observing Members.

Consortium for Drama and Media in Higher Education	Department of Drama and Theatre Studies, Royal Holloway and Bedford New College, Egham Hill, Egham, Surrey TW20 0EX ☎ 01784 443922 fax 01784 431018
Contact	Professor Richard Cave, Chairman
Contact (for general administration)	The Hon. Secretary, c/o British Universities Film & Video Council, 55 Greek Street, London W1V 5LR ☎ 0171-734 3687 fax 0171-287 3914 e-mail BUFVC@open.ac.uk

The Consortium was founded in June 1974 by a group of teachers from universities and other institutions of higher education with support from the BUFVC. It is a representative body, with membership open to all institutions of higher education and other national and international bodies having an interest in the Consortium's work.

The objectives of the Consortium are to co-ordinate the use and exchange of information on audio-visual materials for the teaching and study of drama and related topics at university or equivalent level, and to facilitate the production of such materials by members through grants made from the Central Production Fund. The Consortium is also concerned in representing nationally and internationally the interests of members in the documentation and availability of audio-visual materials which may be used in the study of drama; and in forming links with similar organisations.

An elected Management Committee, consisting of a maximum of 16 representatives of Ordinary Members, is responsible for the conduct of Consortium affairs. Administrative services are provided by the BUFVC. The Consortium's prime source of funds derives from members' subscriptions, the greater proportion of which is placed into the Central Production Fund. From this grants are made, at the Management Committee's discretion, to assist in the production by members of audio-visual materials considered suitable for teaching or research in the field of drama and associated topics at university level. Co-operative projects between members are especially welcomed.

Apart from the Annual General Meeting, the Consortium, from time to time, arranges conferences, screenings and other events for members. *Theatre in Focus*, a series of monographs on world theatre history accompanied by slides for lecturing purposes, is published by Chadwyck-Healey Ltd. The Consortium co-operates with the BUFVC in producing catalogues of drama material. A newsletter, published three times a year, is issued free to members. It includes information on recently published audio-visual materials and related literature, news of conferences and similar events and, affords an opportunity for members to contribute articles and details of their own activities.

There are two categories of membership, subscriptions for which fall due on 1st August each year: Grade A – Ordinary – open to any institution of higher education in the UK and Ireland, annual subscription £50.00 and Grade B – Associate – open, at the discretion of the Management Committee, to any UK body which would not qualify for Ordinary Membership, and to overseas bodies, annual subscription £25.00. All members are entitled to participate in any events organised by the Consortium, normally at a reduced rate, and receive substantial discounts on all Consortium-produced materials. All members are encouraged to apply for grants from the Central Production Fund, although Associate Members are eligible only in conjunction with an Ordinary Member.

The Council for British Archaeology/ BUFVC AV Media Working Party

British Universities Film & Video Council, 55 Greek Street. London W1V 5LR
☎ 0171-734 3687 fax 0171-287 3914 e-mail BUFVC@open.ac.uk

Contact Cathy Grant, Hon Secretary

The joint CBA/BUFVC AV Media Working Party was founded in 1977 at the instigation of Professor Vincent Megaw, then Professor of Archaeology at the University of Leicester. Its function was to co-ordinate the listing of audio-visual materials on archaeology suitable for use in education, to review such materials as these became available and to hold occasional one-day screenings of films and videotapes. As a result of its activities the CBA has published three editions of its *Archaeology Resource Book* (the third edition in conjunction with English Heritage), and the BUFVC has greatly expanded the number of materials on archaeology listed on its computer database AVANCE. Two major screenings, *Archaeology in Focus 1* and *2*, have been held. Representations were made to the television companies asking them to release more of their archaeology programmes into general distribution. Over 190 new programmes, British and foreign-produced, have been reviewed. Since those early days film has largely been overtaken by the videocassette and general licensing schemes for off-air recording are now in operation. These and other factors have inevitably widened the objects of the Working Party.

In 1988 the Working Party, with the generous sponsorship of the Channel 4 Television Company, instituted the biennial Channel 4 Film and Video Award within the framework of the British Archaeological Awards. The 1988 Award was won by YOUR CHURCH – A THRESHOLD TO HISTORY (English Heritage/University of Leeds/Council for British Archaeology co-production), the 1990 Award by ACROPOLIS NOW: THE PUBLIC FACE OF THE STATE (BBC Open University Productions), and the 1992 Award by a programme from the series DOWN TO EARTH (Thames Television). From 1994 onwards separate awards were given for broadcast and non-broadcast programmes, and the first winners of these were TIME TEAM: ISLAND ON THE LAKE (Videotext Communications for Channel Four Television) in the broadcast category and PATHWAYS TO THE PAST (Dyfed LEA) for the non-broadcast category. As well as the winners two runners-up in each of these categories received BAA Certificates. The number of entries for the awards has grown significantly from year to year and it is hoped that this trend will continue for the next Award in 1996 (see award rules on page 305).

The late 1980s/early 1990s have seen the Working Party become involved in activities on the European continent. Mike Corbishley, Chair of the Working Party, attended the First International Archaeological Film Festival held at the Pyramide in Paris in November 1989. In November 1992 the the Working Party organised and hosted an international six-day festival called *Archeos: The Second International Festival of Films on European Archaeology,* held at the British Museum. In December 1994 Mike Corbishley organised a screening of films at the World Archaeological Congress in New Delhi and it is hoped that such international festivals will be held every few years.

The Working Party meets once a term in spring (February or March), summer (June), autumn (December) – usually, but not always, at the BUFVC offices in London. Present membership of the Working Party comprises: Mike Corbishley (English Heritage), Chair; Cathy Grant (BUFVC), Honorary Secretary; Don Henson (Council for British Archaeology); Richard Morris (Council for British Archaeology); Philip Sugg (Independent Film Producer) Ray Sutcliffe (Film Producer); Peter Webster (University of Wales College, Cardiff); Alex West (Ancient Eye Productions); Dr Marek Zvelebil (University of Sheffield).

InterUniversity History Film Consortium (IUHFC)	Department of History, Queen Mary and Westfield College, Mile End Road, London E1 4NS ☎ 0171-775 3388 fax 0181-980 8400 Telex: 893750
Contact	Dr John Ramsden

The InterUniversity History Film Consortium has in membership the universities of Birmingham, Leeds, Liverpool, Nottingham, Salford and Wales; Queen Mary and Westfield College, University of London; College of Ripon and York St John.

The Consortium is a self-governing group of subscribing institutions of higher education which came together to enable teaching historians to make films for their own and each others' use; to foster a more scholarly approach to the use of film as visual evidence; and to arrange conferences and publications in this field. Member institutions receive copies of all films made by the Consortium and have the opportunity to make films themselves in rotation. Films are on general sale in the UK on VHS (625 PAL) video format, and some titles are available for hire on 16mm film format.

Films made by the Consortium have been in two series, the BRITISH UNIVERSITIES HISTORICAL STUDIES IN FILM and the ARCHIVE SERIES. The historical studies include THE SPANISH CIVIL WAR, THE MUNICH CRISIS, THE END OF ILLUSIONS, and THE WINTER WAR (all on international affairs in the 1930s and 1940s). The series has also included THE GREAT DEPRESSION (mainly on Britain in the 1930s) and FASCISM (a comparative study using film material from British, German and Italian archives). The most recent films in the series have looked directly at the influence of film and at its strengths and limitations as evidence: A CALL TO ARMS investigated the relationship between British newsreels of the 1930s and the campaign for rearmament, and IMAGES OF THE SOVIET UNION looks at the way in which the Soviet Union was put across to British cinema-goers during the Second World War.

The films of the historical studies series are not unlike television documentaries in approach – using a narrator, still pictures, graphics and maps, and in some cases interviews, alongside visual material drawn from the newsreels and other films of the period in question. The selection of the material, the script and the editorial decisions are all taken by professional historians in the Consortium. Each film runs for about 50 minutes and is accompanied by a booklet written by the compiler(s) of the film.

The archive series assembles pieces of raw film, usually uncut items from contemporary newsreels, so that in teaching situations the raw material itself can be shown. There is no narration or music, but a booklet analyses the film extracts used and sets each item in context. Films in this series have included biographical studies – NEVILLE CHAMBERLAIN and STANLEY BALDWIN – and a collection of items entitled THE ORIGINS OF THE COLD WAR. Recent films include OUR GREAT ALLY FRANCE, drawn from British newsreel stories about France between 1938 and 1940 and THE KOREAN WAR which uses newsreel coverage from 1950 to 1953 to explore the political complexity of the Korean War. Each film runs for about 30 minutes.

The Consortium organises conferences about every two years, many of which have been at the Imperial War Museum in London, and the proceedings of these conferences have usually been published as edited volumes of essays. These include *Politics, Propaganda and Film* (eds Nicholas Pronay and Derek Spring, Macmillan 1982) and *British Cinema and the Second World War* (ed Philip Taylor, Macmillan 1988). The most recent conference, in July 1993, was on the post-war British media.

The British Universities Film & Video Council handles the sales of all IUHFC video productions.

The International Association for Media in Science (IAMS) c/o Wellcome Centre for Medical Science, Wellcome Trust, 210 Euston Road, London NW1 2BE
☎ 0171-611 8596 fax 0171-611 8765

UK Contact Michael Clark

Founded at Zaragoza in April 1992, IAMS is the successor to the former International Scientific Film Association (ISFA), established by Jean Painlevé in 1948. IAMS's interests are centred in three main aspects of the use of film, television and multimedia in science and technology, namely, their use in science education (including distance learning), in certain specialised areas of research, and in the wider popularisation of science. However, IAMS also has interests in distribution, documentation, media management and the use of audio-visual programmes as an alternative to animal experimentation. IAMS has also drawn up and promulgated a series of guidelines for the good organisation and conduct of scientific film festivals. Members with special interests in medical and health films also now benefit from a reciprocal membership arrangement with the World Association of Medical and Health Film (WAMHF).

One of the most valuable aspects of the former ISFA's work was in bringing together scientific film-makers from both sides of what was 'the iron curtain'. Meetings were held regularly in the east and west throughout the life of the Association. The ISFA meetings provided a valuable forum for the exchange of ideas and an opportunity, even during the height of the Cold War, to view film and television productions which were otherwise inaccessible. This function still continues, but of course the overall political situation has changed considerably during the recent years.

IAMS holds an annual congress, the most recent being in conjunction with the British Association's annual Festival of Science at Loughborough in September 1994. Other than the United Kingdom, 13 countries were represented including Greece, the USA, Chile, and the People's Republic of China. In addition to its own meetings, IAMS is represented on the juries and organising committees of a number of other film festivals including the Ronda Festival (Malaga, Spain), the annual Rencontres de l'Audiovisuel Scientifique in Paris, Videomed (Badajoz, Spain) and the

329

Liège International Medical Film Festival.

Membership to IAMS is open to academic institutions, charitable organisations, professional associations, public bodies, film and television companies, distributors and private individuals. Although wholly international in character, the working language of the Association is English. The Association is funded entirely from membership fees and receives no public or corporate funding. The permanent office, formerly located at the Onderwijs Media Institut, Utrecht, is soon to be moved to the campus of the Italian National Institute for Energy Research near Rome.

Membership

There are currently 82 full members in four classes representing 17 countries (12 European, two Asian, three North and South American). The largest memberships are Italy (18), Germany (11), Spain (11), Netherlands (8) and the UK (7).

President

Dr Jan Tijmen Goldschmeding, Audiovisueel Centrum, Vrije University en VU-Ziekenhuis, Van der Boechortstraat 1, 1080 BT Amsterdam
☎ + 31 20 444 9161 fax +31 20 444 9160

General Secretary

Werner Grosse, Institut für den Wissenschaftlichen Film, Nonnenstieg 72, D- 37075 Gottingen, Germany
☎ +49 551 50240 fax +49 551 5024400

Treasurer

Michael Clark, Wellcome Centre for Medical Science, The Wellcome Trust, 210 Euston Road, London NW1 2BE
☎ 0171-611 8596 fax 0171-611 8765

Abbreviations and Acronyms

These abbreviations refer to entries contained within this handbook. For a comprehensive listing of abbreviations and acronyms refer to the *Handbook of International Film, Television and Video Acronyms* edited by Matthew Stevens (Flicks Books, 1993).

ACCM ....Association for Communications, Culture and Media

ACU ....Association of Commonwealth Universities

ADSET........Association for Database Services in Education and Training

AEI ....Association Européene Inédits

AETT ....Association for Educational and Training Technology

AGOCG......Advisory Group on Computer Graphics

ALT.............Association for Learning Technology

AME ....Association for Media Education

AMFIT........Association for Media, Film and Television Studies in Further and Higher Education

ARLIS ....Art Libraries Association

ASA ....Advertising Standards Authority

Aslib ....Association for Information Management

ASME ....Association for the Study of Medical Education

AV ....audio-visual

BABEL........Broadcasting across the Barriers of European Language

BAFTA ....British Association of Film and Television Arts

BBC ....British Broadcasting Corporation

BBFC...........British Board of Film Classification

BCC.............Broadcasting Complaints Commission

BCS ....British Computer Society

BFFS............British Federation of Film Societies

BECTU ....Broadcasting, Entertainment and Cinematograph Technicians Union

BFI...............British Film Institute

BIDS............Bath Information Data Services

BIMA ....British Interactive Multimedia Association

BKSTS.........British Kinematograph, Sound and Television Society

BMA ....British Medical Association

BNFVC ....*British National Film and Video Catalogue*

BNIF ....British Nuclear Industry Forum

BSAC ....British Screen Advisory Council

BSC ....Broadcasting Standards Council

BSIP ....Brain Sciences Information Project

BUFVC ....British Universities Film & Video Council

BVA ....British Videogram Association

CBA ....Council for British Archaeology

CCETSW ....Central Council for Education and Training in Social Work

CD-i ....compact disc interactive

CD-ROM ....compact disc - read-only memory

CERCI.........Centre for Educational Resources for the Construction Industry

CHEST........Combined Higher Education Software Team

CIMTECH..National Centre for Information Media and Technology

CITB............Construction Industry Training Board

COIC...........Careers & Occupational Information Centre

CPBF...........Campaign for Press and Broadcasting Freedom

CTI ....Computers in Teaching Initiative

CVCP.........Committee of Vice-Chancellors and Principals of the Universities of the United Kingdom

DBS ....direct broadcasting by satellite

DfE ....Department for Education

DNE...........Department of National Heritage

DTI.............Department of Trade and Industry

EAVE..........European Audio-Visual Entrepreneurs

EBS.............Educational Broadcasting Services

EFDO..........European Film Distribution Office

ELT ....English language teaching

ENB.............English National Board for Nursing, Midwifery and Health Visiting

ERA.............Educational Recording Agency

ETA.............Educational Television Association

ETV ....Educational and Television Films

EUROAIM ..European Association for an Audio-Visual Independent Market

EVE ....Espace Vidéo Européen

FAME ....Film Archive Management & Entertainment

FAST...........Federation against Software Theft

FIAF............(Fédération Internationale des Archives du Film (International Federation of Film Archives)

FOCAL ....Federation of Commercial Audio-Visual Libraries

GRECO.......Groupment Européen pour la Circulation des Oeuvres

HDTV ....high-definition television
HEA............Health Education
    Authority
HEFCE ....Higher Education Funding
    Council for England
HEFVL ....Higher Education Film
    and Video Library
HENSA ......Higher Education National
    Software Archive

IAMS ....International Association
    of Media in Science
IBT..............International Broadcasting
    Trust
ICA ....Institute of Contemporary
    Arts
ICCE ....International Centre for
    Conservation Education
IEEE ....Institute of Electrical and
    Electronic Engineers
IT ....information technology
ITC ....Interactive Technologies
    Courseware
ITC ....Independent Television
    Commission
ITU..............International
    Telecommunications
    Union
IUHFC........InterUniversity History
    Film Consortium
IVCA...........International Visual
    Communications
    Association
IWF ....Institut für den
    Wissenschaftlichen Film,
    Göttingen

JANET........Joint Academic Network
JISC ....Joint Information Services
    Committee

KETV ....Kent Educational
    Television
KSP ....Kent Superior Pictures

LAITG ....Library Association
    Information Technology
    Group
LWT............London Weekend
    Television

MAP-TV.....Memory Archives
    Programmes Television
MBS ....MEDIA Business School
MCPS..........Mechanical Copyright
    Protection Society

MIDAS ....Manchester Information
    Datasets and Associated
    Services
MOMI.........Museum of the Moving
    Image
MUTV.........Manchester University
    Television Service

NAHEFV ...National Association for
    Higher Education in Film
    and Video
NAG ....National Acquisitions
    Group
NCC............National Computing
    Centre
NCET.........National Council for
    Educational Technology
NCVQ........National Council for
    Vocational Qualifications
NFTS...........National Film and
    Television School
NIACE........National Institute of Adult
    Continuing Education
NISS...........National Information
    Services and Systems
NSCTP.......National Short Course
    Training Programme

OHP............overhead projector
OUDCE ......Oxford University
    Department for
    Continuing Education

PACT ....Producers Alliance for
    Cinema and Television
PCC.............Press Complaints
    Commission
PRS..............Performing Rights Society

RHS.............Royal Horticultural Society
RNIB...........Royal National Institute
    for the Blind
RoSPA ....Royal Society for the
    Prevention of Accidents
RSPB ....Royal Society for the
    Protection of Birds
RSPCA........Royal Society for the
    Prevention of Cruelty to
    Animals
RTITB ....Road Transport Industry
    Training Board
RTS..............Royal Television Society

SAFE...........Scottish Archive Film for
    Education
SCAA..........Schools Curriculum
    Assessment Authority

SCALE........Small Countries Improve
    Their Audio-Visual Level
    in Europe
SCET..........Scottish Council for
    Educational Technology
SCSST ....Standing Conference on
    Schools Science &
    Technology
SFC..............Scottish Film Council
SIMA ....Support Initiative For
    Multimedia Applications
SOURCES ..Stimulating Outstanding
    Resources for Creative
    European Screenwriting
SRHE ....Society for Research into
    Higher Education
SSVC...........Services Sound and Vision
    Corporation

TALC ....Teaching Aids at Low Cost
TFVA ....Training Film and Video
    Association
TLTP ....Teaching and Learning
    Technology Programme
TRRL...........Transport and Road
    Research Laboratory
TSA ....Trust for the Study of
    Adolescence
TVE ....Television Trust for the
    Environment
TVL ....Technical Video Library
TVS ....Technical Video Sales

UBI..............Understanding British
    Industry
UCL ....University College London
UKAEA ......United Kingdom Atomic
    Energy Authority
UKERNA ...United Kingdom
    Education and Research
    Networking Association
UNRWA.....United Nations Relief and
    Works Agency for
    Palestine Refugees in the
    Near East

VLV.............Voice of the Listener and
    Viewer

WAVES ......Women's Audio-Visual
    Education Scheme
WFTV ....Women in Film and
    Television
WTN ....Worldwide Television
    News

Index